the
Upward
Spiral

the
Upward
Spiral

GETTING LAWYERS
FROM DAILY MISERY
TO LIFETIME WELLBEING

HARVEY HYMAN, J.D.

Published by
LAWYERS' WELLBEING, INC.
Piedmont, California

THE UPWARD SPIRAL:
Getting Lawyers from Daily Misery to Lifetime Wellbeing

For information contact:
Lawyers' Wellbeing, Inc.
104 Olive Avenue
Piedmont, CA 94611

Library of Congress Cataloging-in-Publication data available upon request.

ISBN 978-0-9841139-0-3
10 9 8 7 6 5 4 3 2 1

Printed in the United States of America

Cover Design: Dotti Albertine, www.AlbertineBookDesign.com
Interior Design: www.AlbertineBookDesign.com
Cover Photo: Getty Images/Kamil Vojnar

Contents

Part II ◎ HOW TO CREATE LIFETIME WELLBEING

Acknowledgments

THIS BOOK EVOLVED during my recovery from major depression and played a positive role in my recovery. By sharing the manuscript with others, as it grew and changed, I was sharing myself as I grew and changed. I would like to acknowledge the people who helped me in various ways during this project, without whom I could never have completed it.

Thanks go to my wife Lael Carlson and my two children Simone Hyman and Elliott Hyman for loving me, accepting me and believing in me no matter what. Thanks go to my father Julian Hyman, M.D., my brother Steven Hyman, M.D. and my sister Mona Hyman Rubin for continuously praising my efforts and encouraging me to keep going.

Thanks to the California Lawyer Assistance Program for helping me during the early stage of my depression when I did not know how to help myself. Thanks to the following mental health professionals for showing me so much compassion, taking such great care of me and teaching me so much about overcoming depression: David Feifel, M.D., Ph.D.; the staff at Herrick Hospital's program for adults with mood disorders; Bruce Johnston, M.D. and Rick Trautner, M.D.

I would like to thank disability claims adjuster Mary Kate Thorpe at UNUM for her compassion, concern, competence and professionalism in handling my claim for disability benefits under my individual policy.

I would like to thank the people who read specific chapters and gave me their thoughts and suggestions for how to improve them: Steven Hyman, M.D. (chronic stress, alcoholism; Jeffrey C. Friedman, MHS, CSAC (alcoholism); Claude Munday, Ph.D. (depression); Paul Quinnett, Ph.D. (suicide); and Aymee Coget, Ph.D. (happiness).

Thank you to Dotti Albertine for designing such a beautiful book cover. Thanks also to editing consultant Charlotte Cook for giving me some excellent pointers on how to edit my book, and to copyeditor-proofreader Flo Selfman for her accomplished assistance with the manuscript.

This is my book. I take full responsibility for its accuracy, so if there are any mistakes, please don't blame the folks who assisted me in some fashion.

Preface

YOUR WELLBEING really matters to me. I wrote this book to help you become a healthier, happier lawyer with a clear vision of your life's purpose that connects you with others in a meaningful way and fuels deep inner contentment.

I began practicing law in 1982 in New York. For 25 years I worked my proverbial butt off for my clients, most of that time as a solo practitioner in plaintiff's personal injury in the California Bay Area. I certainly had my share of success, but I also experienced tremendous stress that prompted me to feel sorry for myself, to drink too much, to feel depressed and to express irritation at opposing counsel, family members and strangers driving other cars in traffic.

I always hoped my attitude would improve. I always hoped I would learn to enjoy law practice and not leave the office feeling drained, irritated and unfulfilled. Although I was very active and vocal in fighting for my clients' rights and interests, I was passive when it came to learning how to achieve wellbeing. Although I was always looking for ways to handle my clients' cases more effectively, I never sought out techniques to effectively manage stress or to become a more positive, hopeful and joyful lawyer. Nobody ever popped out of the woodwork to offer to teach me these things.

Between August 2006 and August 2007, I faced some huge and unexpected emotional traumas in my personal life—my mother's sudden, unexpected death from a rare brain virus and my daughter's extended hospitalization for an eating disorder. Because I never learned to truly feel and outwardly express my emotions, I didn't grieve. Instead I became extremely anxious. But I didn't know I was anxious. I somaticized the anxiety into the physical sensation of constant tightness in my chest. My doctor suspected a heart problem and had me undergo an EKG and a treadmill stress test, which both came out negative.

During that same time frame, I was shifting the focus of my law practice from traumatic brain injury cases (which had become way too expensive for a solo practitioner like me to litigate anymore) to bicycle injury cases. Bicycling had tremendous appeal for me personally and professionally. That year I spent at least as much time bicycling as I did practicing law. I loved the physical sensations of bicycling. I also imagined that the more I biked, the more I would benefit professionally by learning about the subject matter of my new field of litigation.

The problem was that I wasn't earning money when I rode my bike, and this led me deeper and deeper into debt. Only later would I learn from my psychiatrist that I had become hypomanic in response to the emotional stressors in my life. In my state of hypomania I saw nothing amiss with riding my bike for hours during a workday and borrowing heavily from the equity line on my house to pay the office overhead and case costs. One day in August 2007 my wife told me our equity line was used up and our money was gone. She wondered what I was going to do to fix this problem.

Hearing this news snapped me like a piano wire. I immediately underwent a strange physical contraction. Every muscle in my body tightened up. I couldn't breathe. An inner voice I had never heard before suddenly emerged. The voice told me I must die for what I had done to my family. This punitive voice told me die in relentless, nonstop fashion and literally tortured me. I had to be hospitalized twice for major depression with suicidal ideation, once that August and again in November 2007. The psychiatrist who treated me during my second hospitalization gave me a drug called Seroquel that stopped these "obsessive suicidal ruminations."

When I left the hospital the second time, I was a shell of my former self. I had lost my self-confidence and I looked skeletal because I had dropped twenty pounds. I was frightened because I didn't know how my family would survive financially and I had no vision of what I would do with myself. Thank God I had self-paid health insurance to pay for medication and therapy. Thank God for Mary Kate Thorpe, the disability claims adjuster at UNUM insurance company. She honored my claim for self-paid disability insurance benefits. These monthly payments enabled my family to meet our basic monthly expenses for two adults and two kids in the Bay Area.

Since discharge from my second hospitalization, I have devoted myself completely to recovering from major depression and becoming a healthier, happier, more balanced person. First I attended a hospital-based day treatment program for depressed adults for one month. Upon discharge I saw a psychotherapist once weekly, did group therapy once weekly and exercised six days a week. I began Buddhist meditation classes in February 2008 and I have meditated every day since then. I have read very extensively about depression, psycho-pharmacology, alcoholism, stress, stress management, suicide, suicide prevention, Buddhism, meditation, positive psychology, the cultivation of gratitude, the practice of forgiveness and sustainable happiness. In the summer of 2009 I began the daily practices of deep breathing and Kundalini yoga.

Although I still have anxiety with chest tightness, I have come a long, long way. I am a much more compassionate, kind, friendly, open and spiritual person than I was before. I used to find things to complain about every day. Now I'm glad and thankful to be alive. I no longer focus attention on what I don't have or don't get. I feel and express gratitude for all the good people and good things in my life. I'm more patient. I don't snap at people. I don't pretend to have all the answers. I talk less and listen more. I'm less immersed in my own head. I enjoy hearing about other people's dreams and encouraging them to live their dreams.

I've enjoyed helping my wife with her graduate school studies in speech language pathology. I've taken time to help coach and cheer for my son Elliott in soccer and basketball, and to volunteer frequently in his classroom. This summer I took him to the Southwest to see fossilized trees, dinosaur footprints, a meteor crater and the ruins of Anasazi cliff dwellings at Canyon de Chelly and Chaco Canyon. He's such a smart, funny and social kid—a great traveling companion. We had a blast.

I'm teaching my daughter to drive. I adopted a rescue dog named Coffee that she wanted, and I take good care of the dog so she can pursue her activities. I'm incredibly proud that she triumphed over her eating disorder and that she's learning to become a competitive high school diver with aspirations to win a college scholarship. I walk Coffee on the nature trails of the East Bay Regional Park where I see deer and hear owls hoot. My relationship with my wonderful children and my time in nature have been healing.

During recovery from major depression I read a great many books and articles about mood disorders and substance abuse among lawyers. I was shocked and saddened to learn that one out of every five of our nation's 1.2 million lawyers suffers from major depression or alcoholism. This made me realize I could be of service by making my experience of recovering from depression a gift to you. My book is meant to get you past the daily misery of law practice that has plunged you into depression or alcoholism, and help make your life an upward spiral.

Based on all I have gone through, I can personally assure you of one thing. You *can* leave misery behind and achieve sustainable wellbeing in your law practice and life. Once you read this book and adopt the new attitudes and behaviors I'm recommending, you will find what I have found—a renewed experience of being a lawyer infused with wellbeing.

Wellbeing is more important than the things our society most prizes, such as material wealth, fame and longevity of years. Wellbeing refers to a state of optimal mental, physical, emotional and spiritual health. Wellbeing includes genuine career satisfaction from the ethical pursuit of personally meaningful work; rich social connectedness marked by peaceful, nurturing friendships; and involving oneself in community activities and spiritual activities that give one's life a larger meaning than the pleasure of personal consumption.

A person who experiences wellbeing is whole. His feelings flow freely, without blockage or tension. He is in tune with his inner emotional life and the emotional lives of those around him. He is compassionate toward himself and others. He has found balance in the pursuit of his livelihood with time for self-care, self-reflection, play and joyful exploration of his interests and passions. He is happy, and regards his life as one that is well-lived and worthy.

Misery is the opposite of wellbeing. Misery is intense personal suffering generated by frustration, confusion, conflicts with others, lack of career satisfaction, lack of meaning, social disconnection and a sense of failing at life. Misery triggers depression and substance abuse.

People in our society feel obligated to be happy, or at least to fake happiness when they're miserable. For many years I faked feeling good when I was miserable. Why? Because I knew that no clients would hire me if I was outwardly miserable. I knew that my parents wanted me to be happy, and I didn't want to disappoint them. And I knew that my spouse and children needed me to focus on them and their needs rather than on my own suffering.

Like other lawyers in my situation, I assumed it wasn't possible to practice law without being miserable and I could tolerate misery because it wouldn't kill me.

Eventually I crashed and went into a major depression that did almost kill me. My condition would have killed me had I not been helped in many ways by many kind, caring people. And with that I found a new understanding of life.

Before my depression I saw the world as a competitive, dog-eat-dog place and acted accordingly. Depression rendered me as vulnerable, helpless and dependent as a newborn. But, instead of being scorned, I received an abundance of warmth, caring and support. Doctors, nurses, staff, family, friends and even other lawyers came to my rescue. To recover from depression required me to change how I lived, what I lived for, and how I related to myself and others.

Today I am a much happier person who sees the world in a positive light. My new world is one in which people can bring out the best in each other and help one another reach our potential to create, contribute, share, inspire, love, laugh and play.

My experiences led me to write this book for your benefit. Even though I don't know you personally, I care about you and want to help you avoid what I had to go through. I want to see you flow and lead a happy life rather than drown in a sea of stress.

You may ask, is it really that bad? Unfortunately, yes. Survey data shows that more than half of all lawyers are so unsatisfied with their careers, they would change careers right now if they weren't trapped by economics. The American Bar Association (ABA) estimates that 20% of all lawyers nationwide are alcoholic, which is double the 10% rate of alcoholism in the adult U.S. population. Lawyers have the highest divorce rate of any occupation. They die by suicide at twice the rate of the general population and rank near the top of all occupations in their rate of suicide.

In 1990 Bruce Sales, a psychologist at the University of Arizona, co-authored an epidemiological study on all lawyers practicing full-time in the State of Washington. The results showed that 18% were alcoholic and 19% had major depressive disorder (MDD). This 19% rate of depression (which he believed held steady for lawyers across the country) is markedly higher than the 6% average for the general population. Later studies by Connie Beck, Ph.D., have confirmed a national rate of 19% for depression among lawyers. In 1990 a group at the Johns Hopkins School of Public Health published an epidemiological study of the rate of MDD in 103 occupations using DSM-III criteria. They found that lawyers had the very highest rate of MDD and were 3.6 times more likely to have MDD than other persons generally employed full-time.

My research has shown me that lawyers are conditioned to engage in distorted thinking which generates unnecessary anger, aggression and conflict. My book is intended to help you see and treat other lawyers as fellow human beings who deserve consideration, respect and cooperation, even though you oppose each other's assertions of fact or law in a given case. Once we learn to resolve legal disputes peacefully and empathically (without hate and anger), we will serve our clients well without getting overly stressed, falling into despair or becoming ill.

Practicing law in a peaceful, constructive spirit will enable us to conserve enough time and energy to develop many other aspects of our lives and reach our full potential as individuals, spouses, parents and grandparents. When we no longer invest all our precious energy to arguing every last petty point with opposing counsel, we are free to devote time to meet our physical, social and spiritual needs. The scope of our lives will broaden and allow us to meet all our human needs in a network of social support. This will enable us to thrive. We will live life in an upward spiral rather than the downward spiral of depression, chemical dependence and suicidal thinking.

To avoid random, arbitrary switching back and forth, I have decided to use "he/his" in place of "he/she" and "his/her." I mean no offense to female lawyers by this choice. I will also use "lawyer" in place of "lawyer/attorney/counselor" throughout my book.

PART I

THE DAILY MISERY
OF LAW PRACTICE

CHAPTER ONE

How come so many lawyers are so miserable?

Lawyers and Dysphoria

DYSPHORIA is the opposite of euphoria. It comes from the Greek term *dysphoros,* which means difficult to bear. A person experiencing dysphoria has no joy. He is ill at ease, anxious, restless, uncomfortable and irritable. As adults, few of us expect our jobs to make us euphoric. But we do hope work will let us provide for our families while bringing some measure of meaning and satisfaction into our lives.

When our jobs are nothing more than what Studs Terkel called "a Monday-to-Friday sort of dying," we're in deep trouble. In *How Lawyers Lose Their Way*, authors Jean Stefancic and Richard Delgado tell us that surveys show 6 out of 7 working people in America regard their jobs as "moderately satisfying," while only one-third of lawyers do. The rest are unhappy, and a majority of them would leave the profession if they could manage it economically.

The Lawyer's Career Change Handbook by Hindi Greenberg and *Running from the Law* by Deborah Aaron both document the shocking extent to which lawyers are dissatisfied with their careers. Greenberg mentions a poll by *The California Lawyer* indicating that seventy percent of practicing lawyers would not go back into law if they had a chance to do it all over again. When lawyers hit their forties and fifties, career dissatisfaction can easily turn into depression. That is the time in life when adults expect to have achieved their goals and feel on top of things. During those years, lawyers are most likely to have suicidal fantasies and to die by suicide, says Joan E. Mounteer in her article "Depression Among Lawyers" in *The Colorado Lawyer*, Jan. 2004 (Vol. 33, No. 1, p. 35).

EIGHT CAUSES OF LAWYER MISERY AND THEIR SOLUTIONS

(1) Materialism

Studies of happiness in America show that during the last fifty years our standard of living has continued to rise. We are producing ever more billionaires and millionaires. Yet our national level of happiness has kept dropping over the same period. Material enrichment has gone hand in hand with spiritual impoverishment and an epidemic of depression. Making lots of money is neither a source of lasting happiness nor a cure for suffering. Young people today are ten times more likely to be depressed than their grandparents were.

In *The Pleasure Center*, Morten L. Kringelbach, Ph.D. says professional people who sacrifice pleasure to work the long hours needed to generate wealth have made a poor choice. They are no more content than people with modest incomes, while being more tense and having much less leisure time. Kringelbach says we are happier over the long run from spending time with friends and enjoying good food, music and sex than from loading up our bank accounts.

In *The Last Self-Help Book You'll Ever Need*, psychologist Paul Pearsall, Ph.D., says that most "successful people" suffer from a spiritual vacuum and they are languishing. They pursue success arduously as something outside themselves, leaving them agitated, drained and exhausted. Many big earners don't experience work as creative play and don't find it enlivening, energizing or inspiring. None of their financial kills brings them real prosperity, the inner prosperity of the heart that makes one glad to be alive, glad to experience the beauty of nature, glad to help others and glad to give and receive love and affection.

The ostentatious rich have a compulsion to impress others by the size and luxurious decoration of their home, the amazing view from their office, their designer clothes and new sports car; but they have no vision that goes beyond them, no sense of higher purpose in work that links them to meaning. When beauty comes from the look of your expensive kitchen appliances, not your soul, life is hollow.

Pearsall says doing meaningful work that contributes to the community is fundamental to human health and happiness. Meaningful work takes the focus off gaining money and status for ourselves, keeps us mindful of our impact on others and motivates us to make the world a better place. When work is a species of giving, not of taking and acquiring, it becomes a way of savoring a well-lived life and feeds the soul. Pearsall calls success that is focused solely on getting money and status for oneself "toxic success"—breeding shallowness, disconnection, loneliness and depression.

Lawyers are more prone to toxic success than other occupations are. While doctors can take pride in lives saved, scientists in discoveries made, and teachers in lessons taught, lawyers measure success by the money they have won and made. Yet making money a supreme value has not brought us wellbeing.

In *Money and The Meaning of Life*, philosopher Jacob Needleman warns us not to use money to define ourselves. He says we have become "time poor" because we give up most of our precious time to make more money than we need. We are, he says, drones who are not in business to live, but beings who live for their business. We aren't consciously living our lives, we are being lived by our lives because we have sacrificed control to something completely external, the making of money.

Needleman says money should remind us of our

dependence on each other and of a greater common purpose for our species. Instead, making money has become an end in itself and the making of money is conducted all too often in an atmosphere of impatience, negativity and cunning.

Solution: Stop measuring your value by your net worth. Doing so ignores your true value as a spiritual being. In 2009 a German billionaire threw himself in front of a train and died, because he couldn't bear losing some of his companies and his lifestyle when the recession hit. Beyond a certain amount, the accretion of money and luxury goods can't make you any more comfortable or happy than you already are. The effort involved is pointless due to "hedonic adaptation," which means people quickly become accustomed to and take for granted the new luxuries in their lives. The toys of the ego (expensive houses, cars and Oriental rugs) pale in comparison with the joys of love, friendship, generosity and service. The German billionaire failed to grasp this point.

It's possible to be a successful lawyer and still devote some time to assist others.

You can help battered women get a restraining order or help poor families get social security benefits. You can help low-income tenants in rent-controlled housing avoid sham evictions to raise rents. You can incorporate or advise worthy nonprofits that serve community or charitable interests. Some lawyers help unjustly convicted people avoid the death penalty, while working to establish their innocence through new forensic techniques. Other lawyers help build new legal systems in less-developed countries, observe the fairness of their elections or monitor the prosecutions of their political dissidents. Find a way to use your legal skills to help others, one that does good and feels good, but doesn't overburden your law practice.

(2) **Isolation, Loneliness and Touch Deprivation**

Lawyers and soldiers are both engaged in relatively constant conflict. The difference between them is that soldiers are fighting for their country (or at least for the idea that their country needs and supports them), and soldiers work in mutually supportive "companies" that have each other's backs. Thus soldiers feel a sense of belonging and solidarity. Lawyers work alone to represent individual clients. The clients keep changing over time. The clients can be critical of their work, resentful of their fee and may fire them at any time or even sue them for perceived mistakes. This way of working makes lawyers feel lonely.

The following factors isolate lawyers:

- The physical design of law firms sticks most lawyers in small offices and cubicles. They spend much of their time in these sealed containers, interacting with machines to generate phone calls, e-mails, letters, faxes, motions, briefs and billing records. Lawyers are not provided with a room for group activities where they can get together for meditation, yoga, exercise or socializing to relieve stress. They are not encouraged to go outside where they can walk together and get sunshine and fresh air.

- Lawyers work in a highly adversarial environment, where letting information slip can be dangerous, so they trust nobody and their guard is always up. They don't want the other side to know the weaknesses of their case, and they don't want anyone to know when they are sick, depressed or having problems with substances.

- Lawyers are afraid of being fired, disciplined by the State Bar or sued for malpractice if they make a mistake. Many of them practice with a defensive mindset which leads them to cover their butts and blame others when anything goes wrong. This is the opposite of collaborative work that joins people together.

- Lawyers are expected to be constantly productive and earn their keep in law firms that spend huge sums of money on rent, decoration, staff and technology. At large firms, associates are expected to bill an inhuman number of hours.

To work anywhere close to the prescribed hours, associates must sequester themselves from family and friends. In *How Lawyers Lose Their Way*, the authors conclude that working these crazy hours is physically exhausting, induces guilt over missing family time and gets associates to lie about their hours, since no human being can actually work that much and still have time to eat, sleep, use the bathroom and commute. The authors mention a survey done in 2000 showing that 45% of big firm associates would give up $30,000 to $50,000 of their salaries to cut their billable hour requirements by five hundred hours a year (amounting to 9.6 hours per week), but as of that time the vast majority of big firms were not prepared to allow such a cut.

The other area of deprivation is physical touch. The work that lawyers do is wholly cerebral, and the manner in which they relate to others is strictly regulated by laws and customs that prohibit touching. Yet we rely on touch for a physical sensation of our world and for many of life's pleasures. We are primates, a group of higher mammals with sensitive fingers, who spend much time kissing, hugging and grooming. In *The Pleasure Center*, Morten Kringelbach reminds us that touch is crucial to human bonding, emotional stability and happiness. Working hard and long hours in a state of physical and social isolation with complete touch deprivation is no formula for happiness.

Solution: The physical layout of law firms has to be changed. Offices and cubicles can be opened to admit light, air, co-workers and visitors. Common rooms for group activities should be constructed. The billable hours system must be reformed so the jobs that lawyers do are less oppressive, more flexible and more life-serving for them. Stanford University Law School students have created Law Students for a Better Legal Profession to protect lawyers who choose reduced working hours for more balanced lives to avoid stigma and become partners. Students at UC Hastings College of the Law in San Francisco just formed Project for Attorney Retention (see www.pardc.org).

New methods to bill for the work of full-time lawyers will increase their time away from the office for family time, socializing, exercise and recreation. Some practicing lawyers have demanded that their law firms give them the option of working part-time. Part-time lawyers will not rise to the top in the traditional sense, but so what? They will lead more balanced, socially connected, happier lives.

Socializing isn't just good for business, it's good for your morale and your health. Don't leave it for the rainmakers. Let go of your compulsion to work, and try to eat lunch with someone every day, unless you're in trial. These people could include co-partners, co-associates, legal staff, friends, relatives, clients, experts and others.

Solo practitioners can reduce loneliness by joining other solos to create a small firm. Even moving to an office that is part of a suite of solos will mitigate loneliness by creating opportunities to chat. Get feedback frequently. Whether you're a solo practitioner or not, but especially if you're a solo, meet often with a group of other lawyers for camaraderie, emotional support and advice on how to handle difficult legal issues and difficult clients.

All lawyers should meet regularly with their clients. Let them know what issues are coming up. They may have information you weren't aware of that you can use to obtain a better result. You can gauge their attitude toward key decisions that must be made down the road. Meeting with your client will create a friendly, trusting relationship. The more often you meet, the more you will be in mental, emotional and social sync with your client. This will increase his support for you and cut friction.

With regard to touch, we can't kiss our clients when they do well in deposition or hug the judge when he makes an evidentiary ruling in our favor. Yet we can incorporate some acceptable touching into our law practice. We can shake hands. We can pat backs. There may be times we can put our arm around someone's shoulders. We can also drop our stiffness and physical reserve outside the office with our spouse, children and friends. This will break the imprisoning crustacean's shell so many of us have grown, and allow us to share the pleasure of normal human contact.

(3) Too Busy To Live Life

Lawyers set their agenda for each workday with a "To Do" list on a computer, Blackberry or legal pad. They don't schedule time for reflection on what's most important or how to do it most efficiently, but strain to get it all done. And they grade their day based on how many items they actually completed. Yet lawyers always fall behind.

As the day unfolds, new items must be added to the list and other items pushed back for another day. A lawyer's compulsion to finish the list generates a rushed, pressured quality in the way he speaks, moves and relates that alienates other people. When lawyers finally leave the office, they often feel as if they accomplished very little. Out of guilt, lawyers bring work home instead of settling down to a leisurely family dinner to reconnect with each family member. Being a prisoner of time makes them feel trapped, oppressed and irritable. Jack Kornfield summed this up well by saying, "When we get too caught up in the busyness of the world, we lose connection with one another—and ourselves."

In his letter to Paulinus titled "On The Shortness of Life," the great Roman Stoic Seneca said: "It is not that we have a short space of time, but that we waste much of it. Life is long enough, and it has been given in sufficiently generous measure, to allow the accomplishment of the very greatest things if the whole of it is well invested. But ... it is squandered in luxury and carelessness [or] devoted to no good end ... The part of life we really live is small. For all the rest of existence is not life, but merely time."

Seneca spends much of the letter lamenting that so many people waste their lives by obsessively pursuing pleasure (food, wine or sex), advancing their own ambitions in the realm of social climbing or politics or sacrificing themselves to advance the material interests of an employer. Such people take no time to "see themselves" or "give ear to themselves" and acquire self-awareness. Unlike Seneca's heroes (men like Pythagoras and Aristotle), they do not lead meaningful lives that contribute to the welfare of others or leave a legacy which benefits others.

Solution: Yes, law firms will suck the life out of you if you let them, but setting up a solo practice is not necessarily the antidote to feeling like there's never enough time for yourself. Seneca rightly suggests that we take time to reflect on what we really want out of life, and to pursue it without guilt. Periodically set aside time to mull over the bigger questions like:

- What am I trying to accomplish with my law practice?
- Am I enjoying my law practice?
- If not, what can I do to make it more meaningful and enjoyable?

On a daily basis ask yourself, what is this case all about, what is the message I want to convey and how can I best go about presenting it? Before you meet with anyone, ask yourself why am I meeting with X, how can this meeting benefit us and how can I maximize this benefit in the shortest possible time?

Become intentional and act with a purpose in mind that serves you and those you are trying to help. When you are intentional, you become more time-efficient and more productive, and you have more time to enjoy leisure and family activities. This in turn gives you a feeling that you have mastered time, rather than allowing time to master you.

Intention is important, but so is attention. Many lawyers make no effort to train and discipline their attention, so it wanders. The result is wasted time. In *Blind Spots*, author Madeleine L. Van Hecke, Ph.D., says distraction is a big problem for adults, not just children. She challenges us to hold one thought in our minds for even five seconds. People who meditate and notice how their minds operate see her point.

While you're working, do you fret over troublesome past incidents, worry over anticipated future events that may never occur, ponder your next meal or plan your next vacation? How often have you been woken from a reverie during a law firm meeting by someone calling your name or joking, "Earth to (your name)"? Do you find yourself doodling on a legal pad at your desk? Do you get so zoned out that you frequently misplace objects and waste time trying to relocate them?

Don't immediately think Ritalin. Loads of intelligent adults have trouble discerning what is happening around them in the absence of mindfulness training. In *On Being Certain*, neurologist Robert A. Burton, M.D., remembers being part of a group of very smart people (all physicians) shown a video about basketball players by a neuropsychologist. They were asked to note how many times each team passed the ball. None of them noticed a man dressed in a black gorilla costume walk across the floor over a period of nine seconds. When this was pointed out and they got to see the video again, they were flabbergasted. Meditation practice is the best way to develop mindfulness—a mental state of heightened awareness that is free, all natural and involves no drugs. Try it.

Time is wasted also when you take on too much. Be clear and assertive in turning down matters that do not deserve your time. Fairness dictates that energy exchanges between people are equal. Don't take calls from people who constantly seek favors but never offer help. Don't agree to participate in long meetings that cannot possibly benefit you.

Time gets wasted by having to put out fires you create unconsciously. Whenever you act with rudeness or lack of appreciation, people will come back with complaints that will take up your time. Do you walk past your paralegal every morning without saying, "Hello. How are you?" Do you fail to return a particular client's calls? Do you speak harshly to your associate for the most minor mistakes? If so, then you will have to face a hurt, angry person sooner or later. Remaining sensitive to others and showing them the same respect you want for yourself will avoid time-wasting, stressful encounters where you get confronted by people you have wounded.

(4) Boredom and Discouragement

Angeles Arrien, author of *Gratitude: The Essential Practice for Happiness & Fulfillment*, says one universal human addiction is the need for intensity. By intensity, Arrien means we think that really being alive means we need to be excited and pushed to our limits all the time. We don't get much of this in routine law practice. We get stuck having to fill out the same old forms, file routine motions and handle routine cases. We must sit through endless depositions filled with irrelevant, unimportant background questions. During litigation we see the other side make the same arguments and use the same tactics we have experienced countless times before in similar cases.

Much time is spent filling out and reviewing billing records. The incredible length of litigation can be a drag. Some cases go on for years. It's hard to maintain interest or see progress when intensive activity is episodic, combined with long periods of inactivity on cases. When we get bored, we feel discouraged. We look out the window and wonder what it would be like to be an astronaut, a chef, a race car driver, a gambler, a cop, a drug dealer, even a pole dancer or the Roto-Rooter man ... anything but a lawyer.

Discouragement comes in when one snag after another blocks progress on case resolution. There are insurance companies that keep changing defense counsel every time you're nearing settlement. Due to court congestion, you can show up fully prepared for trial on multiple occasions only to have your client's trial continued. How about finally getting all parties to agree to mediation, but being unable to find a date when all of them can attend with their lawyers, or repeatedly setting up mediations that get cancelled at the last moment?

Solution: Shape the circumstances of your work to create flow. Mihaly Csikszentmihalyi, an expert on flow, defines it as the experience of firing on all cylinders and performing at your peak without conscious effort. He says that artists, research scientists, concert pianists, rock climbers and elite athletes love what they do because they experience flow. These people engage in activities that are self-validating and self-rewarding. They don't require praise from anyone else. A painter knows when he's got it right.

Flow activities involve setting clear goals, intense concentration, immediate feedback (like knowing when you have struck the wrong piano key) to help you stay on track, operating entirely in the present moment, emptying one's head of all distractions (which would result in death for a rock climber) and losing oneself joyfully in the process of the activity—so that hours can go by as if they were minutes. Flow means an ego-less state in which things go right automatically because you have fused your consciousness with the task at hand. It's the opposite of being self-conscious and worrying about being judged.

Morten Klingberg calls the same mental state "fluid absorption." When people are in this state, they lose all consciousness of self and experience profound pleasure in the absence of external reward. Whether you call it flow or fluid absorption, what these men are talking about is adult play. Whether you are a child or an adult, play is its own reward, and it's so fun and so engrossing, you don't even realize you're learning new things or mastering complex tasks while doing it.

So how do you get your work to flow? Take more control over work and enrich it. It's crucial to set your practice up so that you can safely delegate routine, mind-numbing tasks to competent, reliable people. With regard to tasks that call for original thought in the realm of case investigation, factual presentation, legal theory, trial tactics or other matters, do the following:

- Enrich your work. You can attend seminars or case workshops to deal in greater depth with your issue. You can find an academician or forensic expert to consult. You can subscribe to periodicals that deal with the subject matter you handle, such as a brain injury lawyer getting issues of *Neurology*. You can read blogs and contact the lawyer-authors of the blogs to find out more about how they handled the same situation.

- Challenge yourself by raising the standards of your work to the very highest level. Instead of just cranking out the product, see how superior you can make your thinking and writing.

- Enliven the process of conceptualizing an issue by meeting regularly with a practice group in person, over

the phone or via webcam. Find lawyers who specialize in
the same cases you handle, form a group and spur each
other to new heights of insight and creativity.

- Get out of your rut. It isn't conducive to inspiration to
  sit in the office all day surrounded by the constant drone
  of computers, phones, and faxes; breathing the same
  stale air; and seeing the same people wearing the same
  clothes, saying and doing what they usually say and do.
  Find a colleague, get away and take a hike someplace.
  The exercise, fresh air and opportunity to chat without
  office distractions can really stimulate your imagination.
  Some lawyers even float in a float tank to fire up their
  creativity.

(5) Negativity

Lawyers learn pessimism and cynicism on the job and this is
a major reason for their misery, says Martin E.P. Seligman,
Ph.D., in *Authentic Happiness*. They are trained to see bad
events as constant, permanent and pervasive features of the
world. This pessimism helps them succeed in transactions,
because they scan the horizon for every conceivable "snare
and catastrophe" that could sour a deal, and they plan ahead.
This characteristic blinds them from seeing and appreciating
the good in others, in themselves and in life itself. Lawyers
have difficulty trusting and are on constant alert for the dark
underside of innocent situations.

Cynicism is another source of misery for us. By believing
we are surrounded by nothing but fools, incompetents, char-
latans, cheats and scoundrels, we are left all alone in a bleak
world. There's no one worth befriending. Cynicism is a way
of seeing others as incapable of sincerity, virtue or altruism.
The cynic assumes that all human actions are motivated by
self-interest, that people are basically dishonest, they lie easily
and won't keep their promises.

Some lawyers grow up cynical because they were raised in elitist families that characterized outsiders as inferiors and put them down. They often attended elitist colleges and law schools and went to work in elitist law firms that pumped them up by devaluing others.

Negative energy also arises frequently from negative comments lawyers shoot at one another. How many promising days fell flat after you and opposing counsel traded nasty, biting comments about each other? Why do lawyers make such comments? They can reflect problems with anger, depression, poor socialization, poor communication skills or alcoholism. But sometimes they represent a deliberate tactic. Some lawyers use rude and insulting statements as a tool. They use them to make their adversary look incompetent in front of a judge or jury, to distract him, to cause self-doubt or to drive a wedge between him and his client (e.g., "Come on, Dave. You know I think you're a fine lawyer, so why on earth would you waste your time representing a phony like that?"). If we allow the negative energy from such comments to sit inside us and accumulate, we can become depressed.

Solution: Meditation can help overcome these problems. The daily practice of meditation creates deep calm, relaxation and peace. The present moment is a time of sheer aliveness free of all striving, strife, regret and fear. Meditation enables us to focus on the present moment instead of dredging up and obsessing over rude comments made in the past or engaging in anxious thoughts about our future encounters with lawyers who disturb us.

Meditation connects us to the universe, making us feel like an integral part of the whole, whose value cannot be diminished by anyone else's negative comments. Meditation takes the drama and importance out of negative comments from others. We start seeing them as misguided and unfortunate rather than evil. Once we are free of the need for the approval of others and the sting of their negative comments, a huge source of misery has been lifted from our lives, as Henri J.M. Nouwen points out in *The Inner Voice of Love*.

Just as pessimism can be learned, the same is true for optimism. You can practice seeing the best possibilities in ourselves, others and the situations that life presents. In *As You Think*, James Allen tells us that allowing your mind to operate without any instructions to think positive thoughts allows it to operate in default mode. The mind's default is permeable to every negative thought generated by your own brain and those of others. Negative thoughts threaten our survival and tend to be more powerful than positive ones. Nouwen says, to stay positive we must envision a positive future for ourselves and put mental energy into making it happen. There are many techniques for manifesting a positive future. Wayne Dyer suggests taking time each day to sit quietly in a private place and imagine the life you want while chanting the sacred word AH, which refers to the source energy all great religions have termed God.

(6) Formalism and Intellectual Aridity

Lawyers use their left brains (the logical, sequential, linear and analytic part of their intelligence) to carry out their work. They rarely access their right brain (the creative, artistic, holistic side), their feelings or their bodies at work. They function like disembodied brains floating in a glass case on wheels, like something out of a sci-fi movie. Why?

In *How Lawyers Lose Their Way*, Stefancic and Delgado say it's because the law is a "formalistic" system. By "formalism," they are referring to the mechanical method dictating how law students are educated, how lawyers develop and present their cases, how law firms are operated and how judges decide cases. For them, formalism means having to ignore every relevant source of information that bears on making a just decision in a given case, except the rules of law derived from, and consistent with, precedent.

Formalism is tunnel vision. Formalism relies on internal factors to make legal decisions while blocking out ideas from anthropology, psychology, sociology, history, economics, ethics and philosophy. Out go ideas from the imaginative and artistic realm (art, literature, poetry and theater) or the spiritual realm (myth, mysticism and religion). Stefancic and Delgado say that formalism makes lawyers unhappy, because it is an arid, sterile way of dealing with legal issues that is largely devoid of creativity, inspiration, and intellectual content, and is unable to serve the common good.

So what exactly is formalism? Stefancic and Delgado define it as a system of legal reasoning in which regularity, uniformity and predictability are the supreme virtues.

Formalism confines the decision-maker to a relatively small number of matters or "elements," ideally of an easily ascertained sort. If it's this kind of case, then I must apply this rule, and only material elements A, B and C are relevant, not D, E and F.

How many times did you spot a "gray area" in the law where precedent did not speak to your client's issues, and ask the court to go beyond precedent? How many times did the court refuse to do it? These authors note that formalism is a rule of exclusion, while life is diverse and unruly. They disapprove of formalism, because it hammers reality into existing doctrines and precedents and prevents lawyers from using their personal knowledge and creativity to expand the law. Lawyers with active minds are constrained by formalism. The challenge is to keep your mind alive and express yourself rather than letting formalism choke your spirit.

Solution: Prior to legal formalism, the law had a rich and impressive tradition of scholarship. We can and should move past a left-brained system of reasoning akin to placing coins in slots. It's time to incorporate right-brained thinking into the legal system. Such thinking is intuitive, flexible, creative and holistic. Things will change for the better when we start using our right brains in all aspects of legal practice—from court decisions to law firm design, staff recruitment and organizational structure.

Right-brained thinking will give as a new sense of openness, possibility and empowerment as we face the issues that arise in our work.

(7) Substance Abuse

When law practice has you feeling down, discouraged and depressed, it's easy to reach for a drink, a sedative or a painkiller. It's easy to regard these substances as comforting friends who know your secret life of pain and can melt it away. This short-term fix is not a long-term solution. Substance use becomes addictive and over time progressively erodes your health, independence, productivity, dignity and social relationships. Use of alcohol and drugs to beat the blues only compounds and worsens depression, and puts your job and law license at risk.

Solution: Chapter Five is devoted to understanding and treating alcoholism. The second half of this book is devoted to cultivation of a healthy mind, body and spirit, which will prevent you from craving substances to cope with stress and feel good.

(8) Denial of Feelings

When ending a bad marriage, you can make matters worse by screaming at, slapping or punishing your spouse by hiring a pit bull lawyer. The healthy way is to get in touch with the suffering both of you experienced and allow yourself to feel compassion for yourself and your spouse, so you can both move on. To heal the pain you must you must feel it. Suppressing it only generates anger, blame and attack.

Externally, lawyers like helping clients, establishing a reputation or marketing themselves. They don't set aside quiet time to feel the holes in themselves, those empty places carved out by old pain from life's disappointments, like failed relationships. They use alcohol, drugs, gambling, sex or other addictions to fill those holes, so they can keep functioning. Eventually they crash.

In *Love & Survival*, famed cardiologist Dean Ornish, M.D., owns up to being something of a workaholic to avoid intimacy. He talks about the isolation and loneliness he felt, even while surrounded by admiring patients who thanked him for saving their lives or being applauded by fellow cardiologists at conventions. How could that be?

It's because Dr. Ornish was busy lecturing and speaking, not listening. He was telling people what to do, not participating in conversations with an open heart. In the book he wrote just before *Love & Survival*, Dr. Ornish admitted to being extremely depressed at age nineteen and seeking to flee the pain by seriously contemplating suicide. The doctor was astonished that most of the people who read the earlier book thanked him primarily for talking about that experience of facing and surviving his suicidal crisis. He learned that only when he had the courage to share a deep part of himself in an open way was he able to connect with others. Lecturing from a podium didn't do it.

Dr. Ornish's experience has relevance for us. As a group, we are among the least self-revealing people. We hold in our emotions of doubt, fear, worry and confusion; the stress, frustration and anger; and the desperate need we feel to connect with others and get their support. We suck personal information from others through subpoenas for records and depositions, but we hide our personal lives. We keep a poker face to hide our feelings and appear more confident and in control than we actually are. We wear that mask of total self-assurance when we instruct and advise clients on what to do. Is it any wonder our clients may feel uncomfortable with us and that we experience a sense of alienation, of being cut off from others?

Solution: Share your feelings with others. Self-revelation creates understanding, empathy and trust between people. We like people who are open and vulnerable with us and who are willing to share their own disappointments, imperfections and fears. I am not suggesting that you confess your life story to each client. That would be inappropriate and would over-whelm the client. Rather, use your good judgment to share relevant bits of information about yourself that might make particular clients feel less alone with their burdens.

You and your clients need each other's support, but clients will only reach out to a human being, not a statue. Stop lectur-ing and listen. Just listening (without doing anything more) makes clients feel you care about them, and makes them like you. Clients who like you will not bombard you with calls to criticize you for every little thing and they are much less likely to sue you if you make a mistake.

When you socialize with other lawyers, don't always talk shop. Try sharing your feelings about the ups and downs of your practices and your lives, your hopes and dreams and your struggles. This will invite support and helpful feedback. It will create a sense of community that will buffer you against misery.

CHAPTER ONE: SUGGESTED READINGS

Jean Stefancic and Richard Delgado, *How Lawyers Lose Their Way* (Duke University Press, 2005)

Deborah L. Arron, *Running From The Law* (Ten Speed Press, 1991)

Paul Pearsall, *The Last Self-Help Book You'll Ever Need* (Basic Books, 2005)

Hindi Greenberg, *The Lawyer's Career Change Handbook: More Than 300 Things You Can Do With A Law Degree* (Collins, 2002)

Morten L. Kringelbach, *The Pleasure Center* (Oxford University Press, 2009)

CHAPTER TWO

The causes behind, and cures for, the lack of civilized professionalism

Why Civilized Professionalism is of the Utmost Importance

CIVILITY, which comes from the term civilization, refers not just to politeness and courtesy, but encompasses the idea that conduct affecting others should conform to society's agreed set of rules for social interaction. Lucinda Holdforth, author of *Why Manners Matter*, says that manners are not a social mask that we can conveniently put on and take off as we please, but an essential part of our humanity.

Incivility, which derives from the Latin root *incivilis* (meaning "not of a citizen") involves social behavior that is ill-mannered, rude and disrespectful. To act with incivility is to reject society's code for acceptable behavior. If social interaction were a sport, an uncivil act would amount to a flagrant foul.

The Defining Characteristics of Incivility

Incivility is a form of unprofessional conduct. While it's okay to be assertive, it's not okay to be uncivil. How do you distinguish incivility from other types of conduct? My view is that incivility has these essential features:

- It's conduct that is not reasonably necessary to carry out a legitimate legal objective, such as proving the elements of a claim or defense.

- It's conduct motivated by a desire to cause psychological distress to another lawyer by taunting, mocking, belittling, embarrassing, humiliating, degrading or diminishing him.

- It's conduct that involves treating another lawyer dismissively, as if he didn't count—conduct that violates another lawyer's need to be respected as a person and acknowledged as a fellow professional with equal standing.

- It's conduct that the perpetrator would find intolerable and unacceptable if practiced against him by the victim.

The Flaunting of Incivility is Common Today

Far from seeing incivility as wrong, many lawyers use it to coerce other lawyers into giving them what they want. The idea is to make yourself so obnoxious that opposing counsel will give in to avoid spending time with you. Unfortunately this tactic works far too often.

Years ago I went to opposing counsel's office for my client's deposition and saw many framed letters on his walls. Each letter came from a fellow lawyer who accused him of being a rude, mean and inflexible jerk. This man was so proud of distressing other lawyers that he posted their complaints like a badge of honor. A colleague of mine, a plaintiff's trial lawyer, related another example to me. One Friday afternoon he noticed a well-dressed man loitering for hours outside his office door. Finally, he stepped outside to ask, "May I help you?" The man responded, "No. My orders from the firm that hired me are to wait until 4:59 p.m. on Friday to serve you with legal papers from their office in this case." Clearly the strategy was to burden my colleague's firm with work and keep them stressed all weekend. Nice.

Why the Restoration of
Civilized Professionalism Matters

Lawyers have always been highly educated people well-versed in how government operates, how laws are made and enforced, what rights people have and how these rights are to be protected. You would expect such people to speak to one another with courtesy. Yet lawyers often use mockery and ridicule to disparage each other while addressing the court. This conduct not only alienates judges, jurors and the public, but also makes law practice painful. Having suggested to some of my colleagues that they abandon incivility and adopt civilized professionalism in its place, I have encountered certain objections. The main objection is that in such an environment they would be rendered ineffective as advocates. I wholeheartedly disagree.

My view of civility can be understood through these propositions:

- Lawyers can effectively present their client's position and effectively rebut their adversary's position without incivility. Rudeness, personal insults and abusive tactics are not required to represent your client with all due vigor and competence.

- Treating opposing counsel or his client uncivilly is unethical. It violates the concept that all people have dignity and are to be treated equally (i.e., no worse than we would have them treat us). This concept is enshrined in our common religious, philosophical and constitutional principles and universally accepted.

- Treating opposing counsel or his client uncivilly out of the belief that you must do this to be effective is not only mistaken, but causes emotional, psychological and even physical harm to the victim and to the perpetrator, as Chapter Four (stress and mental health) will demonstrate.

- Lawyers who practice incivility are misguided, rather
  than evil, and should be educated to change their ways.

Who is Responsible for Incivility?

The lawyers who use incivility cannot be blamed for inventing the practice. They first learned incivility was okay from their law school professors who ridiculed all students who were unprepared for class or gave a wrong answer. Once in practice, they observed judges giving the same harsh tongue-lashing to the lawyers who botched oral argument. They also witnessed partners and senior associates using rudeness and ridicule in depositions, motions, trial briefs and during argumentation and cross-examination in trial. To be successful, we modeled ourselves after mentors who practiced incivility.

The Positive Benefits of Civility

The quality of our relationships with other people plays a huge role in determining if we will be healthy and happy. Christopher Hansard, an expert on Tibetan Buddhism, put this well: "Relationships are the foundation of humanity. We derive our nourishment from them, learn from them, and thrive through them. Every human being wants to relate to other human beings; it is an essential part of who we are as individuals and as a species. And the way in which we relate to others determines how happy we are, how long we live, and the choices we make. Through our relationships we discover our place in the world and our reason for being here."

When people are civil and respectful toward each other, an atmosphere is created in which everyone feels valued and safe. People feel comfortable asking questions, sharing opinions and speaking their minds. The best teachers encourage their classes by telling them, "There are no stupid questions in here." The worst teachers squelch curiosity and exploration by the use of ridicule.

The Harms of Incivility

Sarcasm, the use of cutting and often ironic remarks intended to wound, infects the act of communication with anxiety. Because people fear being sliced to ribbons if they speak their thoughts freely, they may remain silent, attack first or disguise their thoughts. Honest communication requires an atmosphere of mutual respect and safety. No one benefits from incivility, because even the lawyers who are most prolific in dishing out rudeness get it back in spades. They provoke normally polite, courteous lawyers into becoming snarling tigers ready to use their sharp teeth and claws.

You may ask, isn't rudeness harmless when directed toward adults? Aren't lawyers people with tough hides who can take it as well as dish it out? This is a myth. No armor protects lawyers against incivility. And the emotional and psychological tone of our work environment is critical to our level of mental health and happiness. Alfred University Professor of Philosophy Emrys Westacott put this well when he wrote: "Precisely because rudeness is quite common, it is not a trivial issue. Indeed, in our day-to-day lives, it is possibly responsible for more pain than any other mortal failing."

The Verbal Abuse Scale (VAS) is a 70-item instrument based on answers to a self-report questionnaire. In the broadest sense, VAS assessment looks at the criticism content of speech, as well as the way it is delivered, e.g., by yelling and screaming, how it is received and processed, and what psychological effects it has on the recipient of the abuse. VAS assessment brings out details with respect to types of verbal abuse, cognitive appraisal, stressfulness, emotions, coping and long-term results. The VAS has been applied to surgical nurses who work for verbally abusive surgeons. Not surprisingly, studies show that nurses who get yelled at feel bad and do not perform as well. A score greater than 40 on the VAS is associated with significant elevation of suicide risk, because of increased depression and dissociation.

If you worked for a highly critical partner who verbally tortured you while you were an associate, what do you think your VAS score was in those days? What is your VAS score while you appear before cantankerous judges? How about when you litigate against a pit bull lawyer who seethes with anger and uses words like darts? Wouldn't it be wonderful to go to work each day expecting civilized debate within a cooperative process of dispute resolution instead of hurtful incivility?

The California State Bar Has Officially Recognized Incivility as a Problem

On July 20, 2007, the State Bar of California adopted a set of voluntary guidelines to promote civility between attorneys called "California Attorney Guidelines of Civility and Professionalism." Section 1 of the Guidelines says: "The dignity, decorum and courtesy that have traditionally characterized the courts and legal profession of civilized nations are not empty formalities. They are essential to an atmosphere that promotes justice and to an attorney's responsibility for the fair and impartial administration of justice."

Had there not been an obvious breakdown in the tradition of civility, the Guidelines would not have been necessary. The Introduction to the Guidelines makes it clear that they are voluntary and aspirational, rather than new rules for attorney discipline. But the Introduction stresses that the obligations of lawyers include "civility, professional integrity, personal dignity, candor, diligence, respect, courtesy and cooperation, all of which are essential to the fair administration of justice and conflict resolution."

The massive explosion of state and federal appellate decisions on imposition of sanctions against lawyers is a testament to the trend toward abuses. Hindi Greenberg, author of *Lawyer's Career Change Handbook: More Than 300 Things You Can Do With A Law Degree*, has counseled some 14,000 lawyers dissatisfied with their jobs or law in general. She estimates that less than half of all lawyers really like what they do for a living. What is the connection between the "interpersonal nastiness" of our uncivil times and this high level of career dissatisfaction? Ms. Greenberg suggests that the pit bull mindset held by many contemporary lawyers plays a significant role in the erosion of law's appeal.

HOW TO COMBAT INCIVILITY
AND RESTORE PROFESSIONALISM

Redefining Our Notion of
"Adversary" in Legal Proceedings

I've told laypeople that working in the current attack-dog environment has caused lawyers exceedingly high rates of depression and alcoholism. I suggested to them that lawyers would benefit personally by learning to treat each other in more compassionate and humane ways than they do now. I asked if that made sense.

Some laypeople said they strongly agreed with this idea. Yet others scoffed. They told me that law is an inherently "adversarial" profession, one in which the lawyer most likely to win is the one who is most aggressive, least accommodating and most relentless in securing victory for his client. The laypeople who saw law as an adversarial system said that when a litigant really wants to win a legal dispute, he will invariably hire the toughest, most obnoxious lawyer he can find. These laypeople dismissed the concept that lawyers should be civil, cooperative and concerned for each other's welfare. They asserted that such values are misplaced since they would neutralize the aggressiveness lawyers must have to succeed within the system, and would deprive the public of the lawyers they really want. Of course, I disagree.

The pro-adversary argument begs three questions:
1. Can advocacy prevail only when accompanied by incivility?
2. Is the domination of our legal system by rude, hostile lawyers socially desirable and beneficial?
3. Does the cost of victory outweigh the gain when you look at how pit bull lawyers raise the duration, cost and stress of litigation by disputing everything and stipulating to nothing?

Let me give you an example to ponder. I was privy to a hallway conversation a number of years back in which I learned that Lawyer X's father died during trial and Lawyer X orally moved the court for an order continuing the trial for a few days so he could attend his father's funeral out of state. But opposing counsel, Lawyer Y, vigorously opposed the motion. The trial judge not only granted Lawyer X's motion, but scolded Lawyer Y for incivility and heartlessness in the face of a fellow professional's personal tragedy.

Did Lawyer Y really need to oppose the motion, to represent his client effectively? Isn't it likely he hurt himself and his client by his heartless conduct? So why did he do it? Anyone who would deny a lawyer a continuance to attend his father's funeral suffers from a misunderstanding of the word adversary. If you look word up the word "adversary" in any dictionary, you will see two definitions.

The first is a morally neutral one such as "one who opposes, resists or contends with you." In legal disputes, this would refer to parties taking opposed positions on issues of fact or law. This is perfectly legitimate and even expectable since reasonable minds do differ about a great many things, especially the law.

The second definition of adversary is "enemy" with synonyms including "devil" and "Satan." Too many lawyers believe they cannot effectively serve their clients unless they attack the honor, character, motives and veracity of the other side. This belief is mistaken and rests on a needless blending of the two definitions of adversary.

We could make a lot of progress by disentangling "one who opposes" from "enemy" in the context of legal proceedings. Everyone participating in the legal process is a fellow human being with the same basic needs, including the needs for consideration, respect and compassion. The party and lawyer on the opposing side are not alien life forms or "others" to be figuratively destroyed in the combat of litigation. The world we live in is the world we project with our minds. We can live in a fortress of self-righteousness in which we assume a position of superiority and judge others as bad and wrong. We can also live in a world where all people are interconnected and the law functions to heal some of the disputes between them.

Redefining What it Means to Win

The whole notion of "winning" needs to be reevaluated. In most legal disputes there is a huge range of possible outcomes. How you define a win depends more on perspective than anything else. Through discernment of common ground and compromise, opposed parties can both win. When a client's vision is colored by hate and vengeance, and the lawyer adopts this vision, litigation dissolves into war. As lawyers, we are gatekeepers to the legal system. We should refuse to play along with a client who wants to go beyond securing his legal rights by punishing the other party. When you reject a fair compromise to level a crushing defeat on the other side, the consequence is loads of excess hours invested in needless work.

EIGHT CAUSES OF UNCIVIL INTERACTIONS AND THEIR SOLUTIONS

(1) Convenience

In many aspects of life we give lip service to rules, meaning we acknowledge that it makes good sense for everyone to follow them, but we break them whenever no one in authority is looking. A common example is running red lights. Adults know they can collide with another car and hurt the occupants of that vehicle, as well as the occupants of their own car, if they run a red light. Yet if they are in a hurry, the intersection is momentarily clear and there is no police car visible near the intersection, they will sometimes run a red light. Why? It's more convenient to run the red than brake to a stop, wait for the light to go through the whole cycle and try to make up the lost time once you resume travel. Some lawyers think it's a whole lot easier to treat other lawyers like garbage than to take time to listen to their concerns and find respectful ways to accommodate their legitimate ones.

Solution: Use self-discipline to cultivate patience when speaking with other lawyers. The famous Beckman and Frankel study in the late 1980s showed that the average time it took a physician to interrupt his patient during an interview was 18 seconds. Based on my observations, lawyers take less time to interrupt each other. Let the other lawyer speak his mind, before you jump down his throat. He will appreciate being heard and you will be in a position to truly understand where he's coming from, which creates the potential for collaboration in place of the usual attack/counterattack. If he cuts you off repeatedly, then advise him you want time to finish articulating your position. If he refuses, you can tell him it's pointless to continue the conversation unless he's willing to listen.

(2) Imitation

Humans learn nearly everything by example and imitation, a process called natural learning. We learn to speak English as children not by studying the language but by listening to adults use it in everyday life. We learn to behave by watching how our parents respond to other people and we take our cue from them.

In the Hollywood version, success is what matters, irrespective of how it was achieved. Indeed, popular TV shows and movies about law practice seem to focus on the most ruthless lawyers and portray them as having acquired the most power, influence and money as they wreck other people's reputations and lives. Lawyers, who pin their whole future on making partner in aggressive law firms, may be asked repeatedly to rationalize exceptions to their ethical standards to get the results and bring in the fees required for promotion to partner status.

What if your mentor at work is a powerful and wealthy attorney who revels in the use of SOB tactics and practices them without any pangs of conscience. You can imitate him in hopes of pleasing him, rising in the firm and making lots of money. You can also ask for a different mentor or leave the firm. Yes, some young lawyers do quit in this situation, but many stay and become someone they never intended to be. If you let your employer define who you are, you may wind up as a Darth Vader.

Solution: Imitation occurs unconsciously, unless you choose whom to imitate. Be very careful whom you imitate, and don't be afraid to leave a Darth Vader mentor. While writing this book chapter I contacted Dr. Marco Iacoboni, author of *Mirroring People* and the discoverer of the mirror neuron system in the human brain. This is the neural circuitry that underlies the human capacity for empathy. The mirror neurons are what enable one human being to discern what another is thinking and become affected emotionally. When I reached Dr. Iacoboni I asked him if he thought lawyers were so uncivil toward each other because they found ways to suppress their mirror neurons.

He responded by saying that mirror neurons work by mirroring what members of the group are doing. Thus, if a majority of lawyers tend to be aggressive, rude and uncivil, it will create an example for others to follow and the culture of rudeness will perpetuate itself. For incivility to stop requires the lawyers reading this book to begin a new practice of civility. In time, other lawyers will imitate these pioneers. Preaching does no good. We need role models.

(3) Careless Use of Language

Next time you drive, please notice how frequently you use negative terms to label other drivers (the people who drive too slowly in front of you or cut you off in traffic). Do you call them jerks, idiots, morons or unprintable names? Are your kids in the car when you use these labels? Now notice how often you use similar terms to describe opposing counsel when he does things that irritate you.

We can't use negative labels about other people without being affected. Benjamin Whorf, co-creator of the Sapir-Whorf hypothesis, said that the vocabulary we use influences both the content of our thinking and our behavior. When you keep calling opposing counsel a shark, a jerk or a whore, that's how you will think of him and that's how you will treat him.

Solution: Become more mindful of your language and clean it up. You can find much less negative terms to describe opposing counsel. If you can't find anything positive to say, then at least use neutral descriptions that focus on his actions rather than his character, his motives, his IQ or his value as a person. Instead of saying he's evil, you can say he's mistaken, confused, ignorant about the facts or lacking a broad perspective.

(4) Loss of Personal Accountability

Prior to the baby boom generation, there were much fewer law schools and lawyers. Our predecessors knew each other socially, and these friendships inhibited them from winning at all costs and burning bridges with colleagues. Knowing each other made them personally accountable to each other for their conduct.

Although collegiality still exists (particularly in specialty areas where the same folks appear day in and day out before an administrative board), it's the exception rather than the rule. What's changed? The explosive growth of law schools caused an explosive growth in the sheer number of lawyers. Today the greater number of lawyers makes for an impersonal atmosphere, anonymity and a dilution of individual accountability. So has the rise of factory firms with high turnover rates where multiple attorneys work on the same case in succession. Predicting they will never see opposing counsel again, or at least not for a very long time, lawyers feel less incentive to take the time to know each other and establish good rapport and good feelings as the basis for future relations.

Solution: Every lawyer we meet for the first time is a stranger but also a potential friend, or at least a potential collaborator in the civilized resolution of a claim. If you will take the time (over the phone or in person) to chat with the lawyer on the other side during the earliest stage of litigation, and get to know him, the atmosphere of impersonality that breeds lack of accountability will be dissipated.

(5) Dramatic Decrease in Percentage of Solo Practitioners

In a speech given in 2005 by David Watkiss to the International Academy of Trial Lawyers, it was noted that between 1949 and 2005 the percentage of lawyers in America who practiced alone went from 60% down to 30%. Solo practitioners tend to be more vulnerable and more humble than lawyers working for firms. They have limited resources. They depend on friendships for referrals. To survive, they need to juggle time deadlines. Solos could not survive without the willingness of opposing counsel to extend their deadlines for discovery, filing motions, disclosing experts, etc. To secure that willingness, they must be friendly and make concessions.

It's probable that the decline of the solo has played a part in the erosion of legal professionalism. Lawyers in big firms have a lot more muscle to flex than solos do, and I have seen them run solos ragged because they can and they think it benefits their client. Psychologists who study group behavior say that group members subordinate their identity to the group, and become willing to abuse individuals in order to serve the purposes of the group.

Solution: The economy is causing big firms to break up into smaller separate firms and this could soften some of the arrogance that goes with working for a big firm.

Yet, big firms will continue to exist and the number of solo practitioners will continue to decline in concert with the ever-rising costs of the law business.

Each of us has to make a choice. We can keep the status quo or we can decide to be accountable for our behavior and treat other lawyers as we would wish them to treat us. You can be a mensch while working for a big firm regardless of the huge resources ready at your disposal.

(6) Salary Inflation Bred Ego Inflation

In the 1980s and 1990s intense competition between large firms for the best legal talent coming out of law schools caused an astronomic escalation in starting salaries. The Padawans became instant Jedi with no time for acquiring wisdom, maturity or humility. Salaries will temporarily come down in our current recession, but the damage to professionalism was done and it continues.

Solution: The education, training and mentorship of young lawyers must be designed to counteract the ego-inflating effects of big salaries. Being able to afford the newest Mercedes coupe doesn't authorize you to treat other people like deckhands on a garbage scow. Law professors, supervising partners and judges can demonstrate the value of and the necessity for courteous, respectful behavior. Was the San Francisco Giants clubhouse a better place to be with or without the narcissistic Barry Bonds seated on his throne-like chair watching his own big-screen TV?

(7) Retaliation

Lawyers pride themselves on "not taking crap" from other lawyers. They will strike back when subjected to rude comments or offensive behavior. Like brings forth like.

Retaliation refers to what one person does in response to an act or series of actions by another which he perceives as causing harm to himself or those he cares about. Statements like, "I was tired of this guy jerking me around," "I had enough of his arrogance" or "It's about time he got some of his own medicine" reflect retaliation.

Law practice today is more rife with tit-for-tat retaliation than our nation's highways.

Solution: The number one cause of traffic accidents is discourteous driving, such as failing to yield to other cars while merging or failing to yield for pedestrians. State driving laws represent an effort to force drivers to be courteous on pain of expensive tickets. Most of the states that have lawyer civility guidelines make them aspirational, not mandatory. Hence, it's up to us to practice courtesy. Just as courtesy on the road prevents crashes and saves lives, courtesy at the office prevents retaliation and saves your nervous system from stress overload.

(8) Confusion About Zealous Representation

Beginning in our first year law school class in professional responsibility, we heard the phrase "duty of zealous representation." What does zealous representation actually mean? Does it mean concealing your strongest evidence (the proof that could lead to early settlement) until trial? Does it mean never granting a harmless continuance? Never agreeing to a stipulated order in response to an incontestable motion?

In July 2007 California enacted a set of aspirational guidelines for increased professionalism and civility among the state's lawyers. In 2008 the State Bar held a panel discussion on the guidelines. Lawyers in the audience told the panel they were not likely to follow the guidelines because the guidelines weren't mandatory and it was more important to zealously represent your client than to be nice to opposing counsel. They couldn't accept the possibility that professionalism and competent representation could go together.

Solution: These lawyers missed the point. It's entirely possible to remain courteous and still make a winning motion for summary judgment. It's entirely possible to remain polite during a cross-examination of your opponent's expert that demonstrates he has no solid basis for his opinions.

AN EXTENDED DISCUSSION ABOUT
THE ROLE OF STEREOTYPES IN CAUSING
LAWYER vs. LAWYER INCIVILITY

In human affairs, rational decision-making is the exception rather than the rule. Most of our decisions are based on gut feelings, stereotypes and biases that arise from beneath the level of conscious awareness. In *The Naked Brain*, neuroscientist Richard Restak, M.D., says our brains have two separate systems for decision-making, which arose at different times during human evolution.

The old system, known as the limbic system, is controlled by the amygdala, an almond-shaped structure that lies deep within the brain in the medial temporal lobe. The amygdala was designed to help us survive by triggering an instantaneous fear alarm when our lives were in danger, as when a saber-toothed tiger on a rock above us began snarling. The amygdala prompted the "fight-flight" response that pumped adrenaline to power our ancestors to run away or stand their ground with a rock or spear. As human evolution progressed, and isolated clans of hunter-gatherers settled down into agrarian civilizations, the amygdala took on new roles. Initially it began to evaluate less direct and more remote threats. Later on the amygdala came to evaluate all objects of sensation, thought and emotion as being attractive/repulsive, pleasant/unpleasant or desirable/undesirable.

One hangover from the Stone Age amygdala is our negativity bias toward strangers. Restak says it left us with the tendency to like other people who look, speak, and act like us, and to dislike people who differ from us in these ways. Experts in social cognition call this "implicit bias," because it operates on an unconscious level in all persons, no matter how liberal, progressive and egalitarian they are in their conscious thinking. Unconscious racism, sexism, ageism and other isms come from the older, unconscious brain system.

The newer, cognitive system for decision making is wired into our prefrontal and frontal lobes. This new neural equipment is what enables us to consciously analyze information gathered in our working memory and come to a decision based on analytic reasoning using principles derived from rules of logic, social ethics and so forth. Because it is a conscious process, not an automatic one, it creates the possibility of seeing when we are acting hypocritically due to an implicit bias and choosing not to do so. If we realize, by ourselves or with help, that we are acting in a biased way, we can inhibit the bias and treat the person with the fairness and respect he deserves. We can train ourselves to stop openly approving of racist and sexist jokes that keep implicit stereotypes alive.

The Shyster Stereotype

The public has a stereotype of lawyers as being greedy, self-centered and dishonest shysters. I'm convinced that some of us have unconsciously adopted this stereotype. If I'm right, this means that when opposing counsel disagrees with you, you will subconsciously see him through the shyster stereotype. Next time another lawyer opposes you, take a deep breath. Don't react immediately on an emotional level. Take a moment to gain some rational perspective on his argument. Is he really just a no-good shyster or is he another lawyer who may have a valid point or at least a reasonable argument?

There is no one racial, national, ethnic, religious or occupational group that behaves all one way all the time. Search your mind. If you are reacting to a stereotype and not to the person in front of you, you are dealing with a fiction. Let the stereotype go, and deal with the real person.

The Us/Them Stereotype

Us/them refers to any split between the parties that a lawyer chooses to highlight in a case. Us/them is based on perceived differences in the character of the parties (honest vs. deceitful, careful vs. careless), their economic status (corporation vs. individual, rich vs. poor), their educational status (school of hard knocks vs. elite college), occupational status (blue collar vs. white collar), etc. Lawyers will use these us/them stereotypes in jury selection, opening statement and closing argument to the extent permitted by the Court over objection of opposing counsel. They do this to enlist sympathy for their client and inflame prejudice against the opposing party.

Yet lawyers are affected by the same us/them stereotype in how they perceive, evaluate and react to each other. Whether it's a clash between a solo practitioner and a big firm, between the plainly dressed graduate of a middling law school vs. the sartorially splendid lawyer from Harvard or between lawyers of different genders, sexual orientations, ages or races, the us/them stereotype can make their interactions highly conflicted.

The really important thing is that we find ways to make these unconscious biases against each other conscious, and that we choose to act based on mutual respect and civility rather than be controlled by the biases. Neurologist Richard Restak says we need "not be slaves to the automatic responses mediated by our amygdala and other components of our brain's emotional circuits; instead, thanks to the frontal lobes of our brain, we have the power to create for ourselves a new and empowering reality."

Dr. Restak also says, quite admirably, that: "If social neuroscience has one basic tenet, it is this: Since we spend most of our time either thinking about or engaging with others, our brain's most important function is to free us from the prison of our own minds and enhance social communication."

The Problem of Hiring Assholes
Who Demoralize Other Employees

Law firms can be so blinded by the star quality or money-making potential of a lawyer that they hire him despite being told he's the biggest asshole in the universe. This doesn't serve anyone's interests in the long run.

In *The No Asshole Rule*, author Robert I. Sutton, Ph.D., describes the damage that "assholes" do as managers of corporations. He argues they should be screened out during the hiring process, and fired if they make it through, no matter how much money they generate for their employer.

Sutton's discussion is relevant to our topic for two reasons. First, although not all law firms are corporations, many law firms refuse to terminate asshole partners because they are skilled rainmakers. Second, any lawyer, not just a rainmaking partner, can be an asshole. Even a new associate can plague his law firm by verbally abusing subordinates or by treating the lawyer, paralegal or secretary on the opposing side like garbage. To preserve civility, it's important to know who the assholes are and how to deal with them.

Sutton says that on the spectrum of human character, the two poles are the "mensch" and the "asshole." He defines mensch as "a person [who] is persistently warm and civilized toward people who are of unknown or lower status." A mensch leaves other people feeling positive and energized. Sutton defines the asshole as a person who saps others of their energy and self-esteem through the accumulated effects of many small, demeaning acts that make the victim "die a little" during every encounter. Assholes cause harm by demoralizing employees, lowering their attendance and performance, and making them miserable enough to quit.

Sutton says there are two main types of assholes: those who act like raging maniacs and those who inflict harm covertly in a backstabbing way. He has a "Dirty Dozen" list of actions that assholes use to inflict damage on underlings:

1. Personal insults
2. Invading one's personal territory
3. Uninvited physical contact
4. Threats and intimidation, both verbal and nonverbal
5. Sarcastic jokes and teasing used as insult delivery systems
6. Withering email flames
7. Status slaps intended to humiliate their victims
8. Public shaming or status degradation rituals
9. Rude interruptions
10. Two-faced attacks
11. Dirty looks
12. Treating people as if they are invisible

Solution: Do you have people with too many of these asshole characteristics at your firm? Sutton advises that if you've allowed an asshole to slip through your hiring process, then "banish the creep as soon as possible." In Sutton's view, the best employers have a no-asshole rule that they vigorously and consistently enforce. At such companies, "employee performance and treatment of others aren't separate things. Phrases like talented jerk, brilliant bastard, or an asshole and a superstar are seen as oxymorons."

How to Act When Cornered by an Asshole Lawyer

In *The Civility Solution*, P.M. Forni offers some rules to live by that will help you deal with the rudest people:

1. Don't personalize rudeness—it's unlikely to be about you even if it's directed to you.

2. Be aware that rude behavior comes from various sources (i.e., sleep deprivation, depression, stress, illness, insecurity, etc.).

3. Respond with calmness rather than behavior that escalates rude behavior.

4. "An eye for an eye" is a poor approach; don't buy into another's insecurity and make it your own.

5. Self-righteous behavior only reflects poorly on you; don't use the opportunity to demean another.

6. Try to address the underlying cause of the behavior ("I can see you are very stressed. Maybe I could help if you tell me what's bothering you.").

7. When necessary, set limits tactfully and assertively, not aggressively.

8. If the conversation remains irrational, know when to quit.

9. Don't assume rudeness is a permanent part of someone's personality. It is a pattern of rudeness that determines character, not one mishap.

10. In the end, always let empathy—the ability to read others accurately—be your guide in understanding rudeness, knowing how to respond to rude individuals and knowing when to leave the scene.

Monitoring Yourself for Assholism and Making Amends

Sutton correctly says that all of us have an inner jerk waiting to come out, one that occasionally appears despite our best intentions. He asks each of us to do a personal "asshole audit." Apparently there is an electronic device called the MIT Jerk-O-Meter that attaches to your phone and registers your level of jerkosity by speaking style and tone of voice, but it was never marketed to the public.

Sutton prefers his own 24-item questionnaire at the end of his book called *Self-Test: Are You A Certified Asshole?* He says that admitting you sometimes act like an asshole is the first step toward awareness and self-control. If you can't think of any times when you have acted like an asshole, then you might be a Major Asshole.

Buddhists don't call themselves assholes. They speak of times when they acted without mindfulness, compassion or kindness. Noticing this, they ask forgiveness from the one they offended, forgive themselves for their lapse and commit themselves to doing better the next time.

How to Solve the Problem of Lack of Civilized Professionalism

Are you willing to admit that winning is not the only thing, that we have other duties and these include litigating in a way that preserves our integrity and honors the dignity of others? Why even bother being a lawyer if this destroys people's happiness, including your own?

Let's face it. There are forces directing you not to be civil. Your employer, your clients and your family need money. You want to win to get them the money and garner their approval. Case management judges are putting tremendous time pressure on you in each one of your many cases. If you screw up, you disappoint the people you care about and you may get disciplined, sued or both. The stakes are high.

Does this mean civility is a luxury you cannot afford? The answer is no. Our legal system is a great achievement and proud symbol of a civilized society. We cannot tolerate the decline of civilized professionalism any longer or it will be gone for good.

Being civil means that representing your client doesn't require or authorize you to insult people or speak rudely to them like lower life forms. Being civil means that you speak less and listen more. It means you take the time to get to know people rather than rush to judge them. It means you allow yourself to be guided more by inner empathy than by inner anger and rage.

Being civil means showing respect for others amidst the tension of conflict in our legal practice. It requires adjusting one's attitude so that building relationships becomes a higher priority than tearing them down. Civility means treating all people as if they mattered and treating no one like an object to be manipulated, destroyed or discarded.

Monitoring One's Own Level of Civility

We monitor our blood pressure and our weight to stay healthy. We monitor the level of gasoline in our car along with the oil pressure so our car doesn't break down. We monitor our bank account so we don't bounce checks. It's time we monitored our civility and the civility of our colleagues. We can make a pact with colleagues to remind us when we are acting in an uncivil fashion, to bring us back to our senses. You can keep a civility journal, writing down each instance in which you were uncivil and what you did to correct it. Toss out the notes at the end of each day, and pat yourself on the back for finding ways to correct your own uncivil behavior. Eventually you won't need the journal because you'll be civil all the time, even during the strongest civility challenges.

Start Fresh in Law School

Law schools teach content areas (like contracts) and practice skills (like client interviewing and cross-examination), but to my knowledge they do not teach the value and importance of civility and have their students practice civility through demonstrations, participation in mock exercises and the like. It is high time we instituted this change.

CHAPTER TWO: SUGGESTED READING

P.M. Forni, *The Civility Solution: What To Do When People Are Rude* (St. Martin's Press, 2008)

Albert Ellis, *The Myth of Self-Esteem* (Prometheus Books, 2005)

Robert I. Sutton, Ph.D., *The No Asshole Rule: Building a Civilized Workplace and Surviving One That Isn't* (Warner Business Books, 2007)

Lucinda Holdforth, *Why Manners Matter: The Case for Civilized Behavior in a Barbarous World* (C.P. Putnam & Sons, 2007)

CHAPTER THREE

The epidemic of destructive anger

Constructive Versus Destructive Anger

THE PROBLEM OF ANGER for lawyers is that too many of us express destructive anger, the sort of anger which aggravates disputes, complicates our work, shoots our stress hormone levels way up and poisons our enjoyment of life. Constructive anger is healthy and useful. To understand how and why destructive anger has reached epidemic proportions and how to reduce it, we have to distinguish between the two kinds of anger.

Constructive anger is episodic, not chronic. It is linked to a specific situation rather than generalized. It gets expressed at the right time, in the right way at the right person. It serves to solve an existing problem rather than create new ones. Constructive anger is sometimes part of normal grief following loss. Sometimes it is a way of getting in touch with thwarted needs and making people aware they are thwarting rather than meeting your legitimate human needs.

Constructive anger can be a way of communicating your passionate and well-founded conviction that someone has treated you, or people you care about, in an unjust or unfair manner, coupled with a request to them to stop. Constructive anger affirms one's personhood and benefits others. It is not accompanied by violence. When people like Mahatma Gandhi, Mother Teresa or Martin Luther King, Jr., got angry, they spoke from conscience and did not become violent or urge others to use violence.

Destructive anger is chronic and generalized. People who suffer from destructive anger get angry all the time. Frequently their anger is disproportionate to the triggering offense and is aimed at innocent bystanders. The same person who becomes enraged at garden variety traffic (something that affects everyone) may also punish someone who happens to move ahead of them by tailgating, honking and giving them the finger.

Fred Luskin, an expert on the psychological processes of anger and forgiveness at Stanford University, says that chronic anger arises from a past wound to the self that has never healed. The wound hasn't healed because the wounded person hasn't grieved or hasn't stopped grieving and has never resolved the hurt and let go of it through forgiveness. An angry person will tell you that long, long ago someone else (usually a parent) ruined their lives (e.g., by verbally criticizing them, favoring another sibling or not being supportive). The angry person doesn't see that he is crippling himself by the self-limiting story he has fashioned about his life, by holding onto anger and by suffering the consequences of his continued anger.

The angry person doesn't notice or much care that everyone on this planet gets hurt. All of us get sick, age and die. All of us hear "no" when we ask for things. All of us get disappointed and rejected at times. The angry person doesn't see life is a mixture of no and yes, of pain and joy, of cruelty and kindness, of ugliness and beauty, of defeat and triumph. He focuses narrowly on his own wound and draws fresh anger from it, over and over again. He can find things to complain about even on vacation in Hawaii.

The angry person has no concern for hurting others. When he becomes angry he dumps his anger on anyone who happens to be nearby. He actually believes the harm done to him long ago justifies his harming others now. He has no self-discipline. If he feels harmed by someone he will automatically play it forward by screaming at someone, by verbally cutting them or otherwise. He has no compassion for himself or others. He sees himself as a broken victim and sees others as sources of irritation. Seeing the world through the lens of anger, he has no hope for a better future and refuses to open his heart to love.

By choosing not to forgive, the angry person is choosing misery over happiness. He could grieve his loss, move on with his life and enjoy what is good in the world rather than seek out what's wrong and complain about it. He could open his eyes to see and appreciate all the good things people have done for him, even his hated parents. Instead he allows his mind to drift back to the old harm and get angry all over again. He thinks to himself, "My life sucks, so I'm going to make your life suck too."

The person addicted to destructive anger has made it a habit. It becomes a response to all of life's minor inconveniences, irritations and annoyances, rather than a rare response to a rare event involving some massive, traumatic violation of his rights. His current anger is why his life sucks, not the old wound, whatever it may have been.

Chronic anger is emotionally harmful to others and corrosive to the self. In *Why Manners Matter*, Lucinda Holdforth puts it well when she says: "When you lose your self-control, when you explode in rage or anger, when you abandon your manners, you are not proudly revealing yourself, you are losing something, some key element of your personhood."

Destructive anger is not exclusive to lawyers. It cuts across all occupations, socio-economic levels and levels of education. What working in the legal profession does is provide angry people with loads of triggers and opportunities to become angry. It also provides them with built-in excuses for being angry. Some lawyers claim they can't be effective unless they're angry or that opposing counsel won't respond to anything except displays of anger.

Every thrust of destructive anger tends to draw a counter-thrust. We are at a choice point in the sense that the dam of civility can't hold back much more anger before bursting. There is still time to prevent us from spawning a culture of anger, one in which stomach-churning, jugular-vein-popping anger has become a virtue and cooperation has become a vice. Our health and happiness as individuals depends on turning things around. So does the ability of our profession to serve its clients.

More and more people are turning away from physicians to complementary and alternative medicine, because they regard physicians as cold, uncaring and ineffective. Because of our anger, there is an increasing number of people who don't want to deal with us and regard us as ineffective. They are seeking out self-service methods of handling legal matters using Nolo Press books and do-it-yourself legal web sites.

Law is an Angry Profession

Chronically angry people have higher rates of hypertension, heart disease and stroke than calm people. A study published in 2009 showed that when physically healthy people develop heart disease, the angry ones have much worse outcomes. While you may think anger is helpful to or even necessary for achieving success as a lawyer, you're wrong. Anger sours your mood, undermines your health, splits up marriages, ends friendships and limits your ability to obtain cooperation from opposing counsel.

In May 1997 a psychologist who counsels lawyers wrote an article for the *Legal Times* stating that lawyers are irritable people with high rates of divorce, domestic violence and alcoholism. He observed that lawyers use anger to motivate themselves to do their jobs, to build a stronger sense of self, to increase certainty in ambiguous situations and to relieve depression by providing a jolt of energy. He also observed that anger becomes as addictive as alcohol or drugs and has the same capacity as chemical addiction to destroy a lawyer's job, health and family life over time.

Psychologists who write about the personality style of lawyers say a majority of lawyers are introverts, thinkers and judgers. As a group they are less social, less feeling and less accepting of other people. Psychologists say that lawyers attempt to dominate other people rather than joining with them as equals. Martin Seligman, the foremost figure of positive psychology, has administered written tests to a great many lawyers and found that they share the psychological trait of pessimism. When you expect opposition, rejection and disappointment, you're likely to get it, and the more you get it, the angrier you're likely to become.

What image comes to mind when you hear the word "lawyer"? Certainly the capacity to argue passionately, persistently and cleverly for one's client. Yet you also think of a person who is irritable, accusatory, sarcastic and quick to anger. These two lists of characteristics have no logical correlation. Passion, persistence and cleverness can go along with positivity and a happy mood. Why then are so many lawyers so angry and what can we do to transform their anger to more positive emotions? In this chapter I'm going to look at what anger is, how it damages our health, what causes lawyers to be so angry and how we can overcome anger to improve our health and functioning.

Defining Anger, Exploring Its Properties and Describing Its Different Kinds

Anger involves negative thoughts of blame and negative feelings of hatred. Anger frequently provokes verbal confrontation that may include name-calling, obscenities and threats. While sarcasm is a product of irritation and annoyance that is largely a mental phenomenon, anger has a strong neurologic component. It is associated with distinct physiologic changes, bodily manifestations and facial expressions.

While it may be hard to detect mild anger, strong anger is obvious. The really angry lawyer is staring and red-faced. He may be pacing or trembling. He may be spitting saliva with his words, clenching his fists, pounding the table or finger-pointing. His heart is racing and his blood pressure is spiking. He's on the verge of losing it and going into an uncontrollable rage, but is able to stop just before tumbling over that edge.

In *Rage*, Ronald T. Potter-Effron, Ph.D., distinguishes rage from anger. A rage is marked by total or partial loss of one's conscious awareness, one's sense of self and one's behavior. Dr. Potter-Effron calls rage a transformative experience that involves temporary dissociation of personality. He also says that rage blanks memory formation, so that people in rages tend not to remember much of what they said and did.

A really angry lawyer is not dissociated. He remains conscious of what he's experiencing, saying and doing and he's still able to control it. Philosopher Robert C. Solomon of the University of Texas at Austin says that anger involves a series of choice points. At each one, the angry person can choose to back off and walk away or go for it and let his anger rip.

Far from fearing their own anger, some lawyers prize it. They prize it because they believe it makes them so powerful and scary, they are more likely to get their way. Every time you allow an angry lawyer to intimidate you into dropping a demand or position you feel is justified, you are teaching him that his anger is okay.

Candace Pert, Ph.D., author of *The Molecules of Emotion* and *Your Body is Your Subconscious Mind*, says we can't be healthy unless we are emotionally expressive. But health lies in the middle between the pole of rigid people who suppress their emotions, and the pole of indulgent people who think it's okay to have a total emotional catharsis in public whenever they feel like it.

Like all emotions, anger is a neurological-physiological event on one level, while being a conscious process for choicefully engaging with the world on another level. While anger may be a knee-jerk response in the very first instance, it doesn't remain so. All of us have time to think about the consequences of staying angry before we act. Thus, it's a cop-out to say, "Opposing counsel made me so angry I couldn't help it when I punched him in the face." As sane adults, we all have responsibility for our emotions.

Our emotions, including anger, help make us human. There's nothing wrong with getting angry now and then for a good reason and expressing your anger appropriately. In *Positivity*, Dr. Frederickson reminds us that the "1" in the ideal 3:1 positivity ratio stands for negative emotions like anger that represent an appropriate reaction to a specific situation. If we have no capacity for anger, we are zombies. Without the capacity for anger, we are not grounded and will not offer any resistance to things like overt racial harassment, the physical abuse of a child right in front of us, or our government's decision to fight an unjust war accompanied by the torture and killing of civilians.

But it's different with gratuitous anger—the sort you see when a lawyer walks around like a tinderbox about to explode and goes off indiscriminately at the slightest provocation. Dr. Pert points out that healthy displays of emotion (such as love) bring on a feeling of wellbeing that comes from increased blood flow to the frontal cortex, which is richly endowed with opiate receptors, whereas explosive anger shuts down blood flow to the frontal cortex and produces feelings of great discomfort.

Physiological Self-Harm From Anger

Intense anger puts people in an altered state. It involves changes in the condition of one's brain along with changes in cognition, physiology, emotion, behavior and physical posture. The fight-flight response behind anger increases heart rate, respiration rate and delivery of glucose to the voluntary muscles. The fight-flight reaction tunes down blood circulation to the body's core, digestion and rational thought. The elaborate, complex frontal lobes we developed at the peak of our evolution are not needed for the primitive defense system evoked by anger.

When we get really angry we lose our eloquence and our cognitive flexibility. We say some very stupid things and keep repeating them as if we had just lost 50 IQ points. Does anyone remember White Goodman, the owner of Globo Gym, the insecure, hyper-competitive and nasty character played by Ben Stiller in the movie spoof *Dodgeball?* When he got mad, which was often, he came out with such goodies as "Cram it up your cramhole, LaFleur."

Stress medicine and neuroscience research have provided us with important information about the damage anger does. Recurrent anger keeps the level of the stress hormone cortisol high in our bloodstream. Chronic elevation of cortisol is a cause of depression, anxiety, atrophy of the hippocampus (the part of the brain that helps encode long-term memories), cardiac stress, fat deposition in the belly and poor sleep.

The Psycho-Social Self-Harm From Anger

Angry people suffer more from their anger than the people they lash out against do. Our attitudes are to us as the atmosphere is to the earth. The earth's atmosphere is less dense, more spacious and lighter than the solid earth, yet it is a continuation of the earth and part of the environment that all earthly beings live in. The moods of people are like emotional weather, with happy moods like bright, clear and warm days and angry moods like dark, stormy days. If you're angry most of the time, people will avoid you to avoid your emotional weather system, and you will suffer having to live in your own bad emotional weather.

In *Staying On the Path*, spiritualist Wayne Dyer has some great quotations to get us to think about anger. Here are my favorites: "Buddha said, 'You will not be punished for your anger. You will be punished by your anger.'" "Loving people live in a loving world. Hostile people live in a hostile world. Same world. How come?" "You get treated in life the way you teach people to treat you." If you are always pissed off, you are inviting others to treat you the same way, so don't be surprised when they do.

Anger and kindness each create their own karma.

Angry people invite conflict, loneliness, alcoholism, homicide, suicide and a host of health problems like high blood pressure, heart attack and stroke into their lives. Mark Twain said aptly that, "Anger is an acid that can do more harm to the vessel in which it is stored than to anything on which it is poured." In *As You Think*, James Allen put it this way: "How many people do you know who sour their lives, who ruin all that is sweet and beautiful by explosive tempers, who destroy their poise of character and make their blood boil."

Angry lawyers rationalize their conduct by telling themselves that "nice guys finish last." Yet everyone exposed to their anger is appalled. Juries will hand a verdict to the other side, no matter how weak his case is, just to teach the angry lawyer a lesson. Just as no school kid liked the schoolyard bully, and always dreamed of seeing him get his pants pulled down, adults are weary of lawyers who shout insults instead of sticking to the point.

The Don Rickles approach of making the other guy look pathetic is no substitute for substantive knowledge and real expertise. In my experience, judges are never more upset than when opposing counsel keep trading tit-for-tat accusations of unprofessional conduct in the course of a hearing or trial. How many times does the poor judge have to hear one lawyer accuse the other of "deliberately attempting to mislead the court" before he throws up?

THE CAUSES OF ANGER: THE COGNITIVE SOURCES

The Need for Certainty

In *On Being Certain,* neurologist Robert Burton, M.D., says the human mind vastly prefers certainty over uncertainty. This is because the feeling of certainty is accompanied by a surge of dopamine into the limbic area of the brain that produces pleasure. The brain circuit responsible for this dopamine delivery is called the reward circuit, and it's the very same circuit activated by drinking alcohol, consuming opiate drugs or having sex. Dr. Burton says the evolutionary purpose of the brain's reward circuit in vertebrate animals was to promote their survival.

In bony fishes and reptiles, the reward circuit produced a feeling of pleasure when they successfully killed and ate their prey and when they successfully mated by having a climax. In human beings with hugely developed frontal lobes, the feeling of knowing—of being on the right track in solving a complex mental puzzle—can produce great pleasure in mathematicians, scientists, engineers, architects, medical diagnosticians, lawyers and others.

How the Brain Produces the Feeling of Knowing

When people analyze data, they can either develop a feeling of confusion or a "feeling of knowing" what the data means. Corporate CEOs, politicians and lawyers love the feeling of knowing. Once they have it, they will recommend a course of action and vigorously push people to take it based on the conviction they're right. The fact that they're mistaken won't stop them.

In *Kluge* by Gary Marcus and *How We Decide* by Jonah Lehrer, the authors establish that more often than not our society's experts and pundits who make predictions are wrong. Simply because you have a feeling of knowing does not mean you're being objective about reality or that people with divergent opinions are wrong.

Dr. Burton says objectivity is a myth and so is the idea that one line of reasoning is clearly superior to another. He is convinced that lines of reasoning appeal differently to different people based on how their genetic code shapes the way their brains process information. Dr. Burton says the function of the feeling of knowing is to provide the internal motivation to keep going when working on complex problems. He cautions us not to view our sense of certainty as a cosmic endorsement of the truth of what we're certain we know.

In *The Pleasure Center*, Morten Klingberg says that much of what drives human decision-making are emotions and non-conscious processes. The reasons we give for our decisions come after the fact, much like window dressing. Since we're not conscious of how we decide, we feel certain we have reasoned our way to a conclusion and we identify our rationalizations as the reasons for the decision. If we admitted our decisions had a large non-conscious, non-rational component, then we would be more humble and more accepting of disagreement with other lawyers. We would not see their divergent opinions as direct affronts to our rationality. We would be less likely to go into fight-flight mode when they presented different views.

Anger Generated by Opposition

While nobody enjoys being told they're wrong, some people take it as a challenge to fight. Jonah Lehrer, author of *How We Decide*, says the human mind has something called "loss aversion." One aspect of loss aversion is that we don't want other people taking away our certainty, our conviction that what we believe is true. Consistent with loss aversion is the human tendency to like people who agree with us and dislike people who oppose us.

Society has authorized the killing of people who challenge assumed truths, including Socrates and Christ. In legal practice, we don't want people showing our ideas to be false and making us lose face. Legal disputes that challenge a lawyer's certainty he's right can trigger discomfort, anger and aggressive self-defense.

The parts of the brain that light up when we get angry include the orbito-frontal cortex, the amygdala, the insula, the hypothalamus and the habenula. Onset of anger is accompanied by the hypothalamus signaling the pituitary to signal the adrenal glands to secrete stress hormones. These consist of short-acting adrenaline and longer-acting cortisol. These stress hormones raise our blood pressure, increase our heartbeat and respiratory rate, stoke our muscles with glucose and get us ready to fight. To stop anger and its hormonal cascade, we must cultivate calmness and detachment.

Lawyers who get angry when anyone challenges their beliefs are failing to inhibit their anger circuits from firing, despite having adult frontal lobes that should be capable of doing this. Meditation strengthens the frontal lobes. It induces calm and patience. It can go a long way into helping us see our own irrational thought patterns that provoke anger. Recently I was waiting for email replies from three different people. I regarded all of them as taking too long to get back to me. I assumed all three of them were mad at me. Since I couldn't find any rational reason for them to be mad at me, I began feeling angry at them for being mad at me without cause.

The next time I sat in meditation I saw how silly that chain of thoughts was and I let the whole thing go. I told myself it was up to them whether to reply and when to reply, and most likely all of them were very busy. After stretching, I went to my computer and checked my e-mail. Guess what? I had replies from all three. Each of them apologized for being late and each of them explained they had been exceptionally busy.

Teaching Your Brain to be Angry

Neuroscientists say that "neurons that fire together wire together." It's a well-established principle of neurology that every time you repeat an action in a similar situation (such as pouring yourself a stiff drink when you get home from the office), you're changing your brain to groove the behavior pattern. The underlying physiologic change is that the brain circuit for the behavior is strengthened by addition of new synapses or thickening of existing synapses.

When the photocopy machine malfunctions or your secretary files a brief with a typo, do you get so pissed that steam blows sideways from both ears? You can fire the secretary and lease a new copier, but the underlying anger problem will not disappear until you decide it's time you changed. We are what we do. If you keep raging over everyday situations at the office, your brain will develop ever stronger anger circuits and become a biological anger machine.

THE CAUSES OF ANGER: PSYCHOLOGICAL SOURCES

Depression and substance abuse are major sources of anger for lawyers. Anger is a hallmark of depression and a chief symptom. Alcohol can drive anger by lifting the lawyer's suppression of his rage, by leaving the lawyer in a state of guilt and shame while recovering from a night of drinking and by causing the lawyer to lose business or be subjected to discipline. Here are other key psychological sources of anger.

Family Upbringing

What characteristics does an angry family have? Potter-Efron says: "They think a lot of anger is normal and expected. Nobody listens until someone gets angry. They try to solve their problems with anger. Someone is almost always angry at someone else. There is at least one feud a day—the scorecard will show who hates who today. There is a whole lot of yelling, screaming, threats, banging on tables, hurling of objects. In order to be heard you've got to get angry. Each family member has trained the other to listen only to anger."

In *Freeing The Angry Mind*, C. Peter Bankhart, Ph.D., tells us he has provided therapy to angry men for thirty-five years. He sees anger as a product of low self-esteem from shaming parents, the inability to accept or love oneself and falling into the trap of seeking approval from others. No amount of approval from others will ever substitute for self-acceptance, and more often than not other people do not express approval as much as you want it, when you want it and in the form you want it. He believes that the purpose anger serves is to distract angry men from the deep sense of shame they feel inside. Angry men are cut off and isolated from others, because they have no empathy for themselves or other people. In the absence of empathy, there can be no connection.

Lack of Positivity in Relating to Fellow Lawyers

In *Positivity*, Barbara L. Frederickson, Ph.D., provides a guide to human flourishing, which explains how we can flourish and why so many of us do not. During 2005 she worked with Marcial Losada, Ph.D., a psychologist and mathematician, to establish and verify the accuracy of "the positivity ratio." They were able to show scientifically that human flourishing occurs when a person's ratio of positive to negative emotions is 3:1 or higher; that life is good, not great, at 2:1; and below 1:1 a person will be clinically depressed.

During the 1990s Losada observed and filmed meetings by sixty different business teams. He tracked three kinds of data about the people in these meetings. Were the people's statements: positive or negative; self-focused or other-focused; and based on inquiry (asking questions) or advocacy (defending a point of view)? He then analyzed which of these sixty business teams were high-performing, which had mixed success and which were floundering. High-performing teams were profitable, had high customer satisfaction and were well-regarded by superiors, peers and employees. Floundering business teams were losing money, were poorly regarded, and left all with whom they did business dissatisfied. Losada found that 25% of the businesses were high-performing, 45% had mixed success and 30% were floundering.

The high-performing teams had positivity ratios around 6:1, while the low-performing teams had ratios of 2:1. To tease out the hidden elements of flourishing, Losada plotted the data on a moment-to-moment basis during the course of observing the meetings. He quantified how each team member affected the behavior of others, and ended up using the term "connectivity" to refer to how attuned or responsive team members were to one another.

Losada discovered that high-performing teams had the highest connectivity. The members of these teams asked questions as much as they defended their own views. They directed their attention outward as much as inward. Low-performing teams showed far lower connectivity. Their members asked almost no questions and demonstrated almost no outward focus. Mixed teams were in the middle.

When Losada ran his complex equations on the data coordinates of the business teams, he found that the high-performing teams generated a trajectory that spiraled, bounced and twisted in what mathematicians who study dynamic systems recognize as a butterfly-shaped pattern. The butterfly wings generated by the high-performing teams were tall (consistent with high positivity ratios) and stretched wide (consistent with high levels of inquiry and outward focus). The butterfly wings that emerged from the low-performing were shorter (consistent with lower positivity ratios) and narrower (consistent with lower levels of inquiry and outward focus).

When Frederickson and Losada reviewed and analyzed the data, they found the high-performing teams with the healthy, vibrant butterflies were constantly generating fresh, creative ideas. They were on the upward trajectory of infinite possibility. Frederickson and Losada found that the low-performing teams had lost their good cheer and flexibility. They were extremely negative and stuck in a rut. They were self-absorbed. They had stopped listening to each other or caring about what the other had to say. They only wanted to defend their own view, which they did over and over. Their meetings went nowhere and just repeated themselves in an endless loop. While high-performance teams keep spiraling up, low-performance teams keep spiraling down until they hit a dead end.

Losada's mathematical results were consistent with Frederickson's theories from experimental psychology. They reconfirmed that positivity broadens our minds by getting us to stay open to new ideas, focus outward and ask questions; and that positivity brings connectivity (attunement with others) and success in life (including business).

The majority of lawyers display negativity in their dealings with each other. They are certain of the correctness of their own ideas and stay closed to the ideas proposed by opposing counsel. They come on strong advocating their views and ask few, if any, questions of opposing counsel about his views. They are antagonistic to and disconnected from opposing counsel. This is why so many cases get stuck and go nowhere until they are resolved under duress at the last moment due to the proximity of trial. This is also why so many anger flashpoints occur during litigation. It is very frustrating to be stuck in this kind of rut and all too easy to blame the other lawyer, and discharge your frustration by lashing out in anger at him. Certainly there is hope here. Lawyers can learn to be more positive in their dealings with each other.

The Need To Be Right

If you cannot feel good about yourself unless your ego is stroked and being right is your favorite form of ego-stroking, you're setting yourself up for a great many angry encounters. Have you dared to disagree with a know-it-all? What happened? Did he respond with a harsh personal attack that questioned your IQ, integrity, motives or competence to practice law?

Know-it-all lawyers can't inhibit their need to make others agree with them even when the other is a judge who clearly has had enough. Have you ever seen a judge tell a lawyer that he understands the lawyer's point but has ruled against him anyway, and doesn't want to hear another word out of him? Yet the lawyer keeps on badgering the judge and won't give up. The judge gets more and more upset and finally warns the lawyer he will be sanctioned or held in contempt if the lawyer does not sit down and shut up. But the lawyer remains at the lectern jabbering away until the judge's gavel smashes down and the order of sanctions or contempt is issued from the bench.

A lawyer who must always be right feels compelled to confront and defeat the people who are wrong. If they resist, he becomes angry and blames their "wrongness" for his anger. Was Moby Dick the cause of Captain Ahab's persistent hate and rage? Did Ahab benefit from pursuing Moby Dick across all the Seven Seas?

Buddhists will tell you that the person who becomes angry because of a judgment in his head that someone else is wrong is in a state of delusion which masks, instead of uncovers, reality. Imposing your mental constructs on reality, instead of perceiving reality and accepting it, is a common way to cause conflict and suffering. Mark Twain said, "The rule is perfect: in all matters of opinion our adversaries are insane."

Judges can lose it just as much as the lawyers who appear before them. Newspapers across the country reported one example in 2007 involving an administrative law judge in Washington, D.C., named Roy Pearson. He sued the Chung family, the owners of his neighborhood dry-cleaning shop, for $54,000,000 when they accidentally lost his pants.

In his opening statement Judge Pearson said he had relied upon the sign in the shop window saying "Satisfaction Guaranteed," and that the loss of his pants constituted an historic wrong. As he put it, "Never before in recorded history has a group of defendants engaged in such misleading and unfair business practices." The trial judge in his court trial ruled against him, awarded court costs to the Chung family and invited them to move for an award of attorney's fees.

The Compulsion to Control

Some people grow up seeking to manipulate and control others to get what they want. They do not trust others to meet their needs. They are driven from inside to control the outcomes of relationships and situations (including lawsuits). Many of them are perfectionists. Typically, perfectionists are people raised by parents who used shame and blame to push them to extremes of achievement for the sole psychic benefit of the parents. These kids were never praised for excellence, but were scolded for mistakes.

As these children grow into adults, they continue living in fear of making mistakes.

They're always looking for mistakes, instead of focusing on what's going right in their lives. To avoid the pain of shame, they develop a rigid, straight-jacketed personality style with an emphasis on orderliness, predictability and control. They are people who do not like spontaneity. They are intolerant of mistakes in others, and point out the mistakes of others in a harsh, anger-provoking way.

No one likes to be controlled and much anger in the legal profession is generated by battles over control. I have participated in many battles over what discovery requests must be complied with, what deposition questions must be answered and what the permissible scope of expert testimony will be in trial. Some lawyers gave it their best shot and then let go. The control freaks made everything a painful ordeal marked by personal attacks, repeated trips back to court and ever-escalating anger.

The motto posted over the blackboard in the group therapy room where I did my day treatment for depression was: "Things are not as they ought to be. Things are as they are." Buddhists say that acceptance is the key to freedom. When you cease struggling against what cannot be changed, you are free to make the best of what exists in the present moment. Difficult situations can teach us new lessons and strategies that ultimately broaden our resources for life. If we stay grounded under pressure and look for the best option in a difficult situation, we are likely to feel a mixture of pride in salvaging some good, and gratitude that we came out okay.

The acceptance model is helpful for the practice of law. You can prepare and argue your client's case to the very best of your ability, but the final decision will be made by a judge or jury, and that decision will be based upon things that are outside your control. Examples could be venue, social trends that imprint the outlook of jurors, the judge's evidentiary rulings, the performance of witnesses, the chemistry between witnesses and jurors, an unexpected change in testimony during cross-examination, the illness of and replacement of a key juror and so forth.

For your own mental health, you have to let go, let it be and acknowledge it is out of your hands. When the result comes in, whatever it is, know that you gave it your best shot. Try not to berate yourself, find fault with others and boil over with anger if the outcome was not what you wanted. Know that things happen for reasons we cannot foresee and cannot understand at the time. There is a great folk tale that illustrates that the universe is wiser than we are:

A man in a village had one son and a fine mare. The mare ran away one day and the villagers said it was sad he had such bad luck. The man said "There is neither good luck, nor bad luck. Let's see what happens." A few days later the mare returned with two fine stallions and the villagers praised his good luck. One day his son fell from the horse and shattered his leg. The villagers said it was sad he had such bad luck. The man said "There is neither good luck, nor bad luck. Let's see what happens." A few weeks later, soldiers came to the village. There was a war, and they took every able-bodied young man in the village away to fight, save the son with the shattered leg.

Distortion of the Need for Respect

Every lawyer wants to be respected and appreciated for his efforts. This is a universal human need. Lawyers who get dismissed, talked down to or ridiculed by other lawyers get angry. How often have you had a conversation with a colleague in which he is still seething after perceived maltreatment by another lawyer? The affected colleague will obsessively go over the details of the incident, because it assaulted his dignity and pushed his buttons. He can't let go of it, because someone else has attacked him where his pride lies: in his intellect, his writing skills, his speaking style, etc.

Although we demand respect, we don't always give it. Too many lawyers see themselves as Masters of the Universe at the top of the occupational and financial food chain. They feel angered by any gesture that shows less than full regard for their own perceived importance. Arrogant anger is associated most with lawyers who act as unilateral decision makers, such as judges and arbitrators. They may become so puffed up by their power that they mock, scold or bully the lawyers who appear before them right in front of the lawyer's client. Lawyers are terrified of telling judges to refrain from this conduct or of reporting them, because of the potential harm the judge could do their current case and future cases.

Be sensitive not just to your need for respect but to the need that others have to be respected. See respect in terms of reciprocity. To get it from others you need to give it to others. Acting this way will prevent many heated exchanges that accomplish nothing beyond getting you and opposing counsel worked up.

Narcissism

Why is that some lawyers keep triggering anger in others by insensitivity in what they say or how they say it? In *The Civility Solution*, P.M. Forni says educated people are becoming more self-absorbed. According to Forni: "In 2006 about two-thirds of American college students scored above average on the Narcissistic Personality Inventory, a test aimed at measuring narcissism. This is a 30-percent increase since 1982, the year the test was administered for the first time. When the healthy pursuit of self-interest and self-realization turns into self-absorption, other people can lose their intrinsic value in our eyes and become mere means to the fulfillment of our needs and desires. Our self is king, the world at its feet, and we are not inclined to be considerate and kind."

The Paradigm of Using Harm To Win Cases

Law practice today is based on harming, much like boxers trying to knock their opponent out by causing the other to sustain a cerebral concussion. Each side uses records, subpoenas and investigators to dig up as much dirt as possible on the other side. In the process of unearthing the dirt, they interview co-workers, relatives, neighbors and friends—alerting everyone to the lawsuit and even rekindling old grievances. The idea is to keep stockpiling harm until someone cries "uncle." The more harm each side does, the more the other will strike back. Eventually you have a legal proceeding with the same dynamics as a war. When things reach that point, even the best mediators are not able to do very much for the parties.

Anger and Projection

We navigate our world by making assumptions and concocting stories about other people, an unconscious process called projection. Having been a plaintiff's lawyer for twenty-five years, I can tell you that many plaintiff's lawyers perceive defense lawyers as jerks who blindly assume all plaintiffs are malingerers or exaggerators. This is a view built up out of a tapestry of negative experiences that gets projected onto new lawyers as new cases get off the ground. It's inaccurate and unhelpful. It provokes conflict.

By the same token many defense lawyers see plaintiff's lawyers as greedy people who manipulate clients to siphon extra money out of insurance companies or as naïve people who allow themselves to be manipulated by greedy plaintiffs. Same kind of projection, but this time moving in the reverse direction.

Both projections generate anger. The biggest problem with these projections is that they obscure the individuality of the real person you're dealing with in any given case, and you're reacting to the projection and not the person. Anything the person does that confirms the projection gets noticed, whereas anything he does contrary to the projection gets ignored. Only when we drop the projections and treat each person on his own merits can we defuse the anger that stems from projections.

Are you angered when opposing counsel does not return your calls? What about an opposing counsel who challenges everything you say, who responds negatively with a point-by-point rebuttal to all your letters and who always has to have the last word? What about opposing counsel who responds to your every action by claiming it's unethical and threatens to report you to the State Bar if you do not retract it? When faced with lawyers like this, it's easy to assume they are cold, friendless, angry people engaging in spite tactics. If you assume this, you're going to be angry every time you have to deal with or even think about the other lawyer.

Better to examine the truth of your assumptions. Sure, opposing counsel is irritating, but is he as bad as you assume? Perhaps the reason he argues with everything you say is that he's highly insecure and desperately craves your respect, so he attacks you to show his competence and win respect. Perhaps he's not a total jerk, but he was trained at his law firm to act this way and he is expected to write reports to the insurance company showing how tough he was toward you. Sometimes we make assumptions about what motivates irritating behavior and we are way off. Perhaps the reason opposing counsel never returns calls is that he suffers from depression, ADD or alcoholism. Perhaps he has cancer and is so tired from radiation therapy that he is hardly ever in the office, but he's keeping it secret so as not to scare off existing and potential clients.

A while back, I found myself going into hate mode in a bicycle injury case defended by a lawyer working for a local government entity. I thought I had a clear liability case, because my client broke his hip when the front tire of his bike hit a 3-inch ridge of street pavement the town had known about, but failed to cut down, for 18 years pre-incident. The defense lawyer denied all liability and asserted a long list of governmental immunities.

From the git-go he was not only objecting to all my discovery requests, but was dumping an endless series of special interrogatories, document requests and requests for admissions of fact on me. His discovery requests kept coming in waves along with his thick lists of discovery objections to everything I wanted. We got into a kind of fax war, in which every half hour or so one of us would send an angry fax to the other laced with terms like ridiculous, ludicrous and absurd to describe each other's positions. I finally had enough.

I called the other lawyer and said in essence, "Look, this is going to be a long, complex and hard-fought litigation—and we have a choice between constantly bashing each other and raising each other's blood pressure, or trying to find ways to work together so the case goes more smoothly and is not a huge thorn in our sides. Life is too short to have this level of angry sniping. Let's try again."

He said he wasn't enjoying our war of words either, and agreed to start our relationship over in a more collegial way. Our conversation lifted the dark cloud over the case and let some light in. When I came to my office in the morning or after my lunch break, I no longer found a scathing fax from opposing counsel, and I could finally relax a bit. From then on, we did work together and we ended up settling the case for an amount that pleased me and my client, and which was acceptable to the group that self-insured his small city.

SOLUTIONS TO THE ANGER EPIDEMIC IN THE LEGAL SYSTEM

Knowing You Have a Choice of How To Respond

Whenever someone does something that triggers the anger message within you, remember you always have a choice of how to respond. One way is to allow the anger to rise up and control you, so that you explode verbally or physically (e.g., by giving someone the finger). The other way is to take a breath, see the anger, remember what anger does to you and then decide in the moment to release it harmlessly. There are two websites that offer audiotapes on how to release anger in the moment. Leonard Scheff, a Tucson lawyer, maintains www.transforminganger.com. The other one is found at www.compassionpower.com

Ask Questions

Don't retreat into yourself, hold to your position like an abalone and ignore what opposing counsel thinks. Ask him questions. Find out what he believes and why.

Mental Flexibility is Your Best Ally—Use It

Without mental flexibility you cannot open your mind to the validity of what anyone else is saying and you cannot compromise. Mental flexibility is an antidote to anger. Bryon Katie says that defensiveness is "the first act of war" in human communication.

If you question what I'm doing or saying, I always have a range of options. I can say, "Thank you for your input," or simply pause, take in what you said, consider it and respond after some honest self-reflection. I can ask you to clarify what you mean and provide me with some evidence in support of your point. I can politely disagree and tell you why. But if I'm stuck in anger, I will automatically defend myself by verbally cutting you to shreds without ever considering if you have made a legitimate point. We always have a choice but we won't see it if we're angry.

The only way to detach from the certainty you're right and the behavioral rigidity that goes with it is to adapt a new premise. The new premise is that at this time, based on the information you have now, you take position X about situation Y, but that you reserve the right to modify position X when you learn more facts about situation Y. The new premise must include the possibility that your inner feeling of really knowing the truth (even the conditional truth) of situation Y may be mistaken. When you can operate on this premise, you have gained the broader perspective necessary to stop taking argumentation over the truth personally and escape the feelings of strong anger that arise when someone challenges your point of view.

Acting As If Others Were Worthy of Respect

The mere act of being respectful toward other lawyers during debate would help reduce the anger epidemic. When we choose to act as if we respect other people, our attitude changes toward them. We feel less estranged, less polarized, and more connected. There is more to talk about and less to yell about.

Practicing Gratitude to Increase Social Connection

An effective way to reduce self-absorption and increase social connection is to cultivate gratitude. When you're grateful, you are truly thankful for (rather than taking for granted) the good things in your life. This includes being alive, breathing, having wonderful people in your life who love and support you, your state of good mental and physical health, your good fortune in living in a free and democratic country with a Bill of Rights, your good fortune in having a fine education, your high earnings as a lawyer, etc.

You can also open your heart by being thankful for what you don't have—like brain cancer, heart disease, AIDS, poverty, homelessness and so forth. Gratitude helps you recognize that in a flash any or all of the good things in your life can disappear and this recognition increases your appreciation for them. In this way you recognize that just the slightest twist of fate could have you change places with the homeless man with his hand out whom you pass each morning without ever greeting him or giving him money. You can also inspire your compassion for others by performing random acts of kindness during the day. If you want to learn more about how to practice gratitude, I suggest you read M.J. Ryan's *Attitudes of Gratitude* and *Thanks! How Practicing Gratitude Can Make You Happier* by Robert Eammons, Ph.D. Joanna Macy, Ph.D., has a website devoted to cultivation of gratitude for life (www.gratititude.org)

Learning to Build Relationships Instead of Arguing People Into the Ground

For far too long lawyers have based their sense of personal power on knowing things, being right and insisting that others agree or pay the price. Far from doing us a favor, this concept has caused little else but conflict, fear, anger and stress.

Aristotle said that our ability to persuade others is based less on *logos* (the reasons we give them to do what we want) than on *ethos* (how much others like us based on how well or ill we treat them) and *pathos* (our success in getting them to identify with us and care about us). Lawyers spend too little time doing things to make others like us and trust us and too much time listing reasons for people to take action.

When a client comes to a lawyer, the lawyer could keep his questions to a minimum and give the client the freedom to fully express himself. If he did, the client would feel respected and cared for, and would have warm feelings toward his lawyer. If people know you care about them, they will respond well to requests. If not, they won't. When you have no relationship with someone, you will not get far telling them why they should do something. Their autonomy is more important to them than the power of your logic.

Lawyers and clients argue all the time over what amount makes for a good settlement. The lawyer emphasizes practicalities and money, while the client talks about his desire for a day in court. They can go round and round annoying each other.

Remember that arguments are simply a way, a strategy, to get people to do something. If you get fixed upon a strategy that doesn't work, and you keep pushing it against ever stronger resistance, the only result is conflict and high blood pressure. Consider using *ethos*, and building cooperative relationships. The more your client respects, trusts and likes you, the more likely he will follow your advice, even if it goes against his preconceptions and inclinations. When you befriend your clients and really get to know them, you cannot help but understand them and their point of view.

You are also susceptible to changing your thinking about resolution and finding new ways to resolve a case that better satisfies your client, yet still leaves you feeling satisfied. Why? Because you are now including your client in your thinking about how best to resolve his case rather than figuring how resolution would best serve your self-interests. Your client is emotionally aware of this. He can look through your rational arguments and feel instantly whether you care about him or not. He will be more flexible if he knows you care about him, not just about yourself.

Learning to be More Tolerant

In *Do It Anyway: Finding Personal Meaning and Deep Happiness by Living the Paradoxical Commandments*, Kent M. Keith says, "People are illogical, unreasonable, and self-centered. Love them anyway." Why? Keith says good lies beneath other people's difficult exteriors, and if we see beyond their faults we can find that goodness and link up with it. When we link our goodness to their goodness we build strong, healthy and mutually rewarding relationships.

Although we assume people oppose us because they dislike us and want us to feel pain, such an assumption is often wildly off base. People refuse each other's requests for a great many other reasons. It can be as simple as having different temperaments, different styles of problem-solving (cognition vs. intuition) or different ideas as to what is appropriate behavior based on growing up in different families or cultures. Sometimes breaking through the crust of mutual irritation can be done by asking, "How come you did you that?" or "How come you said that?"

Learning not to take everything personally is a very helpful practice. At one point in his career Abraham Lincoln was dropped from a legal case, and Henry Stanton added insult to injury by saying something to the effect that Lincoln was nothing but a tall, dumb, country hick lawyer. Lincoln could have smoldered in resentment, but when he had to choose a Secretary of Defense, he chose Stanton, who did a great job.

Stanton stood in awe of Lincoln's ability to forgive and his leadership qualities. Stanton went on to say that Lincoln was the greatest leader of men of all time. How could Lincoln let go of what Stanton said? He was probably able to see himself from the viewpoint of a man in Stanton's shoes, and not take it to heart. The cognitive basis for learning not to take negative comments personally is that the comment is not objective truth, but simply a reflection of the speaker's state of mind, which may be distorted by confusion, bias, envy, anger, etc.

OVERCOMING ANGER AT LONG LAST AND TRANSFORMING YOUR LIFE

Figuring Out if You Have an Anger Problem

Admitting you have an anger problem is the first step. If you suspect you have an anger problem, you probably do. There are many telltale signs of an anger problem. Potter-Efron mentions some of these examples:

Feuding with family members and no longer talking to some of them.

Feeling unusually lousy, annoyed, upset and bothered during the big holidays like Thanksgiving and Christmas.

Repeatedly getting disciplined at school and work.

Repeatedly getting fired from jobs.

Losing friends one by one until you're alone.

Becoming a different person when the beast within is set loose—becoming unusually suspicious, paranoid and nasty; getting in trouble with the legal system for screaming, disturbing the peace or physically battering someone; paying money for the harm you do, be it divorce

and child support, a lawsuit for property damage or a lawsuit for causing bodily injuries.

Feeling transient guilt and shame after abusing others, but then
reverting to your old ways.

Having stress-related illnesses like headache, chest pain, hypertension, ulcers, gastric reflux or irritable bowel.

If you really want to know if you have an anger problem, C. Peter
Bankhart counsels that you ask your family if you have a problem with
anger, and then listen non-defensively without lecturing, denying or
explaining.

Seeing Your Footprint of Anger

Just as we leave carbon footprints by what car we drive, we leave anger
footprints from the fits of anger we have inflicted on others. Bankhart
wants the angry person to know that his failure to inhibit anger causes
him to wound and alienate everyone around him, even his spouse, his
kids and the other people who are trying to love him. Bankhart asks
angry people to stop, to realize they will die and to ask themselves if they
would be satisfied with the lives they lived if they died today. Better still,
he asks them to write their own obituary from the perspective of the
people they screamed at, threatened and struck (verbally or physically). If
done sincerely, these exercises could help, but they will do nothing until
the angry person has first admitted he has anger problems.

Hitting Bottom

Potter-Efron says cracking the denial of an angry person isn't easy
and it may be necessary for him to hit bottom before he can be helped.
Potter-Effron's take is that: "Angry people stay mad because they
don't know what else to do. They've been angry for so long, that's all
they're good at. They have become anger specialists." The angry person
responds to life through the lens of anger. His motto is: "Never forgive
and never forget." He attracts other angry people and repels people
who want love, joy, fun, friendship, peace, ease, rest or relaxation.
Anger is what's familiar. It's all he knows. The concept of living life in
a compassionate way, of letting things slide, of forgiving and trying to
work things out is alien.

Anger is a crude weapon. It can only control some people, and only for so long. Using anger for power and control, in the face of evidence that people are afraid of you and don't want to be around you, is a mistake. Yet angry people are like one-trick ponies. They keep using a failed strategy. Their theme song is "You make me mad. It's your fault." As long as they refuse to accept responsibility for their choices and actions, nothing will change. Sadly, some die angry and others change only after an episode of anger gets them into catastrophic trouble. It would be far better, if you have an anger problem, to admit it right now before it's too late, and begin therapy.

FINDING YOUR WAY OUT OF ANGER TO PEACE

Take a Moment to Unclench Your Body and Breathe

What are the physical signs you are tensing up and thus shutting down? Holding your breath is probably number one. Muscle tension in your forehead, jaw, neck or shoulders would be number two. Mental correlates would be saying to yourself, "This idiot doesn't know what he's talking about," "What a load of crap" or "Does he really expect me to buy this garbage?"

Let's focus right now on the physical manifestations, something you can deal with in the moment. Invariably, when you're angry you're restricting your breathing and clenching your muscles. One way to break the cycle is to stand tall, soften your belly and take a series of slow, deep breaths into the lower belly that fill your lungs with oxygen. Make sure your belly is expanding above and below your navel. You can also massage your head, jaw, neck and shoulders with your own hands. Making circular motions over your forehead and cheeks really helps. Just doing these things will help you unclench and allow your mind to open.

Learning How To Listen with an Open Mind

When lawyers are not talking out loud, we tend to talk a mile a minute in our heads while scribbling furiously on a yellow legal pad waiting to demolish every point the other speaker has made. Rather than listening, we are preparing to confront. In order for two people to relate to each other, they have to take turns being still enough and quiet enough to become what Eckhart Tolle calls "an aware presence" that can take in what the other is saying, feeling and trying to communicate.

Lawyers are obsessive chatterboxes. We interrupt the other person repeatedly so we can make our points. This irritates the other person and prevents us from entering into authentic dialogue. When you're away from the office, how many times do you cut off your spouse, kids and friends when they are trying to get a word in edgewise? How quickly do you do it? Doctors wait an average of eighteen seconds. What about you? Because of the internal mental noise of your own thoughts, are you so distracted that you can't hear your kids when they try to talk to you? How do think that makes them feel? This would be a great time to practice being an aware presence.

Becoming a better listener requires calming your own mind, becoming still and really allowing the other person the opportunity to speak without commenting or chiming in. It also helps to have what Buddhists call "beginner's mind." In this mindset it's perfectly okay to say "I don't know." It's nearly impossible to be angry about someone taking a contrary position, if you honestly admit that there is no clear answer to a particular question or that, at the present time, you don't have enough information at your disposal to answer the question.

A beginner's mind is one that is open rather than closed, one that is looking everywhere for information applicable to the topic instead of racing to exclude as many sources of information as possible. The beginner's mind is the opposite of the mind of the jaded expert who is convinced he knows everything there is to know about a given subject. Ever cross-examine someone like that? How did the jury respond when you showed him to have flawed assumptions or knowledge gaps?

To listen well means not reacting swiftly with defensive anger, but just listening, asking for time to consider what was said, writing it down and then later on, when you have time, thinking about what the other said. Byron Katie says if someone calls you a name (say stubborn jerk) you feel anger well up inside along with an immediate need to deny the accusation, defend yourself and attack the other person. Her approach is to "write it down" and meditate on it. Wholly aside from whether the name-caller has ever acted stubbornly, she will consider whether there have been instances where she has acted stubbornly and not shown any flexibility.

Typically Katie can recall one or more instances where she was inflexible toward the person calling her names. This helps equalize their relationship and enable her to work to repair the situation. She says, "I have learned that my enemy is my friend and my friend is my friend." What does that mean? A friend will always support you, which is great, but an enemy may sometimes help you grow by telling you the unadulterated truth about yourself. If you treat it as a painful slap and slap back, you learn nothing. If you treat it as an invitation to self-discovery, you can grow.

Accepting the Inevitability of Disagreement

How is it that supposedly rational people with advanced training in the law can each be certain they are right while espousing polar opposite opinions or conclusions? To some extent it's how our brains are wired. People's unique genetic code predisposes them to accept or not accept certain types of formulations, propositions and value statements about our shared world. Just because someone disagrees with us does not make him wrong or stupid or willfully perverse. To blame others for feeling certain of their opinions—when we disbelieve them precisely because we feel certain of the rightness of our own opinions— is a form of blindness.

How many of us have shriveled our faces in disgust, sighed audibly, put one hand to our foreheads and nodded our heads from side to side, while recounting what it was like to listen to someone else talk? Do you remember the pained, nauseated expression on Al Gore's face during the televised debates while George Bush was answering questions?

Let's face it. It's hard emotionally to listen to someone else speak who expresses views that are poles apart from our own. We react to such people as if they just landed from Mars and we'd like to send them back. Yet the fact remains that they are people just like us, and if we are to understand them and engage them constructively, we cannot dismiss them, loathe them or wish they would just go off someplace and die.

Preventing eruption of anger when you're dealing with other lawyers who disagree requires acceptance. A person who is short but wants to be tall because he thinks he can only be happy if he's tall has a choice. He can spend his whole life being angry over being short, or he can accept his shortness, make the best of things and create a life in which being tall doesn't matter.

In time he may forget he is short or even laugh about the silliness of thinking only tall people can be happy. It's the same when dealing with disagreements. There are many roads to Rome. You don't have to convince your adversary he's wrong to get your client justice, nor is it your job to do so. You are not the "thought police." Disagreement between lawyers is just the way it is.

If you start out by accepting that your adversary has a different position, and you respectfully acknowledge it, you can still prevail by showing that his position is based on a mistaken view of the facts or the substantive law, that there are insurmountable procedural barriers to raising it, or insurmountable evidentiary barriers to proving it. Just state your position in a positive way without denigrating your adversary. You don't need to add negativity by saying his position is absurd or ludicrous. You gain nothing by such talk. All you do is stoke your own outrage and force your opponent to counterattack.

Eckhart Tolle says the human ego defines itself in opposition to others, because the ego's sole concern is its own happiness, which comes from feeling superior to others. This feeling of superiority arises from stories the ego tells of how it has bested others in competition or how others have unfairly abused it. The ego has an inherent tendency to see the rightness of its preferred values, principles, and policies, in contrast to the wrongness of those espoused by others. Why is this?

Tolle says this is a matter of egoic self-preservation. If we were willing to see the legitimacy of other people's viewpoints and our hearts were set on cooperating with others and remaining in peaceful relationships with them, we could function without individual egos. Anger is useful to reenforce the separate ego, but not useful in promoting community. When you go through a patch of feeling angry all the time, start paying attention to your ego and its stories. Question the value of your anger and the truth of the ego's stories about the villain du jour in your life.

The Benefits of Healing the Mind From Anger

The fundamental principle of Buddhism is non-harming. Zen monk Thich Nhat Hanh says in *The Heart of Buddha's Teachings,* "If our mind has craving, anger, and harming we are like a house on fire. If craving, anger, and harming are absent from our minds, we produce a cool, clear lotus lake." The less angry you become, the clearer your mind becomes, and the more your innate wisdom emerges, so you know what to do in various situations. Even Thich Nhat Hanh gets angry, but he doesn't stay angry. He tells of a time when he got very angry over hearing about some wartime atrocities, but he chose not to speak in anger. He sat down quietly and breathed deeply. He realized that both sides in the conflict had suffered deeply, and his anger disappeared. Can you see the benefit of non-harming as a central life value? Can you see that everyone alive has suffered—even opposing counsel and his client?

Learning Some Humility

Being humble doesn't mean being weak, helpless or pathetic. Being humble means having real perspective on oneself—neither inflating nor deflating who you are. With humility goes the ability to make an accurate assessment of your strengths and weaknesses of character, the varying levels of knowledge and skill you have in different parts of your life, etc. A humble lawyer can be a great lawyer while remaining able to laugh at himself and enjoy doing so. Ego-inflated lawyers who pompously speak of how excellent they are in all aspects of their character, abilities and skills provoke disgust. Ego-inflated lawyers who put people down provoke anger. Stay humble when dealing with other lawyers and you will avoid angry confrontations.

Humility also means recognizing that all cases belong to your clients. You get to give advice, but your client gets to decide whether to settle and for how much. Do you see clients who question or challenge your recommendations as a proverbial pain in the ass? When such a client calls or visits you, do you expect defiance and say to yourself, "Oh, no, not him again!" Could be that you're intolerant of anyone questioning your competence to get the job done best.

While your client is speaking, do you think to yourself, "This guy never went to law school. He's totally off base and doesn't have a clue. He's going to end up ruining his case if he doesn't start listening to me and following my recommendations. I better send him a letter explaining what my recommendations were, and documenting his refusal to follow them in case I get sued."

Bristling with anger when your client has the temerity to ask you why you're doing certain things is not helpful. If you care about your clients as persons, you must care about more than winning their cases. You should care about their feelings and needs. Clients need to be heard, to be respected and to be included in decisions that affect them.

When a client respects you enough to hire you, doesn't it make sense to respect him and work with him, rather than treat him as an incompetent and lecture him as if he were in grade school?

Dacher Keltner, Ph.D., a psychologist at U.C. Berkeley, has done scientific studies on compassion. Dr. Keltner found that what people most appreciate about each other is kindness, not financial success or physical attractiveness. He also found that pride is a turn-off, because it goes with selfishness. When he asked groups of people whom they associated with kindness and whom they associated with pride, they put lawyers in the pride category. Proud people are easily offended and quick to anger.

Anger-Free Law?

Let's face it. Only totally enlightened beings like the Buddha can get through the day without any anger. Law will never be an anger-free career. But great strides can be made in reducing the current epidemic of destructive anger in our profession. Recognizing the negative effects of your anger on your body, your thought process, your health, your relationships and your career is a start. Understanding that anger comes from within empowers us to reduce it.

Look within to see if you suffer from the need to be right all the time, the compulsion to control situations, perfectionism, believing that harming the other side will benefit you or assuming that others are evil or stupid because they disagree with you. Learning to breathe and do self-massage when tense, to feel humility, to feel gratitude and to become a better listener will help. Meditation can help you to watch your anger and let it go. If your main source of suffering is anger, I recommend seeing a psychotherapist who specializes in helping people with anger or joining an anger-management group. Doing both would be even better.

CHAPTER THREE: SUGGESTED READINGS

Ronald T. Potter-Efron, MSW, Ph.D., *Angry All The Time* (2nd ed.) (New Harbinger Publications, Inc., 2004)

M. J. Ryan, *Attitudes of Gratitude: How to Give and Receive Joy Every Day of Your Life* (MJF Books, 1999)

Mark Bender, Ph.D., *Black Ice & Banana Peels: Getting A Grip On Your Mind* (Longbow Press, 2002)

Jeffrey Brantley, M.D., *Calming Your Anxious Mind* (2nd ed.) (New Harbinger Publications, Inc., 2007)

Neale Donald Walsch, *Conversations With God: An Uncommon Dialog* (Book 1) (Penguin Group (USA), 1998.)

C. Peter Bankhart, Ph.D., *Freeing the Angry Mind: How Men Can Use Mindfulness & Reason To Save Their Lives & Relationships* (New Harbinger Publications, Inc., 2006)

Harry G. Frankfurt, *On Bullshit*, (Princeton University Press, 2005)

Ronald T. Potter-Effron, Ph.D., *Rage: A Step-by-Step Guide to Overcoming Explosive Anger*, New Harbinger (Publications, Inc., 2007)

Dr. Less Carter, *The Anger Trap* (Jossey-Bass, 2003)

CHAPTER FOUR

The role of chronic stress in causing anxiety, depression and memory dysfunction

IN THIS CHAPTER I am going to explain the brain's mechanisms for detecting danger and producing states of fear, anxiety and depression. Evolution wired the capacity for fear into the brain so animals could flee or fight when confronted with life-threatening situations. In cases of imminent danger to life or limb, fear is normal and helpful. It does its job quickly and then lets us return to our normal activities once the danger is past.

Anxiety is a pathological state marked by worry which is grossly excessive in its intensity or duration, or by worry which is purely mind-generated and has no correlation to an objective threat in the external world. Anxiety renders us incapable of working efficiently or enjoying life. It causes emotional suffering to lawyers along with physical damage to their brains, hearts and other organs.

By understanding where anxiety comes from, lawyers will be more able to recognize it and get treatment. They will be more able to cut it off at the pass and prevent it from taking over when it begins to escalate. They will be more motivated to learn calming techniques like meditation, deep breathing or laughter yoga.

Anxiety—From Useful Danger Detector to Tormentor

Animals are subject to anxiety in the face of real, physical threats, like a herd of wildebeest crossing a river filled with hungry, biting crocodiles. Human beings are very different. We can suffer tremendous anxiety from purely social interactions of the most innocuous variety, such as a raised eyebrow from a supervisor at work. We can even be attacked by our own minds, as when they harshly disparage our self-worth over trivial mistakes or imagine terrible things happening to us in the near future without a solid factual basis. Referring to dread over future events, Mark Twain said that, "Most of the worst events in my life never happened."

Law Practice Washes the Brain in Stress Chemicals

Some fortunate people go to work anticipating pleasure. How about a well-loved college professor about to lecture fresh-faced young people filled with curiosity about the art, literature and philosophy of ancient civilizations? He anticipates lecturing to an audience who will admire him, applaud him and gratefully soak up his words of wisdom. Our professor does not anticipate anyone standing up to fiercely challenge his credentials to teach, his honesty or the accuracy of his knowledge.

It's different with lawyers. As we drive to work we anticipate facing hostile conflict. At work we get it in spades. As we drive home we tense up remembering something that opposing counsel did or said that really pushed our buttons. Thus it's possible for us to experience stress going to work, working and coming home from work, all in one day. This can cause insomnia or make our sleep restless and fitful. We may even relive the day's stressful events in our dreams.

While all of this is going on, our bodies are undergoing myriad physiologic changes getting us ready for mortal combat. Whether we realize it or not, we are bathing our bodily tissues in the stress hormones adrenaline and cortisol that are changing our heartbeat, respiratory rate, metabolic rate, digestion, blood pressure, blood flow patterns and brain function. When we continuously bathe ourselves in these stress hormones, we actually cause damage to a part of the brain inside the temporal lobe called the hippocampus (named after the Latin word for seahorse because of its anatomical shape).

The hippocampus is one of the most important and most complex modules within the human brain. It encodes long-term memories and makes learning new information possible. Because of the extreme complexity of its cells, it is very sensitive to physical damage from such traumas as oxygen deprivation, hypoglycemia, fever and high levels of blood cortisol. Lawyers subject to chronically high stress levels are likely to suffer hippocampal damage, with decreased ability to form new long-term memories and learn new skills.

Lawyers Need to Understand How Stress Affects Them

Some occupations have a high level of built-in stress that appears ineradicable, like air traffic controller. Law is a profession that generates far more stress on its practitioners than is necessary to get the job done well. A central thesis of this book is that we can and should treat each other with more sensitivity, consideration, courtesy and respect to reduce the high levels of stress we have been inflicting on each other.

Law practice can be a daily pressure cooker. Worries about our dealings with judges, senior partners, peers, clients and opposing counsel can occupy much of our thinking. Will we be adequately prepared for our meeting? Did we handle ourselves well? How were we evaluated? Will we get the outcome we hoped for or not? Did we screw up, and, if so, how will this affect us?

Out of anxiety lawyers over-prepare for depositions, hearings and trials. We don't trust our innate wisdom. We don't trust that the words will be there when we need them, so we write them all out and rehearse them. You can develop self-trust if you take risks. Next time you have to make an oral argument in court or give a speech, try doing it spontaneously at home after grounding yourself by taking some deep breaths. You may be amazed.

The concept of doing our best and then letting things happen as they will because we cannot control how others respond is very helpful in reducing anxiety. Lawyers are very results-oriented, yet no law says we have to be. Why not focus on how much effort you put into a project and the quality of your work. A results-only orientation trivializes these things, yet these are the things under our control, not the result.

Variations in How Lawyers Handle Stress

How any two lawyers handle stress is variable. Your brain development, the emotional warmth and consistency of your mother-child bond, your genetic temperament, your habitual response to stress, your present load of stress, your degree of control over the stressors, your current state of physical and psychological health and the presence or absence of social support to help you through the stress all shape what kinds and levels of stress you can endure before being overwhelmed.

How Stress Affects Our Perception and Performance

In *The Naked Brain*, neurologist Richard Restak, M.D., says the human brain functions differently in different social situations; e.g., situations that make us happy and relaxed vs. being upset and tense. The brain of a relaxed person is going to look very different on a brain scan from the brain of someone feeling significant anxiety. Their brains will have different kinds, amounts and distribution patterns of neurotransmitters flowing between neurons.

The relaxed lawyer and the stressed lawyer will have different capacities for attention, memory, learning and task performance. In the very same setting they will experience different physical sensations, emotions and thoughts that correlate with their prevailing mood. The lawyer able to handle stress understands it's only temporary, that he isn't to blame for the situation and that he can ride it out. The lawyer who folds under stress mistakenly believes it will never end, that he's done something to invite the stress into his life and that there is no hope of enduring it. By virtue of different mindsets, one is hopeful and the other feels helpless in the same situation.

Happiness and Stress Both Shape Your Brain

The expression one hears today, that happy moods make for happy neurochemistry and bad moods make for bad neurochemistry, has some truth to it. Your prevailing mood (relaxed and happy vs. anxious and unhappy) physically reshapes the fine structures of the brain at the cellular and subcellular level. Neuroscientists tell us that receptors for neurotransmitters in the cellular membranes and synapses between brain cells are both plastic, and are continuously shaped by the inner chemistry of our moods. Thinking positive thoughts and experiencing positive emotions affects brain structure in a way that makes us far more able to cope with stress than routinely engaging in negative thoughts and experiencing negative emotions.

How the Brain Processes Stress—
Two Different Neural Alarm Systems

Evolutionarily the older and more primitive danger detector in the human brain is called the amygdala. It's part of the limbic system—the emotional portion of the brain that converts sensory information into emotions beneath the level of human consciousness. There is one amygdala lying deep within each cerebral hemisphere near the anterior temporal lobe. Each one is a small, almond-shaped cluster of brain cells that is hooked up to the thalamus. The thalamus, the sensory gateway of the brain, relays sensory data at lightning speed to the amygdala, and much more slowly to the fronto-temporal lobes where we engage in rational problem-solving.

The amygdala produces the feeling of fear. On a physiological level it activates the sympathetic nervous system, increases arousal and vigilance, causes the release of cortisol and activates fight-flight responses that promote survival in response to a threat of attack. Speed trumps accuracy in responding to danger. Because of the need for speed, the images that go from the thalamus to the amygdala tend be crude.

We are much better off mistakenly jumping away from a crooked stick that cues "rattlesnake!" to our amygdala than waiting around to tell the difference and risk being bitten. The amygdala protects us by sounding the fear alarm before we even know what's happened. Horror movies and suspense movies get much of their power from activating this part of the brain. When we realize we have jumped out of our seats over nothing, we laugh and the laughter releases our fear.

The frontal lobes are new on the evolutionary scene. They appraise danger too, but much more slowly. Using conscious memories, conscious comparisons and rational thought, the frontal lobes make their own independent determination if danger is present. They rank it in terms of the level of threat (minor, moderate, serious or extreme) and when it's likely to cause harm (immediately, later, much later). They analyze all relevant data about the potentially harmful object including past personal experience, stories about it from others, book knowledge, logical extrapolation and so forth.

The frontal lobes have the capacity to inhibit and override fear messages coming from the amygdala. For example, someone with a dog phobia who is learning to overcome his fear of dogs can learn to coach himself to crouch down near a dog and pet it even when he's experiencing fear and has the urge to flee. If the fear is too great, our dog-phobic can take a beta blocker until he's interacted with enough dogs and survived to master his irrational fear and remain calm in the presence of dogs.

The Role of Serotonin in Calming Anxiety

In the normal brain serotonin is released to combat stress, stabilize mood and keep us calm. Serotonin deficiency in the brain is associated with anxiety, irritability, aggression, homicide, depression and suicide. When researchers examined the brains of people who died by suicide, they found very low levels of serotonin.

Where does serotonin come from? The brain and the gut manufacture it from the amino acid tryptophan contained in turkey, pork, beef, eggs, milk and cheese. The part of the brain that makes serotonin is a cluster of cells in the brainstem (medulla oblongata) called the dorsal raphe nuclei (DNR). The DNR transmits serotonin to the amygdala, hypothalamus, basal ganglia, frontal lobes and other areas of the brain.

Like all neurotransmitters, serotonin is released from vesicles (little sacs) at the axon terminals of the brain cells that make it. These cells are called serotonergic neurons. Axon terminal is a fancy name for the tip of the long thin axonal tubes lying farthest away from the body of the brain cell—the body being the fat part of the cell containing the nucleus. Axons lie on the opposite side of brain cells from the feathery dendrites that have a highly arborized network of elements like sea fans. The narrow, empty space between the axon of one nerve cell and the dendrites of another is called the synapse.

Depending on the type of brain cell, the axon of one cell will synapse with the dendrites of 100 to 10,000 or more other brain cells. Since the brain has approximately one hundred billion neurons, the sheer number of synapses is literally mind-boggling. It supposedly exceeds the number of stars in the known universe.

When serotonin is released, it flows across the synapse between neurons and binds to receptor sites on the dendrites of adjacent neurons. In this process not all molecules of serotonin are used up. There is a serotonin transporter protein called 5-HTT that pumps unused serotonin back into the vesicles at the axon tips for later use. The movement of serotonin back into axon terminals for storage and reuse is called serotonin re-uptake.

The gene on the 17th chromosome that makes 5-HTT comes in two forms, the short and the long. The short form allows too much serotonin to be dispersed, broken down and go unused. Without enough serotonin, the amygdala and the frontal lobes are in an overstimulated state, the opposite of the tranquil, happy state we all want to feel as much of the time as possible. Prozac and Zoloft are thought to reduce depression by preventing dispersion and breakdown of serotonin and keeping more of it in the synapses.

People inherit one copy of the serotonin transporter gene from each parent, so they can have two long, two short or one of each. There is a growing body of literature asserting that people with two short copies of this gene are likely to be chronically aroused, fearful and ruminative (meaning they replay negative thoughts over and over in their minds). The same body of literature asserts that people with two long copies of the serotonin transporter gene have more serotonin in their synapses and they are more protected against anxiety and depression in stressful situations.

Avshalom Caspi and colleagues published a study in *Science* in 2003 in which they compared depression rates in three groups of New Zealanders in response to major life stressors. The group with two copies of the short form serotonin transporter gene suffered double the rate of depression than the group with one short and one long copy and still higher rates compared to the group with two long copies.

There is little doubt the short copy of the gene that makes 5-HTT is important, but is it really the "anxiety gene" as one researcher has said (see "The Character Code" by Turhan Canli, an associate professor of genetics in the department of psychology at Stony Brook University in the February/March issue of *Scientific American Mind*)?

In June 2009 Neil Risch and colleagues at the University of California, San Francisco, Medical Center published a review paper in the *Journal of the American Medical Association* asserting there was no evidence of a link between the short copy of the serotonin transporter gene and the risk of depression.

Risch and colleagues did not undertake their own controlled study of depressed patients, but looked at information from 14 other studies involving 14,000 people. They concluded it was stressful events, not the gene mutation, that was responsible for depression. Avshalom Caspi (who was at King's College of London in 2003 and is now at Duke University) criticized the Risch paper which he said ignored evidence supporting his original research.

The truth probably lies somewhere in the middle. In Dr. Caspi's 2003 study, people with the short form of the gene only exhibited an increased risk for depression if they experienced significant negative events in their lives. They did not develop depression merely because they had two copies of the short version of the gene. His research exemplifies the interaction of genes with environment. For anxiety, depression and addiction, genes are important as a tendency or a vulnerability, but they are not destiny. People can use techniques to cope with stress and boost happiness in their lives that have a real impact.

Stress Tolerance—Genes, Personality and Selective Vulnerability to Anxiety

Behavioral neuroscientists say that about half our conduct can be accounted for by our genes and the rest by personal decision-making or free choice. Why? Because, unlike animals, we have enormous frontal lobes that enable us to override instincts. How do our genes play out in influencing things like stress tolerance and vulnerability to anxiety? They do so by setting our personal thermostat for stress. People with serotonin deficiency from the short copy of the transporter gene are more easily stressed. So are people with hyperactive amygdalas.

The sensitivity of the amygdala varies from person to person, due largely to genetic reasons (excepting people with PTSD from childhood abuse, serving in wars and so forth). If we analogize the amygdala to a smoke detector, it would be super-sensitive in a neurotic person who is anxious and worried much of the time, and somewhat desensitized in a calm, emotionally stable and self-confident person.

In the neurotic, the amygdala would sound the fear alarm many times when there was no threat (smoke without fire), something called a false positive. In the emotionally stable person it might fail to go off in the face of some threats, something called a false negative. Neuroscience is beginning to uncover genetic differences between people who have easily aroused amygdalas and people who do not.

A huge new area of research is focusing on the genetic factors that influence personality and mood. An Australian team of researchers in psychology and neuropsychiatry led by Sarah Whittle has come up with a model of three basic human temperaments that correspond with differences in brain processing of social interactions. (Whittle S., Allen N.B., Lubman D.I. and Yucel M., *The Neurobiological Basis of Temperament: Toward a Better Understanding of Psychopathology* (Neuroscience & Biobehavioral Reviews 30(4): 511-525, 2005)

By temperament Whittle et al. are referring to "endogenous basic tendencies of thoughts, emotions and behaviors" that are "observed in infancy, are genetically influenced and are modestly but significantly preserved across the lifespan." Their three temperaments are Negative

Affect, Positive Affect and Constraint. Constraint involves modulation of the other two temperaments.

According to Whittle, a person with Negative Affect approaches new people, things and situations with inhibition and avoidance, and has a propensity to experience a wide range of negative moods such as fear, anxiety, sadness and guilt. A person with NA will tend to have a larger than normal amygdala which is active more of the time, and makes NA people prone to anxiety disorder, panic attacks, phobias and PTSD.

A person with Positive Affect is actively engaged in the world and has a propensity to experience a wide range of positive moods such as joy, happiness, enthusiasm and pride. NA people are sensitive to punishment while PA people are sensitive to reward. People with Constraint demonstrate control over impulses and emotions and the ability to delay gratification to achieve a goal. They are diligent, persistent, reliable and responsible.

The prefrontal cortex (PFC) represents the anterior tip of the frontal lobes just above and behind the eyes. The dorsolateral PFC on the right side of the brain plays a major role in inhibiting negative thoughts. In people with Constraint, the right dorsolateral PFC is significantly more active than in people with NA who suffer from depression, anxiety or both. The dorsolateral prefrontal cortex on the left side of the brain is associated with production of positive thoughts. It's highly active in PA people and relatively inactive in NA people.

Understanding the Role of the Amygdala in the Work Setting

We all have amygdalas with differing levels of sensitivity and activity which appear to correspond roughly with our personality type. I noticed that some of my clients just shrugged off car crashes while others became so apprehensive they stopped driving, or even riding in, cars for a substantial period of time. Desensitization therapy for people with PTSD works by calming (reducing the activity of) the amygdala in particular situations.

One out of every five lawyers is alcoholic or suffering from major depression. It's probable that these lawyers have amygdalas that are more sensitive and more active than those of their colleagues. If they worked in a different occupation that did not involve such high levels of chronic stress, they might well be healthier and happier people. The issue becomes how can we lower the level of stress in law practice so that this large group of bright, talented, creative, well-trained people can contribute without suffering so terribly?

How Does the Amygdala Initiate the Fight-Flight Response in Our Brain?

The Central Nervous System (CNS) consists of the brain and spinal cord. The CNS has a voluntary nervous system that we use to contract or relax our muscles under conscious control. The CNS also has an autonomic nervous system (ANS) which regulates the body functions we need to survive, like heartbeat, blood pressure, respiration, digestion and elimination. Although we can affect parts of the ANS through biofeedback, the ANS operates on its own and does not require any conscious input from us.

The classic understanding of the ANS is that it functions like a homeostatic computer to keep thirst, water intake, fluid levels, electrolyte levels, urinary output, etc., in a state of equilibrium. The ANS has a sympathetic nervous system (SNS) that produces adrenaline for emergencies, and a parasympathetic nervous system (PNS) that produces acetylcholine to calm us down. The SNS is activated by the amygdala when we confront a fear-producing stimulus. The PNS is activated by things like napping, gentle stretching, meditation or yoga.

The hypothalamus is the supreme commander of the ANS, its Captain Kirk. Though small (it is a pea-sized organ lying in front of the hippocampus), the hypothalamus regulates key bodily functions including temperature, sex drive, thirst, hunger and aggression. When the amygdala rings the fear alarm, the paraventricular nucleus (PVN) of the hypothalamus goes into action by sending corticotrophin-releasing hormone (CRH) to the pituitary gland. This prompts the pituitary to send adrenocorticotropic hormone (ACTH) into the bloodstream. The ACTH binds to receptors in the adrenal glands atop the kidneys, which prompts the adrenal glands to release stress hormones into the bloodstream that kick off the fight-flight response.

The hypothalamus, pituitary and adrenal glands are collectively known as the HPA (hypothalamic-pituitary-adrenal) axis. Neuro-pharmaceutical research is investing heavily in studies of the HPA, because it is believed that HPA dysfunction may be the cause of mood disorders that don't respond to antidepressants like Prozac and Zoloft that boost serotonin.

The adrenal glands manufacture two types of stress hormones from cholesterol—fast-acting adrenaline and slower-acting cortisol. Scientists classify cortisol as a glucocorticoid because it affects the availability and utilization of glucose. Cortisol is also a natural anti-inflammatory. Hydrocortisone cream for control of skin rashes and itching is a pharmaceutical preparation that uses cortisol. The hippocampus has more glucocorticoid receptors than any other part of the human body. This explains how stressful memories can be imprinted so strongly as to remain vivid and frightening years after the event. It also explains why overproduction of cortisol from chronic stress can damage the hippocampus by flooding it with cortisol.

What Happens Inside Our Bodies Once the Fight-Flight Response is Initiated?

Once the adrenal glands have begun pumping adrenaline into the bloodstream, our bodies respond quickly with the following types of changes: increase in heartbeat, arterial stiffness, blood flow and blood pressure to deliver extra glucose to our skeletal muscles for fighting or fleeing; digestion slows down; blood platelets become stickier to coagulate the blood in case of wounds; and opioid compounds are released to blunt pain from wounds. We also experience sweaty palms and feet, neck hairs standing on end, goose bumps on the limbs and a powerful urge to freeze, flee or fight.

Stress Hormones in the Workplace—
Friends or Foes?

Adrenaline initiates the classic fight-flight response, and tends to be cleared quickly from the system. Adrenaline helps the gazelle escape from the lion with a short burst of incredible speed. Cortisol is slow to build up and slow to dissipate. While elevated, adrenaline stirs excitement, and even feelings of power. Elevated cortisol tends to make us feel bad and can induce negative thoughts and depression.

People who are highly stressed and depressed have high levels of cortisol. In normal people cortisol builds slowly at night, reaching a peak around 6 to 7 a.m. when increased cortisol wakes them up. Cortisol levels then begin a decline so people feel tired and go to bed at night. In depressed people cortisol production reaches a peak around 2 to 3 a.m. That's why depressed people wake up in the early morning and cannot go back to sleep without drinking alcohol or taking medications like Ambien, Ativan or Klonopin. The infomercial industry plays to depressed people awake at those ungodly hours.

When stress hormones are released from the adrenal gland, they cross the blood-brain barrier and bind to steroid receptors in the amygdala, the hypothalamus and the hippocampus. When the fear stimulus is short-lived, like arguing a motion in front of an imperious federal judge for five minutes, the hippocampus will signal the hypothalamus to stop releasing CRH, which turns off the HPA axis and stops the secretion of stress hormones. Things are different when the fear stimulus never ends, because you're working under conditions of chronic stress in a law office. Under those conditions the amygdala is constantly activated and it will keep triggering the HPA axis to release cortisol into the bloodstream.

Normally the pituitary can slow the release of CRH from the hypothalamus by secreting a hormone called vasopressin. But when too much CRH is secreted, vasopressin loses its braking effect and the pituitary will keep telling the adrenals to secrete stress hormones. Persistent high levels of CRH and ACTH with persistent high levels of adrenal gland secretion will ultimately cause the adrenal glands to atrophy and shut down. This condition, known as adrenal exhaustion, is associated with fatigue and muscle weakness.

If you're feeling stressed and fatigued most of the time, I suggest you ask your doctor to check you for adrenal fatigue. This is especially true if you're getting normal hours of sleep but wake up without feeling restored or refreshed. Other indications of adrenal fatigue include lowered immune function, thirst, craving for sweet and salty foods, diminished libido, muscle thinning and sensitivity to cold.

Chronic Stress, Depression and Pain

Do you feel pain in the absence of trauma, inflammation or objective evidence of a painful condition? Such "psychosomatic" pain is a classic marker of depression. Recent brain imaging studies have shown that depression can increase pain perception because the amygdala in depressed patients is hyper-excitable. It becomes highly active when depressed people anticipate pain or feel mildly painful stimuli that would not bother other people.

The Connection Between Chronic Stress, Bad Memory and Hyperanxiety

If your memory is slipping, it may be due more to stress than ageing. Just ask neuro-endocrinology researchers Robert Sapolsky, Ph.D., and Bruce McEwen, Ph.D.

Dr. Sapolsky is a Stanford neurophysiologist who won a MacArthur "genius" award for his work which he popularized in *Why Zebras Don't Get Ulcers*.

Dr. Sapolsky began his research around 1990 by studying what happened to monkeys kept in cages with aggressive males who tormented them to establish dominance. At the end of the study the monkeys were sacrificed and autopsied. Along with stomach ulcers, the weaker males showed shrinkage of hippocampal volume in otherwise normal brains. Ongoing research has shown that stressed-out monkeys with shrunken hippocampi are learning-disabled. Monkeys and humans need their hippocampus to remember information and learn new concepts, skills or procedures. Hence we must decrease workplace anxiety to protect our brains.

Our Minds Can be Happy Homes or Stress Factories

The Dalai Lama wants us to remember that every second of our lives is a precious, never-to-return opportunity to be happy and to contribute to happiness of all beings by sharing our unique talents. Sadly, too many lawyers spend their time in a state of fear, grievance, anger and depression or engaging in flight from these negative emotions by abusing substances. To solve this problem, we must understand the link between consciousness and the physiology of stress.

What happens "out there" in the world isn't separate from how we experience the world through our minds. Our minds pattern all sensory input. If we adhere to old patterns of negative thinking that stamp experience in a fearful, worrisome cast, then we will spend lots of needless time in the red zone of amygdalar overactivity with elevated cortisol.

Pessimism, Optimism and Explanatory Style

Martin Seligman, Ph.D., the father of positive psychology, says that all persons develop an "explanatory style" during childhood which they carry into adulthood. This is the habitual way they explain why events happen. It comes from observing how their parents respond to, and what parents say in the face of, stressful events like disappointments or losses. It comes from whether parents encourage them to keep going when they're facing challenges or just give up. It comes from how much praise vs. criticism they get from their parents. If, no matter how hard they try, their parents keep criticizing them, they will develop a pessimistic explanatory style.

Pessimistic children are easily discouraged and give up quickly because their explanatory style is to believe that nothing they do matters. Seligman says they have learned to be helpless, because whenever they encounter the normal setbacks of life, the small ones or the big ones, the word in their hearts is no. Optimistic children are hopeful and resilient. They bounce back from setbacks and keep going. The word in their hearts is yes.

Seligman says thinking causes feeling and feeling causes behavior. The difference between them lies in explanatory style, which boils down to what you believe when adverse events occur.

When something bad happens pessimistic people see it as permanent, pervasive and personal. Permanent means it's not a temporary condition but will last a lifetime. Pervasive means it doesn't affect just one part of their lives, but their whole lives. Personal means it's a reflection of what is in them, rather than an external circumstance. For example, let's say you're a pessimist who loses a trial early in your career. In the face of this adverse event you believe you will never win another trial; the loss proves yet again that you are a loser in every aspect of your life and the loss was entirely your fault and had nothing to do with the credibility of the parties or with the attitudes and behaviors of the judge, jurors or witnesses.

Optimists see bad events as temporary, limited and impersonal. The optimist would believe the loss in trial was due to particular circumstance that will not always exist and will not prevent him from winning a trial in the future, that one loss in trial does not render him incapable in all of his many other activities and the loss was accidental (due to circumstance) or the fault of others. He does not condemn himself. He is able to go on and try again, and by virtue of trying again, he gives himself the chance to win and feel good.

Two bits of remarkable information. First, Seligman has tested many different professions and the only one which had pessimism as a common explanatory style was lawyers. Since pessimism triggers the self-condemnation and the feeling of being helpless in response to stressful events, it's small wonder lawyers have such a high rate of depression. Second, Seligman not only believes pessimists can learn to be much more optimistic, he has written a book describing how to do it. It's called *Learned Optimism*.

Seligman's book has a test to help you determine if you're pessimistic or optimistic. He goes into great depth regarding explanatory style and how to modify it so you can become what he calls a flexible optimist, one who is hopeful about his chances but not blind to reality.

Quieting the Stressed Mind

When an event occurs in your law practice that creates strain—the emergence of a new challenge that must be faced—you can either go into a fearful, defensive mindset or look for constructive ways to efficiently solve the problem. The first option involves a movement away from the real situation out there and inward into your mind, where your mind will begin to brew a potent cocktail of stress hormones. Under stress you might say to yourself self-agitating things like "Not again" or "Why me?" or "When am I ever going to catch a break?"

However, you don't have to get sucked in. You can take a few deep breaths, focus your attention on your breath and relax. You can now accept that something unpleasant has happened without personalizing it. You can refocus your attention on the details of the situation with the intent of solving the challenge and with the belief that you can do it. In this case strain will not produce stress. Until you create a habit of blocking the conversion of strain to stress, you will backtrack now and then and get under stress. It's OK. Just gently remind yourself to do better next time.

Stay Mindful of Your Stress Level and Make Adjustments

When we work in a stressful environment with no effort to "check in" with someone about our stress level and make adjustments when it's too high, we're likely to run into trouble. Lawyers who do nothing to monitor their stress are like the frog placed in room-temperature water that is gradually heated to the boiling point. Because the increase in heat is gradual, the frog doesn't notice the change until it's too late and by then he's been cooked.

Having a therapist or a therapy group is expensive and does cut into your time, but it's well worth it. In lieu of therapy, a daily practice of meditation or yoga can work since they involve an opportunity to listen to your mind and body and relax.

If you're feeling overly stressed, you may be secreting excess cortisol. To find out for sure, you can have your doctor order a simple urine test. Every time you have to pee over a 24-hour period, you pee in a container stored in a cool place (like a basement, garage or refrigerator). The lab will tell your doctor if your cortisol is elevated. Mild elevation is consistent with anxiety or depression. To reduce blood cortisol through diet, check *The Cortisol Connection Diet* by Shawn Talbott. If your urinary cortisol is mildly elevated, your doctor will probably ask you to undergo a saliva or blood test just to make sure you don't have a tumor. But the odds would be against it, since tumors are associated with a very significant elevation of cortisol.

Reduce Your Cortisol Naturally by Laughing

Michael Miller, M.D., a cardiologist at the University of Maryland School of Medicine, recommends fifteen minutes of mirthful laughter a day to prevent heart disease. Chronic stress increases blood pressure and causes blood clots that clog coronary arteries by increasing the number of blood platelets and increasing their stickiness. Laughter reduces blood pressure, platelet count and platelet stickiness.

Lee Berk, M.D., at the U.C. Irvine College of Medicine, has analyzed blood samples taken from adult subjects before and after undergoing laughter therapy (consisting of watching funny videos). He also tested the blood of subjects who had anticipated enjoying the videos two days before they watched them, to compare the physiologic effects of laughter with anticipation of laughter.

His published results were astounding. Laughter and the anticipation of laughter both boosted positive mood by stimulating endorphin production; decreasing levels of tension, anger, depression, fatigue and confusion by reducing the levels of the stress hormones adrenalin and cortisol in the blood; and boosting immune system function by increasing the production of gamma interferon, B cells that eat bacteria and T-cells that kill viruses and cancer cells.

Psychologist and "joyologist" Steve Wilson, M.A., the co-founder of The World Laughter Tour, encourages us to laugh because laughter increases useful energy for work, play and creativity, whereas wallowing in stress saps energy by diverting it into the fight-flight response and obsessive worries. Patty Wooten, R.N., and Ed Dunkelblau, Ph.D., call laughter a vitamin for the soul. They extol laughter because it distracts and distances us from painful events and gives us the emotional detachment we must have to cope and recover. It is emotionally cathartic and has the capacity to neutralize and release feelings of anger, tension and fear. By giving us joy it opens a window to the rest of our lives and reminds us life is still worth living and we can continue to experience wonderful moments no matter what losses we have suffered.

If you want to laugh more and you're not sure how, you can watch funny movies on DVD, watch comedy on TV, go to comedy clubs or take a laughter yoga class. You can celebrate World Laughter Day, which is the first Sunday of every May. You can join a happiness club through the American Happiness Association. You can join the Association for Applied and Therapeutic Humor (AATH).

Dr. Laurence J. Peter, author of *The Laughter Prescription*, suggests that you: adopt an attitude of playfulness in which your mind is open to uncensored, iconoclastic, silly or outrageous thoughts; think funny by seeing the flip side of every situation; laugh at the incongruities in everyday situations, whether they involve you or someone else; only laugh with others for what they do, not for who they are; and laugh at yourself with acceptance of and delight in your own weaknesses, idiosyncrasies and conceits.

The Disparate Effects of Smiling and Frowning on Cortisol Levels

Although feelings (like those of happiness, sadness or anger) do influence facial expressions, facial expressions also influence feelings. In her book *Happy For No Reason*, Marci Shimoff discusses studies that show that smiling boosts endorphin production, decreases cortisol secretion and leads to feeling happy. French physiologist Israel Waynbaum has shown that frowning kicks off secretions of cortisol and adrenalin.

A Final Note of Encouragement

It's ironic that we lawyers always have a plan for discovery, mediation and trial, but most of us have no plan for how to manage our workplace stress. We just keep going and hope things will work out for the best. The failure of lawyers to self-manage stress leaves them vulnerable to anxiety, depression and the addictions to soothe psyche-ache. Abdicating responsibility for our own mental health is the road to self-destruction.

Please take responsibility for feeling good. You're worth it. You are here for a reason. The universe went through a lot of trouble to bring you right here right now. The world needs you at your best. So does your family. While depression can get severe enough to spark suicide, there is no ceiling on how good you can feel if you really want to be happy. Martin Seligman says traditional psychology is aimed at helping troubled people feel less troubled, while positive psychology—the newest branch of psychology—is helping well people experience increased levels of satisfaction. Barbara Frederickson, author of *Positivity*, says that each new level of positivity we reach creates the potential for ever higher levels. Start today by frowning less, smiling more and laughing more.

CHAPTER FOUR: SUGGESTED READING

Martin E.P. Seligman, *Learned Optimism: How To Change Your Mind And Your Life* (Pocket Books, 1990, 1998)

Joseph LeDoux, *The Emotional Brain* (Simon & Schuster, 1996)

Robert Sapolsky, Ph.D., *Why Zebras Don't Get Ulcers: A Guide To Stress-Related Diseases and Coping* (W.H. Freeman, 1995)

CHAPTER FIVE

Why so many lawyers are alcoholics

Lawyers and Alcoholism—
The Nature and Scope of the Problem

IT'S HARD TO IMAGINE why so many lawyers become addicted to alcohol, given all of its downsides, which include: sleep disruption, hangover headaches, confusion, memory loss, blackouts, stomach ulcers, cirrhosis, liver cancer, high blood pressure, heart disease, strokes, DUIs, car crashes, complaints to the State Bar, disciplinary actions, legal malpractice lawsuits, loss of spousal affection and divorce.

Yet by the conservative estimate of the ABA, twenty percent of all lawyers are chemically dependent on alcohol, which is double the rate of the general population. Alcoholism is a major problem for our profession.

Lawyers put themselves under constant time pressure and stress. They don't structure their workday to include periods of rest, meditation, exercise or relaxed socializing. If your pendulum is at one extreme the whole workday (nonstop busyness), no wonder it swings to the opposite extreme when you leave the office (guzzling alcohol).

George Bernard Shaw said, "Alcohol is the anesthesia by which we endure the operation of life." The lawyers who find no joy in their workday justify drinking as a numbing agent that enables them to survive their jobs. I've been sober since June 2006. But when I was drinking I used to say to myself, "All I do is work (in the bleak, painful sense). I might as well have a drink and a moment of feeling good." When my wife tried to tell me I had a drinking problem, I became angry because I saw her as trying to take away the one thing that soothed me.

Law practice, in its present form, is a career that not only generates the blues, but also affirms the propriety of drinking. Lawyers use alcohol to reward themselves for periods of sustained hard work, to court new employees, to celebrate legal victories, to bond with colleagues and friends and to show off their wealth and good taste by the fine stuff they drink.

Alcohol consumption is deeply woven into the fabric of their daily lives in and out of the office. It's very hard for them to quit because they cannot imagine life without it. In virtually all cases they do not perceive its destructive impact on their health or career until a true crisis occurs that compels their attention.

Before the crisis hits, the alcoholic lawyer can always find reasons to keep drinking. He may enjoy the taste of his favorite intoxicant, be it fine red wine, microbrew ale or aged, malt Scotch. He can convince himself he is more friendly, witty, charming or attractive while stewed. Red wine drinkers can even fall back on the French advertising campaign that touts red wine as an arterial cleanser that reduces the risk of heart attacks.

The Medical Model of Alcoholism

The medical model of alcoholism was developed by the American Medical Association and Alcoholics Anonymous (AA). It says that alcoholism is an incurable, progressive and potentially lethal disease that involves a craving for alcohol and an inability to stop drinking after the first drink. The medical model says alcoholism is not caused by having a weak will or an immoral character. Rather, it develops mainly in people who have a genetic predisposition (shown by a family history of alcoholism), especially when these people are under stress.

Alcoholism is perpetuated by the denial of the alcoholic and the lack of attempts at intervention by his family, friends and co-workers. An enabler is a family member, friend or co-worker who stands by and does nothing while seeing the alcoholic drink himself into a personal hell marked by being fired, getting divorced, crashing his car or being arrested for DUI. Although alcoholics drink to ease their personal emotional pain, they compound their suffering by causing harm to themselves, their families, friends and co-workers, which is why enabling them to drink is a losing strategy.

Alcoholics become dependent upon and habituated to alcohol. Over time they have to drink more of the usual or move onto harder, more potent forms of alcohol to get back to the state of euphoria they crave. This is called "chasing the high." Alcoholics can become so tolerant of alcohol that when they are arrested for DUI, their blood alcohol content reads out at 2.8 or 3.1. Such alcoholics must be helped in rehab centers, because their withdrawal symptoms can involve confusion and delirium, and the painful symptoms of withdrawal can motivate them to resume drinking.

The Failed Strategy Model of Alcoholism

The psycho-social model of alcoholism sees it as a failed strategy to deal with personal distress. Cognitive behavioral therapy (CBT) is based on the recognition that alcoholics keep drinking because of wrong ideas called cognitive distortions. These distortions include such thoughts as "I am unlovable," "Nobody cares about me," "I always mess up relationships," "I always bungle work assignments," or "Alcohol is my only real friend."

CBT is a method of teaching alcoholics to see through these cognitive distortions by finding their own evidence to contradict them. For instance, an alcoholic can disprove he is "unlovable" by writing down the names of family members or friends who have unequivocally demonstrated their love for him on past occasions. When the false idea arises and the pressure to drink follows, the alcoholic can use this evidence to neutralize the potency of the idea and free himself from the craving to take a drink.

People whose lives fall below their expectations can suffer frustration, envy, anger and depression, especially when they engage in comparisons with peers who seem more successful and more happy. There are three ways of dealing with the discrepancy between the life you expected and the life you have. You can lower or modify your expectations, you can work harder or smarter toward achieving your expectations, or you can get drunk and stop caring.

Many people refuse to change their expectations of an ideal life, but take an "all or nothing" approach to reaching it. On New Year's Eve, or other times, they say to themselves something like, "From now on, I'm going to run every day and lose weight" or "I will spend more quality time with my spouse." The commitment about running was too demanding. The commitment about more quality time was too vague. Each time a person fails to live up to these sorts of commitments, because the demands of life make them impossible to keep, they lose more trust in themselves. Finally, they don't believe themselves anymore when they commit to changing anything about themselves, and this makes them ripe for alcoholism.

Life is on a continuum from two unsustainable end points, 100% despair and 100% euphoria. Many people naively entertain expectations of constant euphoria and get very down when life keeps proving difficult or frustrating.

As you sit at your desk to review a stack of motions to compel discovery and impose sanctions, you might begin to fantasize about an all-expense-paid trip to Hawaii for one month. When you snap out of your reverie and realize this ain't gonna happen, you get angry about having to sit there and draft the opposition papers (moving you closer to despair). You're then tempted to have some wine at lunch to move away from despair and closer to euphoria. This is how addiction to alcohol can develop—as a little treat to make you feel better after each unpleasant law office experience.

The Most Serious Negative Effects of Alcoholic Drinking on Your Life

The effects of too much alcohol on mood, behavior, interpersonal relationships and occupation are highly destructive. According to the DSM-IV Guidebook, "Substance-Related Disorders are among the most common and impairing of the mental disorders." The DSM-IV is the fourth edition of The Diagnostic and Statistical Manual of Mental Disorders. Psychiatrists around the world rely on The DSM to diagnose psychiatric problems for treatment and billing purposes.

Alcohol disrupts the formation of new memories, because it impairs the functioning of the hippocampus, the area of the brain that encodes long-term memories. The more alcohol in your system, the bigger the disruption of memory formation.

A study at the University of Kentucky published in 2009 concluded that people over 50 are less able to metabolize alcohol. When drinking the same amount as a younger person, they end up with a higher blood alcohol concentration and are more affected. They are less likely to realize they are impaired and do worse on tests of performance. As for middle-aged lawyers, the number of lawyers remaining in practice over age 55 will swell over the next two decades as Baby Boomers hit their sixties and seventies. They will need to be very careful about alcohol.

Alcohol consumption compromises your balance and coordination by impairing the function of your cerebellum. I have caught more than one falling adult at a party where alcohol was served. Lucky for them I was sober. Alcohol affects your frontal lobes by blocking their capacity to inhibit socially undesirable behavior including anger, cursing, violence and laughing or crying for no apparent reason.

Alcohol interferes with liver enzymes. The ethanol in alcoholic beverages actually burns and scars your liver tissue on a cellular level. Heavy drinking plays havoc with your basic biological functions like eating, sleep, socializing, sexuality and aggression.

Alcoholics have a harder time falling asleep; they wake up feeling more tired and they are less able to overcome sleep debt than people with disrupted sleep from other causes. There is something toxic in alcohol that triggers an inflammatory response. At night the sleeping alcoholic's blood has abnormally high levels of immune substances (Interleuken-6 and tumor necrosis factor). Scientists believe this causes poor, un-refreshing sleep which keeps alcoholics in a kind of jet-lagged state of consciousness during the day.

Heavy alcohol consumption compromises the immune system and increases the risk of cancer of the liver, esophagus, throat and larynx.

Alcohol consumption can aggravate and worsen many diseases and conditions including epilepsy, hypertension, diabetes and depression. Alcoholics have a lower life expectancy unless they find a way to become sober and stay sober before it's too late. They die from acute alcohol poisoning, cirrhosis of the liver, pneumonia, diabetes, cardiovascular disease, stroke, head injury from falls or fights, fire, suicide, homicide and dementia.

According to the National Council on Alcoholism, over 100,000 people die each year from alcohol-related causes, including accidents that involve cars, boats and bicycles. To learn more about the dangers of drinking, the signs that you are exceeding safe limits and strategies to stop or to reduce your drinking, check the National Institutes of Health website at www.nih.gov.

Alcohol Exacts a Greater Health Toll on Women

Women have less water in their bodies than men. They are less able to metabolize alcohol than men and get intoxicated more quickly. Drinking is more likely to damage a woman's health than a man's even if she has been drinking a shorter time. Alcoholic women have death rates 50% to 100% higher than men from causes as diverse as suicide, accidents, dementia, stroke, heart disease, cancer and liver disease.

Women who consume two drinks per day raise their risk for breast cancer. Heavy drinking raises a woman's risk of sexual assault and unwanted pregnancy. Women who consume more than seven drinks a week are considered to be at risk of alcohol dependence.

Who is Most at Risk for Developing Alcoholism?

Risk factors for having alcohol problems include genetic predisposition (especially if a parent, sibling or grandparent suffered from alcoholism); whether a parent modeled alcoholism as a way of life and tried to get you to drink while you were growing up; being male; beginning to drink alcohol before the age of 16; mental illness involving depression, mania or anxiety; cultural influences; peer pressure; membership in certain ethnic groups (e.g., Eskimos and Native Americans); and stress caused by membership in certain occupational groups (lawyers), easy availability of alcohol (bartenders) or both (chefs). One third of all alcoholics report having had alcoholic parents.

Studies by psychiatrist Victor Hesselbrock at the University of Connecticut School of Medicine show that drinking prompted by bad moods is a risk factor for alcoholism and depression. Based on data collected from 5,000 men and women over 30, he observed that primary depression (depression first, followed by alcoholism) is more common in females, and primary alcoholism (alcoholism first, followed by depression) is more common in males.

Risk Factors Peculiar to Lawyers

Lawyers who become alcoholics commonly engaged in heavy drinking during law school and even high school. They share risk factors common to all alcoholics, but have some of their own.

These include: having the cash to afford the good stuff; working in a high-stress occupation; working in isolation; being a paid worrier; fear of being sued if they screw up; having a personality with features of perfectionism or obsessive-compulsive disorder; coming home to angry family members who resent their long hours at the office; and working in a field that courts clients, toasts new ventures and celebrates success at fine restaurants with abundant liquor, wine or both.

Alcohol and Depression

The need to self-medicate with alcohol is associated with unipolar depression, bipolar depression, panic disorder, PTSD and ADHD. Dr. Alison Goate, Professor of Genetics, Psychiatry and Neurology at the Washington University School of Medicine in St. Louis, has linked alcoholism and depression to a region on human chromosome 7.

It is well known that many depressives who respond well to SSRI drugs like Prozac or Zoloft feel better after drinking alcohol. Both substances affect the emotional part of the brain, and both reduce emotional pain. Alcohol works by boosting dopamine, while SSRIs work by boosting serotonin.

Alcohol and Anxiety

F. Scott Fitzgerald, a famous author with a great deal of drinking experience, expressed the sequence of going from the first drink to a state of drunkenness as follows: "First you take a drink, then the drink takes a drink, then the drink takes you." Alcohol is like a magical elixir that helps you momentarily forget all your troubles and your worries, but all elixirs come at a price.

This one powers down the parts of your brain that feel shame, worry about future consequences and knowing when to exercise tact and discretion. Still worse, this elixir powers down memory, so you don't know why everyone is giving you the cold shoulder the day after the annual office Christmas party.

The anxiolytic effect of alcohol (its capacity to replace tension and anxiety with sedation and euphoria) is a consequence of how the ethanol in alcohol affects brain physiology. Ethanol increases the supply of gamma amino butyric acid (GABA), the neurotransmitter that calms the brain. It increases the flow of dopamine (a pleasure-inducing neurotransmitter) to the amygdala (the brain's fear center). Ethanol also increases release of opioid compounds that dull pain.

Some of the anxiolytic effects of alcohol come from reducing the transmission of glutamate to the NMDA receptors on brain cells. Glutamate has a general role as an excitatory neurotransmitter in the brain. The right amount keeps brain cells humming, while too little turns them off and too much can kill them. Glutamate also has a special role in the brain, which is to help encode long-term memories by docking to the NMDA receptors. When you drink alcohol, the ethanol in your blood blocks the NMDA receptors so you can't remember what you did. If Lawyer Bob always hated his boss Lawyer Dave, and he got drunk at the firm's Christmas party, he could conceivably argue with Dave, punch him in the jaw and not remember doing it the next day when he got his pink slip.

Alcoholic Drinking,
Brain Shrinkage and Dementia

While athletes prize their muscles and their ability to run or jump, lawyers prize their brains and their ability to think. Imagine what it would be like to have a significant cognitive impairment that wiped out part of your ability to remember, to figure things out or to craft arguments. Imagine that you have done this to yourself by voluntarily ingesting a mild poison on too many occasions. How would you feel?

While there is no definitive medical evidence yet that alcoholic drinking can trigger early onset Alzheimer's Disease in susceptible people, there are researchers looking into it right now. We do know that approximately one-fourth of all cases of non-Alzheimer's dementia are caused by chronic, heavy alcohol consumption.

Everyone is born with a huge excess of brain cells (neurons) that is called neuronal reserve. A normal human being is born with approximately 100 billion neurons. The function of neuronal reserve is to provide extra cells that can take over for neurons that have been damaged or killed off by stress, aging, disease, trauma or exposure to toxic substances. Heavy drinking kills brain cells and decreases neuronal reserve. If a lawyer with decreased neuronal reserve from alcoholic drinking sustains a brain insult that would not disable a healthy brain (such as a mild stroke or a mild concussion), he may well experience problems with cognitive functioning.

The volume of the human brain shrinks an average of 1.9% per decade as aging brain cells "retire." The conventional wisdom for a long time has been that light-to-moderate alcohol drinking is good for the brain, because it prevents stroke and has no effect on brain volume. Recent studies from highly respected sources call these "facts" into question.

On December 5, 2003, a group at the Johns Hopkins Bloomberg School of Public Health led by Jingzhong Ding, Ph.D., published a paper in *Stroke*. They describe using an MRI scanner on 1,909 men and women age 55 and older whose drinking habits were categorized as: never drank, former drinker, occasional drinker (less than one drink per week), low drinker (1-6 per week) and moderate drinker (7-14 per week).

Dr. Ding's group found that moderate drinkers had statistically significant shrinkage of their white matter brain volume without any corresponding benefit in terms of reduced frequency of stroke. What caused this atrophy of white matter in moderate drinkers? One possible mechanism is a dietary deficiency of Vitamin B12 which is necessary to produce the fatty myelin sheathing for the axons that make up the bulk of the white matter.

On October 14, 2008, Carol Ann Paul, M.S., and her colleagues at Wellesley College published a paper in the *Archives of Neurology* on their analysis of 1,839 adults (average age 60) from the Framingham Heart Study. They wanted to test the theory that light drinking may protect against age-related decrease in brain size, because it allegedly reduces the risk of all cardiovascular disease, including stroke. But what they found was a significant, negative linear relationship between alcohol drinking and total cerebral volume, meaning that the more you drank the smaller your brain.

How does alcohol kill the neurons that comprise the gray matter? The known mechanisms include inflammation, increase in tumor necrosis factor, thiamine (B1) deficiency and buildup of reactive oxidative species (ROS). Thiamine is needed for the health of tiny blood capillaries in the hypothalamus. Alcohol-induced deficiency of thiamine damages these blood vessels and causes a condition called Wernicke-Korsakoff's Syndrome marked by confusion, poor short memory and inability to learn new information.

ROS are highly reactive, oxygen-bearing molecules that can damage and kill brain cells. Alcohol increases the amount of ROS in our circulating blood and impairs the ability of anti-oxidant substances to combat ROS. Loss of brain cells and brain volume shrinkage from alcohol are not harmless, but are associated with decline in cognitive function that can be career-impairing or career-ending.

The Puzzle of Alcoholism

Imagine how you would feel if your drinking caused your spouse to sleep in a different bed and not speak with you except when strictly necessary to operate the household or take care of the children. What if your kids acted like they feared you, hated you or both? What if you wrecked your car more than once? What if you got arrested for DUI more than once? What if you had to leave a job with a law firm more than once because of errors or omissions that resulted from drinking? What if you got sued for malpractice because of your drinking?

What if your doctor warned you that you were risking liver failure and death if you kept drinking? How would you feel if you started blacking out while drinking and finding yourself in strange places and strange situations without any memory of how you got there? What would it be like to wake up in jail for disturbing the peace, DUI or fighting with someone the night before, and no matter how hard you tried, you could not remember the circumstances? Would you give up alcohol for good?

The amazing answer is that even with these compelling reasons to join AA and abstain from further drinking for the rest of their lives, a certain percentage of alcoholic lawyers will keep right on drinking as if their lives depended on it. Why? Richard Carlton can shed some light here. He runs the substance abuse education programs for the State Bar of California, Lawyer Assistance Program.

Carlton says that alcoholics have gotten so used to feeling good only when they are drunk and gotten so used to using alcohol as their coping mechanism for the stresses of life that they cannot see any alternative. The people stuck in this terrible corner are people educated at the finest colleges and law schools; people who passed the onerous challenge of the State Bar exam; people with families to support and cherish; people who own large homes and new cars; people who are pillars of their communities and occupy high-visibility positions in community organizations. What keeps them prisoners of the bottle?

What Are Cravings and Where Do They Come From?

Carlton says that the heart of addiction is the inability to stop drinking no matter how hard one wills himself to stop. When craving for a drink hits, the alcoholic's knowledge that drinking is harmful and his willpower to resist it both fail. The alcoholic lawyer feels weakened and degraded by making and breaking hundreds of self-promises to quit.

What exactly is craving? In *The Craving Brain*, Dr. Richard Ruden defines it as, "an uncomfortable, intrusive, obsessive thought that can initiate action to obtain the specific object or activity." Do you sometimes experience a need for alcohol, drugs, sex or gambling that is so intense, it pushes everything else out of your conscious mind and pulls you helplessly toward the substance or activity like the undertow at the beach?

Richard Ruden has treated thousands of addicts and heard their stories. In summing up the commonalities between them, he says: "Obsessive thoughts, the inability to resist and the inability to stop, accompanied by feelings of powerlessness and inadequacy are the elements of individual stories of addiction, no matter what the substance or activity involved." Elsewhere he says: "Gotta have it—or perish—is the message the brain sends out. Perish without a piece of cake? Without a codeine tablet? Yes. Ancient biology underlies their behavior." The ancient biology to which Ruden refers is the brain's reward circuit.

The Brain's Reward Circuit

Two of the main brain circuits that drive human behavior are the fear circuit which triggers anxiety and escape behavior in the face of danger, and the reward circuit which triggers approach-and-consume behavior in the presence of objects known to produce pleasure based on past experience.

The reward circuit first appears hundreds of millions of years ago in the brains of prehistoric, bony fishes. Those fishes morphed into amphibians that morphed into reptiles and dinosaurs. The reward circuit was well-developed in prehistoric reptiles. Paul McClean, who elaborated the concept of the limbic system in the 1950s, said that reptiles are motivated to fight or flee by fear, but they are motivated to eat or mate by anticipation of pleasure. The human brain incorporates these circuits and behaviors.

In reptiles, pleasure-motivated behaviors were rapid, automatic responses to smells and sights. When a hungry reptile smelled food, he hunted, killed and ate. When a male reptile saw and smelled a female reptile in heat, he mounted her and copulated. Reptiles had no frontal lobes to put a brake on these responses and give them choices. Their brains were designed for instant action. All sensory input went directly to the limbic area via the thalamus (to motivate action by anticipation of pleasure) and to the basal ganglia (to initiate muscular action).

In human beings, sensory inputs go not just to the limbic area and the basal ganglia, but to the fronto-temporal lobes. It is by virtue of our frontal lobes that we can analyze data, project consequences of different courses of action, make choices and exert conscious control over action sequences. Theoretically we should be able to see the bad consequences of drinking alcohol and stop drinking.

How the Reward Circuit Causes Addiction

At the base of each cerebral hemisphere there is a cylindrical band of white matter that connects with the medulla oblongata (the brainstem) through the pons. These white matter tracts are called the cerebral peduncles. The bottom (ventral) portion of the cerebral peduncles is called the VTA (ventral tegmental area). When a human being experiences pleasure (from eating, sex, alcohol or drugs), it's because the VTA has secreted dopamine into an area of the forebrain called the nucleus accumbens. The nucleus accumbens is extremely sensitive to alcohol and opioid drugs.

After enough pleasurable experiences with a given substance, our brains encode the association between the object and the pleasure and learn how to successfully obtain it and consume it. After a while, the VTA pumps dopamine into the nucleus accumbens based solely on the anticipation of pleasure from consuming the object in the future.

Associations that become etched in the addict's memory include any sights, sounds or smells tied up with pleasurable consumption of alcohol or drugs. Just being with certain people, walking past a tavern, driving past a winery or hearing the tinkling of ice cubes in a glass can trigger cravings for alcohol. Memory and learning drive self-destructive addictions just as they drive positive behaviors that contribute to our survival. When learning is connected with alcoholism it is termed "pathological learning."

In the non-addicted person, the frontal lobes have a wide-open focus. They are able to see many choices and possibilities. They are able to distinguish between actions and substances that help or hurt us. They are able to weigh consequences and make decisions that protect us. In the addicted person, the reward circuit overrides the frontal lobes and hijacks our evolved brain. The way we see the world is changed. The focus of our frontal lobe's attention becomes narrowed to getting and consuming the substance at any cost. We use our vast intelligence to score the substance rather than to practice law, relate to our family or pursue other healthy activities.

When researchers allow rats to choose between food, water and direct self-stimulation of the VTA (by pressing a lever), the rats will choose the powerful source of dopamine release and die of exhaustion or dehydration while pressing the lever.

Humans are no different. Alcoholics skip meals in order to drink. They blow off work and family engagements to drink and get themselves in deep trouble, yet they keep on drinking.

An anxious person is someone with an overactive fear circuit. An alcoholic is someone with an overactive reward circuit that has placed his frontal lobes in a state of complete servitude. The urge to consume alcohol supplants all other behaviors. The reason AA helps is that the group functions as a prosthetic frontal lobe. In moments of weakness, the alcoholic can call his sponsor or go to a meeting, and he will be helped to resist the craving to drink.

Withdrawal Behavior

Right next to the cerebral peduncles is the locus coeruleus, a cluster of neurons at the base of the fourth ventricle on the anterior pons. It produces noradrenaline and norepinephrine. When the alcoholic hasn't had any alcohol for a long time, he will undergo a withdrawal response that prompts extreme craving and a desperate search for alcohol. The same is true of a heroin or cocaine addict.

The increasing physical and mental tension, the hyper-viligant searching for the substance and the distorted thought that "I will die if I don't get my substance soon" all come from the locus coeruleus priming the nucleus accumbens and the frontal lobes with adrenalin. The message from the locus coeruleus is, "I've got to get my fix now and I don't care who I have to lie to, cheat, steal from or rob to get it." An alcoholic lawyer who gives in to his craving by having a couple of jumbo martinis at lunch shortly before an afternoon court hearing or deposition is setting himself up for an embarrassing display that could lead to discipline.

The older idea that alcoholism is driven by avoidance of the anticipated pain of withdrawal has lost favor. This is because of the large number of alcoholics who are detoxified and who go for years without drinking, long past the time when withdrawal symptoms could arise, and suddenly relapse.

These sudden relapses seem best explained by pathological learning, because they are triggered automatically and unthinkingly by chance exposure to people or situations that reminded the alcoholic of the pleasure of drinking. Even years after the alcoholic has stopped drinking, his frontal lobes are still over-weighted toward drinking cues and away from healthier choices. One reason AA groups urge their members not to drop out when they have been sober for years is that they have no protection against sudden relapse. If they stay in the group and are bombarded by daily warnings not to drink anymore, they are less likely to fall off the wagon.

Stress and Addiction

While the pathological learning model of alcoholism is firmly established, the question remains why the draw of alcohol is so incredibly strong in some people, while others can take it or leave it. This appears to be the product of genetic susceptibility to stress, and the presence of significant stress in one's life. Richard Ruden is convinced that chronic stress drives addictions. Ruden's examples of stress include dishonor (a well-publicized act of corruption, cowardice or betrayal); a bad marriage; low self-esteem; loneliness; chronic pain; wartime experiences that cause PTSD; or living in a bad neighborhood with grinding poverty, street violence, early death and drugs everywhere.

These conditions deplete serotonin and make us miserable, motivating us to escape from misery any way we can. For those of you who are genetically susceptible to addiction, drinking your first drink or taking your first hit of cocaine can be a revelation. The nucleus accumbens (which is made extra-sensitive by stress hormones) gets a blast of dopamine from the VTA, and suddenly all the anguish and misery are gone, and replaced with euphoria.

Two salient facts about human behavior are that people need a refuge from stress, and people tend to repeat what works (even if what works is at a cost). When you associate alcohol with your refuge, and when it "works" in the sense of momentarily giving you complete relief from suffering, you're going to keep drinking.

Lawyers are deluged with work that has high stakes for their clients and their firms and they are always under pressure. They worry about failing. They work in a "discipline and punish" environment, where doing well for your client or your firm is expected and your victories are taken for granted, whereas any screw-up is visited with harsh punishment—everything from dirty looks, to verbal attacks, to loss of stature and privileges, to discipline and malpractice claims.

So lawyers drink to boost their dopamine. When all the alcohol is metabolized and their nerves start fraying, their locus coeruleus pumps out noradrenaline and they start getting that itchy, crawling feeling that erupts into a craving. On a neural level they now resemble a very hungry and irritable reptile stalking food with his empty belly growling. The only difference is that the reptile must have food soon or he really will die, whereas the alcoholic only believes he will die if he doesn't get a drink soon.

Neurons that fire together wire together. The more times you consume a substance to escape stress, the more the neural pathways of addiction are strengthened, the more your brain adapts to the substance and becomes dependent. Ruden says the repetitious use of alcohol at times of stress to gain relief is what creates more neural wires going from the reward circuit to the frontal lobes than from the frontal lobes back.

Eventually the signals from the frontal lobes are not strong enough to inhibit the craving for the relief brought by alcohol consumption.

Alcoholism Flourishes in the Land of Denial

Alcohol is a drug and drunkenness is a form of overdosing. Alcoholism is an addiction to alcohol. Alcoholics who have not admitted their powerlessness to stop drinking without outside help and who have not become sober are in denial. Alcoholics in denial have dozens of superficial rationalizations to assist them in denying their self-destructive addiction. They may think they're only an alcoholic if drinking has rendered them divorced, unemployed and homeless. This common view is grossly mistaken since only 1% of alcoholics have reached that point of severity, says Mark Willenbring of the National Institute of Alcohol Abuse and Alcoholism.

Alcoholics use myths to prop up their denial. Some say, "I can't be an alcoholic if I just drink beer or just white wine." Some say, "I can't be an alcoholic because I don't drink at lunch, and I wait to have my first drink after work." Others say I can't be an alcoholic because I don't drink at all on Sundays. Others say, "I can't be an alcoholic, because "I'm Jewish" or "I'm...(you fill in the national, religious or ethnic group)."

Alcoholics come in every size, shape and color. In AA's pamphlet *Living Sober* it is stated:

"We have found that anybody who has trouble of any sort related to drinking may have the condition called alcoholism. This illness strikes without regard for age, creed, sex, intelligence, ethnic background, emotional health, occupation, family situation, strong constitution, eating habits, social or economic status, or general character. It is not a question of how much or how you drink, or when, or why, but of how your drinking affects your life—what happens when you drink."

What All Alcoholics Have in Common

Alcoholics vary greatly with regard to such things as what time of day they drink, how frequently they drink, and whether they get happy and sleepy when they drink vs. getting angry and belligerent. Some drink everything in sight (even cough syrup), while others may drink only white wine, red wine, champagne, Scotch, bourbon, gin or vodka. None of these differences matters. You can destroy your liver and ruin your life with expensive premium wine just as easily as with rotgut vodka, Night Train or aftershave.

Two things that unite all alcoholics are an inability to stop drinking after the first drink and what AA calls an "allergy" to alcohol. The inability to stop drinking means the alcoholic loses control and becomes powerless once he takes a drink, even if it has been 10, 20 or 30 years since he took his last one. At AA meetings you will hear about real people from your community "going out" or "falling off the wagon" after decades of sobriety, only to die within days or weeks of out-of-control boozing. When you lift the lid off that Pandora's Box, watch out. It's not pretty.

The allergy refers to the fact that alcohol affects the drinker like poison—it damages his body, his physical health, his mental and social functioning, and so on. A non-alcoholic can have a drink or two and stop there. He can drink when he pleases without getting mentally and physically sick, and when he stops he feels no craving for more. The fantasy that drives many sober alcoholics back to boozing is the illusion that this time around they will be able to stop at one drink, because they know the risks. If you're an alcoholic, this simply won't happen.

What it Means to Hit Bottom

At AA meetings a "share" is when a person tells a story from his life that he finds personally meaningful and hopes will help others in the group. At AA meetings you will hear people share about the moment they finally got it and invariably this was the moment they "hit bottom." To hit bottom is to sink so low that all pretense you're not an alcoholic gets torn away.

For some people that moment was a shameful arrest for drunk driving, spousal abuse, child endangerment, etc. For others it happened when they were fired from a job, evicted or served with divorce papers. Sometimes denial was punctured through tough love, as when a spouse says "You're an alcoholic.... You either go to AA and stop drinking or this marriage is over and I'm taking the kids." At one AA meeting I attended, the speaker said he saw the light when he passed out from drinking, woke up and said to himself, "I'm fucked and I don't have a plan."

If You're Not Sure, How Can You Tell if You're An Alcoholic?

Lawyers reading these essays may wonder if they are alcoholic. What are some of the telltale signs? The National Institutes of Mental Health says any men who consume more than 4 drinks a day or more than 14 a week, and any women who consume more than 2 drinks a day or 7 drinks a week are alcoholic. Do you drink some form of alcohol (beer, wine or hard liquor) every day? Do you view drinking as something necessary in order to enjoy a meal? Do you select restaurants based on their wine list? Do you spend a lot of time in liquor stores, bars and wineries? Do you drink to celebrate success or to console yourself when you fail? Do you drink alone?

Do you get increasingly fidgety and irritable during the day waiting for your chance to drink? Do you see alcohol as a reward for working? How about for the stress of raising children? How about for any kind of deprivation or suffering? Do you drink in order to unwind or decompress when you get home from work? Do you drink in order to sleep at night? Do you see drinking as a way to put your law practice completely out of mind, so you can truly relax? Do you drink in order to relax so you can have sex?

Do you associate friendship with drinking? Do you select your friends based on whether or not they drink? Do you use alcohol to become more bold, charming and seductive with the person you fancy at a party or a bar? Have you ever skipped meals in favor of drinking? Do you have to drink more to feel the same effects? Do you end up drinking more than you planned? Does it take longer to clear your head or recover from a hangover in the morning?

Have you been late to or missed meetings, depositions or court appointments because you drank too much the night before? Do you experience difficulty remembering what you did or said the night before while drinking? Have family, friends and colleagues expressed concern about your drinking? Do you find yourself vowing not to drink or stopping at one drink, but then drinking to excess anyway? Have you been involved in one or more car crashes while tipsy? Have you been arrested for one or more DUIs? If you have answered yes to a lot of these questions, the odds are good that you're an alcoholic, painful as that sounds.

If you still have doubts, then attend an AA meeting and listen to the speaker's story of how he finally recognized he was an alcoholic and what his life was like before he became sober. If you find striking similarities between his story and the story of your life, chances are that you're an alcoholic. People in AA say that showing up at a meeting is no accident, and if you attend one, the chances are you're an alcoholic even if you don't accept it at the time. Just to make things certain, I strongly encourage you to ask for the opinion of your spouse, your close friends, your physician and your psychiatrist or therapist if you have one. This will only work if you commit to being non-defensive.

Alcoholics Anonymous Can be Your Salvation

AA will take in anyone with a sincere desire to stop drinking. While it does not have a monopoly on getting alcoholics into recovery, it does have a proven track record of success. It's very effective when you attend meetings regularly and you participate with true sincerity by "working the steps" with a sponsor. Regular attendance at meetings provides a constant reminder of how awful, out-of-control and self-destructive your life will become if you give in to the temptation to resume drinking. It provides a regular dose of inspiration from sober alcoholics who express gratitude for their long-term sobriety and for major improvement in their overall quality of life.

The Reach of Alcoholics Anonymous

AA began as one tiny group in Akron, Ohio, in 1935 as the last-ditch attempt by two extreme alcoholics (William Wilson aka Bill W. and Bob Smith, M.D.) to stop drinking before they died of the effects of ethanol. Today AA has 76,000 groups worldwide. The third edition of the Big Book published in 1976 sold 19,550,000 copies. The fourth edition of the Big Book was printed in 2001.

AA always was, and continues to be, completely self-supported by the voluntary contributions of its members. It takes no position on political, religious or other public issues. Its sole focus is on getting alcoholics sober. As of 2006, AA estimates it has helped over 2,000,000 alcoholics recover.

The Twelve Steps of AA— What They Are and Why They Work

AA offers its members powerful support and fellowship as they work the 12 steps to achieve sobriety and sustain it for life. The 12 steps are:

1. We admitted we were powerless over alcohol—that our lives had become unmanageable.

2. Came to believe that a power greater than ourselves could restore us to sanity.

3. Made a decision to turn our will and our lives over to the care of God as we understood Him.

4. Made a searching and fearless moral inventory of ourselves.

5. Admitted to God, to ourselves, and to another human being the exact nature of our wrongs.

6. Were entirely ready to have God remove all these defects of character.

7. Humbly asked Him to remove our shortcomings.

8. Made a list of all persons we had harmed, and became willing to make amends to them all.

9. Made direct amends to such people wherever possible, except when to do so would injure them or others.

10. Continued to take personal inventory and when we were wrong, promptly admitted it.

11. Sought through prayer and meditation to improve our conscious contact with God as we understood Him, praying only for knowledge of His will for us and the power to carry that out.

12. Having had a spiritual awakening as the result of these steps, we tried to carry this message to alcoholics and to practice these principles in all our affairs.

The First Step

AA believes that alcoholics are obsessed with alcohol and cannot stay away from it without help. AA also believes that alcoholics have an allergy to alcohol that makes them sick when they drink it. Step One, the personal admission that you are powerless over alcohol and cannot manage your own life, is the beginning of your journey in AA and the first step toward sobriety.

AA says you cannot take Step One until you have suffered "absolute humiliation" and recognized that your personal inability to stop self-destructive drinking has bankrupted you socially and spiritually. In *The Twelve Steps* and *Twelve Traditions*, it is stated:

"We perceive that only through utter defeat are we able to take our first steps toward liberation and strength. Our admissions of personal powerlessness finally turn out to be firm bedrock upon which happy and purposeful lives may be built. We know that little good can come to any alcoholic who joins AA unless he has first accepted his devastating weakness and all its consequences. Until he so humbles himself, his sobriety—if any—will be precarious. Of real happiness, he will find none. Proved beyond doubt by an immense experience, this is one of the facts of AA life. The principle that we shall find no enduring strength until we first admit complete defeat is the main taproot from which our whole Society has sprung and flowered."

To seriously entertain the concept that you really are an alcoholic is not just unpleasant. It's downright frightening, which is why so many people deny they are alcoholics. Why is it so frightening? Because there's a harsh stigma attached to being an alcoholic. Because it means you're not really in control of your life as you always thought. Because it means you will die young unless you change your behavior and stop drinking. Because it means you have to look at yourself in the mirror, admit you have been hurting yourself and others by your alcoholic behavior and take responsibility for change. Because it means you will have to give up drinking forever, and you will have to eat, sleep, work and socialize without the anesthesia of alcohol.

Steps Two Through Five

Once you admit you've failed to control your drinking and ruined your life, you're ready to seek help from a "higher power" and turn your will over to that higher power. In Steps 2 and 3, you're effectively renouncing the idea that you know more than others and you're better able than anyone else to take care of yourself and the people who depend on you. You're reaching out to something beyond your own knowledge and willpower to stop your free fall into self-annihilation.

This something can be God, as you envision and understand him, be it as Spirit, Source or otherwise. The higher power you reach out to can be AA or your AA chapter. In Steps 4 and 5 you are bid to make a "fearless and searching moral inventory" of yourself and then admit to God, to yourself and another human being the exact nature of your wrongs.

Regarding Step 5, the *Twelve Traditions* states: "All of AA's Twelve Steps ask us to go contrary to our natural desires. They all deflate our egos. When it comes to ego deflation, few Steps are harder to take than Five. But scarcely any Step is more necessary to longtime sobriety and peace of mind than this one. AA experience has taught us we cannot live alone with our pressing problems and the character defects which cause or aggravate them. If we have swept the searchlight of Step Four back and forth over our careers, and it has revealed in stark relief those experiences we'd rather not remember; if we have come to know how wrong thinking and actions have hurt us and others, then the need to quit living by ourselves with those tormenting ghosts of yesterday gets more urgent than ever. We have to talk to somebody about them."

What Will It Take To Get You Into AA?

As a group, lawyers tend to have a rather high opinion of themselves. They regard themselves as being smarter, more knowledgeable and more capable than other people, and they are used to relying on themselves. After all, they got themselves through college, law school and the dreaded Bar Exam of their chosen State. They are experts in the law who are paid dearly for their legal advice (some of them as much as $800 per hour), and they have withstood many difficult, high-stress challenges from other lawyers, judges, juries and witnesses.

Maybe you've also had articles published, lectured to groups of people or even won an important appellate decision. Maybe you regularly earn a high six-figure or even a seven-figure income. Maybe you're interviewed by the press for your insights into important legal issues. It would be hard not to have an inflated opinion of yourself. Yet this ego-inflation is a trap that enables you to keep denying your powerlessness over alcohol and its destructive impact on your health, your law practice and your relationships with family, friends and colleagues.

Getting Sober and Staying Sober through Self-Help Organizations

Staying sober is much easier when you attend AA meetings because AA members cheer and clap for each other's efforts to stay sober and they tell hair-raising stories of what will happen if you "go out," which occurs when you stop going to meetings and start drinking again. Lawyers have a hard time with AA at the beginning because it's hard for them to admit weakness or ask for help, it's hard for them to listen instead of talk, and many are resistant to spirituality of any kind. This can and does change over time. After a while, you can put your ego aside, listen to what others say and reap huge benefits.

Really succeeding in AA means more than just showing up at meetings. You have to get an experienced sponsor you like and work the 12 steps with sincere commitment. Getting a sponsor and working the 12 steps is the real meat of AA. How you handle yourself outside meetings plays a huge role as well.

To reduce your risk of relapsing, you should avoid going to bars with old friends. You should consider asking your spouse not to keep liquor at home or drink in front of you. It's important to develop a reliable alternative to alcohol that you can drink at conventions, awards dinners and cocktail parties lawyers throw. Sparkling water is refreshing and much better for you than Diet Coke.

Alcoholics with a Dual Diagnosis

Approximately five percent of lawyers are depressed and alcoholic or drug-addicted.

For this group, being in AA is not enough. When your compulsive need to drink stems from a mental illness (e.g., phobia, generalized anxiety disorder, unipolar depression or bipolar disorder), it's going to be necessary for you to take appropriate psychoactive prescription medication to get and stay sober.

On the very last page of the AA publication *Staying Sober* are the cautionary paragraphs titled "However, some alcoholics require medication...."

"At the same time that we recognize this dangerous tendency to re-addiction, we must also recognize that alcoholics are not immune to other diseases. Some of us have had to cope with depressions that can be suicidal; schizophrenia that sometimes requires hospitalization; manic depression; and other mental and biological illnesses. Also among us are epileptics, members with heart trouble, cancer, allergies, hypertension, and many other serious physical conditions.

"Because of the difficulties that many alcoholics have with drugs, some members have taken the position that no one in AA should take any medication. While this position has undoubtedly prevented relapses for some, it has meant disaster for others... It becomes clear that just as it is wrong to enable or support any alcoholic to become re-addicted to any drug, it's equally wrong to deprive any alcoholic of medication which can alleviate or control other disabling physical and/or emotional problems."

How to Deal With Cravings

Some people who join AA aren't quite ready to give up alcohol, and so they join, drop out, rejoin and drop out again like a yo-yo. But others make a strong inner commitment to stop drinking once and for all, and they stay sober for decades while regularly attending meetings. What's remarkable is that decades of sobriety are no guarantee against the return of cravings. The craving for alcohol can erupt suddenly and return like a nightmare, even in someone who has been sober for twenty or thirty years. For people in AA, the way to deal with cravings is to rush to a meeting.

Alternatives to AA

Some people won't join AA because of its insistence on giving up your will to a higher power. Such people declare they are atheist, agnostic or turned off by anything smacking of religion. What can non-spiritual people do to deal with cravings once they have stopped drinking?

You can try the path of investing in your health. The idea is to get so healthy (by running, cycling or swimming) that you have a built-in resistance to polluting your body temple. Along with exercise, start eating right, put back the weight you lost while drinking and take vitamins to cure your deficiencies of niacin and chromium. You may eventually look so good, feel so good and have so much clear-headed energy that you'll be very reluctant to throw it all overboard for a drink. AA members would not endorse this approach as it omits the 12 steps and regular attendance of group meetings. But I have seen it work for some people, at least for the time I knew them.

The cognitive-behavioral method is spelled out in Dr. Horvath's

Sex, Drugs, Gambling & Chocolate. Dr. Horvath says that although cravings are very intense, they will not kill you or even harm you, and they will go away rather quickly if you don't give in. The belief that "I will die if I do not have a drink right now" is false, and you can prove it by outlasting the mental episode of craving.

Cravings disappear quickly because people are easily distracted and their concentration on any one point fatigues rapidly. Try to think of a pink elephant as long as possible. How many seconds did it take on a timer for new, different thoughts to spring up in your mind?

I have experienced intense sugar cravings for items like chocolate or ice cream. I go through a moment where I feel that I must have them now, that I cannot live without them and all my problems would go away if I just ate some now. Then I get distracted. The phone or the doorbell rings. My dog nudges me because it's time to walk or feed her. Maybe I notice the clock and it's time to leave to pick up my son at soccer practice.

Once I'm distracted, the air soon leaks out of my tire, and I notice the craving is gone. I breathe a sigh of relief and go on with my business. Some people are successful in knocking out a craving by drinking a glass of sugary fruit juice, drinking ice water to make them feel full or chewing gum.

What if your craving for alcohol or drugs is incredibly intense, and won't go away no matter what you do? If you're in AA, it's time to get to a meeting or call your sponsor. If your sponsor's not available, you can call co-members of your AA group to get help making it through the crisis. If you're not in AA, use CBT. Don't tell yourself, "I can't live without alcohol…. If I don't have a drink right now I'm going to go crazy or drop dead."

Do tell yourself, "I can get through this. I really don't need the alcohol. It's the diseased, alcoholic part of my brain trying to tell me what to do. I don't have to listen. It's a false message, like the dashboard blinking red when the car is working. I've successfully ignored this false message in the past and I'm going to do it again. If I listen to this false message, and drink, I'm back in the clutches of alcoholism again, and I refuse to go there. I will not be fooled. I am much better off without drinking. This craving won't kill me, but I will die if I resume drinking."

Have Compassion For Yourself

Last, but not least, do not judge yourself a failure simply for experiencing cravings. Meditators know we do not control our thoughts, but we can control our responses to our thoughts. We can choose to enact them, to suppress them or to watch them passively as they arise, make their presence known and then disappear harmlessly off our mental screen of awareness. You're not a failure simply because you think a glass of red wine would be nice right now. You don't have to endorse that thought by getting into the car and driving to the liquor store. You can watch it like a cloud. It will disappear. All things pass, including gas and cravings.

Controlled Drinking

Controlled drinking refers to an effort to drink less on a consistent basis by someone who recognizes he has a problem with alcohol, but refuses to give up drinking. The premise of controlled drinking is that people who had alcohol problems in the past are not destined to drink more and more and go out of control if they drink small amounts pursuant to a plan.

AA is totally against the concept of controlled drinking, which runs counter to the experience of their members and their conception of alcoholism as a progressive and lethal disease that can only be held in check with complete sobriety through attendance at meetings and working the 12 steps. I personally do not endorse the idea of controlled drinking for alcoholics. The situation appears different for some former alcohol abusers who try controlled drinking under vigilant medical supervision.

But if you want to try it, there are plenty of books on the subject. There are even Internet support groups that seek to help problem drinkers control their drinking. In the Netherlands there is a site called www.minderdrinken.nl which translates as Drinking Less. In

May 2009, Heleen Riper of the Trimbos Institute in the Netherlands reported that 19% of problem drinkers who used this free, interactive website for over six months were able to reduce their drinking to more "low risk" levels.

Using Medications
to Achieve Sobriety or Stay Sober

Are there FDA-approved medications that can help an alcoholic stay sober? Yes, but to be effective they must be coupled with attitudinal and behavioral changes to reduce stress and the maintenance of a strong psycho-social support network. It's crucial to have someone such as a trained spouse to supervise the alcoholic's compliance with his doctor's orders to take a prescription drug. It's also crucial to have a physician monitor your liver function, because the drugs that help alcoholics stay sober can damage the liver in some patients and alcoholics are a population with higher than average liver damage in the first place.

An older drug Disulfiram (Antabuse) works by making you feel very hungover for 30 minutes within 5-10 minutes of taking a drink. The symptoms include facial flushing, increased heart rate, shortness of breath, nausea and vomiting. This will cause people to abstain from drinking alcohol to avoid these unpleasant consequences.

Normally alcohol is metabolized by liver enzymes, first to acetaldehyde and then to a harmless substance, acetic acid. Antabuse works by blocking the conversion of acetaldehyde to acetic acid, causing a buildup of 5-10 times the normal amount of acetaldehyde in the blood stream. Since acetaldehyde is the agent primarily responsible for hangovers, one drink taken after ingestion of Antabuse will cause a severe hangover.

Antabuse is absorbed so slowly that its effects can last up to two weeks. Side effects include shortness of breath and numbness or tingling of the lower legs. Antabuse should not be taken within 12 hours of having a drink. Antabuse inhibits the metabolism of dopamine and should be taken in small doses to avoid excess dopamine in the brain.

It should not be taken with stimulant drugs like amphetamines, Wellbutrin, Ritalin or cocaine that block the conversion of dopamine to norepinephrine. This is because it will flood the brain with an excess of dopamine, triggering agitation and paranoia. Antabuse does not work for everyone, but can be very helpful in maintaining sobriety for some alcoholics. Controlled studies have shown it to be more effective than a placebo to a statistically significant extent.

There are two newer drugs considered to work more effectively than Antabuse which have different mechanisms of action. These are Acamprosate (Campral) and naltrexone. Both drugs work by reducing the craving for alcohol, and they have been shown to prevent relapse to heavy drinking as part of an overall treatment program.

The brain has excitatory neurotransmitters that cause neurons to fire and inhibitory neurotransmitters that cause them to stop firing. The most common excitatory neurotransmitter is glutamate and the most common inhibitory neurotransmitter is GABA (Gamma-aminobutyric acid). The ingredient in alcohol that produces relaxation and euphoria is ethanol. It activates the receptors for GABA which quiets the brain.

Acamprosate blocks activation of GABA receptors by ethanol, and in so doing it blocks the desired effects of drinking, the sense of ease, release and pleasure that replaces the tight, anxious and worried state of mind that alcoholics want to escape. Acamprosate was approved by the FDA in July 2004. The most common side effects are headache, diarrhea, flatulence and nausea. Acamprosate is used to spare severe alcoholics from the worst consequences of withdrawal from alcohol, delirium tremens and death from a sudden surge of glutamate in the brain, a substance that is toxic to neurons when discharged in excess.

The healthy brain produces opioid compounds that act as anesthetics in blocking painful stimuli. Cocaine addicts are people whose brains are deficient at producing opioids. There is evidence that part of the craving alcoholics have for drinks containing ethanol is that alcohol activates the opioid system in the brain. The drug Naltrexone is an opioid antagonist that blocks the action of ethanol on the opioid system, so that drinking alcohol no longer has a payoff. This reduces cravings and tends to stop alcoholics from losing control after the first drink.

Studies have shown that Naltrexone alone is slightly better than Acamprosate at preventing relapse to heavy drinking and that the two drugs combined are better than either one alone. Studies have also shown that participation in a supportive therapy group plus Naltrexone is better than using the drug alone.

Another drug that shows promise with regard to reducing the alcoholic's anxiety and his craving for alcohol during withdrawal is Topirimate (topomax), an anti-convulsant, mood stabilizing medication. A study published in the *Lancet* shows that use of Topirimate makes it easier to withdraw from alcohol by reducing brain levels of dopamine and causing relaxation. Excess levels of dopamine in the brain are associated with schizophrenia and mania, two forms of mental illness marked by agitation.

However, there is one caveat. In January 2008, the FDA issued an alert to physicians that 11 anti-seizure medications (including Topirimate) were found to double the risk of suicidal thoughts and behaviors. The FDA reached this conclusion by analyzing almost 200 studies of the 11 anti-seizure drugs, some of which have been on the market for decades. The studies tracked almost 28,000 people given the medications and an additional 16,000 given placebos. The FDA found that patients taking the drugs faced about twice the risk: 0.43% experienced suicidal thoughts or behavior, compared with 0.22% of those taking a placebo. However, the number of actual suicides was very low—just 4 of the 27,863 subjects taking the drugs and 0 in the placebo group.

Don't Forget About Your State Bar or Your Employer as a Source of Help

Many states have confidential programs for substance-abusing lawyers that provide structure, fellowship, group therapy and referrals to specialists. In California there is a state run Lawyer Assistance Program (LAP) and a private program called The Other Bar that uses a 12-step approach to treatment. Large law firms have what are called EAPs, employee assistance programs, which provide confidential assistance to partners, associates, paralegals and secretaries with substance abuse issues. There is help out there if you are ready and willing to seek it out.

The Timing of Your Decision
To Seek Help For Alcoholism

Don't wait until you've blown a statute of limitations or misman-aged a client's trust fund and the State Bar prosecutor has mailed you a notice to defend yourself in a disciplinary proceeding. If you first enter treatment because your defense lawyer suggests it, it looks like a defense tactic. The best time to enter treatment is before you screw up and when there is still a chance of avoiding any screw-ups by getting sober first.

The Landmark Needs Assessment Study of 2003
— Identifying the Barriers to Getting Lawyers
into Alcoholism Treatment

We know that 1 out of every 5 lawyers is an alcoholic, yet only a fraction of them seek help they desperately need and manage to stay sober. Why is that? One person who has shed some real light on this is Jeffrey C. Friedman, MHS, CSAC. Friedman is a psychologist who works at Cottonwood Tucson, a state-of-the-art rehab facility in Arizona that treats people with addictions.

Friedman has successfully treated many lawyers over the years, but noted that as a group they seemed to be particularly difficult patients. He was motivated to collect information to find out how to best struc-ture rehab treatment for addicted lawyers so they were most likely to succeed in their effort to recover. In 2003 he conducted and published a survey called *An Assessment of the Needs of Lawyers in Behavioral Health Treatment*. The publication relied on survey data, interviews of chemical dependency/behavioral health therapists who had treated lawyers, and a review of existing literature on treatment of lawyers for addiction.

Friedman sent 460 Key Informant Questionnaires to the Lawyer Assistance Programs in all 50 states and 11 Canadian Provinces. He had staff at the state and provincial LAPs distribute 460 confiden-tial Target Questionnaires to lawyers who had previously engaged in chemical dependency. From the survey materials sent, he received completed Key Informant Questionnaires from 63 staff members at state LAPs and completed Target Questionnaires from 112 lawyers. After collecting and reviewing this data, Friedman convened a focus group discussion of the data with staff from various LAPs, including the then Chairman of the ABA's Commission on Lawyer Assistance Programs, John W. Clark, Jr.

Here is what he learned. While all addicts are in denial and resist treatment to some extent, lawyers have particular characteristics that pose special barriers to getting them into treatment:

- Lawyers are trained to argue and rationalize, so their denial is often highly developed and deeply entrenched.

- Use of the Socratic method of argument with professors creates a tendency to argue about everything and "a kind of cultivated contrariness" that makes it difficult for lawyers to admit to problems and allow others to guide them back to health.

- Lawyers tend to have big egos and to see themselves as part of a well-educated elite that is simply too smart to become addicted.

- Lawyers are trained to keep secrets. Their fear of admitting to alcoholism or drug addiction is that once the secret gets out, they will lose their good reputation among peers, judges and potential clients; that they will possibly lose their license; and either way, their career and livelihood will be ruined.

- Lawyers are very self-reliant. They are used to being in control and giving advice. They feel uncomfortable in the role of helpee and often resist taking the advice of others.

Out of all these, Friedman found the biggest obstacle to accessing care was the lawyers' belief they could handle their addiction problem on their own, and the second biggest was fear that disclosure of their problem would ruin their reputation and career.

With regard to obstacles to recovery during the treatment process, here is what he learned. (1) Lawyers tend to be shut off from their emotional life, and rely on intellectualization as an ego defense. They routinely question the credentials, experience and ability of treaters and use verbal challenge to test the validity of treatment-related information. Uneducated treaters retreat in the face of these challenges. (2) Lawyers do not want to feel weak so they maintain a public image of complete competence even when their addiction problem is destroying them. Even in treatment, they cannot "let down" unless they meet with other lawyers and judges they respect who acknowledge having the same addiction problem and share their stories of disaster, recovery and hope. This argues in favor of group treatment with peers.

Friedman put together a list of Clinical Implications to improve treatment of addicted lawyers. Here is his list:

- The use of highly trained and experienced clinicians with strong verbal skills and ample ego strength, who won't be overwhelmed or intimidated by highly intelligent and often aggressive personalities.

- A strong psychiatric component able to diagnose and treat co-occuring disorders such as depression, bipolar disorder and PTSD.

- The ready availability of respected and successful recovering attorneys who can serve as role models and mentors for lawyers in treatment. This should include patient access to lawyer-specific 12-step meetings.

- An ability and willingness to engage in ongoing interface with LAP programs with respect to continuing care after discharge from rehab.

- A strong experiential component (e.g., psychodrama, gestalt therapy) to engage patients on an emotional level.

- A sophisticated explanation of medical aspects of chemical dependency, including access to professional journals and articles.

A Success Story—
A Lawyer Who Faced Alcoholism and Won

Trial lawyer J. Gary Gwilliam of Oakland, California, just published a memoir of his forty-year career called *Getting a Winning Verdict in My Personal Life*. Mr. Gwilliam had his share of major triumphs in the courtroom and as a leader of trial lawyer organizations, but he chronicles a twenty-five-year struggle with alcoholism, two painful divorces and nearly lifelong estrangement from his biological father and stepfather. The book ends on a hopeful note.

Gary became sober, happily married (his third time around) the right woman for him, and managed to heal his relationships with his two fathers. He also describes his fundamental change in attitude about winning and losing, which was crucial to overcoming alcoholism and becoming a happier, less-stressed-out person. While suffering from alcoholism, he saw winning trials as a source of pride and losing as an unmitigated source of shame, something that made him want to drink to numb the pain.

When he lost a trial, his response to was to work harder and drink more.

His drinking got so out of control that the people who most cared about him staged a tough love intervention that saved his life and turned him around. His newer, healthier view is that he has no control over the ultimate outcome of any trial. All he can do is his best.

Whatever happens will happen and it will happen for the right reasons, reasons that he and his client can learn from and even benefit from. Mr. Gwilliam understands that our contribution as human beings transcends our won and loss record in trial and how much money we earn for our clients and ourselves. It embraces how well we empathize with, listen to and counsel our clients. It embraces our quest to acquire psychological insight and spiritual wisdom. It embraces our willingness to show respect for diverse viewpoints and learn from others, including the clients, judges, juries and other lawyers we deal with every day.

Nutritional Support for Alcoholics

While you're working to get sober, you can cleanse your liver by eating foods which break down the fat in your liver and prevent fatty liver disease. Peanuts, which contain as much resveratrol as red wine or wine grapes, have been shown to break down fat in the liver, in a recent study at the University of South Florida. Peanuts contain oleic acid, the same heart-healthy stuff that makes olive oil protective against heart disease. They are very rich in p-coumaric acid, which helps protect against atherosclerosis by shielding cholesterol from oxidation. This effect is heightened by roasting the peanuts.

Alcoholics desperately need protein and niacin in their diets. Peanuts are high in both. So eat peanuts or peanut butter every day. The Internet has great recipes to provide variety. If you're allergic to peanuts, you can take resveratrol supplements. They have also been shown to break down fat in the liver of alcoholics. You can also eat loads of seedless red grapes, which have resveratrol in their skins.

Avocados, asparagus and walnuts are loaded with fiber and a powerful antioxidant called glutathione, which helps mop up the free radicals produced in the liver when the liver breaks down toxins. Other foods rich in glutathione are garlic and onions. Mushrooms are rich in glutamic acid, which the body converts to glutathione.

Heavy drinkers can benefit from eating lots of avocados. A salad using avocados and walnuts with an olive oil dressing is delicious and good for your liver. Black-eyed peas are loaded with protein, fiber and folate (which makes folic acid, an important B vitamin needed for your nervous system).

Certain foods with a bitter taste detoxify your liver and help keep it healthy. These include mustard greens, dandelion greens, broccoli rabe, romaine lettuce and endive. Your liver benefits from a high fiber diet. Warm lemon water is also good.

Studies of dandelion green supplements have questioned their benefit and raised issues about toxicity.

There is Hope

Given the catastrophic consequences of alcoholism on your health, career, marriage and life span, getting help cannot wait. Alcoholism is a disease with a genetic component and a family history component that results from exposure to intense stress in the absence of good coping strategies and social support. It is not a result of weak or immoral character. It is time lawyers accept this, forget about the stigma and reach out for help.

With help things can be turned around. You can recover, stay sober and lead a happy and productive life. In the 2003 Needs Assessment there is a list of articles on rehab that support a high recovery rate for lawyers who do stick with their rehab programs. One study found 70% of lawyers became more open, more cooperative with staff and more engaged in the treatment process over time. Another study reported that one year post-discharge, 91% of professionals reported being free of mood altering drugs.

I spoke with Jeffrey Friedman over the phone, and he told me that Cottonwood Tucson has implemented the list of Clinical Implications in its treatment strategies and has had a very high success rate with lawyers. Yes, we make difficult patients, but when we stick with it, we get better and we turn our lives around. We stop living in our heads and poisoning our livers with alcohol, and we start feeling our feelings and interacting with colleagues, family and friends on an emotional level as well as a cognitive level. This makes for a much deeper, more genuine, and fulfilling life.

CHAPTER FIVE: SUGGESTED READINGS

Alcoholics Anonymous (4th ed.), (Alcoholics Anonymous World Services, Inc., 2001)

Jeffrey C. Friedman, MHS, CSAC, *An Assessment of the Needs of Lawyers in Behavioral Health Treatment* (Cottonwood de Tucson, Inc., 2003)

J. Gary Gwilliam, *Getting a Winning Verdict In My Personal Life: A Trial Lawyer Finds His Soul* (Pavior, 2007)

Living Sober (Alcoholics Anonymous World Services, Inc., 1998)

A. Thomas Horvath, Ph.D., *Sex, Drugs, Gambling, & Chocolate* (Impact Publishers, 2004)

M. Galanter, M.D., and H.D. Kleber, M.D., *Textbook of Substance Abuse* (2nd ed.) (American Psychiatric Press, Inc., 1999)

Chris Prentiss, *The Alcoholism and Addiction Cure* (Power Press, 2007)

Ronald A. Ruden, M.D., Ph.D., *The Craving Brain* (2nd ed.) (Quill, 2003)

G. Andrew H. Benjamin, et al., *The Prevalence of Depression, Alcohol Abuse, and Cocaine Abuse Among United States Lawyers* (International Journal of Law and Psychiatry, p. 233-246, Vol. 13, 1990)

CHAPTER SIX

Why so many lawyers are depressed

What is Depression?

DEPRESSION IS NOT the same as feeling sad because a loved one died, because you got fired from your job or you lost your house and all your possessions in a fire. Feeling sad in these situations is normal, expected and culturally accepted. A person in these situations can feel sad but resume functioning after a reasonable interval by grieving and obtaining support from his family, friends and employer.

Depression is a mental illness that involves intense psychological distress over an extended time frame which significantly impairs the normal performance of one's family, social and occupational roles. Along with other mood disorders, it is the leading cause of disability in Americans aged 15-44. Depression has a spillover effect. It not only causes intense psych-ache to the sufferer, but stresses out his family and work associates and forces them to make adjustments to their lives.

Depression is not the result of being too weak to handle the troubles and losses that are an inevitable part of life. Rather it is an organic, brain-based illness with neuro-chemical imbalances that adversely effects thought processes, mood, behavior and the body. It has a genetic component and tends to run in families, like heart disease and cancer.

It is highly treatable. Some 80-90% of people with depression who undergo treatment improve.

The problem is that many people with depression never get help. Terrance Real, author of *I Don't Walk To Talk About It: Overcoming The Secret Legacy of Male Depression*, says that 60-80% of people with depression (mostly males) do not get treated. According to Real, it's because men see depression as an unmanly condition. They are too ashamed to admit they have it or seek the help they need.

A depressed person sees small obstacles as mountains. He is not only certain he will fail at whatever he tries, but finds ways to interpret his successes as failures. A depressed person feels awful, discouraged and sour. Nothing can cheer him. He is passive, indecisive and vulnerable to impulsive thoughts of ending it all because he can't bear his suffering. A depressed person is tired and sluggish, but can't sleep through the night. He tends to wake up around two a.m., after which he tosses and turns. He is apathetic. He loses interest in food, sex, exercise, people, work and the activities he once enjoyed. After a while, he neglects self-care and personal hygiene.

No matter how punctual and reliable they were when well, people who are depressed will forget and miss appointments or show up late. They take no joy in beautiful sunsets, delicious food or other pleasures of life. There is a flattening of affect with a loss of emotional expressiveness, except for episodic anger which functions as a "stay away" sign. Much of the time a seriously depressed person's face is frozen into a gloomy expression that psychiatrists call "the mask of depression."

The most distinctive cognitive symptom of depression is "stink'n think'n." This consists of negative, pessimistic, guilty and harshly self-critical thoughts that make the depressed person feel like a complete failure without the inner resources to improve. The psychological pain of depression has been described as worse than any pain except rabies.

When depressed, Abraham Lincoln called himself the most miserable person on earth. Samuel Johnson said he would consent to have a limb amputated to recover his good spirits when he was depressed. An elderly English clergyman, who had recovered from depression, later badly scalded his genitals, thighs and belly. When asked which pain was worse, he said "I would suffer the scalding a hundred times rather than have a depression again. Every night I pray to God to let me die before the depression returns."

The emotional pain of depression comes from feelings of worthlessness, helplessness and hopelessness that make even the smallest task seem overwhelming. In depression, a very harsh inner critic emerges which engages in self-blame for anything that goes wrong. The depressed person thinks only in worst-case scenarios. All his predictions about the future and his assessments of the past are as dark and bleak as the mind can imagine. Severe depression involves thoughts of self-harm, even suicide. Thoughts about suicide can be sporadic, frequent or constant. Under certain conditions these thoughts can ripen into a plan and be acted out successfully.

The Symptoms of Major Depression

As set forth in the DSM-IV Section 296.1x, Major Depression is diagnosed when a person has 5 or more of the following symptoms for at least two weeks (at least one of which must be depressed mood or loss of interest or pleasure):

- Depressed mood most of the day, every day

- Markedly diminished interest or pleasure in all, or almost all, activities most of the day

- A significant (5%) gain or loss of normal body weight associated with diminished or increased appetite rather than intentional dieting or weight gain

- Insomnia or hypersomnia (excessive sleeping) nearly every day—the typical pattern of insomnia is waking up at 2-3 a.m. and not being able to fall back asleep

- Psychomotor slowing (slowing of thinking, speech and/-
  or movement) or psychomotor agitation (restlessness,
  fidgeting) nearly every day

- Fatigue nearly every day

- Feelings of worthlessness or excessive and inappropriate
  guilt (which may reach delusional proportions)

- Diminished ability to think, concentrate or make
  decisions

- Recurrent thoughts of death, recurrent suicidal ideation
  without a plan or a suicide attempt.

Major Depression is diagnosed when the onset of these symptoms represents a marked change in previous level of functioning. Documentation of the symptoms can be obtained from the personal report of the patient or the observation of others (e.g., family, friend or colleague). There are no laboratory findings that are diagnostic of Major Depression.

Manic Depression (Bipolar I)

Depression is called unipolar when it does not alternate with elevated mood states.

Dysthymia refers to a state of chronic, mild depression that lasts two or more years. Dysthymia is an example of unipolar depression. When depression cycles with a manic mood state, it is Bipolar I. When depression cycles with a hypomanic mood state it is Bipolar II. Depending on the person and his condition, the cycling can be slow, extremely rapid and everything in-between.

Bipolar I involves acute mania with persistently elevated mood, racing thoughts, pressured and rapid speech, going without sleep for days, hyper-sexuality, impulsivity, distractibility, unwarranted optimism, poor judgment and grandiosity. A patient with Bipolar I in his manic phase typically refuses to believe he is ill and resists all efforts to treat him. He can become delusional and psychotic and end up tangling with the police. If he goes back on Lithium, chances are he will mellow out and his mood will stabilize.

People with Bipolar I who are manic and off their medications have a tendency to get very drunk. Barrett Robbins, the 380-pound Bipolar I center for the Oakland Raiders, stopped taking his meds without telling anyone. He went AWOL the night before the Raiders met the Tampa Bay Buccaneers in Superbowl XXXVII in San Diego. Robbins got really drunk and passed out someplace. He missed the game. This had a bad effect on the quarterback Rich Gannon (who had an awful game after a brilliant season) and the team, which lost 48-21. In January 2005 Robbins attempted a robbery and resisted arrest by three Miami police officers who ended up shooting him.

Bipolar I is a tragic illness if it is not controlled by strict medication compliance. With medication compliance Bipolar I patients can do remarkable things. Kay Redfield, co-author of the principal textbook on manic depressive illness, has struggled with Bipolar I for most of her life, yet she is a high-achieving, well-respected researcher, writer and lecturer in the field of manic depression.

Manic Depression (Bipolar II)

Bipolar II involves hypomania, which is a much-toned-down version of mania. Hypomania does not progress to psychosis, require hospitalization or severely impair social and occupational functioning. When manic, people with bipolar II are animated, charming, funny and great to be around, so it may be hard to think of them as being ill. But when Bipolar II patients flip into depression, their depression tends to be much more severe than that of Bipolar I patients, and they are at higher risk of suicide.

Some lucky patients are manic all the time and never slide into depression. I was diagnosed as Bipolar II after my second hospitalization for depression with obsessive ruminations about suicide. I can vouch for the psychiatric observation that depression in Bipolar II patients can be hellish and ferocious.

Differentiating Depression from Anxiety

Depression and anxiety are both mood disorders. They can co-exist. Sometimes anxiety underlies depression, and does not emerge until the depression is resolved with psychotherapy and medication. Some people confuse anxiety with depression when they try to explain what is wrong with them. These two separate mood disorders need to be differentiated because they require different medications.

While a depressed person is sluggish, apathetic and self-absorbed, an anxious person is very jumpy and scanning the environment in a hyper-vigilant way for threats. Anxiety involves heightened fear and excessive worry along with somatic symptoms that may include: sweating, hot flashes or chills, lightheadedness, dizziness, nausea, chest tightness, shallow and difficult breathing, sensations of choking, rapid heartbeat, pounding heartbeat, trembling, pins and needles sensations in the limbs, insomnia and fatigue. Anxiety tends to disrupt concentration at work. Severe anxiety can involve fears of losing control, going crazy or dying.

The Epidemiology of Mood Disorders in the General Population

At some point during their lives, 46% of Americans will have a mental illness. The mood disorders (depression and anxiety) are the most common of all mental illnesses. Women suffer depression at twice the rate of men, and anxiety disorders at three times the rate of men. No one knows exactly why this is so.

Experts attempt to explain the difference in part by the greater willingness of women to disclose their suffering and seek help. But they emphasize the many roles and responsibilities women have. In addition to working and being the primary homemaker, women are also the primary caretaker of children.

Martin Seligman, Ph.D., says depression has become an epidemic. This generation is ten times more likely to be depressed than the generation that lived during World War II. The World Health Organization ranks depression as fourth on its current list of the most urgent public health problems on earth. In the chapter on mood disorders in Kaplan and Saddock's *Comprehensive Textbook of Psychiatry*, it is stated that the disability induced by depression exceeds that caused by pain, hypertension, diabetes and coronary artery disease. It is also stated that 20% of women and 12% of men will have a depressive disorder at some point in their lives, and that many of them will be disabled.

Some 15% of people with depressive disorders commit suicide. The largest groups of depressed persons who die by suicide are adolescents and the elderly. The World Health Organization predicts that by the year 2020 depression will be the second leading cause of mortality in the entire world, affecting 30% of all adults.

Depression and Middle Age—A Special Case

Every person I met in group therapy for depression started out believing they were the only person in America who felt that awful, and because of this cognitive distortion, they got to heap extra blame on themselves for being such a loser. The fact is that depression is extremely common. If you use Google to find a list of famous persons who suffered major depression, you will be shocked. It's a virtual Who's Who in entertainment, literature, the fine arts, sports and politics. Many of these famous people were in their middle years when depression struck.

The April 2008 issue of the *UC Berkeley Wellness Letter* reported that researchers from the University of Warwick in England and Dartmouth College in New Hampshire looked at the happiness levels of two million people from all over the world, which they were able to obtain from published survey data regarding people's wellbeing. What they found was that the probability of depression peaks in the middle years (40 for women and 50 for men), while happiness reaches a low point.

This was true for people who were married or single, with children or childless. The Wellness Letter says midlife seems to be a rocky time for most people, who gradually move into a downswing and then slowly climb out as life goes on. If healthy, people in their sixties and seventies seem to be as happy as young people.

Why is midlife so hard? For some, midlife is the time when we give up dreams we know we can never fulfill. In some cases, midlife depression is precipitated by a drop in the production of male testosterone or thyroid hormones. There is evidence that Vitamin D production drops in midlife and this can contribute to depression. For some people the combined stress of working, taking care of children, and attending to one's parents during their decline in physical and mental health can be overwhelming.

Divorce, job layoffs and the health consequences of overeating, too much alcohol consumption, too few vacations or insufficient exercise can play a role. Not everyone who reaches midlife becomes depressed. Some people feel great in their forties and fifties. The important point is that if you are feeling depressed in your middle years, you are not a freak and you are not alone. You are a member of a worldwide group.

There's no reason to accept depression as the cost of making it to midlife.

Middle-aged lawyers (both males and females) can really benefit from reading Marianne Williamson's book titled *The Age of Miracles: Embracing The New Midlife*. It provides a great deal of wise reflections and positive encouragement for making the best of our middle years.

Epidemiology of Depression in Lawyers vs. Society

In the U.S. the rate of depression in society generally is 6-7%. Multiple studies have shown the depression rate in lawyers to be 19%. Approximately 5% of lawyers have a dual diagnosis, meaning they have depression and they are addicted to alcohol or drugs. (G. Andrew H. Benjamin, et al., *The Prevalence of Depression, Alcohol Abuse, and Cocaine Abuse Among United States Lawyers* (International Journal of Law and Psychiatry, Vol.13, 233-246, 1990)

Overcoming the Stigma of Depression

Depression deserves treatment as much as a broken leg because it is an organic illness that causes pain (psyche-ache) and mental disability in the absence of treatment. Yet society has not reached the point of acknowledging it. One barrier is that the broken leg is visible on X-ray while the imbalance of neurotransmitters in the depressed person's brain is not. Depression also has a long history of stigmatization. Old notions of witchcraft and demonic possession color the modern mind. Depression triggers aversion because it provokes subconscious fears about falling apart. It makes people wonder what would happen to them if, for once, they were honest about their psychological pain and their unmet emotional needs. When you see a person in the grip of major depression, you can't empathize unless you accept that all of us have frailties and sometimes in life we just need help. You have to be receptive, and for some of us that's pretty hard.

To keep the fear at bay, it's easier to say, "Everyone is responsible for his own emotions. There's no reason I can see why Lawyer Bob should be so sad and troubled. If Lawyer Bob just tried harder, he would master his sadness and get on with life." Another way to block recognition of depression is to blame its consequences on the depressed person.

If Bob is drinking heavily to self-medicate his emotional pain, you can dismiss him as a drunk. If he's frequently angry on account of his depression, it's easy to dismiss him as a crank or a grouch. You have to be willing to look past the symptoms and discern the underlying depression in order to help. That willingness requires moving past stigma and moving through our own fears.

What Brings on Depression in the Average Person?

What factors play a role in causing depression in people generally? They include genetic predisposition, personality type, child rearing, endocrine gland tumors, neurotransmitter imbalance, abuse of alcohol or drugs, poor nutrition, lack of exercise, sleep disorders and age-associated drops in production of human growth hormone, thyroid hormone, testosterone and estrogen.

Life events can trigger depression, especially loss—the death of a loved one, divorce, children leaving home for college, a job layoff or business failure. Traumatic brain injury, psychiatric trauma from harassment or a brush with death, and injuries resulting in chronic pain or loss of critical functions like seeing or walking can cause depression. Age-related decline in cognitive sharpness, memory, physical strength and endurance or global functioning can produce depression too.

Depression often results from inability to make successful life transitions. These include things like marriage, buying a house, having kids, moving to a new community, starting or ending a job, changing careers and retirement. In 2008 and 2009 a number of lawyer suicides were reported that had to do with those lawyers being fired from high-visibility, high-paying partnership positions with nothing lined up to cushion the sudden loss of income.

Everyone has a stress threshold, which can be exceeded by one very large stressor or by many small stressors occurring close in time. Some psychologists have suggested that hope plays an important role here. People who are hopeful tend to be optimistic and they can endure more trauma, hardship, loss or even physical pain than people who lack hope. A person's degree of hopefulness can be measured. Although there is evidence that hopefulness is an inborn trait, some psychologists believe that people who lack hope can be taught to be more hopeful.

Factors that Contribute to Depression Specifically in Lawyers

Lawyers are people drawn from every gender, race, nation, ethnicity, religion, culture and sexual orientation. Like everyone else, they are vulnerable to mental illness. Given the consistent level of high stress they endure plus the pressure on them to be strong, stay the course and never fold, lawyers are at higher risk of mental illness than nearly any other occupation.

Lawyers don't want to appear ignorant or equivocal for fear of scaring off clients or signaling weakness to their opponents in litigation. They want to be perceived as knowledgeable, decisive and in control at all times. This mask of certainty hides doubt, worry and fear. None of us knows the answer to the myriad questions that keep popping up. None of us can be sure our choices of strategy and tactics will work. All of us fear losing cases and losing face. Sometimes displays of anger are nothing but an effort to save face after someone has made us feel foolish.

To succeed, lawyers play poker with each other. This means they conceal important facts, opinions and theories about their cases from their adversaries for years. They also stifle their feelings so as not to betray these secrets. They do much the same with their clients and families. No matter how demanding or irritating the client is, if they need the income from the case, they are going to hold onto that client and refrain from sharing their displeasure or asking him to change this behavior.

When lawyers conceal financial setbacks and worries about income, it's because they want their spouses and kids to feel safe and secure. Who listens to their fears? Who encourages them to let their anger out privately? Who holds them together? For the most part nobody does. They tend to be all alone. This is a substantial part of the problem.

When there is a great discrepancy between a person's expectations and his real-life situation, a person is at risk for depression. Because lawyers are high achievers with traits of perfectionism and compulsivity, they often have extremely high expectations and this sets them up for depression. While the pursuit of excellence through trial and error, making mistakes and learning is healthy, perfectionism is pathological.

The perfectionist cannot tolerate mistakes by himself or anyone else. He is extremely harsh and wounding in his criticisms over perceived mistakes. This attitude can cause the perfectionist or those around him to become depressed. Would you like to be the Great Santini's child? Would you trade places with your own child?

Virtually any lawyer who loses a big trial, gets bad-mouthed, loses clients and suffers diminished income is certainly at risk of losing self-confidence and becoming depressed. Sometimes it's not the size of the stressor, but the timing.

Lawyers, like other professionals, go through periods of "building" (when their competence and success are peaking) and "transition" when they are feeling lost, uncertain and vulnerable due to divorce, death in the family or other traumatic events. Minor stressors at work could trigger depression if they strike during a time of transition.

How Lawyers Break Down—
Spotting the Danger Signs of Depression

Very few lawyers see the freight train of depression coming to hit them in time to seek treatment and avoid the worst. Lawyers are very conscientious and task-oriented. As they slide progressively deeper into depression, they try their best to keep going and downplay their symptoms. They also do a great job of managing other people's impressions to make others believe they are still functioning. Often the very last thing to go is their work product. When they stop showing up and they stop producing assigned work, the days of guessing whether they are depressed are over.

It's important to recognize we're all vulnerable to severe depression. Recognizing our vulnerability and seeking help, especially before breakdown, can prevent many a personal and family tragedy. I got blindsided by major depression, and it's my hope to help each of you prevent this from happening in your lives. It helps to know the danger signs and see a psychologist when you recognize them.

Danger signs include: feeling worthless, blameworthy and hopeless; having incessant worry; increasing your drinking or drug use to escape stress; impaired concentration, increased distractibility and making mistakes at work; inability to complete a night's sleep with early morning wake-ups around 2-3 a.m; daytime fatigue and sudden increase or decrease in appetite and weight. Loss of interest in socializing, sex, exercise, hobbies and other normal activities is a sign. Suicidal thoughts are more than a sign. They're a billboard.

Obstacles to Realizing You're Depressed

It's not easy to know you're depressed, since most lawyers are not trained mental health professionals and it's hard to be objective about oneself. The lawyer suffering from depression will focus his attention on the problems at work that are stressing him out. He mistakenly believes that if he can solve them (e.g., settle all the weak cases in his office that are draining so much of his time, energy and money), he'll feel all better. It's also common for the family and colleagues of a mentally ill lawyer to miss the classical signs of depression he exhibits.

Typically they say "he's under a lot of pressure right now, so it's understandable why he's doing X, Y, Z, but when it (and "it" can be a hard-fought trial or a million other things) is over, he should be fine." These attitudes delay the treatment and counseling the mentally ill lawyer desperately needs. If there wasn't such a stigma about having an episode of mental illness, lawyers would think of that possibility closer to first rather than dead last.

Seeing a Psychologist to Find Out and Get Feedback

Are you really depressed or not? If you're puzzled, it's a good idea to see a psychologist. Many of them will give you a free consultation to see if you need their help and if it looks like a good match. They will listen to you non-judgmentally, think diagnostically and let you know if you need therapy. Anything you tell a psychologist is confidential, so you can feel safe unburdening yourself.

Psychologists are there to create a healing, therapeutic relationship in which they can explore the root causes of your distress. They use the DSM-IV for billing purposes, but they do not treat you in a cookie-cutter way based on your DSM-IV diagnosis. They treat you as a whole person.

If needed they can use CBT to help you neutralize the power of negative thoughts. If they think you need time off work or increased social support, they will tell you. They will speak to your boss and your spouse if needed to gain the understanding you deserve. They can refer you to a psychiatrist if they think you need medication to bridge a period of depression. If you are severely depressed and suicidal, they can talk to you about hospitalization.

The Health Consequences of Untreated Depression

In *Why Men Die First*, Dr. Marianne J. Legato says, "Depression can shorten your life. It can be a lethal disease, not only directly, because it causes suicide, but indirectly, because it plays such a strong role in the production of other dangerous illnesses."

Dr. Legato says depression plays a medically proven role in causing coronary artery disease (CAD), hypertension and diabetes—each one of them a major risk factor in causation of heart attacks and strokes. Indeed, the risk of developing CAD is triple with a diagnosis of depression. For people who've had one heart attack already, becoming depressed means they are 3.6 times more likely to suffer a fatal heart attack.

The cover story in the June 2009 issue of the *Harvard Mental Health Letter* talks about the two-way relationship between depression and heart disease. It says "depression is hard on the heart and the arteries that carry its blood supply." The article reports that in healthy people depression doubles the risk of sudden cardiac death and increases the chance of having a heart attack or stroke by 60%. What's the connection?

Depression activates peptides called cytokines that sustain and promote atherosclerosis and the rupture of cholesterol-filled plaques. It also makes blood platelets stickier and more likely to clump. Both mechanisms can block coronary or cerebral arteries. Depression can impair heart rate and rhythm by disrupting the functioning of the autonomic nervous system (either the HPA axis, the renin-angiotensin-aldosterone system or both). Depressed people tend to exercise less, play less, eat unhealthy foods, become non-compliant with instructions for taking medication and withdraw from family and friends. All of these changes in behavior consequent to depression are bad for heart health.

Dr. Legato has a chapter on Andropause (her humorous twist on menopause for men) that should give all men pause to think. She notes that as men age their testosterone level drops (especially after age 50). As a consequence they experience changes in their body contours, physical abilities, mood and attitude toward life. In many cases men have expansion of their breasts and midsection; muscle atrophy; drop in strength; feelings of sadness and irritability; and decreased concentration. A doctor could mistake these andropausal mood changes for depression related to low serotonin, and prescribe the wrong medication (e.g., Prozac or Zoloft). These men would be helped far more effectively with a testosterone supplement.

Middle-aged people of both genders are at risk of social isolation and depression when they lose their vision or hearing but fail to get them checked and corrected. The same is true when they fall and break a hip. As you age it's very important to protect yourself from hip fractures by consuming Vitamin D, walking, doing balance exercises, making sure to have non-rigid flooring and being cautious about sleep medication. Lawyers who take too much Ambien or Ativan can fall and break their hip on the way to the bathroom at night.

Getting Your Hormone Levels Checked

It's common these days for men to get a PSA test for prostate cancer every 1-2 years after age 40, but rare for them to get their testosterone level checked. If you're experiencing depressive symptoms and you're reluctant to try an anti-depressant, then go to your family doctor and ask for a testosterone level check. Our Cro-Magnon ancestors didn't live long enough to experience depression from a drop in testosterone, and if they did, there were no testing labs around.

Do I Really Need Treatment for My Depression, and If So, What Kind?

Let's assume for the moment that you're depressed. Is treatment a necessity? Although untreated mental illness can sometimes go into spontaneous remission, this is an uncertain gamble. Carrying the burden of mental illness all by yourself without appropriate medical and psychological care is not a very good idea. The longer you go without help, the greater the danger of losing your marriage, psychologically damaging your kids, losing your job, starting or escalating a substance abuse problem and dying by suicide.

Appropriate treatment consisting of psycho-pharmaceuticals and psychotherapy can greatly speed up recovery and resumption of normal functioning, thus sparing the patient from needless weeks, months or years of distress and disability. There is no magic bullet for curing anyone's mental illness. All patients must go through a period of trial and error with respect to therapies, therapists and medications. The ride can be bumpy, because it not only takes time for the right meds to work; it takes time to find meds that will work for you.

Anti-Depressant Drugs

Not everyone responds to antidepressants. About one-third of depressed people are not helped at all by these medications, and show no response whatsoever. Among the other two-thirds, about one-third responds well to the medications and one-third responds poorly with undesirable side effects. Assuming you are a responder, you may or may not get a direct hit with the first drug.

Front line SSRI antidepressants that are often tried first include Zoloft, Lexapro, Prozac, Celexa and Paxil. If none of those work, your psychiatrist may try a combination medication such as Effexor or Cymbalta. These drugs combine an SSRI (to boost serotonin) with a tricyclic (to boost norepinephrine). They are called SNRIs (serotonin-norepinephrine reuptake inhibitors). Another approach is to augment a standard SSRI antidepressant with drugs like Buspar, Wellbutrin, Tryptan (the amino acid tryptophan) or Pinoldol (a beta-blocker which slows heartbeat).

If your anti-depressant works, it usually takes 2-3 weeks for any beneficial effects to show up and about 8 weeks for the drug to really start kicking in. Patience is needed when it's hard to come by, because you're miserable and you want instant relief. While you're waiting you can begin battling stress by meditation, boosting exercise and eating more healthfully.

Why is emotional relief from anti-depressants delayed for weeks when aspirin relieves your headache in an hour? Aspirin rapidly blocks the movement of pain signals through the brain, and its anti-inflammatory properties work quickly. For an anti-depressant to change your mood you must create sensitivity to the drug. When serotonin or norepinephrine supplies have been chronically low in the brain, it will take time to grow enough new receptor molecules in the walls of brain cells to process the more abundant supply. This requires changes in gene expression in brain cell nuclei. You will know when your anti-depressant kicks in, because you will start feeling better and may even smile at a joke.

Anti-Anxiety Drugs

Most anti-anxiety drugs are tranquilizing drugs (benzodiazepams) like Xanax, Ativan and Klonopin. Over time people who use them become tolerant and need higher doses to gain an effective response. After a while, they can become dependent and undergo withdrawal if they stop. Because of this side effect, many people with anxiety are afraid to take these medications. However, if the anxiety is strong enough the risk of addiction may be outweighed by the need for relief in the short term. You can also use low doses.

Managing the Side Effects of AntiDepressants

All antidepressants have side effects. This is inevitable because the receptors for serotonin and norepinephrine exist not just in the brain (as is commonly thought), but in the gut, muscles, bones, blood cells and immune system. Anticipating side effects is a problem because there are very few studies on poly-drug interactions. If you're taking an antidepressant in combination with other antidepressants and/or anti-anxiety medication, you will likely face a variety of side effects, some of which may be obvious to your physician and some not.

Drug companies get FDA approval for testing one drug at a time, and they're under no obligation to test the safety of their drug when used in combination with other drugs already on the market. Remember that 70% of all antidepressants are prescribed by non-psychiatrists, who are less schooled in side effects. So be careful.

Some common antidepressants like SSRIs cause weight gain. Why? No one is sure, but there are theories. Serotonin is a natural appetite suppressant. People who are deficient in serotonin not only suffer from depressed mood, but have cravings for carbs (like candy or soda) and comfort foods that combine carbs with fat (like ice cream, pie or fried foods). Once they are on an SSRI (which blocks re-uptake of serotonin already in the brain) and their depression improves, many patients cut back on carbohydrates to reduce the weight they gained while depressed. But this backfires.

According to *The Serotonin Power Diet* by nutritionists Judith J. Wurtman, Ph.D., and Nina Frusztajer Marquis, M.D., you must eat carbs to get tryptophan into your brain, where it is synthesized into serotonin. If you stop eating carbs, you will make less serotonin and your lust for carbs and carb-fat combination foods will soar off the charts.

A book that comprehensively covers the many side effects of taking antidepressants is *The Antidepressant Survival Guide* by Robert J. Hedaya, M.D. By now most consumers of antidepressants have access to side-effect information from TV commercials, Internet sites, blogs, patient support groups and the like. Many antidepressants are known to cause weight gain, fatigue, emotional blandness, difficulty having orgasm, delayed orgasm and other unwholesome changes. Many people put up with these side effects because they don't know how to fix them, they are too overwhelmed by life to take the time to find out, or they accept them as the inevitable downside of a drug that is helping them.

Some of these side effects can seriously interfere with a marriage or long term relationship. Dr. Hedaya mentions a peer-reviewed study in the *Journal of Clinical Psychiatry* showing that 75% of 60 male patients on Prozac could not ejaculate or took a prolonged time to do so. Just as cancer patients need chemotherapy, but press their physicians for drugs to relieve their nausea from chemotherapy, it is legitimate for patients with depression to press their doctors and the pharmaceutical industry for help with side effects.

With regard to nutrition Dr. Hedaya says some antidepressants stimulate sugar cravings. The more sugar you eat, the stronger the cravings get. One of his patients developed a candida infection from all the cookies she ate that were made with white flour. Hedaya says that eating extra sugar causes insulin spikes with release of extra cortisol. The insulin spikes lead to insulin resistance and diabetes Type II. The excess cortisol can trigger depression, the very thing the pill is supposed to mitigate. With regard to eating, he stresses consuming adequate protein every day, since lack of protein for just three days will trigger recurrence of depression.

How much protein? His recommendation for meals is two-thirds carbohydrates to one-third protein. Protein is needed to manufacture the neurotransmitters and hormones that keep our central nervous system operating in a healthy way. He also recommends daily exercise to increase the flow of blood and lymph, tone the muscles, increase aerobic capacity (our ability to take in and use oxygen) and release feel-good brain chemicals like endorphins.

Can I Just Take a Pill or Just See a Therapist? Do I Really Need Both?

Medication is never enough. You have to get psychotherapy as well. At best, medication can scale back the frequency, intensity and duration of troubling symptoms like profound sadness or intense anxiety. But no medications can resolve internal psychological conflicts or objective problems (such as divorce or getting fired) that are contributing to your mood disorder; nor can they clear up the cognitive distortions that stem from mental illness.

Psychotherapy gives you a chance to explore the problems that have contributed to your depressed or anxious mood, to consider a variety of solutions to them, to try out the solutions that seem most promising and to learn which ones help and which do not. Psychotherapy also provides an ongoing, supportive relationship with a therapist who is there to help you, not judge you. Ideally the therapist will help you find your strengths and work with you to use those strengths to bounce back resiliently from your crisis and emerge as a wiser, more balanced, more grounded person.

In *Surviving America's Depression Epidemic*, Bruce Levine, Ph.D., says that depression is a mechanism by which the mind of a sensitive person numbs the pain from an emotional wound. Levine cautions that treating a depressed person with medications alone is harmful, because it shuts down the depressive symptoms (sadness, despondency, lethargy) without any attention to the wound that triggered them. The meds-alone approach aborts the opportunity to engage in a self-healing process with a trained therapist.

While medications alone will not give rise to life-transforming insight, medications can play a positive role in preparing the ground for psychotherapy. When a person is extremely depressed, he is too withdrawn, too pessimistic and too lethargic to participate in psychotherapy in any meaningful way. Antidepressants can lessen the severity of the depression to the point where such a patient can engage in fruitful dialog about his suffering with a psychotherapist.

The one step, two step process of antidepressants and therapy is well described by psychiatrist Gordon Livingston, M.D. in his book *Too Soon Old, Too Late Smart*. Here is what he tells patients who come to him for treatment of depression: "The good news is that we have effective treatments for the symptoms of depression; the bad news is that a medication will not make you happy. Happiness is not simply the absence of despair. It is an affirmative state in which our lives have both meaning and pleasure."

Dr. Hedaya makes the same point in his book when he says all an anti-depressant can do is take away the blues, while leaving you in the flatland between depression and feeling joy. He recommends that while taking the anti-depressant you begin a lifelong process of cultivating joy by walks in nature, use of techniques for physical relaxation, meditation and the pursuit of what you find meaningful in life, be it gardening, a return to the religion of your ancestors or something else. At a certain point you may be able to stop the pills, and rely entirely on your cultivation of joy. Isn't that a wonderful goal?

How Do You Find the Right Psychiatrist?

Next to lawyers, psychiatrists are the group most often accused of having a personality with an uncaring attitude. Yes, there are some psychiatrists with the bedside manner of a refrigerator, but there are others who are warm, empathic and caring. You definitely want to avoid the bad ones (who spend more time discussing insurance and billing than your desperate need for help), because they make everything worse.

Word of mouth is often the best way to avoid the bad ones and find the good ones. This is tricky because most lawyers do not want to advertise the fact that they are mentally ill by asking everyone they know to recommend a great psychiatrist. To get accurate information without tipping off the planet, you can ask your primary care physician.

You can also pick names out of your insurance coverage book, visit two or three and compare them. You can find out which of them has the most experience counseling depressed adults, which has the most appealing treatment approach and which one gets the best patient outcomes. Choose the one who makes you feel the most secure, understood, cared for and hopeful.

Once you find a good psychiatrist for prescribing meds, try to see him regularly and do not accept telephone conferences. You will do best with a psychiatrist who sees you in person to monitor your mood, your behavior and your responses to medication, while having you tested periodically for side effects like elevated blood sugar, high cholesterol or liver damage that you would not experience in the absence of the medication. Some busy psychiatrists do phone consults and this virtually always results in missed information and poor communication with worse outcomes.

The Limitations of Modern Psychiatry

In *Surviving America's Depression Epidemic*, Bruce Levine, Ph.D., says that most contemporary psychiatrists are not healers but technicians who follow a mechanical two-step process. First they diagnose your disorder by applying DSM-IV criteria to your symptoms. If they find out a parent or grandparent had the same set of depressive or anxious symptoms, they nod their head knowingly and feel certain they have bagged the right diagnosis. They seem not to appreciate that the development of depression is mediated by many non-genetic factors.

Second, these psychiatrists prescribe a drug synthesized in a laboratory which has been touted by paid sales representatives as the most effective drug for relieving symptoms of the disorder they have diagnosed. If the first drug they prescribe does not work, they look for other candidates within the same family of drugs. If none of those work, they may try a new family of drugs, and if that doesn't work, they will probably recommend ECT (or transcranial magnetic stimulation if they are at the cutting edge).

Dr. Levine is troubled by this approach of diagnosing symptoms and then prescribing a consumer product (a drug) to shut down the symptoms. He is concerned that today's psychiatrists do not see emotional pain as part of the normal human experience and as an opportunity to learn by transforming emotional pain into energy for healing emotional wounds. He says they have no curiosity about who their patient is as a whole person, and no incentive to delve into his life history to find reasons why he is having particular kinds of emotional pain at this juncture in his life.

Their patients do not feel cared for—they feel like a car that an auto mechanic is tinkering with, and in a way they are right. Their psychiatrist is tinkering with their brain by choosing which medications, at which dosages, are required to get their brain running smoothly again; i.e., operating without the sludge of depression or anxiety that gets in the way of doing what they used to do before the onset of symptoms.

In place of a chemically induced shutdown of painful emotions, Dr. Levine advocates getting in touch with our pain and healing it in a humane and dignified manner that takes account of our whole lives. This accords with the Buddhist approach to depression, as well as that of Native American tribes like the Lakota and Blackfoot.

Dr. Levine says those tribes understood that pain has meaning and can be a door through which the sufferer learns compassion, patience, duty and gentleness. They employed stories and rituals in the healing process to help the sufferer accept that pain is a necessary part of life to help us awaken to what is real and true. I listened to a CD called *Keep Going* by a Native American storyteller on how to cope with grief from the death of one's father; it was spellbinding and inspirational.

I agree wholeheartedly with Dr. Levine that an episode of major depression is a sign that one's mode of living has failed and has become a source of terrible pain. I also agree that major depression can be a catalyst for healthy change when we work with someone to help us examine our lives, to find where we turned down a dead end and to visualize a new course that promises less stress, less constriction, more freedom and more joy.

Does this mean medication is never a good idea, and that psychotherapy alone is always what is needed? No. There are occasions when medication is helpful and some when it's absolutely necessary. If a person has become so depressed that he is ruminating constantly about suicide, medication is life-saving and must be taken to assure the patient remains alive to start the healing work of psychotherapy. This was true in my case when my Bipolar II flipped from hypomania to severest depression. If not for Seroquel, I would not be here to write this book.

Don't Let Shame or Fear of Stigma Keep You from Treatment

Because of shame and fear of the stigma around mental illness, a lawyer may deny he is depressed and pretend it's something else—like being run-down from too much work. He may imagine that if he can just take a week off to go to Hawaii he would bounce right back.

If his law partner or spouse tells him he appears depressed and urges him to start taking an antidepressant, he may balk on the grounds that depression is for weak people and he's not weak. If he finally acknowledges he's depressed and it's not his fault, he may keep it a secret for fear that disclosing it would cost him his job. When he leaves the office to see his psychiatrist for meds or his psychologist for therapy, he tells his secretary he's off to play racquetball.

The John Wayne approach is counterproductive, because the depressed person now has a terrible secret. Instead of being able to provide help and support, the important people in his life are left guessing why he is acting so strangely.

How Shame over Depression
can Perpetuate Depression

Mental illness is every bit as real, as distressing and as impairing as a serious physical illness. No one would blame you for having leukemia, nor would you blame yourself. Logically there are no reasons why a person should berate himself for having depression. After all, it arises from things we cannot control, like our genetic inheritance, our brain chemistry and unforeseen stressors. Yet to this day, many people see mental illness as if it were something shameful, something that marks us as failures in life.

Many depressed people get disappointed and angry at themselves for staying depressed, for sleeping too much, for skipping meals, for socially isolating themselves, for feeling down all the time, for needing medication and for lacking the energy and animation they need to work and care for their families in a competent manner. They never give themselves a break.

Seriously depressed people completely suppress conscious recognition of and self-appreciation for the good things they accomplish during their depressed phase. To encourage them to recover, it helps to teach them how to praise themselves for accomplishing everyday tasks like grocery shopping, doing laundry, changing a light bulb or driving the kids to school.

Forcing Yourself to Get Up and Go
When You Just Want to Sleep

Nobody can survive depression without having compassion for himself. On the other hand, even though you feel too depressed to do anything, you will only start to feel better when you push ahead despite your depression and do something. It will make a difference just to have lunch with a friend, walk the dog, read the newspaper, do a load of laundry or drive your child to school. By celebrating each tiny victory over despair and inaction, you build momentum and regain faith in yourself.

There are modern day examples, one being Terry Bradshaw, the quarterback who led the Pittsburgh Steelers to four Super Bowl victories. He is bipolar and had severe episodes of depression throughout his long and storied football career. He's been quoted as saying there were days when all he wanted to do was stay at home, but he forced himself to get to the stadium and play ball, which took his mind off his depression, raised his endorphin level and made him feel better.

The Spillover Effect of Mood Disorders—Depression Doesn't Stop With You

While you're in the grips of depression, you're not the only one affected. The other people affected include your clients; law partners; the associates, paralegals and secretaries who work for you; and your spouse, children, close relatives and friends.

When a lawyer is depressed, the people who depend on him cannot help but notice he is more withdrawn, less animated, less energetic and less reliable. His focus and concentration will be diminished. If he drinks alcohol, his drinking may increase. He may also be uncharacteristically abrupt and irritable and snap at loved ones. He can cause a lot of hurt feelings at home.

A depressed lawyer puts burdens on his firm. He shows up late and unprepared for depositions, case management conferences or hearings on contested motions; he misplaces files or important documents; he is erratic in returning phone calls from clients, opposing counsel, court clerks, court reporters, investigators and experts; he falls way behind on his paperwork obligations to propound or respond to discovery, and so on. The lawyers covering for him are likely to be stressed out and resentful. When a lawyer becomes depressed, his colleagues and family should be educated about symptoms so they can be more patient, understanding and supportive.

The Need for Colleagues to Detect Depression and Intervene

If a lawyer with depression who is not yet diagnosed is very lucky, a law partner or supervisor with experience in these matters who cares about him will sit him down for a private chat. During this chat the partner or supervisor will get him to recognize his illness and his urgent need for treatment, induce him to start treatment and allow him time off to recover, while transferring his files to other trusted, competent lawyers in the office.

If he is not so lucky, he may get sanctioned or held in contempt by a judge who is intolerant of his impaired performance as an officer of the court and he may commit one or more acts of legal malpractice and get himself and his law firm sued.

A depressed lawyer can alienate clients by not returning their calls, by acting strangely at meetings or by failing to perform as promised. Clients expect a great deal from their lawyers and can be very quick to complain to the State Bar when their lawyers disappoint them.

In this way a well-educated, well-trained and competent lawyer can slide down the road to perdition before he even knows what hit him. For the benefit of lawyers like these, their clients and the law firms they work for, it is imperative to have a program in place to detect mental illness at the earliest possible moment and intervene with a spirit of helpfulness to initiate appropriate treatment.

Among the lawyers most likely to fall through the cracks are solo practitioners. Why? Because they work alone and the last person to realize he has a mental illness is the person with the illness. Some solos do not even have a paralegal or a secretary who could notice the onset of the mental illness and say something.

If they do have an assistant, he may wait a long time before speaking up out of fear of over-reacting or angering his boss and getting fired for speaking up. Other lawyers who fall through the cracks include contract lawyers and lawyers who telecommute. Why? Nobody has much direct, personal contact with them.

The Phenomenon of Covert Male Depression— Ambushed by Anguish

Women are diagnosed with depression twice as much as men and as a group take about twice the total amount of antidepressants as men. Some authorities explain this difference by saying that women's brains contain less serotonin than men's. Yet severely depressed men die by suicide at a rate of 4:1 in relation to women, and low serotonin is a factor that contributes to suicide. Clearly the differences in depression rate and antidepressant use cannot be accounted for by serotonin levels alone. What we do know is that women are more able to admit to having depression and to seek treatment, whereas men either avoid treatment altogether or avoid it as long as possible.

Terrence Real's book *I Don't Want To Talk About It: Overcoming The Secret Legacy of Male Depression* is a must-read for every man who has ever experienced symptoms of depression. Real divides depression into the categories of overt and covert. Women's depression tends to be overt; i.e., something they acknowledge having, something they talk openly about and something that prompts them to seek help. Men's depression is covert, because men are not supposed to be vulnerable and are expected to rise above pain. Men see depression as unmanly and feminine.

To admit to depression is to risk the double stigma of having a mental illness and feminine emotionality—so men's depression goes unacknowledged and unrecognized. Real says that somewhere between 60 and 80 percent of people with depression (mostly men) never get help, which is heartrending since depression is highly treatable with psychotherapy and medication. The men who do get treated wait years to seek help. To be brought low by "their own unmanageable feelings" is a source of shame. Men with covert depression are depressed about feeling depressed and ashamed of feeling ashamed. They don't want anyone else to know.

The personal and social cost of men concealing their depression is unacceptably high. Real says: "There is a terrible collusion in our society, a cultural cover-up about depression in men…. Hidden depression drives several of the problems we think of as typically male: physical illness, alcohol and drug abuse, domestic violence, failures in intimacy and self-sabotage in careers." Real explains the statistic of depressed men committing suicide at four times the rate of depressed women by saying that when men aren't able to rid themselves of depression on their own, they conclude they are "wimps" and can no longer face themselves or the world.

How come men have so much difficulty acknowledging their own depression and getting help? Why don't their mothers, wives, daughters or female law partners see it and say something? Real blames it on gender socialization in our culture, which encourages men to develop their public, assertive selves while banning them from exercising a full range of emotional expressiveness and developing the skills for making and reaping the benefits of deep social connections with others.

Men have remained lone wolves who are pressured to pretend they are tough as nails and pressured to go it alone when they are wounded. The women in their lives may minimize their depression for fear of shaming them. This only serves to perpetuate the harmful social definition of masculinity. Depressed men who cannot bring vulnerable feelings into the open will bury themselves in work, numb their pain with alcohol and disconnect themselves socially from family and friends.

Real calls covert male depression a "chain of pain," which the father unconsciously and unintentionally hands down to the son. There is typically no one momentous incident. Rather there are hundreds, even thousands, of small incidents of betrayal, neglect or abandonment that combine with a biological vulnerability to generate depression.

Covert depression is a disease of self-esteem. The victim did not receive unconditional positive regard from his parents. His sense of self-worth is not intrinsic. It rises and falls with what he does, what he achieves and what he has. He cannot love himself in the face of having the same sorts of imperfections that everyone else has.

Real says that men can live for decades with covert depression until their brittle sense of self-worth splinters against the sharp edge of a particularly painful event, and their covert depression erupts into a Major Depression requiring hospitalization. Until then they get by using workaholism, alcoholism, domination of other people and living within a shell as defense mechanisms; that is, until the Big Depression comes and washes them all away.

Overcoming depression, being the one who breaks the chain of pain, requires time-traveling back to childhood, feeling the awful pain of the lonely unloved boy, enduring it, expressing it, letting go of it, and allowing oneself to touch and be touched. Reaching inside to pull out the childhood pain, and then learning to love oneself from within, to see oneself as the equal of others, no more or less valuable than anyone else, is the way out of the dark forest.

TREATMENTS FOR DEPRESSION OTHER THAN MEDICATION AND INDIVIDUAL PSYCHOTHERAPY

Exercise

Along with medication and psychotherapy, the best treatment for depression hands down is exercise, the more vigorous the better. Depressed people are reluctant to exercise because they feel down and predict that nothing they do will make them feel better. Complying with this prediction, they stop doing all the things that used to make them feel good when they were well, including exercise. People who used to run, swim or ride their bikes 3, 4, even 5 times a week, become reclusive couch potatoes whose only exercise is getting the morning paper, which they don't read and chuck into the recycling bin instead. As depressed people lose muscle bulk and tone and as they gain lots of extra flab, they feel worse about themselves and are less able to envision being active and strong again.

Paradoxically the only way to feel better is to make yourself exercise and partake of other activities you used to love. Exercise increases blood circulation, stimulates deep breathing, oxygenates your body and brain and produces endorphins—all of which contribute to boosting your mood. Once you're exercising you feel less leaden and sluggish. Your body feels alive and energized again. The tangible proof you are recovering from depression is watching yourself exercise, lose weight, regain muscle tone and begin looking like your old self. As your mood and self-confidence improve from exercise, you become more social again and this boosts your mood still more.

A psychologist I know who got herself through college and grad school working as a personal trainer, and who continues to work as a trainer on weekends, says that exercise is one of the absolutely essential keys to recovery from depression.

In his book *play*, Dr. Stuart Brown describes working with a group of seriously depressed women in San Diego. He got them to commit to exercising at 80% of their maximum heart rate for 45 minutes a day, four days a week, on the beach. For the first three months getting them to exercise was a "titanic struggle." Eventually the women began feeling more confident, positive and energized. Only a small number dropped out. By the end of the year, there was a noticeable improvement in the women who stayed. They were able to maintain their improved mood by continuing to exercise.

Using Group Therapy to
Overcome Shame and Gain Acceptance

Lawyers are used to dominating other people by displaying their powerful intellects and verbal skills. When we participate in groups (at work, in the community or the volunteer realm), we take over— identifying problems and offering solutions without letting anyone else get a word in edgewise.

I spent over a year in group therapy and gained great benefit from the experience. In group therapy I was told repeatedly that people want me to listen to them, not cut them off and tell them how to solve their problems. I was also told not to tell stories, but to speak from my heart about my feelings. I have made stronger connections by practicing these techniques.

While it's not possible to make group therapy compulsory for law-yers, it might not be a bad idea. In group therapy, the other people connected to me when I expressed my true feelings and they were able to stay connected to me and validate me even when those feelings expressed pain, loneliness, frustration, confusion, doubt or anger. In the group I learned it's okay to be honest about my feelings and it's okay to be me. I don't have to pretend I'm always on top of things and have control of my life. I have also learned the joy of listening to others and supporting them. It feels a whole lot better than attacking a witness and going in for the verbal kill.

Herbal Remedies for Depression

Although I'm convinced that antidepressant medications are a necessary and useful part of treatment, I've met plenty of people who will not touch medication with a ten-foot pole. Some of these folks use extracts of the St. John's Wort plant in place of meds. Because of flaws in studies of the effectiveness of this plant in fighting depression, the National Institutes of Health undertook a large, well-controlled study that lasted three years. The result was that St. John's Wort was no more effective than a placebo in reducing depression and boosting wellbeing.

No matter what science says, herbal remedies will always be attractive to some people. This is partly due to distrust of synthetic chemicals and of drug companies, which have a profit motive to push sales. It's also due to a feeling of kinship with what is natural. All of this is legitimate. But if your depression is incapacitating or has triggered suicidal wishes, I think it's definitely time to see a psychiatrist for prescription medication.

Caution about drugs is fine since they all have side effects, but at some point it really is self-defeating to avoid a trial of prescription antidepressants. Caution is also appropriate when using herbal remedies. The *Physician's Desk Reference* has one thick volume for prescription medicines and another one for herbal remedies. It is a myth that herbal remedies are perfectly safe because they are natural. Hemlock, Jimsonweed and a variety of mushrooms that will kill you are also natural. Look before you leap.

Massage and Touch

When people become depressed they contract physically, emotionally and socially. They are the human equivalent of a sow bug rolling into a protective ball. They don't want to be touched and they don't want to touch other people. They just want to be left alone.

Paradoxically, one of the best things for them is the soothing touch of another person. A gentle massage from a spouse, partner or massage therapist can begin to break up the body armor and emotional armor that goes with depression.

Humor and Laughter

Humor has its dark and light varieties. When you're depressed, avoid dark humor, since all it does is reinforce depression by reminding you of things like hypocrisy, corruption and the inevitability of doom. Light humor is better medicine. Light humor focuses on our common foibles as human beings in a gentle, affectionate and non-hostile way that gets us to belly laugh. The Marx Brothers movies, the Pink Panther movies (with Peter Sellers or Steve Martin as Jacques Clouseau) or Gary Larson's cartoons are great examples. Belly laughter brings air deep into our lungs and triggers endorphin secretion. It's a wonderful mood booster.

Being human means losing your way every now and then. If you can laugh at your confusion you can survive it. If you can laugh at your pain you can survive it.

Don Piper, the survivor of a horrendous truck accident that flattened his car and essentially killed him, has written several books on finding meaning in traumatic events that shatter one's world. In *Heaven is Real*, he's got a chapter called "We Might As Well Laugh." Despite severe chronic pain in his legs, Mr. Piper still laughs a lot, even at himself. Someone described him at the hospital as "that tall man who limps," and he took on the name as a joke. Good ole Mark Twain said, "Humor is mankind's greatest blessing" and "Against the assault of laughter, nothing can stand."

In *Why Good Things Happen to Good People*, authors Stephen Post, Ph.D., and Jill Neimark mention a study of laughter in Holocaust survivors. Chaya Ostrower of Tel Aviv interviewed 84 survivors and learned that all of them used humor to survive trauma. Humor enabled them to discharge tension built up from the most recent threats to their survival, put those threats in the past and put something good in their lives right now to keep them going.

Laughter is like medicine that restores vitality not just to the sick (Norman Cousins) but to those living in a state of fear and anxiety. The authors mention Teddy Roosevelt and Ronald Reagan, who faced some very tough times, but used jokes and laughter to get themselves through. When Reagan was wheeled into the emergency room for removal of the bullets pumped into him by John Hinkley, Jr., he looked up at his masked surgeons and said, "I hope you're all Republicans."

Post and Neimark caution people to avoid mocking humor. They say that healthy laughter is warming and inviting, not sneering, jeering or hollow. It's the kind that's not at anyone else's expense, and does not embarrass or ridicule. Truly mirthful laughter is associated with health, whereas hostile laughter aimed at denigrating, harming or destroying someone else is associated with poor psychological functioning. Wavy Gravy is a great example. He uses healthy laughter to bond people together into a group that shares the feeling of happiness.

Dr. Madan Kataria, the founder of Laughter Yoga and World Laughter Day (see www.laughteryoga.org), says on his website:

"We are more prosperous today than 50 years ago. We are also 10 times more stressed, sad, lonely and depressed. Depression is the number one sickness, while stress continues to be a major cause of 70 to 80% of all illness. There is a sharp rise in the incidence of cancer and heart diseases. According to medical research, the root cause of most of our sickness is lack of oxygen in our body cells. Laughter Yoga is an effective routine that brings complete physical, mental, social and spiritual wellbeing by instantly reducing stress, bringing more oxygen, strengthening the immune system, fighting depression and creating a network of caring and sharing society."

Too many law offices and legal proceedings are dreadfully formal and dull. You almost wish someone would fart just to lighten the atmosphere. I always cracked jokes with my clients in the privacy of my office, and they appreciated it since it helped make the legal process less threatening and gave them hope they could survive it. I was much less likely to use my sense of humor in depositions, trials or hearings, because of meeting up with testy lawyers who did not appreciate it. The loss of this outlet for my sense of humor was actually a source of pain for me.

Light Therapy

Light therapy started in the early 1980s for people suffering from SAD (seasonal affective disorder). People with SAD become depressed during the fall and winter months when the intensity and duration of sunlight diminishes. This is accompanied by a fall in production of Vitamin D in their skin and by an increase in melatonin.

The increase in melatonin provoked by fewer hours of daylight makes these people sleep longer hours, while changing their mood for the worse. During the fall and winter months people with SAD have a dark, depressed mood and find it difficult to get out of bed and function normally in their required activities. You can raise your Vitamin D levels by eating Omega 3-rich seafoods that are also loaded with Vitamin D (salmon, mackerel, sardines and shrimp), drinking more milk or eating more eggs.

Staring at a light box appears to be very helpful in relieving some people's depression. Why? Because the indoor light from the light box mimics outdoor light and the extra light it gives helps to suppress melatonin production. I have met people, including one lawyer, who swear by light box therapy. My lawyer friend uses a $250 light box for 2-3 hours in the morning before going to work, and he said it has made a huge difference in his life and his ability to practice law. Without the light box treatments he was too depressed and lethargic to go to work.

Although the FDA has not yet approved light box therapy for depression, some studies show it is as effective as or more effective than antidepressant medication for some people with depressive symptoms. The reason the FDA has withheld approval is that other studies show this treatment has little or no effect on depression.

The Mayo Clinic recommends that you try it if you are depressed and you don't want to take antidepressants, if antidepressants don't improve your mood or their side effects are intolerable. They also recommend it if you are pregnant, you lack insurance for mental health services or you want an alternative to psychotherapy.

For people with light-dependent depression, neurosurgeon Larry McCleary, M.D., recommends using full-spectrum lightbulbs such as Chromalux at home and office. Lawyers with SAD should ask their employers to switch out fluorescent bulbs for Chromalux. This should be covered by the ADA. The Mayo Clinic cautions that light therapy may trigger mania in people with bipolar disorder and should not be used if your eyes or skin are light-sensitive or if you take medications (e.g., certain anti-inflammatories and antibiotics) that react badly with sunlight. It also warns that some people may experience side effects including eye strain, headache, agitation, nausea, insomnia, irritability, fatigue, dry mouth and sleep disruptions.

Household Chores

The August/September 2008 issue of *Scientific American Mind* has an article by neuroscientist Kelly Lambert called "Depressingly Easy." She says that rates of depression continue to climb despite a plethora of antidepressant drug choices now available, and this may be due to our incredibly passive lifestyle.

Lambert points out that we use labor-saving machines to do all our chores, leaving us empty time to fill by watching TV. She is convinced that effortful, physical work using their own hands gave our ancestors a payoff in terms of mental wellbeing that we no longer get.

She contrasts the Baby Boomers (with the highest rates of depression compared to any other generation) to the settlers on the American prairie. The settlers thrived by hunting, fishing, growing and harvesting crops, milking cows, churning butter, building and repairing their own homes, making their own clothes and collecting rain water to wash their clothes.

Boomers have fallen into depression living in a world where they buy pre-made meals and heat them up in a microwave, communicate by e-mail, entertain themselves by Web surfing, use machines to wash dishes and clothes, pay people to clean their homes and maintain their yards, and send their kids off to school where someone else reads to them. They spend a lot of their time sitting—while driving, computing and watching TV or videos.

Lambert is certain we lost something vital to our mental health when we began pushing buttons instead of plowing fields. Why? She says our brains are wired to experience a deep sense of satisfaction and pleasure when we use physical effort to produce something tangible, visible and meaningful with respect to contributing to our own survival. Our ancestors could not afford to be "cave potatoes" hanging out all day.

They either braved the dangers of leaving the cave and collecting food by using their wits and their brawn, or they died of starvation. Our ancestors survived because their brains were wired to reward effort and provided them with a pleasurable sense of accomplishment when they caught and skinned an animal for dinner.

Lambert's message is: spend less time drinking Chardonnay and watching ESPN, and spend more time doing activities that require effort to accomplish something personally meaningful, be it washing the car, camping and fishing for dinner with your kids, tending your vegetable garden, chopping firewood, knitting a sweater, working out at the gym, exercising your dog by jogging around the park, memorizing your favorite poem or calling an old friend to chat.

ECT, TMS and DBS

For depressed patients who gain no relief from psychotherapy and antidepressant medication, the typical course of action has been to prescribe ECT (electro-convulsive therapy). The modern version of ECT uses much less electricity than its predecessor. It doesn't cure depression, but is highly effective in snapping people with treatment-resistant depression out of their funk. Maintenance treatments may be required after the initial course, because people with this type of severe depression tend to have recurrence of symptoms.

Because ECT causes mini-seizures, you have to be anesthetized and strapped to a bed. Approximately one third of patients experience significant memory loss. I know a person who had ECT who cannot remember anything from the weeks she was getting the treatment, including her participation in a group therapy program. It's just a hole in her memory. With regard to events happening in the present, it took a while for her memory function to normalize. But the ECT did get her out of suicidal depression, and put her in a position where she could begin to work on her issues in a therapy group. So ECT helps, but it imposes a cost.

It's estimated that approximately four million depressed patients in the U.S. do not respond to medication, psychotherapy or ECT. Transcranial magnetic stimulation (TMS) is one promising new alternative to ECT which uses harmless pulses of magnetic energy into the brain to activate neurons. The technique is to apply small metallic coils to the scalp and zap portions of the pre-frontal cortex that are less active than normal in depressed patients. Unlike ECT, the patient need not be strapped down or anesthetized.

A team of researchers led by John O'Reardon at the University of Pennsylvania, using a group of 300 depressed patients, including a control group, found that doing TCM 40 minutes a day on a daily basis for four weeks produced significant reduction in depression with no harmful side effects. Patients with seizure disorder were excluded from the study, because TCM can provoke seizures in such patients. TCM was legal in Canada and Australia well before it was approved by the FDA for use in the United States in October 2008.

Another technique now used only for treatment of Parkinson's Disease and chronic pain patients is deep brain stimulation (DBS), which works by implanting electrodes into the brain tissue and running a micro-current at different frequencies to stop tremors or relieve pain. In 2003 Dr. Helen Mayberg of Toronto tried DBS on a very small group of patients with treatment resistant depression and had some success. She theorized that these patients had over-activity of Brodman's area 25 and DBS quieted this area down. Since then there have been more small studies in the U.S. with somewhat promising results. At this time the FDA has not approved DBS for depression.

Playing with Children

Anthropologists say evolution made children incredibly cute, so their odds of survival would be increased. When I was severely depressed, playing with my son Elliott (then age 7) was like a wonder tonic. He and I would jump on the trampoline in our backyard with each other and with his friends from next door. The exercise and the silliness and laughter that went with it really picked up my mood.

If you don't have young kids you can still find kids to play with—be they nieces and nephews, kids on your neighborhood sports team or kids in programs like Big Brothers and Big Sisters. When kids smile their gap-toothed smiles, their faces light up and so does the face of every sane adult around them. Their joy is contagious.

In *play*, Stuart Brown, M.D., says physical activity is a great form of play for depressed adults because it bypasses cognitive roadblocks to happy mood. When you're throwing a ball to a dog you don't have time to think about why you're so sad or how you can overcome it. You're just having fun in the moment.

Dr. Brown says lack of play is like malnutrition—it's a health risk to your body and mind. Since lack of play probably contributed to your depression in the first place, it sure makes sense to use play to help you recover from it.

Hanging Out with Friends

During my depression, having friends come over and chat was of utmost importance. When I was depressed I expected people to abandon me, so when friends came over, I got a different message. The message was, "I still care about you." This made me feel better about myself.

Their company was a distraction from depressive thoughts. It was good to hear about outside news, about their lives and the lives of their spouses and kids. Some of the friends got me out of the house. Some of them got me hiking in beautiful spots, which touched me and reminded me that even though I was struggling with depression, I was fortunate enough to live in a beautiful world. I would urge any lawyer suffering from depression to reach out to friends and let them know, so they can visit you and be part of your life when you really need them. Friendship is energizing and uplifting.

In *The Pleasure Center*, Morten Kringelbach expressed the pivotal role of friendship in helping people survive severe depression when he said, "There is always hope—even if it may at times seem like only a glimmer. At the end of the day, it is other people who make it worth staying on and who can help us back to the pleasure and happiness of life."

All Things End, Even Depression

When you're depressed, it seems like you are trudging across a vast wasteland that will never end. But depression does end. If you don't succumb to suicidal urges, you will experience the light at the end of the tunnel. Keep on going. You owe it to yourself, your family, your friends, your law partners and the world. There is just one you and there will never be another. You have a unique role to play in the world, and we need you.

Depression sucks, but looked at in the grand perspective of life, it's a stepping stone in your personal evolution. Without difficult times, without suffering, life is shallow. When you emerge from depression you have a certain wisdom, along with the ability to really appreciate the good stuff instead of taking it for granted.

CHAPTER SIX: SUGGESTED READING

Benjamin Saddock, M.D., and Virginia Saddock, M.D., Editors, *Comprehensive Textbook of Psychiatry* (7th ed.) (Lippincott Williams & Wilkins, 2000)

William Styron, *Darkness Visible: A Memoir of Madness* (Vintage Books, 1990)

DSM-IV (4th edition) (American Psychiatric Association, 1994)

Steven C. Hayes, Ph.D., *Get Out of Your Mind and Into Your Life* (New Harbinger Publications, Inc., 2005)

Don Piper, *Heaven is Real* (Berkeley Praise, 2007)

Terrence Real, *I Don't Want To Talk About It: Overcoming The Secret Legacy of Male Depression* (Scribner, 1997)

John McManamy, *Living Well With Depression and Bipolar Disorder* (Collins, 2006)

Frederick K. Goodwin and Kay Redfield Jamison, *Manic Depressive Illness* (2nd ed.) (Oxford University Press, 2007)

William W. Eaton, Ph.D., et al., *Occupations and the Prevalence of Major Depressive Disorder* (Journal of Occupational Medicine Vol. 32, No. 11, November 1990)

Bruce E. Levine, Ph.D., *Surviving America's Depression Epidemic: How to Find Morale, Energy and Community in a World Gone Crazy* (Chelsea Green Publishing Company, 2007)

Robert J. Hedaya, M.D., *The Antidepressant Survival Guide* (Three Rivers Press, 2000)

John Scharffenberger and Robert Steinberg, *The Essence of Chocolate* (Hyperion, 2005)

Henri J.M. Nouwen, *The Inner Voice of Love—A Journey Through Anguish to Freedom*, (Image Books, 1998)

Julia Ross, M.A., *The Mood Cure* (Penguin Books, 2002)

Judith J. Wurtman, Ph.D., and Nina Frusztajer Marquis, M.D., *The Serotonin Power Diet* (Rodale, 2006)

Sandra Aamodt, Ph.D., and Sam Wang, Ph.D., *Welcome To Your Brain* (Bloomsbury USA, 2008)

Marianne J. Legato, M.D., F.A.C.P., *Why Men Die Early* (Palgrave Macmillan, 2008)

CHAPTER SEVEN

Why lawyers become suicidal

A Strong Caution Before Reading this Chapter

THIS CHAPTER IS MEANT for lawyers who are not struggling right now with intense suicidal thoughts. Please go ahead and read this chapter if you've never had suicidal thoughts, if such thoughts are in the past or if you're having them now, they are fleeting, infrequent and have not ripened into a plan.

But, if you're having frequent, powerful thoughts about suicide right now and you've already begun imagining or planning how you would do it, then put this book down and call a suicide hotline such as 1-800-SUICIDE or 1-800-273-TALK. If you are on the verge of taking action to die by suicide and someone is with you, then have that person drive you to the emergency room. If you're alone, then call 911.

Why is This Chapter Necessary?

The hard truth is that lawyers die by suicide at double the rate of the general public.

Their high stress level, pessimism, social isolation and fears of admitting to depression or reaching out for help all contribute.

Another factor is that lawyers rely too much on thinking to solve problems. You can't think your way out of severe depression for two reasons. First, depression has biological, hormonal, emotional and social components that won't respond to thinking. Second, severe depression distorts thinking and a severely depressed person is extremely likely to see everything within the frame of negativity, hopelessness and doom.

I had precious little time to think. The terrible depression that struck me in August 2007 came on so fast and so hard that I was unable to fight it alone or even conceive of doing so. After just three days of pretending to my family that I was okay, I realized I had to have help right away or I would die. I sought help and got it. It took two one-week hospitalizations, loads of therapy and a bit of tinkering with medication, but I made it.

The good news is that I'm no longer depressed and I don't think about killing myself anymore. Although I'm still being treated for anxiety, I am a much happier person now than I was before my depression struck. I appreciate being alive. I appreciate my family and relate to them much better. I am a more open, sensitive, considerate and compassionate person. I look for the best in people instead of the worst. And I finally have a clear purpose in life that really resonates with me—passing along the wisdom I gained from my painful ordeal with depression and suicidal thoughts.

I got lots of help when I most needed it, but I can't just assume that every other lawyer will be so fortunate. The last thing I ever want to see is another lawyer take his own life because he isn't educated about, or prepared to respond to, his own suicidal crisis when it hits. This chapter is necessary to bring you the facts about a taboo subject that has to come out of the closet and become public information if we are to prevent future lawyer suicides.

The one person I know who has written openly in clear, simple and easily understandable terms about how to prevent your own suicide is Paul Quinnett. His book is called *Suicide: The Forever Decision.* You can buy a copy or download it free from his website, www.qprinstitute.com.

Suicide is the Most Preventable Cause of Death

Former U.S. Surgeon General Dr. David Satcher said, "Suicide is our most preventable form of death." What did he mean by that? Suicide is not a disease like cancer that suddenly shows up without your conscious participation. It's not the consequence of external circumstances like motor vehicle crashes or random street violence. Suicide is the result of the conscious choice of an extremely distressed human being to commit the ultimate act of violence upon himself, the taking of his own life.

Although not everyone who feels a suicidal urge takes his own life or even tries to, the odds of suicide go way down when concerned people intervene. Abraham Lincoln's friends helped him survive a strong urge to commit suicide when his first true love died. Can you imagine America being deprived of Abe Lincoln's leadership during the Civil War?

Every lawyer wrestling with suicidal thoughts deserves the very best help and most prompt help available. Something people can do to help is remove all firearms from their homes, since the easy availability of a firearm can make a temporary suicidal impulse ripen into a completed suicide that would not otherwise have taken place.

The Four Psychological Characteristics of People Who Die by Suicide

The National Institute of Mental Health (NIMH) says that more than 90% of suicides are carried out by people with depression, other serious mental illness or substance abuse problems. NIMH emphasizes that attempting suicide is not a harmless plea for attention, but the direct expression of extreme emotional distress. Sara Goldsmith of the Board on Neuroscience and Behavioral Medicine created a booklet titled *Risk Factors for Suicide: Summary of a Workshop*, published by the National Academy Press. The booklet says: "Suicide occurs only in the presence of severe psych-ache (mental pain). There is a 100% overlap between the commission of suicide and perturbation, upset, unease, anguish and discomfort accompanied by the idea of ending it all."

In *Why People Die By Suicide*, Thomas Joiner agrees that psyche-ache will exert a powerful push on a person to kill himself when his psychological and emotional pain have built up to an intolerable intensity. However, he finds that other ingredients are necessary to get a person to the point of taking his own life. Joiner lists the four ingredients that are necessary for suicide as:

- Failed belongingness
- Perceived burdensomeness
- Hopelessness
- Lethality

Joiner says the need to belong is a bedrock human need which is met by being in one or more stable relationships with people you see frequently who make you feel cared for. Public disgrace, imprisonment, addiction to drugs or alcohol, depression and other factors can cause a persistent thwarting of the need to belong. Joiner says individuals who have relationships that are unpleasant, unstable, infrequent or without geographic proximity are not likely to feel connected or cared about. When such people feel a painful loss of belongingness, they are at risk of desiring to die.

Another bedrock human need is to feel capable. Joiner says that when a person feels he is ineffective and his continued existence is nothing but a burden upon and a threat to the people he cares about, he will feel a desire to die. This can happen in the wake of a scandal, a bankruptcy, a disabling illness or injury and so forth. The perception of burdensomeness can also result from the cognitive distortions of Major Depression.

These two aspects of psyche-ache, failed belongingness and perceived burdensomeness, are severely aggravated by hopelessness. By hopelessness Joiner means a belief that these conditions are stable, permanent and unchangeable. In 1990 A.T. Beck, the creator of the famous Beck Depression Inventory used in so many hospitals, did a study of the relationship between hopelessness and suicide involving nearly 2,000 psychotherapy outpatients. He found that people with high scores on the hopelessness scale were 11 times more likely to die by suicide.

The fourth psychological condition necessary for suicide is lethality. By this Joiner means the person has past experience enduring and becoming increasingly tolerant of pain, to the point where his fear of death is markedly diminished in comparison with "normal" people. Sometimes the past experience of pain comes inadvertently through car accidents, surgeries or both. By reviewing the literature on suicide, Joiner determined that frequently there is a history of childhood physical abuse and prior suicide attempts.

Contrary to popular belief, the more often a person attempts suicide, the more likely he is to get the job done. Joiner says it is not only possible to get used to the fear and pain involved in self-injury but that getting used to it is also a necessary condition of suicide. He points out that heroin addicts and prostitutes, who endure not just shame but frequent physical pain, have an extremely high rate of suicide.

The Extent of Suicide in the General Population

Suicide is an uncomfortable subject, but it's happening every day in our country in attention-grabbing numbers. The American Association of Suicidality (AAS) collects and publishes the data. Every year in the United State 32,637 people commit suicide. That's 89.4 people per day and one suicide every 16.1 minutes.

The largest group of completed suicides per year by far are white males. They account for 70%. Black females are least likely to commit suicide. Suicides are more common than homicides. In 2005 suicide was the 11th most common cause of death in America with homicides being the 15th.

Although women experience depression at double the rate of men, some 3.8 males die by suicide for every 1 female. Experts account for this difference on several grounds. Males are more likely to express anger with violence (including violence directed against the self) because of testosterone. Males are more likely to possess and use a firearm and they are less likely to talk about their feelings with others.

There are 816,000 annual attempts at suicide, or one attempt every 39 seconds. There is one successful suicide for every twenty-five attempts. According to AAS, each completed suicide intimately affects at least six other people. Thus, every 16.1minutes, someone in the U.S. takes his own life and leaves six survivors. For persons who committed suicide before age 75, there were 967,570 potential years of life lost. For the survivors of the failed attempt and the survivors of the person who succeeded, the impact is catastrophic. Everything changes.

The Extent of Lawyer Suicides

In the United States the national rate of suicide in the general population is 11 persons for every 100,000. In 1992 the National Institute of Occupational Safety and Health (NIOSH) reported that lawyers die by suicide at near double the rate of the general population. In 1995 Peter A. Boxer, M.D., and his colleagues at the Cincinnati office of NIOSH published a paper titled *Suicide and Occupation: A Review of the Literature*. The paper discussed data showing that the five occupations with the highest odds ratios for completed suicide by white males were psychologists, pharmacists, physicians, financial service salesmen and lawyers.

In *Preventing Suicide: A Challenge to the Legal Profession* by Skip Simpson and Paul Quinnett (in *GPSolo*, a publication of the ABA's General Practice, Solo & Small Firm Division, Oct./Nov. 2008 vol. 25, issue 7) the authors mention a Canadian study. It said that Canadian lawyers were committing suicide at a rate five to six times higher than the general Canadian population. The study was published in 1997 by the LPAC (Legal Profession Assistance Conference of Canada) based on term life insurance claims made from December 1, 1994, through November 30, 1996, to the Canadian Bar Insurance Association, one of Canada's largest life insurers for lawyers.

The data revealed that suicide was the third leading cause of death for lawyers in Canada, after cancer and heart attacks, accounting for 10.8 per cent of all deaths. This suicide rate calculated out at 69.3 deaths by suicide per 100,000 population. The rate of suicide in the general population of Canada was 10-14 per 100,000 population, indicating a suicide rate nearly six times that of the general populace.

The data identified lawyers and judges aged 48-65 as the group most at risk. This data spurred a massive national, educational intervention to prevent lawyer suicides in Canada and it was successful. The number of lawyer suicides dropped and never returned to those high levels. To my knowledge there has never been anything approaching a massive, national educational campaign to prevent American lawyers from dying by suicide.

What is the status of lawyer suicide in our country right now? In the fall of 2008 Judge Childers, the Chair of the ABA Commission on Lawyer Assistance Programs, noted that over the past two to three years state LAPs have reported a significant increase in lawyer suicides.

The current recession has led to layoffs of lawyers across the country with a spike in cases of Major Depression and suicide that has grabbed headlines. In 1999 the lawyer unemployment rate was 0.6%, but in 2008 it was 2.6% While these rates should decline to baseline when the economy normalizes, more education and intervention are still sorely needed.

KEY RISK FACTORS FOR SUICIDE AMONG LAWYERS

Major Depression, Alcoholism and Dual Diagnosis

A substantial majority of people who commit suicide have Major Depressive Disorder (MDD). In a landmark study in the United States by William W. Eaton, Ph.D., et al., funded by the Johns Hopkins University and published in the Journal of Occupational Medicine (volume 32, issue 11, pp. 1079-87), data collected from over 100 occupations showed that lawyers suffer from MDD at a rate of 3.6 times higher than that of all other persons generally employed full time.

Alcohol is involved in thirty percent of all completed suicides. Twenty percent of America's lawyers are alcoholics. People with a dual diagnosis (depression and chemical dependency) are the fastest growing group of people who die by suicide, and this includes lawyers. A bottle of alcohol or a handful of pills doesn't provide instant courage.

Rather they short circuit the cognitive constraints of the frontal lobes that give rise to caution, fear, shame and guilt. In the fall of 1998 an article in the *American Journal of Psychiatry* asserted that co-occurring alcohol addiction and major depression represent the most dangerous co-occurring conditions for death by suicide.

Since the rates of depression and alcoholism in lawyers greatly exceed those in the general population, lawyer suicide must be an area of great concern and increased prevention efforts. Indeed, it is the ultimate challenge to our profession and to every person who wants to put time and effort into helping his colleagues lead healthier, saner and more satisfying lives.

Middle-Age Blues

According to the ABA, the average age of lawyers in 1991 was 41 and it jumped to 45 in 2000. Stratified by age, the risk of suicide is highest for lawyers at middle age. Why? Perhaps it comes from realizing it's too late to live out your youthful dreams of who or what you wanted to be. Lawyers may take this especially hard since they come from achievement-oriented families that set high benchmarks for professional accomplishment, peer recognition and annual income.

Middle age is the time when adults are stressed by working, raising children and coping with the declining health of their own parents. Middle age is the time when adults suffer major losses, such as the loss of youthful dreams and the death of one or both parents. These losses can be devastating, especially when the person lacks good social support and has no religious or spiritual beliefs that could buffer the losses.

Putting Up a False Front To Conceal Feelings of Sadness, Pain and Helplessness.

In *How Lawyers Lose Their Way*, the authors say lawyers feel lonely which induces them to contemplate suicide at twice the rate of non-lawyers of comparable backgrounds. Isolation is built into the job as things now stand. Lawyers have to spend a great deal of time alone reading documents, preparing and editing documents, doing legal research and preparing for hearings where they will argue to the court and examine and cross-examine witnesses.

They eat in the car on the way to a deposition or munch mindlessly on some food at their desk rather than lunch with colleagues. Their isolation continues at home and on family vacations, because lawyers have so much work they bring work with them. Lawyers who commute by mass transit tend to read or write legal documents instead of chatting with other people. It's as if they were always in Maxwell Smart's "cone of silence," cut off from others.

We've been taught to look behind the smile for the lies, deceptions and ill intent. We have a hard time believing anyone has integrity or means what he says. We conceive of our job as proving the other side is falsifying the facts, claiming things that don't exist or exaggerating what does exist. This bias toward thinking the worst about others also serves to isolate us.

In *Suicide: The Forever Decision*, Dr. Quinnett says loneliness generates suicidal thoughts. If you're lonely you tend to think no one really cares about you, that no one would miss you if you were dead and you couldn't be less alone even if you were dead, so why not just kill yourself? Loneliness may be based on delusional thinking that if you're a good person, other people owe it to you to come to you and befriend you. This isn't how it works in the real world. Passive people are invisible. If you get out there and start interacting socially with others, and especially if you are giving to others, then the friendships will follow.

No matter how hard you work, and no matter how well you succeed in pleasing your clients, you won't have a social life outside of the office unless you invest in it. About a week before he died the famous actor Rudolph Valentino sought out a journalist to whom he confessed he felt incredibly lonely even though millions of fans worshipped him from afar. All of the praise was on a superficial level. He hadn't let anyone really get to know him. Take the time to befriend someone. It's a crucial investment in your mental health that you can't afford to go without.

The Origin of Hopelessness

We already know from Thomas Joiner that hopelessness greatly elevates the risk of suicide. How does hopelessness originate? Paul Quinnett says hopelessness can come about when bad events strike one after the other (like losing a big case, getting sued by the client and getting negative publicity that sparks loss of new business and loss of friends). When this happens, it can seem like there's no way out, no hope that things will ever change again for the better.

Quinnett says hopelessness can also arise from "learned helplessness" which is a condition in which a person becomes convinced that no matter what he does he cannot control, master or alter his environment for the better. It boils down to the feeling that one has no efficacy in the world. Research done on rats showed that normal rats swam to safety when their environment was flooded, but rats who had been repeatedly shocked with electricity no matter what they did to avoid it, felt helpless and just sank in the water.

When we think of lawyers we imagine people who are doers and high achievers. How could they feel helpless on the inside?

Like other over-achievers, lawyers may be covering up feelings of inadequacy. They are compelled to be busy making things happen outside, because they feel valueless inside. This is typically a consequence of how one was parented. It can come from parents who neglected and ignored you; from parents who caustically criticized everything you did and never praised you; or from parents who did everything for you and discouraged rather than promoted your independence.

Learned helplessness can result from trauma or abuse that leaves you with a victim mentality, something that becomes a way of avoiding personal responsibility and finding a way to blame others for your unhappiness. It can come from the development of addictions (such as alcoholism) to numb one's pain rather than face and master challenges. The more times you escape by drinking and wake up to find your life worse than before, the more helpless and hopeless you feel.

For many lawyers, their egos and their sense of personal power go up and down with their bank accounts. If they have just won a big case they are on top of the world. If they have had a string of losses, a bleak period of no decent new cases, or both, they may torture themselves with self-doubt and start to feel like throwing in the towel. Quinnett says that people rewrite their personal histories to confirm the current feeling. This can be very dangerous when you've been on a losing streak.

How should we respond when we've had a really awful year in our lives, a year marked by a stack of negative, painful events that threaten to overwhelm our capacity to endure pain and adapt to loss? Very often these events will be beyond our control, so we should not blame ourselves for them. Often the best we can do is hold on, remember what we stand for and ride out the storm. This is harder for lawyers, because we have cultivated an image of ourselves as the ones who prepare and plan for every contingency, the ones who spot challenges coming, meet them head-on and always find a way to win.

Thus when life rains shit on us (the same as it does on everyone else), we feel confused, powerless and shaken. "Hey, this wasn't in the script. I'm the guy who helps clients with this stuff. It wasn't supposed to happen to me!" Well, too bad. It does. Quinnett rightly says that things do eventually get better, and sometimes much better. If, in a state of depression, we plot out a future in which only catastrophes will occur, we are engaging in "stink'n think'n" and this is a precursor to suicidal thoughts.

In *Positivity*, Barbara L. Frederickson, Ph.D., says that people with resilient personality styles are able to put the brakes on the downward spiral of depressive thoughts and feelings that follow a terrible event like 9/11. How do they do it? Frederickson says they start out initially with the same shock, fear, sadness and anger that afflict everyone else, but within a short period of time they begin to rebound on account of their own positivity.

Positive people never lose hopefulness about the future. After 9/11 positive people followed the news and experienced feelings of hope, gratitude and joy by learning about the sacrifices made by rescuers and the groundswell of compassion and support for victims from people all over the country.

If you're a pessimist by nature, all is not lost. One thing you can do right now is begin learning to be more optimistic. Positive psychologists like Martin Seligman have books and websites that teach learned optimism. You can begin the daily practice of meditation, which buffers the mind against the depression that flows from loss or trauma. You can cultivate a circle of supportive friends, another buffer against depression.

And, when you have to deal with your own personal 9/11, you'll have some resources. You'll have a reservoir of optimism as well as understanding, acceptance and support from your friends. Your friends will encourage you to get the psychotherapy and antidepressant medication you need. If you're alone, you may try to tough it out like the men described in Terrance Real's book about covert male depression.

Lawyers, the Stigma of Suicide and Failure to Seek Treatment

If you became so depressed that you began ruminating about suicide, would you seek help or would you avoid it due to fear of stigma? Simpson and Quinnett say: "We all know lawyers are not immune to personal crises, mood disorders, and substance abuse problems. We also know that many lawyers, while excellent at referring other distressed people for help, are often loath to seek the same help for themselves.... Self-referral takes courage."

The stigma and shame of admitting to suicidal urges means the number of completed lawyer suicides is small by comparison with the number of lawyers who secretly think about it. One state study published at 52 *Vanderbilt Law Review* 871 (1999) indicated that 11% of lawyers had considered suicide at least once a month during the past year. That's a huge number. Since that study in 1999 the kinds of pressures and the intensity of pressures on lawyers has greatly increased, and one wonders what percentage of lawyers are thinking about suicide right now.

People who dance close to suicide but withdraw from the brink before it's too late find out that life can be better. No matter how bad you feel right now, try to remember how much your family loves you and needs you, and how incredibly sad they would be for the rest of their lives if you took your own. The children of a parent who dies by suicide have an extremely higher than normal risk of being depressed and a significantly higher risk of dying by suicide, too.

How the Cognitive Incapacitation of Severe Depression Blocks Reaching Out

Quinnett says that when we're at our lowest, we have the cognitive powers of a "bug at the bottom of a cup." The bug cannot see its way out. Every time it climbs up the smooth, slippery walls it slides back down. The edge is too high to reach by jumping. It's stuck in the cup. From its perspective there is no way out and it falls into terminal despair.

When we're depressed and alone with our depression, we tend to see no way out of our misery and this can drive us to suicidal thinking. This is the time to speak to friends and go into therapy. The old phrase "two heads are better than one" could not be more applicable to our bug-in-the-cup condition. This is when we most need the outside perspective of others.

Quinnett's advice rings very true to me. In 1986 and again in 1998 I got the news that a male lawyer who was sharing a suite of offices with me had killed himself. One was married. One was single. Both were bright, conscientious lawyers who worked very hard but didn't come out of their offices much to mingle, joke and laugh. Neither man told anyone in our suite that he was horribly depressed and having suicidal thoughts. In both cases, the suicide came as a total shock. Had they reached out, the odds are they would be here with us today. Please don't repeat their mistake.

The Trap of Negative Self-talk

Giving our minds free rein to be negative about all we do is a sure way to grind down our spirits and make us feel utterly dejected. The more we engage in negative self-talk, the more we believe it's true and the more we do it. If you call yourself a failure for making a mistake, and repeat that phrase "I'm a failure" enough times, you will begin to construe everything bad that happens to you as your fault.

When something happens that causes you to feel pain, frustration, disappointment or rejection, your mind will automatically seek to blame someone. People prone to negative self-talk will blame themselves. Examples would be, "I've misplaced my pen again. I must have Alzheimer's," or "I can't believe I lost that slam dunk case to a kid right out of law school. I'm too old for this." We need to be very mindful not to do this, because when we do it too frequently or too strongly we can kick off a terrible depression with suicidal thoughts.

A recent article in *Plaintiff Magazine* pointed out that bright, experienced lawyers over 50 who still have much to offer are losing clients for reasons having to do with appearances (not their competence) that they could easily change. The article mentioned wearing thick glasses and outdated clothes; allowing yourself to grow a belly; muttering aloud about "senior moments" when you forget something; failing to attend conventions and meetings to keep referral relationships alive and stay current on new legal trends; and using antiquated technology.

Sadly the 50-something lawyers interviewed for the article all felt their loss of clients and referral sources was an irreversible consequence of an unpreventable, age-related decline in their competence. The clients and referral sources interviewed for the article said they continued to view the older lawyers as competent; they just got the impression that these lawyers had lost their energy and motivation. Clearly these older lawyers had not outlived their usefulness, and they could turn things around with some help from a consultant. Better to wear contact lenses and update your wardrobe than to take your own life.

If you can start noticing your urge to trash yourself, and learn to be kinder to yourself, you will lead a happier life and lower your risk of suicide. In his essay *Listening From the Heart* in *The Wisdom of Listening*, Rodney Smith recalls counseling a very conscientious hospice nurse. After she expressed acute guilt over not being fully present for her dying patients day after day, Smith asked her if she would ever treat her patients with the same unforgiving attitude she used with herself. Upon reflection, she thanked him and said she would be more compassionate to herself in the future.

De-Toxifying Your Negative Self-Talk

In *Toxic Criticism: Break The Cycle*, counseling psychologist Eric Maisel, Ph.D., says that in every case where we are criticized negatively by another we can either flatly reject it, accept it as potentially useful information couched in needlessly abusive language or adopt it in the form of hostile self-criticism.

For example, let's say the senior partner comes into your office and says, "Frank, I'm sure you know your brief in the Jones appeal is due next week. I trust you'll manage to hand it to me for review on time this time." This criticism is based on prior instances of delay, handing in your appellate briefs at the very last moment. Why were you late before? Are you a procrastinator? Are you a perfectionist who neurotically keeps rewriting an excellent brief?

Perhaps you've done nothing to cause delays. Does your firm overload you because you do high quality work, or you're the only lawyer in their appellate department? Is your secretary out sick a lot? Does your firm use temps that keep having to relearn the wheel? Was the photocopying and delivery of the trial transcript in the last appeal badly delayed for reasons beyond your control? Was that trial transcript over 1,000 pages long and did you have to read the whole thing? Everyone has an inner critic. If Frank's inner critic is negative and hostile, he's going to blame himself for being late no matter what the reasons.

Dr. Maisel treats people with low self-esteem from receiving harsh criticism throughout childhood. He says these people readily accept it when others point out their failings, and they believe it is their moral duty to rub their own noses in such criticism and make themselves suffer. These folks engage in self-flagellation that converts an "unfortunate fact" to a "self-inflicted wound." It's almost as if they are taking the place of an overly critical parent who can't criticize them in person because they live far away or died. Do you do this?

Dr. Maisel sees this kind of toxic self-criticism as a "mental mistake." What is the mistake? Taking a neutral "is" statement (such as "I didn't get your time sheets last week") and turning it to a moralistic "ought" statement about yourself that puts you on the losing end of right/wrong, good/bad or proper/improper.

Let's say you found out the salaries your firm was paying various associates, and you went into your boss's office to ask for a raise. He said no, you got mad and started complaining loudly about certain people being paid more than you when your work was as good or better. You were loud enough to be heard and you hurt other people's feelings. You could berate yourself along the lines of "I'm an oblivious jerk always shooting my mouth off," or you could apologize, learn something and move on. Maisel counsels you to forgive yourself and move on, rather than torture yourself in neurotic fashion.

Dr. Maisel's keys for dealing with toxic self-criticism are: (1) It does not help you make your life meaningful or authentic. (2) It does nothing to help you appraise situations accurately. (3) It excuses you from taking responsibility for your life circumstances, because it portrays you as a failure at everything you try. (4) It is maladaptive because it weakens and incapacitates you. (5) It is not a motivator, but rather a disincentive to act.

Non-hostile criticism from others is simply "information from the world" that can help you create a more beneficial outcome. If you take neutral comments from others to heap negative self-talk on your head, you're not doing anything noble. You're making a mental mistake that leads to inaction and depression.

Defeating the Hostile Inner Critic Once and For All

Robert Nozik, M.D., author of *Happy 4 Life*, advocates standing up to your inner critic as if he were a bully, telling him off and demanding that he support what you're doing rather than tear it down. Nozik's approach is simple but effective.

When your inner critic starts bashing you, tell him, "I'm sick of listening to your insults. If you're not ready to speak to me respectfully and help me with life, then go away and don't come back until you are." After you do this a few times you will notice a pronounced change. Your critic will appear much less frequently and will take a friendlier, more positive tone.

Sustainable happiness coach Aymee Coget, Ph.D., recommends using a journal to convert your inner critic (the voice that tears you down) to an inner colleague who helps you. The journal is a pocket-sized notepad that you carry around at all times. Whenever your inner critic makes a nasty remark about you, you write it down on the left side of the page. Then on the right side of the page you rephrase the remark from the perspective of an inner colleague, who seeks to encourage you to feel good and do your best. When you take the voice of the inner colleague you use kindness, respect and fairness as opposed to the mean, hostile voice of the inner critic.

Let's use an example. Today was your wedding anniversary. Your spouse presented you with a lovely card at breakfast, but you forgot to buy one and don't have a card for your spouse. On the left side write down the hostile remark of your inner critic ("You're a selfish pig who never thinks about others, not even your spouse."). On the right, rephrase the remark from the perspective of your inner colleague ("I'm a caring, considerate person who forgot on this occasion to give my spouse an anniversary card. Next time I'll write a reminder in my calendar beforehand.") Keep using the notebook until you have transformed your inner critic to an inner colleague. Begin using the notebook again, if you're under stress and your old inner critic re-emerges.

Changing Your Self-Image
from Negative to Positive

In *Reflections in the Light*, Shakti Gawain encourages people to begin noticing what kinds of images they hold in their minds about themselves at varying times of day. Are you negative and critical or positive and self-affirming? If you're hard on yourself, try her strategy to like yourself more.

Do this by regularly telling yourself positive, appreciative and loving things based on your strengths (the specific qualities you most appreciate about yourself). Gawain encourages us to release old beliefs and make room for new ones. How do you release the old, negative beliefs?

In *Walking In Balance*, Sun Bear discusses a range of ancient ritual practices for getting rid of your psychological garbage. The Mayans would wade into a river and speak to the flowing water of their anger, sorrow, complaints and troubles and let the moving water carry it away downstream. Some Native American tribes would have dancers come into the village and use chanting, beating drums and rattles to scare off negative forces. Afterward a Corn Maiden would come through sprinkling a blessing of cornmeal throughout the village.

You can develop your own personal ritual to assist with your release of negativity. You can burn things that embody your old set of negative beliefs, like an old photo of you looking unhappy or a pessimistic page from an old journal you kept. Use your imagination and try whatever works.

Some people find that energetic healing helps. If you want to give that a try there are many options that include practitioners of Reiki and sound-healers who use voice, instruments, or both, to rebalance your energies. Working with a healer and using your own rituals are not mutually exclusive. Why not do both, especially when you consider that the only thing you have to lose is your negative self-image?

Practicing Self-Acceptance

The opposite of constantly criticizing yourself is accepting yourself. In *Suicide: The Forever Decision*, Paul Quinnett says some of us (and this includes many lawyers) see their lives in terms of complete success or utter failure. This either precludes self-acceptance or puts it on a very fragile footing. We can only tolerate and learn from our mistakes and setbacks if we are prepared to live life with less than perfect success at anything.

Years of working as a lawyer can strip down our self-images. Perhaps we are not as smart and talented as we once thought. Perhaps our memory capacity and energy level have begun to slip. Is all lost? No. If we feel grateful for what we still have and make the most of it, then we can be happy. If we can laugh at the expectations that once tortured us, so much the better. Laughter heals. Whatever we can laugh at, we can defeat.

In trial, the plaintiff's lawyer will talk about quadriplegia as a living hell involving intense, pervasive and permanent suffering that comes about because a person has lost all mobility. On one level this is true.

Yet no matter how physically limited a person becomes, he can rise above the limitation through self-acceptance and even find happiness. In *Walk in Balance*, Sun Bear mentions a man who was in a terrible car accident and found himself in a head-to-foot body cast. When asked how he was doing, he said pretty well since he could still wiggle his toes. Perspective counts for a lot.

Developing An Accurate Perspective About Yourself

Byron Katie has found a formula to give us perspective on our lives. She is an internationally recognized speaker, writer and workshop leader in the area of self-acceptance. She spent years living with severe depression and rage until she developed a method of self-healing she calls "the work." Ever since she cured herself, Ms. Katie has been teaching others the work.

Like the Buddha, Ms. Katie believes all suffering is mental in nature and originates from delusion. She says our suffering comes from accepting the truth of the false beliefs that spring into our minds when we try to explain our experiences in the world. When accepted as true, these false beliefs place us under terrible stress. Healing occurs when we stand up to these beliefs, question them and liberate ourselves from them. The way you do the work is to ask yourself four questions and answer them with complete honesty, after which you do a "turnaround." You can do the work on your own or attend one of her one-week camps. To learn more go to www.thework.com.

The four questions, which can be applied to any belief about yourself, are: (1) Is this belief true? (2) Can I say absolutely that this belief is true? (3) How do I feel when I believe it to be true? (4) What kind of person would I be like if I did not believe it was true? Then you do the turnaround. Examples of false beliefs are: I need more money to be happy, I'm not as smart as I pretend, I'm weak and have no willpower, I'm too fearful, I'm not a risk taker, no one is interested in what I say, no one notices me and people don't like me.

Let's take one example and run it through the work. Let's say you believe you're not a risk-taker and you make this a self-fulfilling prophecy by holding back from action. Ask yourself if your belief that you're not a risk-taker is true. If it is not, go to question three. If you think it is true, ask yourself if you can absolutely say it's true. It's probably not absolutely true, because you can find examples in your life when you took risks. Going off to college, taking the LSAT, going to law school, taking the Bar Exam, interviewing for and taking a job at a law firm, marrying, buying a house and having kids certainly involve risk-taking don't they?

Now ask yourself how believing you're not a risk-taker makes you feel It probably makes you feel small and weak. Perhaps it even contracts your body. Now ask yourself how you feel when you don't believe it's true. Most likely you feel bigger, stronger, more able and freer to accomplish your dreams.

Now turn the statement "I'm not a risk taker" around to "I am a risk-taker." How does this make you feel? Can you give yourself three true examples from your life when you took substantial risks? Having gone through the exercise, you should be in a position to question the belief that has harmed you and caused you to suffer.

The Role of Friendship in Making Life Good and Preventing Suicide

We are social creatures. We all need friends. We are happier when we are connected and when we use our energy, talents and resources to help others. In *The Big Questions*, Lama Surya Das says: "What I have noticed over the years is that the fewer selfish preoccupations I have and the more connected and thus less separate or boundaried I feel, the better things seem to go for me and the more I find in common with others." On one occasion the Buddha's student Ananda suggested to him that friendship counted for as much as half the Dharma (the sum of Buddha's teachings). Buddha replied "No, it's the whole Dharma."

One antidote to isolation is using your non-work time to join with other people in achieving a positive goal through common effort. Volunteering at your child's school, at a homeless shelter, a food bank, a dog pound or something like it would help. The more we enjoy being part of the human race, the less likely we are to want to leave it.

During discussions in group therapy with other adults who had been hospitalized for suicidal urges, all of us agreed the urges grew worse when we were alone, and they receded when we were socially engaged. Being with friends and with co-participants in positive community activities is not simply a distraction from emotional pain or thoughts of self-harm, it is healing medicine. If you're always working, you can't make new friendships or sustain old ones. Better to cut back on your work hours and leave some time for socializing. Friends are more important than money in the bank when you're depressed and the higher the quality of your friendships, the lower the odds you'll ever become depressed.

When you're feeling a bit suicidal, loneliness increases your risk because it stops you from talking to people who care about you, the same people who could help you see through the delusion that no one really cares. I know now that creating and maintaining social networks is as important as breathing and eating. I used to conserve my energy for my job. I would not bother talking to other people if I didn't need to. What was the point?

These days I tend to strike up conversations with all kinds of people and get great enjoyment out of it. Instead of exercising alone, I take a group class. We've all gotten to know each other. We tell spontaneous jokes and crack each other up. Once a week I meditate with a group and then help make lunch for us. I chat with strangers when I walk my dog on the park district trails and this always leads to enjoyable discussions while we watch our dogs frolic. The world feels friendlier because I'm bringing friendliness to the world. You get what you give.

Intervention—What To Do When a Colleague Appears Suicidal

Even psychiatrists, who are trained experts in spotting suicidal tendencies, sometimes miss the boat. For laypeople like ourselves, figuring out if a colleague is at serious risk of suicide is difficult. We may shy away for fear of being wrong or of making things worse by going about it in a clumsy, offensive fashion.

In July 1999 Dr. Paul Quinnett founded the QPR Institute to study, test and develop teaching modules for suicide-prevention strategies. In

2006 he published the QPR method for training laypeople in suicide prevention strategy after having his method peer-reviewed by AAS and the International Association of Suicidology.

In partnership with Eastern Washington University, QPR has trained more than 700,000 adults in the United States and abroad. To learn more log onto www.qprinstitute.com. The acronym QPR stands for question, persuade and refer. Asking your law firm administrator, managing partner or LAP contact person to get the training for firm members is a very good idea. Training can be done on the Internet.

The Experience of Suicidality Can Help Heal the Broken Self

I want to end this chapter by talking about the positive benefits of surviving a suicidal crisis. While the concept that a suicidal crisis could be of any benefit to anyone may strike you as crazy, it is undoubtedly true.

In *Suicide: The Forever Decision*, Paul Quinnett says that none of us is going to get out of this world alive. The clock is always ticking. It's not a matter of will we die, but of when and how. Is contemplation of suicide always a bad thing or can it be useful? Quinnett, who has counseled many hundreds of suicidal patients, says: "Maybe until we look death in the eye, we cannot live life so well. And maybe, after we have done so, we are stronger for it. Maybe only after we have come close to death, can we come close to life…by talking about [dying] we might come to a better understanding of what life is and what we can do with the days we have left."

In *Unstuck*, a book about surviving depression, Dr. James Gordon has a chapter called "The Dark Night of the Soul." Instead of seeing thoughts of suicide as the utter and irreversible failure of a human being, he sees them as part of "natural process of change and progression." Indeed, they represent a kind of cry or call from deep within a person that the life he is leading is unbearable and must stop. Associated with this is the wish to change and move on, but without the support of others, the "leaden weight of depression" can be overwhelming.

Dr. Gordon reminds us that in Antiquity there were myths regarding people or gods descending to the Underworld, facing a period of darkness and then returning to the surface world enlivened and renewed. He reminds us that forest-dwelling African tribesmen and the Native Americans who lived on the plains were only some of the cultures with rituals that enabled youngsters to become adults by facing fears and terrors in a dark place like a cave or tunnel. Dr. Gordon believes suicidal thoughts are a legitimate topic for discussion, and the worst thing we can do is shame people into silence, because that increases the odds they will take their own lives.

Severe depression is not a cul de sac with no escape. It's not an end point. Well-known Buddhist teachers say it can be a teacher which acts as a springboard to meaning. In *The Big Questions*, Lama Surya Das says: "Without dissatisfaction and uncertainty, what would fuel our quest for enlightenment? And without that quest what would human life be worth?" Elsewhere he bids us to respond to despair by asking: "Why this now? What does it mean/signify/indicate? How is this connected?" When a life of automatic routines and complacent acceptance of dissatisfaction, discontent and dis-ease suddenly falls apart, there is an opening in which you can seize the freedom to change for the better.

According to Hippocrates some people experience a "healing crisis," a moment when the forces of debility and death are wrestling with the forces of health and life, and the potential exists for the patient to triumph because his own will to live and to lead a better life win out over the descent toward oblivion. Albert Camus called suicide the ultimate philosophical question, because it demands that we decide for ourselves whether life is worth living.

Suicidal urges are not a purely biochemical event that should be treated solely by antidepressants. The person who feels like killing himself has unwittingly created a life structure that disconnected him from loving relationships, meaning and joy. The impulse behind suicide is not to kill the human being but to kill off the wholly unsatisfying life the human being feels hopelessly trapped within. Even the best antidepressants can't fix this problem. The person in crisis must address the structure of his life and decide how to change it for the better.

The Joy of Choosing Life After a Suicidal Crisis

Surviving the intense loneliness of living with suicidal thoughts is like being rescued from a deserted island. There is an incredible indescribable joy. Remember how Scrooge felt when he realized he wasn't dead, that Christmas Day wasn't over and there was still time to buy a turkey and celebrate the holiday over dinner with the Cratchet family?

I intend to spend the rest of my life passing along my joy and helping to make other people's lives more joyful, including those of my fellow lawyers. No matter how much people kvetch about what isn't working in their lives, everyone has things that are working, things that could be sources of daily celebration. A wonderful book on how to feel more grateful each day for the gift of life is *Thanks!* by Robert Eammons.

CHAPTER SEVEN: SUGGESTED READING

Eckhart Tolle, *A New Earth: Awakening to Your Life's Purpose* (A Plume Book, 2006)

Robert D. Putnam, *Bowling Alone: The Collapse and Revival of American Community* (Simon & Schuster, 2000)

Brian J. Mahan, *Forgetting Ourselves On Purpose: Vocation and the Ethics of Ambition* (Jossey-Bass, 2002)

Sara Davidson, *LEAP! What Will We Do with the Rest of Our Lives?* (Ballantine Books, 2007)

Steven Johnson, *Mind Wide Open* (Scribner, 2004)

Rita Carter, *Multiplicity* (Little, Brown and Company, 2008)

Paul G. Quinnett, *Suicide: The Forever Decision* (Continuum, 1987)

Mark Johnson, *The Meaning of the Body* (The University of Chicago Press, 2007)

Mark Brady (Editor), *The Wisdom of Listening* (Wisdom Publications, 2003)

Albert Camus, *The Stranger* (Vintage Books USA) 1989 (Matthew Ward's English Translation of the 1942 French novel)

Eric Maisel, Ph.D., *The Van Gogh Blues: The Creative Person's Path through Depression* (New World Library, 2008)

Eric Maisel, Ph.D., *Toxic Criticism: Break The Cycle* (McGraw-Hill, 2007)

Sun Bear, *Walk In Balance* (Simon & Schuster, 1989)

Thomas Joiner, *Why People Die By Suicide* (Harvard University Press, 2007)

PART II

HOW TO CREATE
LIFETIME WELLBEING

Chapter Eight

Rehumanizing your relationships
with empathy and ethics

Physicians, psychologists and neuroscientists who study the effects of how we treat other people say that treating others with compassion and kindness makes us happy. Why? One reason is that our brains have been wired by evolution to experience pleasure when we get along well with others or help others. Evolution also wired our brains to feel stressed when we are in conflict with others. Socialization has conditioned us to feel guilt and remorse when we treat others poorly. Too many lawyers get into bitter feuds with each other in their efforts to win cases for their clients. Bitter feuding never made anyone happy, and if they tell you so, it's a lie.

When we treat people well they give us back the peace and cooperation we want.

They make us feel safer and more relaxed. But when we treat people in a rude, aggressive manner, we rightly expect retaliation in kind—and that expectation produces tension, fear and anxiety. We know what's coming.

What makes people healthy and happy is friendship. The evidence for this is pouring in from every corner of medicine, psychology and neuroscience. The longest longitudinal study of health and wellbeing ever conducted began at Harvard in the 1930s. Researchers followed a group of 238 Harvard undergraduates through graduation, career, marriage, divorce, illnesses, grandchildren and the other big events of their lives. The men have been evaluated by means of medical exams, psychological testing, filling our questionnaires and in-person interviews.

Harvard psychiatrist, George Vaillant, M.D., directed the study for 33 years before publishing *Aging Well* in 2002 to share it's secrets. Dr. Vaillant says that you will not be happy if your life is "all about me" or "keeping up with the Joneses." He says that a happy life involves work, play, friendship and love—with love being the most important. Having followed these people for nearly a half century and measured every influence on their moods, he came away believing that having good, close relationships with friends and family is the strongest, most reliable factor in being happy.

Candace Pert, Ph.D., author of *Your Body is Your Unconscious Mind*, says that every cell in the body has molecular receptors for endorphins. The endorphins are a group of neuro-peptides (short amino acid chains) that stimulate us to feel the highest states of pleasure. Substances that cause the secretion of endorphins include Darvon, Percusset, morphine, heroin and methadone. Experiences that cause the secretion of endorphins in varying amounts include cardiovascular exercise, friendship, mother love, breast-feeding, romantic love, sex and orgasm.

Dr. Pert says that the highest "bliss state" (i.e., the state of utmost happiness a person can achieve) comes from positive relationships with other people. So if you want to be miserable, then hate other lawyers and fight with them as bitterly and as frequently as you can. If you want to be happy, then it's time to adopt empathy and ethics to make your relationships a whole lot warmer. Try being empathic. It won't make you less of a lawyer, and it will make you more of a human being.

What is Empathy?

British anthropologist-psychologist Daniel Nettle distinguishes mentalizing and empathy. Mentalizing is the ability to attribute a mental state to another person and accurately predict what he is thinking. We can know the risks and harms that others face by mentalizing and figuring out what's probably going through their minds. Psychopaths who are utterly lacking in empathy can mentalize and do it well.

To empathize is to imagine what another person is feeling and become affected emotionally through this identification. Thomas Aquinas defined empathy as the heartfelt sympathy for another's distress that impels us to help him. When Henry David Thoreau said, "Could a greater miracle take place than for us to look through each other's eye for an instant?" he had empathy in mind—the capacity to project oneself into the mind of another in such a way as to see *and* feel what the other would.

The Psychological Model of Human Empathy

The 18th century British empiricist David Hume said that morality springs from moral feelings, not abstract moral reasoning from premise to conclusion. Rational reasons to act morally do not compel behaviors in the way that feelings do. Rational people acting from self-interest could do things most people regard as extremely unethical. The makers of the Ford Pinto calculated that selling the car with a side-mounted gas tank without any safety devices to lower the risk of an explosion would be cheaper than paying out all the anticipated wrongful death claims and suits.

Yet, when the average person learns that a mugger shot and killed a peaceful person who freely handed over his wallet to avoid violence, will he not experience moral outrage? Will he not instinctively judge the mugger as bad and the mugger's conduct as wrong? Will he not instinctively demand that the killer be apprehended, put on trial and severely punished? There is an old saying that the mind is for seeing what is true, while the feelings are for understanding what's good.

Moral feelings about what's right or wrong arise automatically without reflection. All normal humans regard feeding starving children as good, and inflicting gratuitous cruelty upon others as bad. After all his travels and investigations, Charles Darwin concluded that all humans share the same set of emotions, and that moral feelings are what set us apart from the other animals. He believed they were the same across time, countries and cultures. He said:

"Of all the differences between man and the lower animals, the moral sense or conscience is by far the most important...It is summed up in that short but imperious word ought, so full of high significance. It is the most noble of all the attributes of man, leading him without a moment's hesitation to risk his life for that of a fellow creature; or after due deliberation, impelled simply by the deep feeling of right or duty, to sacrifice it in some great cause."

The Neurobiological Model of Human Empathy —The Mirror Neuron System

How does the human brain produce empathy? The first major breakthrough in answering this question came in primate research. In 1996 a group of Italian neurophysiologists led by Giacomo Rizzolatti discovered what they called "mirror neurons" in the pre-motor area of the frontal lobes of macaque monkeys. The function of these neurons was to enable monkeys to imitate and learn from each other.

When monkey A grasped, opened and ate a peanut, certain areas of his motor cortex lit up on a brain scan. As monkey B watched monkey A grasp, open and eat the peanut, the very same areas of his brain lit up on the brain scan. When monkey A simply waved his arms (a random, non-goal-directed action), monkey B's brain did not light up. Monkey B's brain only matched Monkey A's brain activity patterns when he observed Monkey A engage in intentional, goal-directed activity.

The Italians named the neurons responsible for this phenomenon "mirror neurons," because the brain of the observing primate mirrored what it saw the active primate doing. In 2003, after years of collaborative work with the Rizzolatti group, Dr. Marco Iacoboni published work showing that a mirror neuron system existed in the human brain and that it was responsible for human empathy.

In the human brain, the mirror neuron circuits connect brain cells located in the inferior frontal gyrus of the frontal lobes; the pre-motor strip where actions are planned out; the parietal cortex which provides the spatial context of actions; the limbic (emotional) areas; and the insula. The insula lies deep within the lateral fissure of the brain that separates the frontal and parietal lobes from the temporal lobe. It's the part of the limbic system that integrates sense perceptions with emotional states. Neurologist Antonio D'Amasio says the insula helps make us conscious of our own feelings.

How do mirror neurons work in practice? Let's say person A sees person B struggling to open and get through a door while holding a big load of cumbersome packages that are about to fall. When person B notices person A behind him, he is wanting and expecting person A to assist him by holding the door open or taking some of his packages. This is because he has functioning mirror neurons and he has assisted others in like situations in the past.

If person A had no mirror neurons and he was totally narcissistic, he would not identify with person B or have any conscious desire to help out. He would not imagine himself in B's shoes. He would not ask himself whether in this situation he would want and expect help from Person A. He would feel nothing and do nothing when person B dropped his packages. B's plight would have no pull on him, and would not cue him to helpful action. He might walk past B or even laugh at him.

Dr. Daniel Siegel works at the Center for Culture, Brain and Development at UCLA on the neurobiology of empathy and has collaborated with Dr. Iacoboni. In his book *The Mindful Brain*, Dr. Siegel says the insula enables us to feel what others feel. While the mirror neurons perceive the intention of another to act, it's the insula that alters our emotional and bodily states to match those we see in the other person, and this attunement (which is called resonance) is what enables us to feel what others feel.

Siegel says the insula is thicker in people who meditate on a regular basis, which appears to correlate with meditators' development of high levels of compassion. In *Welcome To Your Brain*, Dr. Aamodt and Dr. Wang say that in normal ten-year-old children the mirror neuron areas are more active in individuals with higher scores on a test of empathy. They believe that autistic children (who can be intellectually strong while lacking in social warmth, empathy and the ability to communicate with others) have poorly connected mirror neurons and a deficient insula, the part of the brain which is active in processing both one's own emotional state and that of others.

Mark Hauser, the Director of Harvard University's Cognitive Evolutionary Laboratory, has written a book titled *Moral Minds: How Nature Designed Our Universal Sense of Right and Wrong*. Dr. Hauser is convinced that morality springs from an innate moral sense that is not dependent upon moral reasoning from moral principles. He believes the mirror neuron system makes ethical behavior possible. That's because the function of mirror neurons is to enable one person to identify with and empathize with another, which inhibits gratuitous cruelty and promotes reciprocity, helpfulness and personal sacrifice for others.

According to Dr. Hauser: "The mirror neuron system is therefore an important engine for simulating emotions and thoughts—for getting under someone else's skin, feeling what it is like to be another human." Its functions "are essential to our moral faculty as part of the support team."

For example, "When we evaluate whether an action is fair or whether inaction leading to harm is justified, we often simulate, in our mind's eye, what it would be like to be someone else. Our first-person experiences of the world are translated into their third-person experiences—what we feel and think is functionally equivalent to what they feel or think. We decide whether something is fair by imagining not only what we would exchange, but what someone might exchange with us. We decide whether it is permissible to harm someone else by imagining what it would be like to be harmed or to watch someone else engaging in a harmful act."

Being Empathic Will Increase Your Success Rather Than Making You a Doormat

Cultivating empathy is the way to overcome the pressure you feel to dehumanize the opposing party and his lawyer in order to win. With empathy you can recognize in a feeling way that the other side is composed of other people just like us with same needs and feelings.

Being empathic does not make you a doormat for more aggressive lawyers.

India's most famous lawyer Gandhi didn't have to fire a single shot to bring the British Empire to its knees. His public display of complete integrity was more powerful than a repressive, brutal regime. Much of the aggressiveness of your adversary comes from his anger over not being heard or respected. Once you really listen and show respect, your adversary will calm down and become your colleague.

The Role of Empathy in Human History Supports Lawyers Being Empathic

Scientists who study evolution say that what distinguishes human beings from other species, and what has enabled us to survive and flourish, is our remarkable capacity for empathy, compassion, cooperation and self-sacrifice for the good for the group. People who believe the survival of the fittest means the strongest, most aggressive animal in the herd lives longer and produces more offspring misinterpret Darwin. The way he meant it, natural selection is a driving force behind evolution in species based upon how well the characteristics of particular animals adapt them to a changing environment.

Darwin said that, as the environment changes, animals better suited to survive those changes, due to chance genetic variation, are the ones most likely to live on. Darwin never meant that the biggest, strongest creature will always win out over the smaller, weaker one. If that were so the dinosaurs would still rule, and human beings (if they existed at all) would be dinosaur chow.

Darwin had ten children, whom he loved dearly. His shipmates on the *Beagle* during their five-year voyage considered him the kindest, warmest person aboard. In *The Descent of Man*, Darwin wrote that sympathy and maternal instincts are not just the foundation of morality, but the sine qua non of evolution, since they ensured that vulnerable young survived to an age where they could reproduce.

Daniel Nettle, author of *Personality: What Makes You The Way You Are*, explains the appearance of "pro-sociality" in human evolution as follows: "Our ancestors lived in small, long-lasting social groups performing collaborative tasks, where the benefit of membership was high, and the cost of being ostracized near fatal. Under such circumstances, it would pay to always be a good group member, and avoid at all costs getting any kind of reputation for anti-sociality. In other words, this situation produces the unusual selection pressure whereby there are strong self-interest benefits to being very attentive to the interests of others, because that makes you a valued and secure group player."

The Benefits of Empathy

Einstein said the most important decision you'll ever make is whether you live in a hostile or a friendly universe. Between the extremes of Christ (who would give a stranger the shirt off his back) and the psychopath (who delights in conning people out of their money) lies the mass of humanity.

The more empathic you are the more the world looks, feels and becomes like a place where we can all get along despite disagreements. The less empathic you are, the more the world looks and feels like a battleground where everyone else's gain is your loss. In this world you're always at risk and can't expect help from anyone. Empathic people express concern for other people and have friends. When they become sick, injured or disabled, people rush to their aid. When narcissistic people fall on hard times, they're forced to deal with survival alone. Caring for nobody but themselves, they get no mercy.

Moving From Empathy to Ethics— What Makes Our Actions Ethical?

Peter Singer is an enormously influential, contemporary philosopher in the area of ethics who now works at the Center for Human Values at Princeton University. In *Practical Ethics*, Singer rejects the pursuit of self-interest as the foundation of ethics, precisely because it lets us rationalize abusing others or violating their rights in situations where doing so secured a more favorable outcome for us. Singer says the real distinction between ethics and pure egoism (I will do only what pleases me regardless of how it affects you) is that ethical principles must embody elements of impartiality and universality.

Ethical decision-making takes account of the existence of other persons; the needs, interests and welfare of other persons; how the actor's actions will impact other persons; and the paramount values of the actor's society. Singer concludes that while ethical decision-making does not exclude consideration of one's own desires and interests, it embodies a desire to do the right thing, to act from a concept of duty toward others. Along these lines, German philosopher Arthur Schopenhauer said that "compassion is the basis of all morality," and the Jewish Talmud asked, "If I am only for myself, what am I?"

Peter Singer uses the psychopath as a contrast to put the ethical life in starker outline. "The psychopath's life can now be seen to be meaningless in a way that a normal life is not. It is meaningless because it looks inward to the pleasures of the present moment and not outward to anything more long-term or far-reaching." What then is an ethical life all about?

Singer says, "To live ethically is to think about things beyond one's own interests. When I think ethically I become just one being, with needs and desires of my own, certainly, but living among others who also have needs and desires.... Essentially, this means that in considering whether I ought to do something I must if I am thinking ethically, imagine myself in the situation of all those affected by my action (with the preferences that they have). At the most fundamental level of ethical thinking, I must consider the interests of my enemies, as well as my friends, and of strangers as well as my family."

A sociopath perceives no dignity in others. He sees ethical rules as an attempt by others to protect themselves and their property. A sociopath will comply with or fake compliance with ethical rules only to get what he wants at the expense of others. An empathic person perceives that all persons have dignity, and sees ethical rules as manifestations of that dignity. So long as everyone plays by the rules, an empathic lawyer maintains the ability to see opposing counsel and his client as fellow persons who are always deserving of respect and fairness no matter how sharply contested their legal dispute.

An empathic lawyer won't seek sanctions for a minor, harmless infraction. But he's no sap. If he learns that opposing counsel has deliberately broken laws pertaining to discovery, evidence or the conduct of trial to gain an unfair advantage, he will certainly bring it promptly to the attention of the court with all due vigor and seek the full protection of his client. On the other hand he won't demand the guillotine if the other lawyer borrows his pen and forgets to return it.

Empathy and Ethics Must Extend
Beyond Our Clients to the Whole Legal System

Being a little empathic or a little ethical is like being a little preg-nant or a little dead. It can't happen. Never will. The Dalai Lama has been asked repeatedly how he developed his incredible level of compassion. He always answers the same way. The Dalai Lama tells people that many times a day he prays that *all beings* should experience peace, freedom, health and joy. He does not restrict his good wishes to the Tibetans and curse the Chinese. He builds his compassion by extending it to every person on Earth. He even thanks the Chinese for challenging his ability to have compassion for all persons.

While the Dalai Lama is a special case (a person who is deservedly a legend and a source of inspiration and hope to millions of people), we don't have to be the Dalai Lama to start acting like him. All it takes is a shift. Right now so many of us practice empathy only toward our clients. We suppress empathy for the other side, because we think giv-ing empathy to our adversary would hurt our client, because he doesn't deserve it or he won't give us any back.

While we strive to be squeaky clean ethically when it comes to dealing with our own clients, we feel tempted to engage in tactics of questionable ethics when it comes to our adversary. We may even cross the line based on the assumption that it's OK, because the other side is getting witnesses to shade the truth in depositions, hiding documents from us or otherwise cheating. But this is just an assumption. How do we really know?

We justify reserving empathic, ethical treatment for our clients and giving the other side hell by telling ourselves our job is to win. We think the people on the other side have a duty to look out for and take care of themselves. This antagonistic, war-like attitude between lawyers on opposing sides is a deviation from our in-born wiring to be empathic and it puts all of us in the red zone of unhealthy, chronic stress.

Functional Magnetic Response Imaging (fMRI) investigation of the human brain by neuro-economist William Harbaugh has shown that charitable donating causes the brain's pleasure center (the nucleus accumbens) to light up. The test subjects who donated money to a food bank instead of keeping it for themselves, experienced what Harbaugh called a "warm glow" as dopamine flowed into their nucleus accumbens. While Jack the Ripper may have had pleasure center activation while killing women, most of us experience the "warm glow" Dr. Harbaugh talks about while doing something good for others. Most of us experience acute stress when we threaten, taunt, oppress, harass or abuse others to win at something. The money may be good, but the victory feels hollow and we leave a lot of unhappy people in our wake.

Three Barriers to Extending Empathy and Ethics Outward From Our Clients

As it now exists, we have a legal system with selective empathy and selective ethics. Our clients receive our best intentions and behavior while our adversaries receive our worst. This one-way street has contributed to the suffering of all lawyers. It's time to identify the barriers to extending empathy and ethics and to dismantle them so all of us can experience wellbeing.

(1) Personal Differences.

Empathy is easy to feel when someone just like us suffers. The lawyers who attack each other seem alike to an outsider, yet to each other they are vastly different. Why? Because they have very different ideas about how their cases are to be resolved, and they tend to notice and magnify petty differences in how they dress, speak, stand, walk, question a witness, etc.

In *The Empathy Gap*, J.D. Trout mentions a brain-imaging study done at Princeton which checked for how people react to images of people from other social and ethnic groups—with pride, envy, pity or disgust. When shown an image of homeless people, the test subjects had no measurable reaction in their medial prefrontal cortex, which signified they did not regard the homeless as part of society.

Obviously the homeless are as human as we are, yet because they are jobless, do not earn money, do not own homes, do not wear nice clothes and do not shower, very few us can empathize with them. Trout says the most effective way to cut through this emotional disconnect would be to spend some time on the street as a homeless person. No Congressman is going to make ending hunger a priority until he feels hungry, and this is unlikely to happen. Congressmen are very well fed.

Lawyers have done a good job of solidifying their sense of difference by creating separate organizations for plaintiff and defense lawyers, restricting lectures to members only and giving awards to members only. How can we bridge these differences? Meditation is a great way to know in the depth of your being that the human family is one and that all differences between us exist on a superficial level. We could try opening up lectures to lawyers from both sides and having retreats where lawyers from both sides spend time under friendly circumstances.

(2) The Risk of Extending Empathy and the Status Quo Bias

No doubt some lawyers worry that allowing themselves to feel empathy for the other side could weaken their resolve to fight for their client. As J.D. Trout points out, empathy is a feeling, but by itself it does not mandate action or give rise to action. He says a major barrier to converting empathy to action is the status quo bias. This refers to the idea that since things have always been a certain way they will always be that way.

Thus lawyers may agree that while allowing ourselves to experience empathy for each other is a good idea, our adversary system has always opposed it, and it always will, so what's the point? The real point is that repeating the errors of the past benefits no one. Empathy opens the heart but does not reduce your alertness, your intelligence, your legal skills or your loyalty to your client and your desire to do well for him.

Empathic lawyers have broad vision and notice a great deal, while angry lawyers have tunnel vision and notice very little. Empathic lawyers are more in control of their actions

than the angry ones who are often out of control and irrational. If you agree it's in our best interest to be empathic to all
people in the legal system, then let's change the system. Don't
let the status quo bias stop you.

(3) The Lack of Moralnets

Peter Singer defines "moralnet" as a group of like-minded
families, neighbors and friends in a community who provide
each other with guidance and support. Moralnets help their
members make ethical decisions in line with what they regard
as the right thing to do. In deliberating which action would
serve justice, moralnets resemble juries, but juries are a mix of
strangers who come together one time for one case, whereas
moralnets function as ongoing communities to help their own
members whenever needed.

Singer notes that with people constantly uprooting and
crisscrossing the country for better jobs, more affordable housing and decent schools, the number of moralnets has steadily
dwindled. He concludes that consequent to the loss of moralnets there has been a rise in crime, drug and alcohol abuse,
domestic violence and mental illness.

Do you have anything resembling a moralnet in your
law practice? When you flag a serious ethical issue in a case
that requires making a choice, are there any lawyers at your
office you can go to for advice? Does your law firm even have
a protocol for dealing with ethical issues or an internal ethics
committee to weigh the pros and cons of alternative actions?
All too often we are on our own in these matters, and taking
the ethical path may seem unappealing because it slows and
complicates the decision and it can involve passing up business opportunities that would bring in easy money but don't
pass the moral smell test. Ethics are a social matter, and ethical
decisions are best made in a social context with feedback from
trusted people.

Ten Ways for Lawyers to Grow Empathy and Ethics in Their Daily Practice

(1) Build a Moralnet to Roundtable Ethical Issues on a Continuous Basis.
This can be done in-house at a large or medium firm. If you are a solo, you can build one by inviting other solos to join. Given the practical difficulties of getting people together, you could use the Internet to create a virtual moralnet. A model for this is www.stickk.com, which was established by a Yale economics professor who wanted social pressure to help him keep to his commitment to quit smoking cigarettes. His website makes use of Commitment Contracts and a virtual society of Internet users to goad people to keep their commitments.

(2) Use the Golden Rule.
Moralnets are useful when you have to make a rather complex decision in the future, and there is time to weigh all the pros and cons with others. Many ethical decisions we are called upon to make are relatively simple and must be made instantaneously. When making such decisions use the Golden Rule and the Hippocratic principle of doing good if possible, but at least doing no harm. If your only reason for contesting your adversary's claim, defense or motion is to do him harm (i.e., putting him through extra time, effort and cost to get what he is clearly entitled to), you are acting unethically.

(3) Meditate on a daily basis to develop compassion for others.

(4) Increase your skills as a listener.
A great book on listening that lawyers can really benefit from is *Are You Really Listening? Keys to Successful Communication* by Paul J. Donoghue, Ph.D., and Mary E. Siegel, Ph.D. The authors say that when others speak we don't take in their

message because we are always distracted by something. We are rushing to get someplace, we are worried the ketchup stain on our shirt is visible or we are replaying an argument we had with a family member earlier that morning. They also say that because of our need to be liked we scan the statements of others for content that praises or affirms us. If another person says anything negative, we are likely to turn off and stop listening even if the negative statement was not about us, because we assume it was about us.

Donoghue and Siegel say that lawyers make poor listeners because they have a tendency to interrupt people and because they are focused on identifying and solving the person's problem, rather than getting to know the person and really listening to his concerns. People want to be heard. They want someone to sit back, shut up and let them speak. This enables them to articulate what they are really feeling, become more conscious of their true feelings and make choices based on them.

Studies show that bartenders make better listeners than trained psychological counselors. When you listen well without distraction, judgment or interruption, the speaker will feel good about you. He will trust and like you. If you keep cutting him off to tell him how to solve his problem, he will dislike you and want to end the meeting. Attentive, supportive listening generates empathy and connects us with others.

(5) Increase your understanding of the perspectives and motivations of others.

Wanting to care about others is a start, but it's not sufficient. In *Blind Spots*, Madeleine L. Van Hecke, Ph.D., stresses that we also have to emotionally grasp other people's perspectives. All too often, we start out with the intention of cooperating with others, but we run into a wall when we misunderstand them or they misunderstand us, because we are "poles apart."

By poles apart Dr. Van Hecke means that the people who are interacting have ways of life, attitudes or sets of beliefs which occupy the opposite ends of a spectrum. Israeli and Palestinian hardliners each believe they are solely entitled to inhabit all the land from the West Bank to the border of Jordan and that the other side should be driven out by any means possible. In their native languages they refer to each others as dogs and pigs.

For people who are poles apart it seems inconceivable how another human being could see the same world so differently. Can this bridge be gapped, and if so, how? Dr. Van Hecke is a licensed clinical psychologist who teaches at North College in Naperville, Illinois, and leads workshops for Open Arms Seminars. Every year she requires her psychology students to write a Poles Apart paper to teach them how to bridge the gap.

The assignment involves identifying a group of people poles apart from the student, and then reading published personal accounts by members of the group or interviewing members of the group. Afterwards, the student must write a paper expressing how members of the group see the world and why they believe what they do. The paper must demonstrate an empathic understanding, not just an intellectual one.

What was fascinating for Dr. Van Hecke when she first handed out this Poles Apart assignment was how frightened and uneasy her students were to take part.

Why? The students feared that if they allowed themselves to really understand in a visceral sort of way how others could believe, think or live in ways that they had always found offensive and deplorable, they would be transformed—they would lose their own values and come to adopt those of the morally repellent group.

This prediction did not come true. What did happen was that the students were able to see the world in a radically different light from the eyes of the group under study, while retaining enough distance to retain their core values and avoid agreeing with the positions and actions of the others.

Dr. Van Hecke says this exercise in empathy enabled her students to experience their polar opposites as human beings who were following their own consciences, without passing judgment on them as being stupid, obtuse, callous, mean or evil. This was transformative in that the gulf between them and their opposites was no longer a divide between clear truth and falsity, pure good and evil, complete rightness and wrongness or justice and sheer injustice. The students who completed the assignment in a sincere, honest way could now see the other as holding a position the other believed in for reasons he found persuasive, while disagreeing with the other for different reasons the students found more persuasive.

(6) Do not allow technology to compromise your empathy and ethics.

Today email is the primary method of communication for many lawyers. Does email facilitate or distort communication? I think we are deluding ourselves when we believe that email is a superior or even an adequate method of communication (except for clerical and scheduling matters). It cannot replace personal contact. How many times have you had a nice conversation with another lawyer after a deposition only to return to your office and get a scathing email from that person which badly misstates the conversation.

Electronic communication is more likely to be polarizing than face-to-face communication. This is because it is written in isolation on a screen and you are not facing the human being you are addressing so you are less likely to inhibit self-righteous irritation or anger. Emails are deceptively easy and quick to write. After indulging your anger by pressing SEND you neither see nor hear an immediate response, but a response will come later that could bring you guilt, regret, even fear. It's always a good idea to save such emails in draft, walk around the block and come back to review them yourself or with a colleague before pressing SEND.

(7) **Read about and reflect upon the lives of empathic people who made personal sacrifices to help others and be inspired by the good they did.**

You can make up your own list. Examples would be St. Francis, Father Damien, Harriet Tubman, Mahatma Gandhi, Raoul Wallenberg, Albert Schweitzer, Andrei Sakharov, Rosa Parks, Martin Luther King, Jr., Mother Teresa, Nelson Mandela and the Dalai Lama.

(8) **See your actions in the context of the larger community.**

It's time to stop seeing the legal system as a set of rules that exist to be manipulated with the most clever to win it all. The reality is that the human community is all inclusive genetically, biologically, socially and spiritually. Our commonalities are enormous. Our differences are miniscule. It's time to see our actions within the larger community, and when we do, it becomes harder to treat some people worse than others.

(9) **See your intellect, verbal skills, education and training as gifts to be shared with others in the community.**

Einstein readily acknowledged that all he did in physics was made possible by standing on the shoulders of his predecessors. Our lives, our bodies, our brains, our intellects, our passions, our talents—these are all gifts. None of us created the events that led to our birth or the genetically programmed cells that gave us our capacities. Our childhoods and our youths were shaped largely by the nurturing of our parents and by the training and opportunities afforded to us by our schools, our culture, our society and our government's policies.

If you don't believe me, consider this. Were you born with a dull, normal or a superior IQ? Did you grow up with a healthy brain or did you inherit an array of learning disabilities? Could you see or were you blind? Did you attend underfunded public schools that had leaky roofs, outdated textbooks and unqualified teachers or did you attend an elite private high school? Were you 18 when our country was at war and had a draft, so that you got shipped off to Vietnam and came home with just one arm and PTSD, or did you turn 18 at a time of peace, prosperity and abundant opportunity for young people?

Did you grow up in a stable home environment with loving parents who hugged you, tucked you into bed at night and read to you? Was your mother a neglectful crack addict or your father a raging alcoholic who beat you and screamed at you? Did your father gamble all his money away or did he put money away each year into a fund so you could go to college? Did you have parents who routinely praised you or blamed and shamed you? These chance variations at play in our lives are but a drop in the ocean of circumstances that determine the nature and extent of the gifts we have been blessed with and the hardships thrust upon us.

Lawyers who take credit for all they have achieved are denying the gift nature of existence. Being grateful for all the gifts we receive on a daily basis will have a positive impact. It enables us to appreciate all those who have helped us get where we are today. Instead of keeping all the fruits of our labor or sharing only with our nuclear family, we become eager to help others. Once we see our mental abilities (such as superior memory and verbal fluency) as gifts, we are motivated to share them, and enjoy sharing them, in a way that benefits others, not just ourselves. Like the ancients before us, if we give thanks for our mental powers, we will nourish them, and they will flow abundantly without ever running dry.

(10) Design a law firm culture that rewards empathic, ethical conduct.

The managing partners of a law firm have the responsibility to set the level of ethics, fair play and compassion toward others expected of their associates and staff. They can build a law firm which places a high value on empathic, ethical conduct or they can build the legal equivalent of Darth Vader's Death Star.

Skeptic Magazine founder and author Michael Shermer has analyzed the implosion of Enron and the flourishing of Google. He traces them to the guiding vision of their leaders. According to Shermer, Enron's Jeff Skilling paid bonuses to people who engaged in ruthless competition and fired people who refused to be greedy and selfish. Google has always been a pro-social company with the mantra "Don't be evil." Google's website has a code of conduct, written by its founders Sergey Brin and Larry Page, which says:

"Being a Googler means holding yourself to the highest possible standard of ethical business conduct. This is a matter as much practical as ethical; we hire great people who work hard to build great products, but our most important asset by far is our reputation as a company that warrants our users' faith and trust. That trust is the foundation upon which our success and prosperity rests, and it must be re-earned every day, in every way, by every one of us....We compete, but we don't cheat." By sticking to this code Google has earned tremendous employee loyalty and business success.

Envisioning an Empathic Law Practice

Being empathic means sincerely considering what your opponents have to say. It means you're open to the possibility they are sharing their perspective in a truthful way to advance what they perceive as legitimate interests. Being empathic means you don't assume your adversary is acting from evil motives or trying to cheat you. It means you give serious consideration to their point of view, ask questions for clarification and take time to respond. You don't say no automatically.

While empathy requires you to imagine yourself in your opponent's shoes, it doesn't demand that you waive important rights of your clients or forsake diligent efforts to secure your client's rights. Empathy doesn't force you to conceal your disagreement and allow your opponent's erroneous arguments to stand in the name of harmony. Cooperation, reasonableness and civility will not emasculate you as a lawyer. Instead, this style of law practice will put you and opposing counsel at ease. It builds rapport, trust and mutual respect in place of discord, distrust and scorn.

What would an empathic law practice look like? You would patiently hear out your opponent even if your initial response is to disagree and feel annoyed. You would routinely grant him reasonable continuances that did not materially prejudice your client. You would direct your conversations with him to the facts and the legal issues, and refrain from making personal comments, especially the kind likely to be perceived as rude, offensive or hurtful.

If sought by opposing counsel, you would embrace the use of procedures that reduce the duration and cost of litigation so long as they are beneficial to your client or do your client no harm. If opposing counsel accidentally sends you confidential material, you would not open and read it, but would promptly notify him of the mistake and make arrangements to return it.

You would not use superior resources to punish the other side simply for daring to oppose you without regard to the merits of their position. You would not win cases by so overburdening the other side with discovery requests, motions and other paperwork as to break their backs. You would not ridicule opposing counsel in briefs or oral argument in hopes of winning a legal point by making him look incompetent. You would refuse to win by painting a false or misleading picture of the adverse party for the decision maker even though you could do it by cherry-picking particular facts and ignoring others.

CHAPTER EIGHT: SUGGESTED READING

Paul J. Donoghue, Ph.D., and Mary E. Siegel, Ph.D., *Are You Really Listening? Keys to Successful Communication* (Ave Maria Press, Inc., 2005)

Jon Kabat-Zinn, *Coming To Our Senses* (Hyperion, 2005)

Peter Singer, *How Are We To Live?* (Prometheus Books, 1995)

Jacob Needleman, *Money And The Meaning Of Life* (Currency Doubleday, 1991)

Marc D. Hauser, *Moral Minds: How Nature Designed Our Universal Sense Of Right And Wrong* (Harper Collins Publishers, 2006)

Daniel Nettle, *Personality: What Makes You The Way You Are* (Oxford University Press, 2007)

Peter Singer, *Practical Ethics* (Cambridge University Press, 1979)

J.D. Trout, *The Empathy Gap* (Penguin Group, 2009)

Lewis Hyde, *The Gift* (Vintage Books, 2007) (25th Anniversary Edition)

Lou Marinoff, Ph.D., *The Middle Way* (Sterling, 2007)

Michael Shermer, *The Mind of the Market: Compassionate Apes, Competitive Humans and Other Tales from Evolutionary Economics* (Henry Holt/Times, 2008)

CHAPTER NINE

Communicating without verbal violence to meet your needs and the needs of others

The Importance of Communication for Wellbeing

COMMUNICATION IS THE MOST frequent and essential activity that lawyers engage in day in and day out. Virtually everything we do involves communication, either expressive (writing, speaking, gesturing) or receptive (reading, listening, observing). Football players throw, catch and run with a ball. We communicate.

Our words matter. What we say can heal or hurt. It can be a balm to the wounds of the parties and bring them closer or act like salt in their wounds and push them farther apart. Whether we use our words to reach out or to spew anger and dump our crap on others, it's crucial to recognize our responsibility for what we say. We decide what comes out of our mouths. It's that simple. Claiming that something the other lawyer did made you say something hurtful is a cop-out which ignores your accountability.

When you use communication selfishly (solely as a tool to get people to give you want you want), communication can backfire by triggering suspicion, resistance, defensiveness and hostility in others. When you communicate as a means of impressing or overwhelming others by showing them how learned, perceptive or brilliant you are, you're likely to succeed in alienating them.

Communication can be used constructively. It can be used to learn about and connect with others. It can be used to find points of commonality with others and to foster cooperation that benefits both sides. When you are truly interested in and open to what others are feeling and what they have to say, real connection is possible. The openness requires that you feel secure and relaxed in the presence of others rather than threatened.

Why might you feel threatened? Perhaps you fear the other will influence or affect you and get you to see the merit of other points of view. While such fears are understandable, if you want to make communication an act of human connection, it is imperative to step out of your tight, closed shell and make yourself vulnerable. For some of us hearing another lawyer dispute our position is like hearing fingernails scratch against a blackboard. This presupposes I'm always right and he's always wrong, so his words amount to intolerable noise. The truth is that there are many ways to interpret the same data, and disagreement is natural, even inevitable. Yet with goodwill on both sides, you can have a civilized, fruitful discussion.

What's Wrong With How Lawyers Communicate Now?

A substantial amount of communication between lawyers is abrasive, unpleasant and either causes or exacerbates conflict. It's common for one lawyer to send another a lengthy letter lecturing him on what a jerk or what a know-nothing he is, and why everything he does or says is wrong. It's common for one lawyer to fire off a letter with a laundry list of punitive measures he will take against the other lawyer if the other lawyer doesn't agree to his terms. These kinds of communication bristle with anger and barely masked violence.

At best, lawyer-to-lawyer communication these days is impersonal and disconnected. Each side makes a little speech while the other side ignores it and scoffs or takes umbrage and attacks it. How many times have you tried and failed to get opposing counsel to look you in the eye and sustain eye contact during mediation while you spoke from the heart about your client? Was he looking away to fiddle with a paper clip, taking notes, doodling or conferring with someone else instead?

An Alternative System of Communication that Connects People

If we are going to make progress we need a system of communication that connects people. The good news is that we don't have to invent it from scratch. One already exists. It's called Nonviolent Communication or NVC for short. It's been used successfully for decades to enhance the lives of individuals and to resolve conflicts that involve everything from gangs to labor unions, major corporations, public institutions and national governments.

A History of Nonviolent Communication

Marshall Rosenberg grew up in a tough Detroit neighborhood where empathy was in short supply and gang violence was common. As a young man he pondered long and hard about what aspects of the human experience bred so much conflict, hatred and violence. He sought a way for people to connect and peacefully cooperate in making each other's lives wonderful, not miserable. This motivated him to get a doctorate in clinical psychology from the University of Wisconsin in 1961. In his last year of the program he studied with Carl Rogers, one of the most influential and highly regarded of all American psychologists. Rogers is best known for developing the client-centered approach to psychotherapy and counseling.

During the 1960s Marshall Rosenberg began developing a new system for communicating to promote peace which he called nonviolent communication. Rosenberg recognized that people's intent behind communication is to get their needs met. For instance, all people need understanding, consideration, respect, trust, acceptance and appreciation. The problem was that how people communicated thwarted the meeting of their needs and degenerated into angry clashes. Rosenberg designed NVC to explain why this occurred, and to teach people a new model of communication that would enable them to avoid bitter conflict in getting their needs met. His hope was to teach communication skills that would affirm and enrich everyone's life.

In 1984 Rosenberg founded the Center for Nonviolent Communication (CNVC). Rosenberg has written numerous books on

NVC, including his best-selling introduction to the practice of NVC called *NVC, A Language of Life* (2nd ed.) released in 2003. Rosenberg's CNVC is an international nonprofit peacemaking organization which now has more than 200 certified NVC trainers in dozens of countries. NVC has many offices in the United States. You can find them at www. cnvc.org.

While NVC acts to help solve conflicts between institutions, anyone can sign up for an NVC course and learn this method of communicating—even lawyers. NVC can be applied to any type of work setting (including law offices). Married couples and parents have used it to repair damage from years of arguing and start fresh.

An Overview of Nonviolent Communication

Rosenberg teaches it's important to feel what is "alive" inside you before you speak. By that he means take a moment, breathe and get in touch with your feelings before speaking. Don't rush impulsively to speak the first words that come into your head, as they may distort, not clarify, what you're feeling. Rosenberg noticed that many people have an impoverished vocabulary for their feelings. They can say I like this or I don't like that, I want this or I don't want that and very little else. To help people articulate their feelings, Rosenberg supplies a long list of feeling words in his book.

For Rosenberg, NVC serves life by using empathy to connect people in a reciprocal attempt to meet each other's needs. In his view life is at its most wonderful when people have so much compassion for each other's needs, they're not only willing to listen to each other articulate their needs, but also help each other get their needs met. Violent communication is communication that blocks the natural flow of our compassion and disconnects us from others. Communication can be violent without speaking of or intending to commit physical harm.

Communication is violent when you speak only to accuse, criticize or verbally attack another. Anytime you use words to coerce, manipulate, abuse or degrade others, you're engaging in violent communication, because you're not respecting the other's humanity and you are not doing anything to serve their interests or enhance their lives. Rosenberg has used the terms "life-alienating" and "life-denying" to describe communication that uses naked power or manipulation to get your needs met, something that turns the other person into an object.

Rosenberg says words can be windows to or walls around our hearts. How? Words are tools that can either meet our needs or thwart the meeting of our needs by generating misunderstanding and conflict. When we listen to another speak, we have a choice between focusing on the surface content of what they say (the who, why, when, where and how) or focusing on what is moving their heart. For Rosenberg our hearts are alive with feelings and these feelings are direct expressions of whether our basic human needs are or are not being met.

For instance we feel joy when people meet our need to be appreciated for our many contributions to our law firm. But you would likely feel anger if you stayed late at the law office every night for two weeks to assist trial counsel behind the scenes with paperwork, but he never thanked you. Rosenberg sees feelings as clues to the status of our needs, much like the red light on our dashboard tells us the oil is low in time to avoid overheating and ruining the engine.

What are examples of universal human needs? A partial list from NVC literature includes: the need for connection (understanding, compassion, acceptance, community, love); competence (mastery, effectiveness, growth); meaning (learning, creativity, contribution, hope); autonomy (choice, space, respect); peace (beauty, ease, harmony); honesty (authenticity, integrity, presence); celebration (joy, play); and physical needs (shelter, nourishment, rest, touch).

Rosenberg says that when our needs are met, we will experience one or more of these positive feelings: hopeful, relieved, comfortable, glad, touched, moved, eager, thankful, joyous, stimulated or trustful. When our needs are not fulfilled, we are likely to feel confused, puzzled, embarrassed, frustrated, distressed, nervous, irritated, annoyed, angry, sad, discouraged or hopeless.

NVC stresses it is wrong to blame others for our feelings, because others cannot cause our feelings. They can only trigger our feelings by acting in a way that meets or does not meet our needs. It is up to us as individuals to recognize what we are feeling and identify why—in terms of which of our needs has or has not been met. Sometimes we need help doing this. That's when it's very helpful to have another person who is trained in NVC ask us questions to prompt us toward this recognition.

Let's say my paralegal arrived later than his usual start time on a big day at the office when I asked him to come earlier than usual. NVC says it would be a mistake for me to say, "You've made me angry by coming in late today." Clearly such a statement would alienate the paralegal. Instead I could say, "When you came in late today you weren't meeting my need for order, so I'm feeling anxious about completing our work on time for a client who is depending on us." The paralegal also needs order in his life. He is likely to get the message and accept it when it's presented that way.

To practice NVC requires that when someone expresses his feelings (e.g., "I'm angry"), we view his feelings as arrows pointing back toward his needs. If you just react to someone's feelings on the surface, you're going to wind up in conflict if the feeling expressed is anger. If my law associate is mad at me because I didn't express appreciation when he stayed late to help me in trial, I have a choice. I can either ask him why he's angry (which gives me the chance to apologize and express the appreciation he was needing all along) or I can react to his anger with my anger. Meeting his anger with my anger will alienate my associate and lead to negative consequences for both of us.

Thus, anger can be helpful or harmful depending on how we respond. Rosenberg says anger can be a gift if it spurs us to ask questions about why someone is angry and helps both of us to become conscious of what need of his hasn't been met. But how the angry person expresses his anger is also important. He can express it with hate by blaming others for his anger and making threats, or he can express it with vulnerability as a window into the pain he feels, because his needs are going unmet.

When people get the hang of NVC they experience genuine communication for the first time in their lives, and it is a revelation. Thomas D'Ansembourg, a longtime practitioner of NVC and author of *Start*

Being Genuine: Stop Being Nice, says of NVC: "The end purpose here is encounters, true encounters between human beings, with no games, no masks, no interference from our fears, habits, and clichés that don't carry the weight of our conditioning and old reflexes—and that subsequently bring us out of the isolation of our telephones, our screens, and our virtual images."

NVC Basics on Listening

To practice NVC you have to be mentally present and not engaged in thinking about the past, the future, other people or other situations. Let's say I'm concerned about my son, a college freshman. He's hanging out with friends I suspect are involved with drugs and I'm worried he's cutting classes, because his grades are so poor. If I'm mulling all that over in my head while opposing counsel is trying to talk to me, I can't possibly hear what he says, grasp it and respond with my full intelligence.

Practicing NVC requires focusing on the other person and experiencing what he's feeling as he speaks. In *Why Good Things Happen To Good People*, the authors quote Theodor Reik to teach us how to have a meaningful conversational encounter: "Listen with your third ear and catch what people do not say, but what they truly feel and think. When we truly absorb another's story, we are saying 'You count. Your life and feelings and thought matter to me. And I want to know who you really are.'"

To be a good listener requires opening out from your inner solitude. Don't interrupt to tell stories of your own. Don't check your iPhone. If you're sitting at a café don't keep turning your head to look at strangers. Do keep eye contact and offer your conversational partner encouragement to continue if this seems to help. You can encourage him simply by an occasional nod of the head, a smile or an audible breath.

Mirroring and Paraphrasing

Rosenberg figured out that mirroring is a very effective technique to enhance peaceful communication. Mirroring is a technique in which the listener says something like "If I understood you correctly, you said…." It shows that the listener is awake, that he's actually listening, that he cares and that he actually got the message.

Rosenberg also stresses the usefulness of paraphrasing. When you paraphrase, you say things like, "From what I heard, you're feeling frustrated because your need to be heard at our law firm's meetings isn't being met. Does that come close to what you're experiencing right now?" Paraphrasing is a way of testing the waters to see if you have accurately felt what the other is feeling and accurately intuited what he is needing. If you're wrong, he can tell you so and you can try again, even multiple times. Eventually you may hit the nail on the head or your paraphrasing will help the speaker figure it out for himself. This will trigger relief and your conversational partner will be grateful for your assistance in clearing up his emotional confusion.

How to Use NVC—The Four-Step Process of NVC

NVC teaches a four-step process for communication involving neutral observation, identification of feelings, expression of needs and requests. The key is to clearly express what's going on inside you without blaming or criticizing the other person.

- First, I observe what the other person is doing without evaluation or judgment about his character, his motives or what sort of person he is.

- Second, I ask myself what I'm feeling right now in relation to what I've observed.

- Third, I determine what I need right now with the understanding that it is my need which has caused my feeling, not the other's conduct. If my need has been met, I can thank the other or celebrate with him if appropriate. If my need has not been met, I go to the next step.

- Fourth, I make a polite request upon the other to take a concrete action to meet my need. The request should be made in a clear way rather than in vague terms.

There is an important difference between requests and strategies. When you make a request you are asking if the other person would be willing to take a specific action to meet your need. The action you ask for is the strategy you have come up with to have your need met. If the other person is willing to meet your need (which is what really counts), he may not want to do it in the way you have asked. Disagreements over strategies are very common, and all too often they bog down and block the process of getting human needs met. Flexibility and compromise are the name of the game if you want to have your needs met.

Let's go through an example to show how it all works. Let's say I've been working really hard at my law office. Finally I finish up my opposition to a massive motion for summary judgment. It's Saturday around two p.m. I'm worn out and need to nap. I get home and go upstairs to my bedroom, but I can't nap because my new neighbor is playing his stereo loudly from his patio. I feel frustrated, irritated, and annoyed because my need for sleep isn't being met. The trigger is my neighbor's conduct.

At this point I have a choice to make. I can slip into evaluating his behavior and characterizing him as a selfish, uncaring stereo-blasting jerk who doesn't give a damn about his neighbors. If I do this I'm likely to get angry and retaliate. I might do it by calling the police or by walking next door to tell him off. I might accuse him of being an insensitive asshole or tell him to move back where he came from since he isn't welcome here. Clearly going that route will raise my blood pressure and won't get my need met.

Instead of letting things get out of hand, I can stop, take a breath and empathize with my situation—here I am sorely needing quiet so I can rest, yet there is too much noise coming from next door. By empathizing with my own need, rather than evaluating my neighbor's conduct, I enlarge rather than shrink my heart. In doing so, I prepare the ground for peaceful communication that may get my need met, rather than alienate my neighbor. By empathizing with myself first, before I say anything to my neighbor, I relax rather than turbo-charge my nervous system. I give myself much greater freedom to respond. Absent giving myself empathy, I'm likely to engage in the stereotypically angry response that will fuel the fire.

Once my heart is enlarged by empathizing with my own need for rest, I'm in a position to empathize with my neighbor's needs. I become more curious than pissed off. What need might my neighbor be trying to meet by playing his music so loud? Perhaps he's partially deaf. Perhaps he's been working hard and he's cutting loose by having a few beers and playing his music loud. Maybe he's an enthusiastic person who loves his music and wants to share it. The only way I'll ever know is to ask him.

The content and tone of what I say to my neighbor as I stride over to his house will depend totally on whether I am reacting blindly out of annoyance and anger or whether I have gone through the NVC process. If I have done NVC I will open myself up to the possibility of finding a way to have both of our needs met. Instead of yelling, "Your music is blowing out my eardrums!" I would disclose how I'm feeling, why I need to nap now and ask him in a polite way if he would be willing to turn the volume down.

This is how it would play out. I would say, "Hi Bob. Welcome to the neighborhood. I'm Jim from next door. Sorry to trouble you, but I'm feeling upset right now, because I've had an incredibly hard week at work without much sleep, and I can't nap because your stereo is too loud. I went into the back bedroom and even used ear plugs, but I can still hear your stereo. I'm desperate to get some rest. Would you be willing to turn the music down for a while so I can nap? I would really appreciate your cooperation."

Bob now understands my legitimate need for quiet, and he is in a position to simply say, "Yes, I'll turn it down at once," or express his needs and work with me to find a mutually agreeable solution that does not involve anger, verbal violence or a fistfight. If I come to his house in a peaceful manner, make myself vulnerable by opening up to him about my needs and make a reasonable request, he's likely to cooperate.

Imagine you are litigating against Jim and Jim doesn't know NVC. Imagine that every time you do anything Jim doesn't like he hits you like a hurricane. Does this sound familiar? How many times have you been on the receiving end of angry, threatening communications from lawyers like Jim? How did it make you feel? Wouldn't you have preferred the more positive approach like that offered by the Jim who knew NVC? The unfortunate thing is that many lawyers do not even know that the NVC approach to communication exists. Now you know and you can teach them.

BARRIERS TO GOOD COMMUNICATION

Locking Horns Over Strategy

Rosenberg found that even when people can agree on which of their needs is to be met, they often disagree about the means for doing so (what Rosenberg calls the "strategy"). While the need is much more important than the strategy, and strategies should be flexible and changeable, many people get hung up arguing about strategies. A land developer who wants to make a profit by the use of the land, and keeps insisting on a particular project that enrages the neighborhood, is fixated on one strategy. He could meet his need to make a profit and meet his neighbors' needs (for peace and quiet or beauty) by building many alternative projects on the same land.

Avoiding Prejudgment Due to Bias

All human beings have implicit biases, which are cultural stereotypes based on membership in groups defined by gender, age, race, ethnicity, etc., that operate beneath the level of conscious awareness. Because of implicit bias we automatically favor or disfavor people after hearing their name or seeing their face.

NCV was intended to be used as a way of fostering the development of empathic relationships for engaging in peaceful discussions about the meeting of two parties' needs. In order to use NVC that way, you have to become conscious of your implicit biases and inhibit them. You have to be able to see the individual in front of you as a unique individual.

Empathic Listening—Being the Giraffe, not the Jackal

Marshall Rosenberg developed a humorous metaphor to guide empathic listening. He says that whenever people communicate, they can be giraffes or jackals. The giraffe is the land animal with the largest heart because it needs a huge heart to pump blood all the way up its seven-foot-long neck to its brain. A huge-hearted animal symbolizes empathy. The jackal is a carnivore, a cunning scavenger and a snarling beast, which symbolizes lack of empathy. Rosenberg says that whenever someone speaks to us we can listen with giraffe ears or jackal ears and that these ears can be pointed in or pointed out.

When giraffe ears are out we listen in a compassionate way to the other, looking past the words to the feelings and to the needs actuating those feelings. When giraffe ears are in we feel compassion toward ourselves in relation to what the other is saying to us or about us. When jackal ears are out, we looking only for the worst in the speaker and we are prepared to shower him in negative stereotypes. When jackal ears are in, whatever the speaker says to us or about us becomes fodder for us to dump negative judgments on ourselves.

In the series of NVC classes I took several years ago, we actually wore giraffe and jackal ears attached to headbands while we conversed. It made everything a bit funny but also more intense, more real.

Here is an example. Let's say a potential new client with a big case chooses another lawyer after interviewing me. If I hear the news with giraffe ears, I can commiserate with myself. I can say, "Too bad. I had a lot to offer him, and I know I would have gotten him an excellent result. But I can understand why he went with the other firm, because it's larger, has more resources, a much ritzier office and more associates to help out on his case. Oh, well, another good case will come along."

If I hear the news with jackal ears I would lambaste myself for blowing yet another opportunity and proving yet again what a total loser I am. Listening with jackal ears feels so bad, it could spark an episode of depression or prompt me to binge drink.

Why Not Ask?

You can read books on how to decode people's emotions from facial expressions, gaze direction, pupil size, physical posture, physical gestures, word choice, vocal tone, handwriting, etc. The problem with all of these decoding systems is that they are only as good as the person using them; they are error-prone and they can blow up in your face. Has it ever occurred to us to just ask another person what he is feeling in a compassionate, non-offensive way? This approach can succeed in unlocking the other's feelings and opening up a beneficial conversation.

How many times have you tried to engage opposing counsel in a discussion about settlement, gotten nowhere and assumed he was a hopeless jerk? Had you asked him why he's unable or unwilling to talk settlement he might have told you something enlightening. Maybe he always wanted to explore settlement but he's been instructed by his principal to try the case or to wait until the eve of trial to talk settlement. Maybe the insurance company is reorganizing its files and none of the temporary adjusters have been given settlement authority. Maybe he feels it's hopeless because there's a minimum policy or the adjuster was only given minimal authority. There are dozens of innocent reasons that could change your attitude if you just asked and found out.

Barriers to Good Listening

Lawyers love to talk because it showcases their knowledge and their power to persuade. They are much less enamored of listening. They believe, quite mistakenly, that they are paid to talk, not to listen. Why? Because they receive a settlement check after a strong oral presentation to a mediator or they get a verdict in their client's favor after a strong closing argument to a jury.

The truth is that they put themselves in a position to get the settlement or the verdict by listening to and learning from their client, fact witnesses, experts and the potential jurors during voir dire. They just don't remember this. What they remember are their own words.

Why don't lawyers listen well? In some cases it's because the lawyer hasn't learned to be empathic. He may have gone into law practice not to listen to people and counsel them, but to make money, to gain social prestige or to crusade against his own version of society's demons. Sometimes the reason for poor listening is poor eyesight, which deprives the lawyer of the capacity to see micro-expressions on another's face.

Another reason for poor listening is hearing loss. Sixteen percent of Americans between the age of 20 and 69 have hearing loss. Men are five times more likely than women to have it. Many men have hearing loss in their twenties and thirties. By their sixties all men do. Sometimes the reason is psychological; i.e., the lawyer is a narcissist. Sometimes it's a neurological condition like ADHD.

In *Mind Wide Open*, Steven Johnson says that the Comprehensive Attention Battery is a test that can probe your different kinds of attention and give you feedback on where you are strong and weak. He says there are neurofeedback trainers who can improve your attention in a desired area of functioning, be it golf, stock trading, law practice, even meditation.

The married couple who created Brain Care, initially to improve the attention of kids with ADD and ADHD, have branched out to helping professionals reach peak levels of performance with their attentional faculties. If you find yourself tuning out and getting distracted when a client, an opposing counsel or the judge speaks, you may not have ADD or ADHD. You could have under-developed attentional capacity for listening. If so, attentional training could help.

Overcoming Fears of Conversational Outcome

Rosenberg says our biggest fear in conversation is that if we ask the other to meet our need he will refuse. Most of us have a hard time with rejection or disapproval. Rosenberg encourages us to ignore those fears and to see the other person's refusal to meet our need as a gift. How could a refusal be a gift? Rosenberg says that when the other person tells us "I can't," or "I won't," he's on the verge of handing us incredibly valuable information about what obstacle he has to meeting our need. All we need to do is follow up and find out why he isn't ready, willing or able to meet our needs.

Knowing this can lead to a peaceful negotiation and a win-win compromise. Even if it does not, you have each learned something important. Perhaps the other person becomes aware, by sharing his "no," that he is afraid of giving because he grew up poor and in fear of his survival because there wasn't enough to go around. Perhaps the other person discovers he is reluctant to help, because he has residues of racism, sexism, ageism or some other "ism" from his childhood upbringing. Either way, you understand him better and he is now in touch with an issue he may choose to work on in the future.

Joining an NVC Practice Group

NVC organizations teach courses but also refer people to practice groups in the community where they can work on their skills. In NVC practice groups, people listen empathically to each other and give each other empathy for what they are going through and feeling. The facilitator gives feedback to the practice group to help them learn and keep them on track. He will help them see when they are cutting off a speaker seeking empathy so they can tell a story about themselves, when they are telling the other what he's feeling rather than asking, when they are giving advice instead of listening and so forth. Such practice groups are extremely helpful.

Changing Your Communication Strategy

NVC will drain the violence and stress from communicating. Using NVC techniques in your daily communications with others will infuse your relationships with empathy and improve them. Whether you're dealing with opposing counsel, your co-partners, co-associates, your staff, your spouse, your kids or your friends, using NVC will enhance and enrich your life.

CHAPTER NINE: SUGGESTED READINGS

Gerald Jampolsky, M.D., and Diane Cirincione, Ph.D., *A Mini Course for Life* (Mini Course Publishing, 2007)

Thomas D'Ansembourg, *Being Genuine: Stop Being Nice, Start Being Real* (Puddle Dancer Press, 2007)

Marshall B. Rosenberg, Ph.D., *Nonviolent Communication: A Language of Life* (2nd ed.) (Puddle Dancer Press, 2003)

C H A P T E R   T E N

How to reduce emotional strain and cope better with emotional stress

The Difference Between Strain and Stress

STRAIN IS ANYTHING that challenges us, be it a bike ride up a steep hill or three days of tense depositions in a sharply contested case. There are some naturally resilient people who love strain and live for it—people like Lance Armstrong. But most of us respond to strain with stress, which means we go into an anxious state of mind. Anxiety constricts our thinking and produces emotional and bodily discomfort, leaving us less able to respond to challenging situations. Chronic stress is what puts lawyers over the edge into alcoholism, depression or both.

Stress is manifested by muscle tightness, constricted breathing, obsessive replaying of scenes or thoughts, difficulty concentrating, restlessness, irritability and decrease in one's mental flexibility, creativity and sense of humor. Examples of negative thoughts associated with stress are, "I can't believe this is happening again. When is my luck ever going to change?" or "What did I do in a former life to deserve this?" or "Why is the universe torturing me?"

Using a positive affirmation to overcome chronic stress is like putting a bandage on a hemorrhage. You can say, "Every day is a new day.

Today is going to be the best day of my life," but when you spill coffee on your clean shirt at breakfast, the spell of hope gets broken, and it's all downhill from there.

Strain can accumulate rapidly from a big event like a trial. Strain can also build slowly from isolated events like a computer system crash, paralegals arriving late, files getting misplaced and unpaid bills piling up.

The Old Model of Stress Management

Old cartoons and comedy films beautifully capture the "last straw" model of stress. In cartoons like Tom & Jerry, Daffy Duck, and Bugs Bunny, the hunted character eludes every effort at capture and keeps turning the tables on the hunter until the hunter's mounting frustration blows his mind and he's ready for the nut house.

In films like *The Three Stooges* and *The Pink Panther*, the domineering figures in charge (Moe and Inspector Clouseau's boss) try everything to assert control over their daft subordinates and fail—ending up with a nervous facial tic and a prescription for a very long rest.

The concept implicit in these funny cartoons and movies was that stress comes from one identifiable external cause, such as a nemesis. Today we know that strain comes from a myriad of environmental causes, some known (traffic, noise, work deadlines, bills, taxes) and some unknown. We also know that stress is a physiologic response to strain that is subject to mental control and is heavily influenced by our attitudes, our natural levels of resilience and use of (or failure to use) coping techniques.

Not everyone is optimistic or naturally resilient, but all of us can use techniques to reduce strain, and thereby avoid or decrease the level of stress we feel when strained.

Techniques to Reduce Strain

(1) Decluttering

Clutter may be worse than procrastination, because procrastinators know what they're putting off, while lawyers with cluttered offices don't know, don't want to know and live in fear of what's in the pile. Many lawyers have incredibly cluttered offices. There are new client files, current client files and closed client files lying on the desk, the credenza, client chairs and even on the floor. There are stacks of unopened correspondence, old phone messages, recent bills, ancient bills (either paid or now in some phase of collection), lawyer magazines and photocopies of unread appellate decisions.

Reducing clutter in your office unclutters your mind and frees you up to focus on something other than the fearful stacks of papers that could have time bombs ticking away inside. Worry over what may be lurking in all that stuff reduces your energy level and can weaken your immune system. Look through it, get rid of what you can and file the rest away so it can be found when needed. It's also a great idea to declutter your personal space at home. Just seeing space in these rooms (for the first time in months or years) can take a great weight off your mind and open you up to new, creative possibilities for using them.

You can declutter your social life. How? By eliminating efforts to get together with people you dislike or see no value in spending time with. Take a look at your social calendar. What percentage of your social appointments involve going out with these kinds of people (due to guilt or a perceived obligation)? Is it 25% or 50%? Eliminate those appointments.

You can even declutter your mind by finding old, worn-out ideas that have ceased to bring your life any value, and tossing them. If you want help from a professional declutterer, and you can't find one by word of mouth, try the national association of professional organizers (www.napo.net).

(2) Preparation for Vacations and Family Visits

A common time for maximum stress is right before a family vacation or a family visit for the holidays. Frequently you have tasks that must be completed before you leave, and this requires frenetic, extra work on weeknights and weekends to perform. Then you realize you'll need time extensions on discovery or other matters, which puts you at the mercy of the opposing counsel you've been battling.

The family is counting on you, but so are your clients. You don't want to disappoint anyone, so you push yourself so hard that when you get to Mexico or Hawaii or wherever you are going, you are fried, frazzled and exhausted. This puts you at risk of drinking too much, if you tend to abuse alcohol, and of being distant, irritable or both toward your family.

Let's really crank up the tension and make this a holiday visit to parents and grandparents in some other state, maybe across the country. Perhaps there is an adult sibling or in-law you absolutely don't want to see. The kids are refusing to go or will go only begrudgingly when coerced or bribed. It's a long plane flight where you have to pay $10 for a tasteless sandwich. The kids say grandma and grandpa are boring, there's nothing to do and they insist you do not leave their side. Since you're stuck entertaining your kids, you can't take in the big-city culture or spend time chatting undisturbed with your folks. Everybody's miserable.

Here's where pre-trip planning really pay off. Ideally you want to line up as much help as you can before the trip so things go much easier. With visits to family on the other coast, you might want to split the visit. Let the grandparents know you'll spend some time with them and some just with your kids seeing cool places the kids will love.

The one thing you want to avoid, besides pre-trip burnout, is having the trip feel like more work than your usual labors at the law office. The trip was a failure if it makes you long to be back at the office instead of giving you the fun and relaxation you wanted. If you're not good at making these sorts of plans, get help from someone who is. It's a good idea not to dump it all on your spouse either.

(3) Preserving Marital Happiness by How You Handle Spousal Phone Calls

For years I treated my wife shabbily when she called me at the office. Why? Because I was so focused in a tense, irritable sort of way on getting tasks done that when she called to say hello, I practically bit her head off. An old friend of mine used the phrase "bum's rush" to describe how he dealt with his mother when she called him at the office. It went like this: "Hi Mom. Great to hear from you. I'm really busy now. Talk to you later. Bye. Click."

This took him about five seconds, and he never broke stride to do it. Do you give your spouse the bum's rush on the phone? If you calm yourself, breathe deeply and access kindness before pushing the blinking button on your phone to take your spouse's call, you will get a warm reception at home rather than one resembling the Ice Age.

(4) Consulting with a Colleague About a Difficult Client to Prevent Disaster

There are some problems in life that can get much worse very fast when you try to solve them on your own. For some people that would include trying to fix a leaky pipe under the kitchen sink or a flat tire on their car. For most lawyers it would include trying to reason with a difficult client who is critical, controlling and grumpy by nature, and who is always telling you what to do and how to do it. Let's say he's been especially difficult of late and you're at the end of your tether.

You're about to explode and tell him off to his face in a way that will predictably cause trouble. If you try to deal with him on your own at this point, you risk creating a huge blowout. Be smart. Call a wise and trusted colleague and chat with him in person or over the phone to lay out the details and get his feedback over how to handle this client. This technique of consulting a wise, trusted colleague works for all similar situations, such as how to deal with an especially difficult judge, opposing counsel or witness.

(5) "Chunking" Your Assignments into Workable Bits

We cannot grasp an entire appellate decision or a new client file in one fell swoop. We have to break them down into chunks of information and slowly digest them with sustained attention. How effectively we comprehend what we read depends on how much information we can hold in our minds. This depends in turn on where we focus our attention.

Yesterday's lawyers single-tasked by writing briefs with quill pens by oil lamp. Today's lawyers use technology like cell phones, iPhones, iPods, laptops and Kindle readers to multi-task. Multi-tasking overburdens our working memory system, and strains our brains to the point where we fail to grasp information. We are forced to keep re-reading material or suffer the embarrassment of getting it wrong.

New York City is famous for its blackouts (when the whole power grid crashes in the summer heat and people are trapped in elevators) and its brownouts. A brownout is when the electricity briefly stops in some parts of the city, then spontaneously pops back on. It's all a matter of degree, but in both cases there's too much drain on the limited source of existing power. The brain is not endlessly powerful. When you multi-task, you are causing brownouts that prevent your brain from fully listening to what others say, fully consolidating or retrieving memories or fully working out problems.

Every day we get ads for products to increase our multi-tasking and invitations to continuing legal education seminars on how to use these products. When lawyers visit our offices and find out we don't have the very latest technology for lightning-speed multi-tasking, they shake their heads as if we were in the Stone Age. Don't become a slave to these products. Use them only when they help you accomplish your goals efficiently. Make sure you take time away from technology to read, think, ponder and converse with others to clarify your thoughts.

Lawyers are driven, ambitious and high-achieving people. We feel compelled to cram as much activity into each minute as seems humanly possible; but at some point our brain capacity is exceeded and we become inefficient. At an MCLE seminar last year, I beheld the symbol of our profession. While the lecturer tried his best to impart the information we paid to hear, I noticed a male attorney seated one table away. He had his laptop open and was simultaneously talking to his office using a Bluetooth ear receiver/transmitter, checking his email and replying to emails.

Ironically, the lecture topic was "How to avoid committing legal malpractice." Hhhhhmmmm. Seems like something worth listening to, especially from a speaker who had 30 years experience defending lawyers in legal malpractice cases. There is no way this guy could have been paying attention to the speaker or taking in what he said, since the lawyer was staring at his laptop screen while engaging in email review and phone conversations. Could this lawyer have done any of his tasks accurately or was he overloading his brain beyond its biological capacity?

Torkel Klingberg obtained an M.D. and Ph.D. from the Karolinska Institute in Stockholm, Sweden, and is now a professor of cognitive science there. In *The Overflowing Brain*, he says the human brain is a communication channel with a limited bandwidth that was set at approximately seven units of information about 40,000 years ago. The process of holding bits of information in the mind long enough to transfer them by writing them down or telling them to someone else is called working memory. Working memory is an intentional process also known as controlled attention, because it involves an effort to remember something. Stimulus-driven attention, like jerking your head around in the direction of a noise, is an automatic response to an unanticipated stimulus. Accident witnesses have such different versions of events because they were not planning on remembering what they suddenly saw.

Remembering names is an intentional process. Do you have name dementia? How many times does a person tell you his name and within less than one second you have forgotten it? Why? It's all about distraction disrupting our limited capacity for working memory. As the person is telling you his name you may be looking at the tray of hors d'oeuvres going by, thinking, "I need to buy paper towels on the way home," or looking at the attractive person across the room. Poof. The man's name is gone.

The first human ancestor to qualify as modern man, by the scientific consensus of anthropologists, is Cro-Magnon. The capacity of human working memory correlates with the demands upon it—the demands related to living in a social group, using language to learn what you need to know, etc.

When the modern human brain developed, Cro-Magnon people were making sophisticated hunting tools out of bone and painting animals on cave walls using pigments from crushed berries. They lived in small social groups varying from 15 to 150. They did not need a huge working memory capacity (equivalent to DSL or cable) to get the job done. The sheer amount of information at their disposal was miniscule related to our time. Their limitation to seven units of information at a time suited them fine.

The modern world bombards people with stimuli and information. Klingberg gives the example of a middle-aged professional in an open-plan office who can see lots of other people, hear phones ring and overhear conversations, while juggling an immense, disparate array of visual and mental tasks. The first might be checking Google or Yahoo for the day's news. Whichever he calls up, it's going to be flooded with headlines, pictures and hyperlinks that can send him on wild goose chases.

Next he checks his email, and begins the time-consuming process of deleting some, putting some away for later and responding to others. Then there's checking the day's calendar, rearranging to-do lists and priorities. Before these tasks can be completed, the phone rings or someone barges into his cubicle, or both. As the distractions build, our professional forgets what he was doing, becomes fretful and tenses up. He asks, "Am I losing my memory?" or "Did I drink too much last night?"

Klingberg says no—this is not dementia. It's the sheer volume of information to digest. It overwhelms our brains when it hits a working memory system built 40,000 years ago and creates a bottleneck. You can't run the volume of cars that travel California's superhighway I-5 today on its two-lane, scenic coast highway (Route 1).

In most human beings the capacity for working memory reaches its peak at age 25 (which was the time of maturity for our ancestors) and then declines. By age 55 most of us have the same working memory capacity as a 12-year-old. Hence we are facing the need to process data growing at an exponential rate with a Stone Age working memory capacity at an age when that capacity is steadily declining.

It's no wonder we're under strain, and that we get stressed just thinking about our jobs. Have compassion for yourself, and make use of every cognitive strategy to help you with this situation.

TECHNIQUES FOR COPING WITH STRESS

Strengthen Your Resilience

Physicians who give their patients the bad news that they have a serious chronic illness (like cancer, HIV or diabetes) notice different responses. Some patients become very depressed, some experience little outward perturbation in their mood and others find a silver lining in their illness. Receiving a diagnosis like HIV creates negative psychological and physiological effects, yet some people are able to counteract them. Medicine has developed the concept of resilience to describe and explain these responses.

A patient who is resilient in the face of a stressful diagnosis like HIV is one who not only avoids clinical levels of depression, anxiety or PTSD, but retains the capacity to experience positive mood states as well. Some people are naturally resilient and tend to bounce back psychologically from anything rather quickly. They are said to have the inborn trait of resilience. Many of us do not have this trait.

Can lawyers be taught to have greater resilience? The work of Judith Moscowitz, Ph.D., seems to say yes. Dr. Moscowitz practices at the Osher Center for Integrative Medicine at UCSF Medical Center where she works with AIDs and HIV patients. She noticed that the partners of AIDs patients who cared for them until their deaths showed markedly elevated symptoms of depression on psychological testing. Yet most of the time they felt good, because they experienced so many positive emotions from loving and caring for their partners and celebrating the shared life remaining to them.

Moscowitz learned that positive emotions can co-occur with the most dire, stressful events and this remains true even while symptoms of depression are significantly elevated. Based on her work with AIDs patients and their partners, she developed the understanding that positive emotions can buffer and even counteract the negative psychological and physiological effects of stress. She became interested in learning whether she could coach people newly diagnosed with HIV to be more resilient.

Based on her review of the literature, Dr. Moscowitz developed a positive affect intervention named IRISS (Intervention for those Recently Informed of their Seropositive Status) consisting of five one-on-one sessions in which a facilitator teaches the individual eight different skills for increasing positive affect. The skills are:

- Noting daily positive events

- Identifying positive events and capitalizing on them by sharing them with others or marking the occurrence in some way

- Feeling and expressing gratitude toward people, Nature or God for one's blessings

- Mindfulness—maintaining non-judgmental awareness of one's situation, which prevents anxiety from taking over

- Positively re-appraising one's situation by reinterpreting the significance of events in a more positive way

- Focusing on one's personal strengths for getting through the challenge

- Setting and working toward attainable goals

- Performing small acts of kindness for others.

Dr. Moscowitz tried the IRISS technique on eleven patients who had been diagnosed with HIV within the past three months. She found significant increase in positive affect from week 1 of the intervention through post-intervention follow-up. She believes the technique has unlimited application, and can be applied not only to persons diagnosed with illnesses other than HIV but to persons suffering from chronic occupational stress like lawyers.

Rituals for Starting and Ending Your Day

How you start and end your day influences your subconscious. Some happy people will start or end their day by experiencing gratitude for all the positive aspects of their lives—love in their family, being employed, having a nice home, good food on the table, good health, good friends, beautiful weather, etc. Aymee Coget, Ph.D., suggests that just before you close your eyes to fall asleep at night you visualize five instances in which you were kind to someone else that day and three instances in which you felt happy. Troubled marriages can be helped when each spouse takes time to dwell on what they love, or at least like, about their partner.

Making Lists That Inspire You

One simple exercise you can start today is to write down five things a day you find beautiful, touching or inspiring. If you do this even for a week, you will begin to notice your mind inclines more to the positive and less to the negative.

Once You're at the Office

Nearly all of us start by checking emails, phone messages or both. This will set a stressful tone for the day. What if you started each workday differently? You could tell your secretary you have a 15-minute ritual that you need to do behind a closed door to prepare you to meet your workday. During the 15 minutes you could meditate. You could form an intention for what you most wanted to accomplish that day and envision yourself doing it successfully. You could sit quietly, breathe gently and put your hand on your heart to get in touch. This is very grounding. You could also do deep breathing to energize yourself with prana (life energy taken in through the breath).

Deep Breathing

The rate of our breathing (the number of breaths we take per minute) and its depth (the volume of air we take in) is regulated by clusters of cells called respiratory centers at the top of our medulla oblongata. The respiratory centers have receptors for many different peptides that convey information about stress and mood. If we're stressed out or depressed, the respiratory centers will produce very shallow chest breathing. If we're deeply relaxed and feeling groovy (as Austin Powers would say), we will breathe easily and deeply into the base of our lungs.

We lawyers are so tense that we hold our breath without realizing it. When we do breathe, we tend to take frequent, shallow breaths. Poor breathing depletes our supply of oxygen and energy along with mental focus. Next time you're in the office make an effort to monitor your breathing every so often. Are you breathing in and out fully and effortlessly or incompletely with strain?

Lawyers are chest breathers, meaning we do not take air deep down into the base of our lungs and toward the back of our rib cage. We breathe only into the top and front of our lungs. The average person breathes 12-14 times per minute, while a practiced deep breather breathes 6 times a minute. The average person suffers from some level of anxiety. The most healthy and revitalizing form of breathing is deep, slow belly breathing. This activates the calming parasympathetic branch of the autonomic nervous system.

Proper breathing saturates our blood with oxygen, increases the elimination of toxins from our blood, increases calmness, increases energy and decreases stress and anxiety. Since we breathe an average of 20,000 times a day we can reap a huge benefit by breathing right. Dennis Lewis has put out a CD titled *Natural Breathing* in which he provides deep breathing exercises and meditations.

On the inhale push the diaphragm downward while expanding the belly forward. Simultaneously push the lower posterior ribs and the lower spine backward. This brings air deep into the bottom of your lungs where most of the blood is pooled to accept fresh oxygen. On the exhale move the diaphragm upward and the belly inward so they press against the lungs and completely empty them.

According to Dacher Keltner, Ph.D., author of *Born To Be* Good, practitioners of loving kindness meditation emphasize the exhale. It is during the exhale that your heart rate slows and your vagus nerve activation increases, which is associated with a sensation of spreading warmth in the chest and increased feelings of compassion.

You can do deep, slow belly breathing while standing up, seated or lying down. If you are standing, Lewis advises to keep your feet apart and tilt your pelvis forward so your back is flat. If you do it lying down you can feel the process by placing your hands on your belly or see the process by placing a book on your belly.

The Body Scan and the Relaxation Response

In *Freeing The Angry Mind*, psychotherapist C. Peter Bankhart describes two methods to get in touch with your body and relax deeply. Both can be done at home or office (with the door closed).

To do the Body Scan, lie on your back in the corpse pose (with feet and hands spread wide, palms facing upward), gently close your eyes and take some slow, deep abdominal breaths. You know you're breathing into the belly when your belly rises on the inbreath and falls on the outbreath. While continuing to breathe deeply begin to scan your body from the feet all the way up to your head. As you come into contact with each body part allow yourself to fully experience whatever feelings and sensations are present without judgment. There might be tension, pain, tingling, coldness, warmth, softness, ease or other qualities. Candace Pert, Ph.D., says that doing the Body Scan strengthens your frontal cortex by focusing attention, and increases blood flow to the parts of your body you're focusing on.

To do the Relaxation Response, alternately clench, then release and relax, the muscles in each part of your body from feet to head. You'll feel elongation, warmth and the release of tension. Bankhart says that over time, most people find they prefer one method over the other. Try both and see which one you like. They're both a better way to deal with stress than cursing at your paralegal, blaring your horn fruitlessly at the driver in front in bumper to bumper traffic or tossing down hard drinks at Happy Hour.

Sex

Sex is an integral part of life. When you engage in sex in a slow, relaxed way with full attention to your partner's pleasure and comfort, and you show your partner caring and respect, you can't help but have a great time. Sex done right is a major contributor to human health and happiness. The practice of law can make us too busy, too emotionally withdrawn, too tense, too anxious or too doped with alcohol to have regular sex with our spouse or partner. This is a big loss for both halves of any couple, and a frequent cause of dissatisfaction, irritation and anger in relationships.

While couples counseling can help, there are practical barriers in terms of time, cost and scheduling that may make it too difficult to pursue, especially when you have kids living at home. One alternative is to find a relative to watch the kids and take a weekend together every couple of months at a resort or a nice hotel. Another is to use such a free weekend to go on a retreat. Some retreats are designed for the sexual healing of couples who have lost their sexual intimacy, while others are designed to enhance sexual pleasure for couples who are intimate but lack the necessary knowledge or skills in this area to reach the bliss that is possible for them.

Walking

Walking nearly anywhere (except a dark alley at night) helps relieve stress. To increase stress relief you can play music on your iPod while you walk, walk with a friend or walk in a pretty spot like a beach or forest trail. Walking stimulates endorphin production while oxygenating and toning the body. It also helps keep your bones strong, unlike prescription medicines for osteopenia and osteoporosis that work by killing off the osteoclast cells that eat up damaged, degenerated bone.

To increase the good physiologic effects of walking you can pump your arms or walk against gravity by going up hills or stairs. Fitness experts encourage walkers to do intervals, which means alternating periods of brisk walking and walking at a normal pace. Regular walking is considered one of the single most powerful preventives against Alzheimer's Disease and other senior dementias.

Yoga

Yoga is great for stress relief. It gently unsticks stiff joints and gently releases tight muscles and muscle fascia which opens up the tissues and promotes better blood flow. With increased blood flow there is increased oxygenation with better elimination of lactic acid and other toxins. When you do yoga on a regular basis you'll receive the benefits of deep breathing, elongation of the body, improved posture, strength and balance.

There are two main types of yoga. Flow involves continuous movement that makes you sweat and burn calories. Iyengar focuses on holding long stretches and uses pauses to switch from one stationary pose to another. Flow activities other than flow yoga are dance, tai chi, qui gong, martial arts and capoeira.

A lesser-known form of yoga is bikram or hot yoga. Bikram yoga is done in a heated studio to make people sweat. The warmth and the sweat increase body flexibility and enable people to bend their bodies beyond their conventional limits. If you do Bikram, drink loads of water and ingest some salt to replace the fluids and electrolytes you will lose. The biggest danger of Bikram is passing out from the heat or from the smell of the men who haven't showered in days.

Yoga Combined with Meditation

Combining yoga with meditation not only soothes and calms the mind, it makes the body more flexible and actually relaxes the blood vessels. When you lead a sedentary life style and eat foods high in saturated fats or transfats, the lining of your blood vessels becomes more stiff, less stretchy and more prone to disease. Can this stiffness be reversed by yoga? Yes. Research by Satish Sivasankaran, M.D., at Yale University published in 2004 showed that consistent practice of yoga and meditation relaxed the endothelial lining of the practitioner's arteries.

Dr. Sivasankaran's study involved 33 people, 10 with cardiovascular disease, at Bridgeport Hospital, one of Yale's research hospitals. The participants were mostly men with an average age of 55. Prior to the start of the study he had them measured for blood pressure, BMI, heart rate, cholesterol and blood sugar level. He also checked the condition of their arterial linings. After six weeks of three 90-minute sessions of yoga and meditation, he rechecked all these variables.

Dr. Sivasankaran presented his findings at the annual meeting of the American Heart Association in New Orleans in November 2004.

Amazingly, there were significant reductions in blood pressure, body mass and pulse rate across the whole group. Those with previous disease showed big improvements in endothelial function. This was a pilot study, and no doubt more studies on this beneficial effect of yoga combined with meditation will be undertaken.

Massage and Stretching

Massage and stretching are both great stress relievers as they knead and release tense, bunched-up muscles and tight muscle fascia. Don't wait until you get your gift certificate for one massage at Christmas. You can enjoy massage year-round for just pennies when you buy a shiatsu massage chair for home use. You can buy a chair massage from a masseuse for 5, 10, 15 or more minutes at many farmers' markets, airports and natural food stores. You can buy a set of massages from a Certified Massage Therapist at a bulk discount. Mark Verstegen's book *Core Performance Endurance* teaches a variety of home stretches for myo-fascial release and regeneration of the health of your muscles.

One of the best techniques for self-massage is using a Styrofoam roller or a semi-soft ball to roll your body parts against. Stretching out tightness in your quads, hamstrings, hip flexors, ilio-tibial band, piriformis and gluteus medius is easy to do and very rewarding, because it reduces stiffness and pain and increases flexibility.

Stretching can be passive, active or both. For passive stretching you can hang upside down, have a partner stretch you or use a ball, chair, bench or other piece of furniture for gravity-based stretching. For active stretching you can use an exercise ball, straps or ropes to assist you in stretching your body parts against gravity in the direction and distance you want them to go. Physical therapists and personal trainers can teach you how to stretch too. Be gentle and don't use force.

Carving Out Slow Time

When is the last time you made something in your kitchen from scratch—bread, soup, chowder or stew? These things take time, unleash your creativity, let you savor the smells and take justified pride in serving up a delicious, home-cooked meal. How about chores? Cutting the grass, trimming the shrubs, doing laundry, walking the dog, repainting parts of your home, are all things that take time but involve you in caring for your home and family.

Better yet, involve your kids in the chores. This may take a small bribe, but it's worth it, because you are doing something positive together. My son requires a small inducement (e.g., new Pokemon cards) to do what he regards as boring chores, but he loves to join me for washing the family cars, baking brownies, painting a fence, and that sort of thing. We once made strawberry lemonade from scratch and sold it for fifty cents a cup from a homemade stand. It was great fun.

Hobbies for Grown-Ups

Hobbies are not just for kids. There are some very fun adult hobbies. They include tai chi, martial arts, golf, tennis, running, long distance road cycling, mountain biking, motorcycle touring, skydiving, cave exploration, snorkeling, scuba diving, camping, hiking, fishing, white water rafting, mountain climbing, ice climbing, nature photography, sculpture, pottery, painting, fiction writing, poetry, foreign language immersion, classical music, jazz, taiko drumming, winemaking, beer making, cooking, baking, adventure travel, scenic travel, cruises, educational travel (led by a university professor who is an expert in a field of your interest), Elderhostel and the like.

Volunteering

There are community volunteer activities that relieve stress and stimulate endorphins such as planting trees, cleaning up litter from a creek, helping the homeless, helping lost and injured wild animals or pets, etc. Donating your time and energy to build low-income housing through Habitat for Humanity feels good and does good. Being a "Big Brother" or "Big Sister" to a child is very rewarding. Helping someone much less fortunate than you is not only good for the soul, but is also a reminder that you are blessed and that your privileged status can end on any given day.

CHAPTER TEN: SUGGESTED READING

Andrew Weil, M.D., *Breathing: The Master Key to Self Healing* (Sounds True) (available on CD from www.soundstrue.com)

Mark Verstegen and Pete Williams, *Core Performance Endurance* (Rodale, 2007)

Eileen Roth, *Organizing for Dummies: Organize Your Office, Your Home, Your Life!* (Wiley Publishing, Inc., 2001)

Judith Moskowitz, Ph.D., M.P.H., "*Positive Affect at the Onset of Chronic Illness: Planting the Seeds of Resilience*" in *Handbook of Adult Resilience: Concepts, Methods and Applications* (Reich, J.W. Zautra, A.J. & Hall, J. [Eds.], Guilford, 2010)

Paul C. Bragg, N.D., Ph.D., and Patricia Bragg, N.D., Ph.D., *Super Power Breathing For Super Energy, Health & Longevity* (Health Science) (22nd printing)

Torkel Klingberg, M.D., Ph.D., *The Overflowing Brain* (Oxford University Press, 2009)

Mandy Aftel, *The Story of Your Life: Becoming the Author of Your Experience* (Fireside, 1996)

Donna Smallin, *Unclutter Your Mind: 500 Ways to Focus on What's Important* (Storey Publishing, 2006)

CHAPTER ELEVEN

Using meditation to become a wiser, calmer, more likeable and more effective lawyer

Why Lawyers Need Meditation

MEDITATION IS A TECHNIQUE that has enormous benefits for lawyers. Lawyers are highly cerebral. They value their analytic reasoning skills over sensation, emotion, feeling and intuition. They are impatient and like to get "right to the point" rather than allow their conversational partner to express his feelings. Lawyers don't take time out to breathe and feel what is in their hearts. They use "head energy" to categorize human experience into problems they can analyze and fix through research, writing and logical argument.

Lawyers love to talk and tell stories but are very uneasy with silence. When meeting with others they do the vast majority of the talking, and very little listening. Lawyers have difficulty letting things be and trusting that things will work. They feel secure when they take control and tell others what must be done. They want to be productive and make things happen.

Buddhist psychology says our private mental experience of reality is what counts, not what it is "out there," assuming anything is really out there separate from the way we know and understand it. Since the world we live in is completely shaped by how our minds construct it, interpret it, and react to it, it becomes crucial to know our own minds. Meditation uses silence and stillness. When we are silent and still we are much less distracted. This gives us the chance to see how our minds operate.

One thing people learn in meditation is that our minds generate thoughts on a virtually nonstop basis, much like the ticker tape at the bottom of the TV news screen. Many of these thoughts are random and represent intrusions into or disturbances of our mental flow and mental peace. As we sit quietly in meditation we may suddenly remember being behind on our bills and start worrying about how, and when, we will pay them. We may recall getting into an argument with our spouse the day before over how much TV the children may watch, and become steamed all over again. We may become irritated, because our house guest is snoring, because we heard someone honking his horn outside or because we've started sneezing because of dust on the floor.

Buddhists call this restless aspect of the human mind monkey chatter. How do random thoughts interrupt and distract us so that we are mentally scattered much of the time? The ratio of negative to positive thoughts in our skulls is stacked very high in favor of negative thoughts. Negative thoughts include worries, memories of or anticipation of unpleasant experiences, irritation over our physical circumstances, judgments casting blame on the self or others and generalized anxieties reflected by thoughts like "I'm going to die one day."

Negative thoughts have a sticky quality. Our minds get caught up in them. We may try to follow the story line to see where the negative thought leads. We may try to push the negative thought away by dismissing it. We may even try to talk ourselves out of the negative thought by convincing ourselves it's a mistake. Either way, we have been sucked out of being present and living life. For those precious, never-to-happen-again moments, we weren't really here. We were someplace else, essentially wasting time.

Lawyers do this even more than members of most other occupations. They are responsible for many clients, some of whom have very challenging personalities. They must get hold of, learn, remember, process, organize and master many facts for each client's case. They must stay on top of the ever-changing issues in each client's case, remain vigilant for and fend off surprise attacks and take full advantage of an opponent asleep at the switch. They are always juggling many balls in the air and if they drop one they fear terrible repercussions. Consequently, their minds are humming like a nest of bees, accompanied by shallow breathing, distractedness and anxiety.

One goal of meditation is to become as calm as the flat surface of a pond that reflects what is happening but does not react to it. This is called equanimity. The more equanimity we have, the more freedom from distraction, perturbation and anxiety we have. Through meditation we may eventually become like an ocean that takes no notice of the little ripples on its surface. This does not mean we have become numb, apathetic or emotionally dead. Far from it.

Advanced meditators experience their feelings very clearly and fully, much more clearly and fully than the confused way most of us do, because we're so caught up in a welter of feelings and thoughts that pull us in many directions at once. As you progress in meditation you learn to heal your own mind by reducing its reactivity. The less reactive you are to events, the more you can access the wisdom of your mind and the compassion of your heart. You gain mental peace and mental clarity which enable you to function at your best.

The Benefits of Meditation for Lawyers

Meditators develop the capacity to be open, receptive and non-judgmental. Wary lawyers fear that taking on those qualities would make them passive, weak and inferior. Yet this wariness prevents lawyers from really hearing what others have to say and it prevents others from trusting them. When a client can see his lawyer is distracted, he's not going to share deeply what is going on with him. The same is true of a witness or a potential juror.

Meditation benefits lawyers because it can counterbalance their one-sidedness and make them more complete human beings who are more in harmony with themselves and others. The agitation and ferocity that lawyers bring to hashing out disputes can be counterbalanced by the calmness and gentleness of meditation. In meditation there is no need to show off your wit and brilliance, and no benefit in doing so.

Your aim is to access wisdom deeper than anything the conscious mind produces. To get there you must become present. To become present requires that you let go of your obsessive mulling over of past events (something that provokes blame and anger) and your obsessive speculation about what the future holds (something that causes worry).

Lawyers feel a compulsion to be busy and productive, to fill every moment of that vast expanse of time we call the workday with tasks to complete. The paradox is that the busier they are, the more empty their days feel. Meditators achieve a sense of the fullness and richness of life not by performing loads of tasks, but by staying in contact with "inner space." You get to inner space during meditation by slowing your breath, by taking your focus off your nonstop stream of random thoughts and putting it on your breath, and by calming and quieting the restless mind. Lawyers who learn to leave their busyness behind and take more trips to inner space, the field of pure awareness, will reap physiological, behavioral and spiritual rewards.

Experienced meditators who spend much time in this emptiness increase blood flow to their frontal cortex, increase the interconnections between their frontal lobe neurons and thicken their frontal cortex. This in turn fuels the growth of their compassion and their wisdom (their ability to reserve judgment and make life-serving choices after due consideration of all options). Guess who winds up with decreased bloodflow to the frontal cortex? Lawyers who are angry all the time at the other lawyers who won't cave in and give them what they want.

Meditators believe in unity and see all persons as one. When they meet another person they can see elements of themselves in that person and find ways to identify with him. Lawyers impose a conceptual grid onto other people. They use either/or dichotomies to characterize others, such as smart/stupid, educated/ignorant, right/wrong, good/bad, reliable/unreliable, truthful/untruthful, etc. Far from clarifying life, these labels obscure reality and cause confusion. These labels do not help us perceive reality clearly or make wise decisions.

Once we have labeled someone as wrong or bad, we start judging him in terms of those labels. We become disconnected and oppositional. These concepts are poor substitutes for the direct experience of reality. The proof is that we agonize constantly over choices in life—from the big to the trivial—at the law office and at home. We are not in touch with our inner wisdom and feel lost much of the time. Trying to reason things out or consulting others doesn't help very much.

It's even worse when a crisis strikes. When this occurs, lawyers are likely to become agitated and angry rather than calm and clear, because they are making judgments and reacting emotionally to their judgments. In a crisis it's better to breathe, relax and take the time to accurately perceive what is really going on and respond from a place of wisdom rather than knee-jerk fear or anger. Meditation can help us get to that place of wisdom inside us so we make calm decisions that end well without all the fussing, fretting and hand-wringing that is so draining.

How Does Meditation Change the Meditator?

Meditation is a technique to keep our minds spacious and clear and to keep our hearts open and compassionate. To use an old book title from Aldous Huxley, it opens all of our "doors of perception" wide. When we meditate we learn to listen to our experience not just with our head, but with sensations and heart. The human brain is constructed in a way that allows our frontal cortex (the rational mind) to block out sensations and feelings. This is useful in that it enables us to override our emotions and change behaviors that hurt ourselves or others. But when we block out too many of our sensations and feelings, we are deprived of our emotional and spiritual connection to others and to the world. We become dried up. We become heartless. We lose our compassion.

Using our minds we can build structures—languages, technologies and cities.

Certainly our minds are very useful, but they are just one medium for relating to ourselves and others. They are not up to the task of handling it alone and they have their drawbacks. Meditation is a technique for slowing and quieting the mind and allowing us to develop a broad field of awareness that notices our thoughts but is not limited by them.

As our awareness grows we develop our capacity to attend to everything in the present moment without distraction. Our sensory perceptions grow sharper. We are less pressured by time. We envision more options for resolving disputes in a peaceful, mutually satisfactory way. The keys to the development of awareness are relaxation and patience. During meditation our focus is inward on the breath. As we sit quietly in a state of relaxation we patiently explore our bodies, our feelings and our minds through awareness. We become a witness to our own thoughts with no compulsion to believe them or act upon them.

If we have a thought like "I need ice cream" during a state of meditative calm, we are not likely to judge ourselves negatively as hopelessly fat or act on the thought by jumping in the car to get to nearest grocery store. As we progress in meditation, we develop mindfulness which is the capacity for non-judgmental awareness of the present moment accompanied by free choice as to whether, when and how we will respond to what is happening. Pavlov's dogs had no space between stimulus and response. Meditators have extra space between thought and action. This gives them extra capacity to handle stress and to release anger that would otherwise erupt into a confrontation with another lawyer.

The Benefits of Developing Heart Energy

The Buddha encouraged his students to develop heart energy and to integrate the energy of heart and mind. What flows from this integration is that your actions (which once were thought-based) become infused with heart. You are much less likely to engage in harmful gossip or slander. You are much more likely to be compassionate, forgiving, generous and helpful. In situations that used to confuse you, you will readily know what to do, and need not consult lots of other people or books for the answer.

In Buddhism the heart is the portal to compassionate awareness that goes beyond thought. Thus, if you have the thought "I hate this guy" (because the other lawyer objected to your direct examination question), you can use your broad awareness to say to yourself, "I'm having a hate thought right now." Then you can take a breath and count to 10 or feel your feet grounded to the floor and let go of the thought. You are now free to deal with opposing counsel without hate.

Heart lets us know that all life is precious, even the life of the most bickering and obnoxious, opposing counsel. Heart tempers the tendency of our thoughts to become aggressive and vengeful when we are blocked from getting what we want, such as a settlement offer at the level we expected. The more time you spend in your heart, the more quickly and easily you will know when your intentions or actions don't pass your own moral smell test. By the same token, the more quickly and easily you will experience forgiveness, peace, satisfaction and joy.

Heartful, Happy Lawyers Fare Better
Than Heartless, Unhappy Ones

People know right away if you're a happy person. In July 2009, J. Antonio Aznar-Casanova of the University of Barcelona in Spain published a paper showing that the right hemisphere of the brain perceives happiness in others more quickly and accurately than the left side of the brain perceives expressions of sadness and fear. People form first impressions of each other based on these instantaneous, unconscious perceptions and the value judgments derived from them ("I like this guy. He's a happy person." or "What a grouch. Who needs a grump like that for a lawyer?"). While the grand purpose of meditation is to achieve wisdom, compassion, inner peace and true connection with Life or Being, an offshoot is that it will make you a whole lot happier. This in turn makes you more likeable, more approachable and ultimately more successful in your dealings with other people.

What Kind of Meditation is Best?

The one that works for you. In this chapter I'm focusing on Buddhist meditation, because that is the only form I have studied and practiced, and it has been a source of great comfort and benefit to me. However, there are other forms used very effectively by Hindus, Kabbalistic Jews and Christians.

What is the Origin of Buddhist Meditation?

Meditation was developed by the Buddha (which means the awakened one) about 2,500 years ago in northern India. His birth name was Siddartha Gautama. He was born a prince, and until age 29 he was raised in a number of different palaces where he was completely spared from the sight of aged, sick and dying people. He was surrounded by the finest luxuries and wanted for nothing. All his desires were met for food, clothes, women, entertainment, you name it. Buddha had his own charioteer. One day at age 29 he slipped out of the palace and had the charioteer take him around. He came upon successively an extremely old person disfigured by age, a sick person ravaged by illness and a corpse. He bade the charioteer explain, and Siddartha learned that all human beings (including himself) would one day experience aging, sickness, pain and death. He was shocked and highly disturbed by this news. Siddartha saw no use in hiding from these inevitable forms of suffering in his parents' palaces.

He and his five friends decided to become renunciants. They renounced all material pleasures and conveniences. They went into the forests of northern India where they lived according to an extreme form of ascetic spiritual practice. They wore the same old, tattered clothes. They held their breath, exposed themselves to pain and ate less than needed to preserve their health, becoming incredibly emaciated and weak. The Buddha did this for five years seeking to become happy by freeing himself from worries about aging, sickness and death. It didn't work. He told his friends he was not going to be a renunciate anymore and took some sweet rice and milk to eat. They criticized him for going "soft" and they left him.

Siddartha made a decision that day—to sit under a Boddhi tree and meditate until he died or became enlightened. By meditation, he meant sitting still, being quiet and looking deeply into the fundamental questions of life. After sitting under the Boddhi tree for a long time, Siddartha became fully enlightened and was then known as the Buddha. Part of his vision was the Middle Way, the wisdom of leading life between all extremes, such as those of complete indulgence versus complete self-deprivation or between living as a monk to flee the world vs. giving all of one's energy to assist the poor and sick. The very first people he taught were his five old friends. He spent the next thirty years of his life teaching the cultivation of wisdom and compassion for the benefit of all beings. His teachings as a whole are called the Dharma, which means the Way. To keep his teachings alive he founded a monastic order called the Sangha. Today the term sangha is applied to any group of people who get together to practice Buddhism, even everyday folks like you and me.

The Buddha never spoke of himself as a god and never spoke of his teachings as a religion. The term Buddhism was invented long after his death by a British professor of religion. The Buddha did not want people to accept his teachings based upon his fame. He always told people to try them out and see if they led to more of the same suffering they were already experiencing or if they led to a new sense of freedom, ease and release from suffering. The Buddha said anyone could follow his teachings anywhere in this world, and it wasn't necessary to become a monk.

The Four Noble Truths

The Buddha's first teachings were the Four Noble Truths. Number one is that life inevitably involves suffering. Number two is that everything changes—all that lives dies; every combination of circumstances that provides us happiness now will sooner or later dissolve; and everything that now depresses, annoys or angers us will also pass away. Number three is that suffering has an identifiable cause which is our attachment to the objects of our desire or our compulsion to push away that which we find unpleasing. Number four is that if we let go of our attachments (which he called grasping) and our resistance to that which displeases us, we will be free from suffering and attain happiness.

The Buddha never said that all of life is suffering and happiness equals escaping from life. He understood life had wonderful moments to savor. Indeed, one of the greatest meditators of our time, J. Krishnamurti, said, "If you cannot experience beauty in the moments of your everyday life, even at the office, then your life is of no significance." But the Buddha also understood that emotional attachment to the goodness of life would always produce a sense of loss, sadness and grief when the object of your attachment (a spouse, a job, a house) dissolved. He wanted people to face this truth. Even today this is hard to do. So many of us lawyers numb ourselves to suffering by addictions to work, alcohol or drugs. The sad thing is that we can't numb ourselves to pain without numbing ourselves to everything else.

What is Mindfulness?

The Buddha taught that gaining mindfulness through meditation was the way. The very term "mind" refers to the act of minding, the act of deciding where to place one's attention. Attention is the function of deeply contacting and absorbing the essence of what one is contemplating. One of the basic premises of mindfulness is that we are what we attend to. This is true in a number of ways, since reality (whether it does or does not exist "out there") is mind-created by being filtered, organized and interpreted by the mind. Secondly, what lies outside of our attention lies outside our conscious concern and will not prompt us to act. Thirdly, what we do attend to not only provides content for our thoughts, but colors our moods.

To be mindful is to be awake and to notice much more inside and around you than you used to before you began meditating. Mindfulness has four aspects. The first is seeing things as they really are. The second is noticing how everything changes. The third is being connected to the present moment, being in the now, rather than allowing one's attention to wander back and forth between the past and future. The fourth is relating to your moment-by-moment experience without distortion and thus without evaluation, judgment or story. As my instructor in Buddhism says, a mindful person is present for his life rather than living in an unconscious manner. By unconscious, he does not mean in a stuporous state or a coma. Rather, he means the person is so immersed in the ceaseless mental chatter inside his skull that he is disconnected from what is actually happening now. Since the past is gone and the future is not here, life only happens now and to truly live is to be mentally present now.

The Buddhists use "monkey mind" to refer to the constant push and pull of the forces of desire, craving, envy, repulsion and anger within our minds that make us like a spectator at Wimbledon turning our heads left, right, left, right, ad infinitum. Monkeys are nervous, wound-up creatures—always twittering, grasping and moving in a blur from branch to branch. In ancient India people would trap a monkey by putting a treat inside a hollowed area scooped out of a coconut that was big enough for the monkey's fist. If he relaxed his hand and dropped the treat, he could free himself, but the craving monkey was so eager to keep and eat the treat that he trapped himself.

When you relax your mind, you are free to notice and enjoy life in the present. In one class we were each given one raisin and told to look at it, smell it, roll it between our fingers and talk about how it got to our classroom. People mentioned preparing the soil, planting the grape vine, watering it, having the sun shine on it, pruning the vines, picking the grapes, drying out the grapes, packaging them in little red boxes, shipping them to a store and so forth. Then we were to play with the raisin on our tongue, after which we gently bit into it and masticated the raisin very slowly—for several minutes. Each of us was able to describe sensations we had.

The sensations included salivating, feeling the raisin skin puncture, feeling multiple bursts of flavor from the raisin as we chewed, smelling the fragrance of the raisin, experiencing the change in texture from hard to soft and finally experiencing the sensation of swallowing the raisin. When we were asked how we normally ate, I joked about mindlessly shoving one chip after another into my mouth while eating a whole bag of potato chips in front of the TV during the Super Bowl. I never looked at the chips or examined their flavor. I just kept shoveling them into my mouth. Other people talked about eating while driving or eating while carrying on conversation without ever noticing what their food tasted like.

At the end of the exercise, our instructor asked us, "How would it be to live all aspects of your life as if you were eating this raisin?" All of us can develop more mental presence and incorporate it more into the moments of our daily lives. By doing so we will enjoy life more, and we will become more likeable. People much prefer to talk to someone who is really listening to them than to someone whose attention is wandering in every direction. When a certain person is greatly liked and you ask his friends why they like him so much, you invariably hear something like, "When I'm with him, he is completely focused on me as if no one else existed, and I feel he really cares about me." That likeable person could be you if you can develop the quality of mindfulness.

Mindfulness and Mental Resilience

In this human life we face all kinds of challenges, shocks and storms. Meditation teacher James Baraz says that when we have never meditated and are wholly lacking in mindfulness, we are like a tall cone-shaped hill with a ball on top. The least wind will roll the ball off. After we meditate for a while and develop some mindfulness, we level off the top of the hill to a flat shape so it takes more wind to blow the ball off. But after years of meditation practice the top of the hill is like a U shape. Now when the wind blows, the ball goes up to the sides but quickly falls back to the center of the U. This is Baraz's metaphor for the development of mental resilience. Mental resilience is not shouting down someone shouting at you. Mental resilience is the ability to handle challenge without reactivity or defensiveness, but with wisdom as well as compassion for yourself and the others involved.

If you lose a hotly contested motion, will you slam your file shut and race out of the courtroom to avoid the other attorney, while feeling like you've just been publicly tarred, feathered and branded the world's most incompetent lawyer; will you demand immediate reconsideration from the judge in a loud, challenging voice that lets him know he got the decision wrong; or will you wait outside the courtroom for the other lawyer and tell him "This isn't over," while making threats about what you will do next? None of these options feel very good, do they? Do any of them serve you or help you? Wouldn't it be great to find some other way to respond—a more positive, less painful way? That's where a regular meditation practice can really help.

What is Needed in order to Meditate?

Many people think they must have some special qualities or talents to meditate, such as being highly spiritual or having remarkable powers of attention. This is not so. My teacher Robin Caton says that as long as you have a mind and you are breathing, you can meditate. She also says it is important not to have preconceptions about what meditation is and what it isn't. Why? For one reason, the experience of meditation is different each time. For another, if you have a definite idea of what it should be, you will judge yourself negatively if your experience doesn't meet the idea. That will discourage you from meditating in the future. Better to see meditation as the experience one has when he sits quietly, pays attention to his breath and watches his mind operate without trying to stifle his thoughts.

Do you need any special paraphernalia? No. You can meditate standing up, sitting on a chair or walking. Many people meditate while seated cross-legged on a rounded cushion with their legs resting on a mat. Some prefer to sit on a small wooden bench with hands on thighs and calves folded under the bench. Do you need an absolutely quiet place where you will never be disturbed? No, since such a place does not exist. A reasonably quiet place where you're unlikely to be disturbed is sufficient. Letting others in your house know you're not to be interrupted is a good idea. Some parents post a "meditating" sign on their closed door. It helps if you can place a flower, an incense burner or a piece of art (such as a statue, poster, tapestry or tanka) in your meditation area to give it a personal touch. Time is more important than externals like the size of the room or the hue and intensity of the ambient light. You need to set enough time to allow yourself to fully relax into a meditative state in which you can move inside into your own "inner space."

Meditation Myths

There are many myths that keep people away from trying meditation or induce them to stop before they ever get the hang of it. One is that meditation requires emptying your mind of all content, so you've failed if you haven't suppressed all perceptions, thoughts, memories and feelings. Another is that meditation exists solely to calm and relax us, like a hot bath, which would mean that feeling frightened or anxious during meditation makes one a failure. Another myth is that the goal of each meditation session is to have a great life-changing insight. Another is that successful meditators are able to sit for hours, and short sessions are of no benefit.

All of these assumptions are rejected by meditation instructors. They will tell you that the mind can never be emptied and it's hopeless to try; that feelings come and go unbidden and we benefit more from investigating negative feelings with curiosity and learning from them than from seeking to eliminate them; that spectacular insights are very rare during meditation even for very experienced meditators; and that it's the quality, not the quantity, of meditation that counts. With all that said, the fact is that with regular meditation practice you will be able to slow and deepen your breathing, relax your body, calm your jittery mind and free yourself from servitude to all the little thoughts that fly by. You will also develop the ability to connect more directly with reality as it truly exists by releasing the need to employ categories, distinctions, comparisons and judgments in order to "understand" reality.

Learning to Meditate

There are books, CDs and Internet courses on how to meditate, which you can use alone in the privacy of your own home. Learning from a teacher in person at a meditation class is more fruitful. The teacher will guide you, inspire you and answer your questions. You can use the Internet to find organizations within your community that sponsor classes on meditation. You can also hire a teacher to come to your home or office to teach you (and perhaps others on your staff). As lawyers we routinely use expert consultants to teach us about a great many technical subjects we did not study in college or law school. Think of a meditation teacher as an expert witness to help you improve the quality of your life. Find one you like. Cost won't be a problem, since meditation teachers charge just a fraction of the experts we hire to prepare our clients' cases for trial.

Special Benefits of Group Meditation

Whether you are a complete beginner or a highly experienced person who has meditated for decades, meditating with others in a group provides special benefits. The single most important one is the energy field generated by all group members meditating at the same time. To understand it you have to experience it. Unless you live in a monastery, retreat center or meditation institute you are likely to meditate on your own most of the time, and meditate with a group once a week. That once a week is a very nourishing time. Group members bond, encourage each other, explore issues of mutual interest and exchange ideas to remove blocks to meditation or to enhance the experience.

How to Meditate—
The Basics of Physical Positioning

I am a beginner in meditation. My knowledge pales in comparison to that of teachers who have thirty, even forty years of experience. For that reason, the idea of me instructing anyone on how to sit while meditating strikes me as funny. Remember that I am urging you to take a class and learn there from the more experienced instructor. On the other hand, while I have your attention, I can pass along what I have learned during daily meditation for the past two years. Perhaps this will make meditation seem less alien or less frightening to you and encourage you to give it a try.

Meditation strikes many lawyers as a strange practice at first, since it doesn't require them to do anything, make anything, fix anything or prove anything. The core of meditation is taking time from daily activities for sitting quietly and focusing inward. It can be done any time of day, but the early morning is especially good because that is a quiet time and it sets a nice platform for your day. Sitting cross-legged on a cushion is comfortable because it elevates your hips above your knees. Lawyers who are expert in yoga can sit in lotus or half lotus. Beginners typically meditate for 15-20 minutes, which can seem like an eternity until you get the hang of it. I prefer to meditate barefoot. If you get cold you can wear socks or even cover your legs and feet with a blanket.

Using Kum Nye, Sound or Mindful Walking
to Prepare for Seated Meditation

Some people prefer to just sit and meditate without any kind of preparation. They get into the mood by slow, deep breathing while seated on the cushion. Other people prefer to prime themselves by chanting or using Kum Nye (Tibetan yoga) for five to ten minutes. Kum Nye was developed to facilitate meditation by opening up one's breathing and one's heart rather than to promote a flexible, strong body. At Nyingma, where I study in Berkeley, they teach Kum Nye along with meditation. For those of us who lack the time or inclination to learn Kum Nye, doing some slow, gentle neck rolls at the start of meditation works well too. Instead of Kum Nye, you can produce beautiful sounds on your own using a Tibetan singing bowl that you can purchase on the Internet for $30 to $40. Listening to the sound gradually fade into nothingness primes you for meditation.

Other people may do a bit of walking meditation before sitting on the cushion. This involves walking very slowly in your meditation space, feeling each foot sink into the ground (which could be a carpet or bare floor). While doing this slow walking you allow your mind to register sensations without trying to interpret them. For example, you take in the temperature of the room, the color of the walls, the softness or hardness of the floor, etc. My instructor says feeling the weight of your feet on the floor will ground you for meditation or for challenging situations in the world. If you're on the phone with or face-to-face with opposing counsel and he says something that really ticks you off, instead of blasting him, you can pause, breathe and feel your feet grounded on the floor. When you respond you are likely to come from a calmer, more reflective place. A grounded lawyer is a balanced lawyer who is not likely to be pushed over or need to violently push back.

The Posture for Seated Meditation

I have been taught the seven gestures posture for seated meditation. Take your seat on the cushion and feel your sit bones pressing against it. Raise your torso up so your spine is erect but not rigid. Keep your belly soft. Shoulder blades should be down, not scrunched-up. Hands rest gently on your knees consistent with the notion of being receptive, not defensive. Your neck is extended without strain as if a string were attached to the top of your head pulling it up. Tilt your head slightly forward, with eyes cast down and chin slightly tucked in. Depending on personal preference, you can close your eyes, or keep them open, with a soft gaze toward a spot on the floor a few feet in front of you.

My instructor says keep your eyes "soft," and by that she means you're not squinting, staring or tensing your eye muscles. You can play with this by allowing the weight of your eyeballs to sink down into your eye sockets. To release tension from the eyes prior to meditation, you can use your thumbs to very gently press against the bony ridges of the upper eye sockets and your index fingers to very gently press against the bony ridges of the lower eye sockets. Keep your jaw soft, with the tip of your tongue touching the upper palate just behind the front teeth. This helps with energy flow during the in and out breaths. The seven gestures posture feels quite good and can be held for a long time. You may notice a tendency to slump, which you can easily correct by lifting your torso.

The physical posture of meditation can produce pain, itching or numbness when held over time. If sitting cross-legged puts too much pressure on your ankles, you can switch legs. If your legs still hurt or feel numb, then take a break and stretch. Sitting quietly is not easy. It's okay for beginners to itch. Advanced meditators not only endure the pain and itching, but make these part of the meditation.

The Core of Meditation

Slow, gentle breathing quiets and warms the body. A quiet body quiets the restless mind, giving rise to an awareness that goes beyond all particular sensations, memories, thoughts and feelings. When I meditate I begin my focus on the in-breath as it moves through my nose and mouth into my belly and the out-breath as it moves from my belly out through my mouth. Whether you focus just on the in-breath, just on the out-breath or on both, the important thing is to relax, place your awareness gently and lightly on your breath and gradually merge your awareness with your breath.

Once you are in synch with your breath, begin paying attention to the gaps between the thoughts in your head or the gaps in the sounds outside you (such as the distinct phrases of a bird singing outside your window). You have reached the place of meditative calm when you are in touch with what lies between and behind the thoughts and sounds that occupy your mind. This emptiness turns out not be an anxiety-producing void, but a place of tranquility, warmth and ease.

Meditation is a journey inward into your body, and a leave-taking from the chattering mind, the mind that is constantly worrying or obsessing about something. As you gain experience, the thoughts in your head become like a radio playing in the background that you're no longer listening to but forgot to turn off.

The chattering mind is characterized by Beta waves on EEG. As you meditate your brain waves are going alpha—they are now slower, more relaxed and more rhythmic. You are creating a sense of peace and a place of refuge, where you can go for wise decision-making when the world outside becomes chaotic or threatening. Although meditators journey inward, they are not cut off from the world. Experienced meditators with well-developed alpha wave patterns are very sensitive to and in touch with the world. Indeed, they feel a stronger, more heart-infused connection with others than non-meditators (except for those who pray regularly).

The Five Hindrances

The Buddha taught that there are five main obstacles to developing and improving one's meditation practice: craving, aversion, sloth, restlessness and doubt. These hindrances to meditation are the very same obstacles that block people from being truly present and engaged in their day-to-day lives, and to enjoying their lives. The Buddha taught that meditation functions like a mirror. It enables us to observe how our minds operate and to transform them by releasing suffering and gaining freedom and joy.

By craving, the Buddha meant any strong desire afflicting the mind such as those for sex, alcohol or food. By aversion, he meant a pushing away of negative experiences during meditation including physical discomfort, money worries or sadness over past life events. By sloth, he meant becoming drowsy during meditation and beginning to fall asleep or actually falling asleep. Restlessness is the state of being agitated and unable to settle down mentally, physically or both. These days restlessness can be due to too many coffees, cokes or other caffeinated beverages. It can come from our habitual level of frenetic, nonstop activity. The fifth hindrance of doubt refers to every species of doubt that can make the project of meditation seem doomed to failure. It can include judging yourself incapable of meditating competently, doubting that meditation will ever benefit you personally or even doubting that meditation works for anyone.

Antidotes to the Five Hindrances

Trying to suppress a craving just makes it stronger. The way to handle craving is to turn your awareness to it in a spirit of detachment, which will lead it to evaporate. For aversion, the Buddha advised using lovingkindness, which is being compassionate toward yourself. By wishing yourself peace, calmness, good health and joy, while focusing on the breath, these negative feelings will dissipate. Drowsiness and sleepiness are a common problem for beginning meditators. The purpose of meditation is the development of awareness, of becoming truly awake to life. You are not meditating to feel like a jellyfish at a New Age spa. If you become sleepy you can help to re-energize yourself by straightening your back, slowly rotating your head, doing some rapid chest breathing, opening your eyes or even briefly standing up. If you do fall asleep, my teacher counsels not berating yourself, but forgiving yourself and going back to the meditation.

Early attempts at meditation can produce boredom and restlessness, especially for Type A people like lawyers, because you're not figuring stuff out or getting tasks done. Sometimes people become bored, because little happens as they sit. Eckhart Tolle says the mind searches for things that are "interesting" and it likes to grab hold of data to analyze, interpret and label. Sitting still can be painful for the mind, which can fail to see the point of the exercise. The mind also likes to feel it is making progress, so it needs a reference point in time.

Tolle says that stillness, which brings us in contact with our deepest self, with who we really are, is timeless. The mind tends to rebel against timelessness, which has no reference point.

When the mind is not given content, it tends to generate its own. Beginning meditators can be visited by a mind-generated show. When I began meditating I would see blobs of color and all manner of swirling shapes. Lawyers may start editing motions or trial briefs in their heads. You can set these inspired ideas aside, refocus on your breath and then write them down after you're done meditating. Some beginners have thoughts related to the meditation process. "Will I ever gain an insight? Am I doing this right? Is this going to help me in any way?" When you're not used to sitting quietly, the passage of time can be as agonizing as water torture. This is restlessness.

The Buddha taught that everything which arises passes away and this is true of sensations, perceptions, thoughts, feelings and desires. Teachers of meditation say it is useless to try and stop them from arising, but if you sit quietly they will pass. By allowing them to pass you prove to yourself that they are powerless to control you and you increase your own freedom. The practice of allowing them to arise and pass develops your ability to resist distraction. Do not waste energy trying to push away bits of mental content. Just watch in a detached way and they will pop like soap bubbles.

It can really help to classify thoughts and feelings. This is done not to suppress them or push them from consciousness, but to take away their potency as distractions. If you're having obsessive thoughts about the past or future, you can help yourself by saying in your own head "thoughts about the past" or "thoughts about the future." You can defuse the potency of feelings as distractions by labeling them. Thus you can say "fear," "anger" or "lust." This helps train you to observe what is going on in your mind. The more you understand your own mind, the better you will become at meditation and the more present you will be in everyday life.

Lawyers are especially vulnerable to the fifth hindrance of doubt. We scoff at opinions as subjective interpretations of data that can be bought and sold. We demand that all assertions of fact be proven by hard evidence that cannot be refuted by any rational mind. We refuse to make leaps of faith or rely on intuition. How are we going to overcome doubts that make us want to ditch meditation after giving it a day, a week or a month? My teacher says to look to inspiring people we know and to consider their wisdom, the remarkable things they have achieved and the lives they have changed for the better. With this inspiration, we can harness the energy to keep going until we begin reaping obvious benefits from meditation.

For me, gaining confidence in meditation is like gaining confidence in running. An out-of-shape person who starts to run after years of inactivity finds the first few runs painful, tiring and discouraging, but if he stays with it, he finds he can endure longer distances with less and less pain and fatigue. Gradually his confidence builds and he comes to enjoy running. It's much the same with meditation.

Progress in Meditation

It takes at least three weeks of daily practice to begin to have the slightest inkling of what meditation is about. The benefits of meditation keep increasing over a lifetime. To really deepen your meditation practice it would help to go on a retreat to a place like Spirit Rock in northern California or the Omega Institute in upstate New York. Not everyone can take the time to go on a meditation retreat because of cost, work obligations, family obligations or both. One alternative is to get a group of friends together and pool your money to pay a meditation teacher to come to your home, or you can join a Sangha and go once a week. A Sangha is a meditation community that rents a room through voluntary payment of "dana."

How to end a Session of Meditation

When I meditate in a group, the leader will use a sound (such as a cymbal or bell) to signal the close of the session. We chant to share the benefits of what we received with the world. My instructor has us chant Om Ah Hum (pronounced OOOOMMM, AAAHHH, WHOM) three times. Each word is chanted in a slow, calm, monotonal way with a brief pause between words. The Om expands head energy, the

Ah opens the channel between head and heart energy and the Hum increases heart energy. When we finish chanting, we bow our heads, put our hands together under our chins in prayer position and dedicate the merits of our meditation to a specific person, a group of persons or to "all beings." I always dedicate the merits of my personal sessions of meditation, too.

Bringing Meditation From the Cushion to the Law Office

It's a good idea not to tell everyone you know that you've started Buddhist meditation. This will generate expectations on their part that you are going to be calm and serene in all situations from now on. The first time you get angry and throw up your hands or yell, they may respond with laughter or statements of mockery like, "Some Buddhist you are!" Stay humble and stay quiet about your beginner's commitment. It will take time for your attitudes and behaviors off the cushion and in the world to change. Yet it will happen. Indeed, the greatest benefits of meditation lie in life transformation. As your skill and joy in meditation increase, the more you will discern how your daily life has improved.

Lawyers give speeches not just in the courtroom but at the office and at home. When someone pushes their buttons, they respond with a speech. The underlying thought could be, "You are being disrespectful toward me." This will trigger a speech from a mental cassette such as, "After all I've done for you, how dare you treat me this way" to a child. To an opposing lawyer it could be, "Disagree with me if you want to. That's your privilege. But you have no right to speak rudely to me like that, you pompous ass. It's lawyers like you that are ruining our profession."

Meditation mindfulness enables us to spot the thought and stop the speech before it begins. The thought is a judgment. The speech that gets triggered by the judgment is a neural circuit that represents a reflexive response. Meditation can help us learn to listen patiently, instead of interrupting angrily, and it can act like a mental circuit breaker which enables us to stop habitual mental patterns that serve only to spark anger within and around us.

Brain Transformation: The Cognitive and Social Benefits of Meditation

Kamal Sarma says, "I like to think of meditation as an insurance policy to protect your most precious asset—your mind. Meditation is about keeping the mind strong, clear and resilient." How does meditation accomplish this? Sarma says it does so by resting the mind and clearing it of trivia. The mind of the busy professional is crammed with much information that is unimportant and irrelevant to his goals. He gets distracted by it. Sarma says that quieting and clearing the mind can only be done through conscious effort while awake—for even during sleep the mind is active in processing information and consolidating memories through dreams.

Why can't we eliminate the distracting, tiresome monkey chatter in some way other than meditation? Vacations won't do it. Naps won't do it. Nothing else will do it. Within minutes of getting back to the office, your mind starts racing again as if it had never stopped. To truly stop the clutter and "traffic," we need to control our flow of thoughts and our brain waves. Meditation is a way to do just that. Through meditation we develop the skills and power to relax and clear our minds, and through this comes rest [along with the] clarity to make better decisions and the ability to focus our minds to the task at hand."

In *Welcome To Your Brain*, the authors mention a study done on eight Tibetan Buddhist monks who spent entire days meditating over a period of years. While the monks meditated on compassion for all beings, their heads were attached to EEG leads and wires. The EEG reading showed brain activity building in a coherent, rhythmic manner suggesting that different neural structures were firing in synchrony. The increase in the synchronized signal was mostly at rates of 25-40 times per second, a rhythm known as gamma-band oscillation.

In some cases, the gamma rhythms in the monks' brain signals were the largest ever seen in people. The control group of beginners at meditation couldn't generate any gamma rhythms. This EEG study is an indication that experienced meditators have a superior level of mental clarity. Facing your daily challenges at the office with increased mental clarity will enhance your comfort, confidence and success.

There is MRI evidence that regular meditation practice enlarges parts of your brain that will improve your social interactions. Harvard trained psychiatrist Daniel J. Siegel, author of *The Mindful Brain*, is the Director of the Mindsight Institute and Co-Director of the UCLA Mindful Awareness Research Center. Based on brain scan studies, he says that regular mindfulness meditation practice generates an increase in the cortical thickness of key brain areas.

These are the medial prefrontal (MPF) area, the insula, the limbic areas and the centers of somatic awareness that project to the MPF as well as the mirror neuron system that regulates how we feel emotionally and somatically during contact with other minds. These areas of the brain are concerned with emotional self-regulation, emotional expressiveness and empathy. Experienced meditators are more able to weather emotionally distressing events without going to pieces, to feel compassion and to express positive emotions like love and joy.

Meditation and Motivation

How many times do you have to tell yourself to do something, say, write a brief, before you feel ready to do it? Five times, ten times? How many times have you had to walk around the block, drink coffee, return phone messages, check your email, clear your desk and do lots of other irrelevant stuff, before you felt ready to tackle a big writing assignment? And then, when you're about one hour into the work, an angry client calls to complain or you get an upsetting fax from opposing counsel, and the bubble bursts. You cannot get back into it.

Can you imagine what it would be like to tell yourself once and only once? Without the distractions of the monkey mind, this becomes possible. For reasons we do not understand, the monkey mind tends to latch onto the negative, and many of the passing thoughts we have during the day carry frustration, doubt, discouragement, greed, envy, resentment and so forth. The monkey mind tells us, "I'm too tired, too upset or too distracted" to start the brief right now. Can you also imagine how you would feel telling yourself how good your work is, what a good lawyer you are and that you have a decent shot at succeeding at your firm? Turning around your patterns and habits of thought requires gaining control of your monkey mind. This is what meditation can accomplish.

Meditation, Mindfulness and Wholeness

No matter how smart you are and no matter how many trials you've won, if you're a tense, uptight, angry person, then other people are not going to enjoy being around you. Meditation will not sap your intelligence or otherwise deplete your ability and willingness to win trials. What it will do is produce a spiritual sense of wholeness that is nourishing, and which makes you a happier person who others enjoy being around.

In his book chapter on *Wholeness and Oneness*, Jon Kabat-Zinn says we can experience our wholeness in meditation. When we do, we are able to come to terms with things as they are, deepen our understanding and compassion and lessen our feelings of anguish and despair.

Imperfect Meditation Is Better Than None

I will be the first to agree that a lawyer cannot function as a lawyer and earn a living while seated cross-legged in a cave somewhere in Tibet to explore stillness with a master of meditation. But there is no need for us to go to that extreme. We can all learn how to meditate wherever we live and we can all make time to practice meditation. Allan Wallace and Jon Kabat-Zinn both say it's not the quantity of time you put in, but the quality.

James Baraz says he makes time to meditate every day, and although his goal is to do it for hours, some days it's just five minutes, or even one minute. He says it's important not to beat yourself up for missing a day or meditating for less than the desired time. Meditation is largely about learning to love yourself and accept your human imperfections, to see the radiance and beauty of life in all its manifestations, in yourself, other humans, trees, butterflies, sunsets, and so on.

Meditation Is Not Just for Hippies—
Top Lawyers Do It, Too

In his book *Making Waves and Riding the Currents*, lawyer Charles Halpern chronicles his career as a founder of the public interest law movement and the first public interest law school, while describing his increasing involvement with and reliance upon meditation, meditation retreats, vision quests and hiking or canoeing in remote wilderness areas, as a way of getting in touch with his deepest self and cultivating wisdom. Halpern is a role model for the lawyer who seeks to become awakened and mindful, and to learn how to heal rather than aggravate conflict.

Halpern says he benefited greatly from Buddhist retreats conducted mainly in silence, where he received teachings that were sparse and simple, so unlike the torrent of words and complex concepts he used as a lawyer. The key principles he learned were the impermanence of all things, non-attachment to desires and outcomes, the interconnection of all beings, compassion for self and others and being committed to relieving suffering.

Over the years, a Buddhist friend named Mr. Sui taught Halpern many important lessons. For instance, he stressed that careful reflection on the stages of one's life utilizing feelings, not just analytic thinking, is a way to remain centered and make good decisions. Indeed any major decision should "draw on the resources of the whole person— their values, emotions, empathy, sense of justice." Sui taught that when responding to highly pressured situations, it's important to maintain one's empathy for all persons involved and not to lose sight of what was really at stake and what was really going on under the surface. He encouraged Halpern to make big decisions by opening his mind like the very widest view camera lens to take in the entire picture, not just a few small details that clamored for attention. Sui advised him to be like a still pond, reflecting the world just as it is, without distortion and without flattening out its complexities or putting any political or ideological filter between himself and the world.

Halpern is a living example of what the awakened lawyer looks like. Describing this new way of approaching law he says it's important not to get caught up in the negativity and combativeness, and better to approach tasks with "clear, relaxed, and mindful attention." Halpern says we don't need more self-righteousness, technical mastery of subject matter, unreflective anger and rigid insistence on legal rights. Rather we need more wisdom, balance, mental flexibility, humor and compassion along with the ability to deal with each other productively in a spirit of respect and good will.

In the Epilogue to his book Halpern gives a long description of what an ideal law firm would look like. "The lawyers would give more time to silence and introspection, and to assuring that their lives could be lived and enjoyed in balance, that career and ambition did not squeeze out family and personal growth. In their professional work, clear seeing would be valued—free from the screens of cynicism and materialism on one side, and ungrounded utopianism on the other. Core values of interconnection, humility and kindness would be reflected in their choice of cases, the way they related to adversaries, and the positions they advocated. They would be as zealous and determined in serving their clients' interests as any other lawyer. They would work with their clients to explore the long-term consequences of the issues they took on. The lawyers would regularly check into the extent that they were honoring their commitment to cultivate wisdom and support each other in that commitment."

Buddhism Is Not a Religion and May Be Safely Incorporated into Your Law Practice

The range of people who have embraced Buddhism as part of their lives is limitless. It includes members of every religious group as well as atheists and agnostics. Buddhism has no requirements for admission, no dogma, no rituals, no uniform and no holidays.

Anyone can add the teachings and practices of Buddhism (which all relate to meditation) into his life at any time. By meditating you gain patience, wisdom, compassion, wholeness and interconnectedness with others and you lose nothing but your current level of high stress, anger and suffering.

CHAPTER ELEVEN: SUGGESTED READING

Tarthang Tulku, *Gesture of Balance* (Dharma Publishing, 1977)

Tarthang Tulku, *Hidden Mind of Freedom* (Dharma Publishing, 1981)

Tarthang Tulku, *Knowledge of Freedom* (Dharma Publishing, 1984)

Mark Halpern, *Making Waves and Riding the Currents* (Berrett-Koehler Publishers, Inc., 2008)

Kamal Sarma, *Mental Resilience: The Power of Clarity—How To Develop the Focus of a Warrior and the Peace of a Monk* (New World Library, 2008)

Jack Kornfield, *Teachings of the Buddha* (Shambala Publications, Inc., 1996)

Daniel Siegel. M.D., *The Mindful Brain* (W.W. Norton & Company, 2007)

CHAPTER TWELVE

Self-transformation using authenticity, life balance and your right brain

THE MENTAL SUFFERING of lawyers has many causes and many solutions. In this chapter I want to focus on correcting our lack of personal authenticity, life balance and use of our right brain capacities.

Many lawyers live unconsciously in the sense they have no clear purpose for their lives, no coherent identity and no definite criteria for deciding how to spend their time. They are on auto-pilot making as much money as they can and winning as many cases as they can using their left brain skills. This is not a unique purpose which grows organically from their individual life experience. It is a role sold by law firms much like bacon cheeseburgers are sold by fast food joints. They're not good for you, but they make a tidy profit for the business.

Law can be practiced in many different ways with many different motivations. You can practice law in a heartless way or in a compassionate and heartful way. You can practice using your left brain only (like Mr. Spock) or you can use the social, emotional, creative and holistic intelligence that lies within your right brain. You can aggravate conflict to maximize your profit and others' pain or you can heal conflict and help heal the people in conflict. You can practice the slash-and-burn way or you can practice with the mindset of leaving the world a better place for your having been a lawyer.

Defining Authenticity

Authenticity evokes the concept of acting from your heart, not your head, from the inner knowing of your true path rather than doing what some boss, advertiser, politician or parent tells you to do. Being authentic is the opposite of adopting "success" behaviors that experts say will lead to higher positions, higher salaries and more peer recognition. These behaviors have little to do with who we are deep inside, and can set up internal conflicts that gradually fracture our identity.

When the Issue of Authenticity Knocks on Your Door

For unhappy lawyers "normal" is going through the motions while performing activities that don't serve who you were meant to be in this life. There are two ways reality can penetrate this numbness and trigger change in the lawyer who is receptive.

One way is the gradual buildup of perceptions that your career is deeply unsatisfying. Perhaps the lawyer clothes look and feel awkward. The office cubicles are too artificial. Communication is too formalized. There's too much emphasis on billing hours. Too much catty talk about other lawyers behind their backs. Too little loyalty. Too much cynicism about people. Too much competition. Too little connection. Too much talk about money in a profession that's supposed to be about rights, responsibilities, justice and equity. Too much bending of ethical rules behind closed doors. Too much pressure. Too little comradeship and laughter. Too much seriousness and gravity. Too little emotional expressivity. Too little joy.

The other way is a single traumatic event that breaks the glass case of denial. The event can be the death of a loved one, an unexpected job layoff, hitting bottom from an alcohol or drug problem or being diagnosed with a serious and potentially fatal illness.

The role of trauma (be it physical, emotional, social or financial) in tearing apart the "old normal" and forcing people to move to a "new normal" has been vividly described by Don Piper in *Heaven is Real*.

Piper says that once the shock of the trauma has worn off, we have a choice between desperately clawing our way back to a past that no longer exists, or accepting that the old normal is gone and making the decision to create the best life we can amidst our changed circumstances while drawing upon the big lessons learned from the trauma. As long as we are "teachable," we can profit from being squashed by life and emerge wiser, more mature human beings with more to offer our fellow humans.

Piper goes so far as to say that horrendous, life-altering trauma can be a gift, one that puts us in touch with who we really are and gives us a clear purpose to live out. For him and the people he's met on his speaking tours, trauma cleared the haze from their eyes, helping them see more clearly and feel more deeply. They were able to articulate a new, broader purpose for their lives that encompassed the change and found good in it.

Piper says he doesn't recommend being run over by an 18-wheel truck, but sometimes that's what it takes to make a good person who is merely tolerating his job and his life into a great person who is deeply content with his job and his life. If you are going through a very painful trauma right now, please remember it may be a gift in the long run.

Spiritual teacher Eckhart Tolle hits upon the same theme when he says that the beginning of a happy, fulfilling life rooted in who we really are is a "failed story." By failed story, he means the situation where the perfect life that someone has envisioned for us (be it Madison Avenue, our parents or our own ego), the one that we always banked on to make us feel complete and happy, comes to grief. It's the time when we realize it will never happen, when we taste it briefly but it's snatched away, or when it happens exactly as we envisioned but it's a huge disappointment.

At that moment when our story crumbles, we may become suicidal. But it is only then that we can let go of the story and free ourselves to live a meaningful life that springs from our higher self. It is only then that we can have compassion for ourselves, for all the time we wasted pursuing the realization of a delusional story of the perfect life that never had the potential to fulfill us. It is only then that we have compassion for others living in the same state of seeking happiness in the future by trying to make their own delusional story come true.

Pursuing Authenticity

Authenticity is living from the deep wisdom of your heart, not from the ever-changing whims of your ego or to gain someone else's approval. People who feel content or who are willing to put up with the status quo (no matter how unsatisfying) are not motivated to pursue authenticity. Let's say you can't tolerate your life as a lawyer any more or you've experienced an adverse event that puts your career in question. These are the circumstances that should put authenticity on your front burner. Yet, the pursuit of an authentic life is a matter of choice.

Why pursue it? Living authentically makes us purposeful and happy. It satisfies our deep yearning for meaning. When we're living authentically we can trust our instincts and be spontaneous and creative in the moment. When we live inauthentically we're likely to become very depressed. A lawyer can become seriously depressed when he realizes the role he's playing is like a straightjacket, rather than a vehicle for full and enjoyable self-expression.

In the June 2008 issue of *Psychology Today,* science writer Karen Wright says pursuing authenticity takes hard work. It takes intense inner concentration to divine what we really believe or how we really feel, and courage to express it openly to people who may or may not agree with you. To gain the required level of concentration, Wright says it's necessary (at least temporarily) to give up the distractions of shallow, short-lived pleasures and focus on achieving long-term happiness through the construction of a durable meaning for one's life.

Wright cites the sacred Hindu text, The *Bhagavad Gita*, to establish that human beings have a duty to realize their full potential in the world, to construct or discover a unique individuality, and thereby to live authentically. She also cites a Hasadic parable, the story of a Rabbi Zusya, a humble scholar who has a deathbed revelation. Zusya says, "In the next life, I shall not be asked, 'Why were you not more like Moses?' Instead, I shall be asked, 'Why were you not more like Zusya?'"

The Human Need for Meaning

As adults we benefit greatly from a clearly defined purpose in life that grows organically from who we are and from our life experiences. When we have such a purpose we can survive periods of tremendous stress as shown in Victor Frankl's book *Man's Search for Meaning*.

Frankl was a Jewish psychiatrist leading a conventional life in Austria when he was rounded up by the Nazis and placed in a series of four different concentration camps, including Auschwitz. In each of the camps Frankl observed fellow inmates quickly wither and die once they had lost their sense of purpose, their belief that their life had a specific meaning important enough to justify persistent efforts to survive in the face of incredible suffering. Frankl's pregnant wife, brother and parents died in the camps along with millions of other Jews, yet he found the will to go on and survived.

The purpose that fueled his will to survive was to outlive his internment and become a witness against his Nazi captors and torturers and the Jews who collaborated with them (the Capos), and to testify at a war crimes trial once the Allies had defeated the Nazis. More than anything, he wanted to see justice done and to prevent another genocide. For that purpose he was prepared to accept anything, to undergo anything.

Following WWII, Frankl returned to psychiatry and treated patients with what he called Logotherapy. The basic principal of Logotherapy was that all of us exist to discover and to pursue what is personally most meaningful to us. He said that man's search for meaning is the primary motivation in his life, and that people who live without meaning are depressed. Frankl said there is no abstract meaning of life that applies to everyone. He taught that each individual has his own specific vocation or mission in life to carry out a concrete assignment which demands fulfillment.

While the modern law office is hardly a concentration camp, it does impose a certain amount of hierarchical control over your comings and goings, your physical appearance, the values you publicly espouse, your speech and your behavior. In time you may come to see yourself as a cog in a machine and lose all sense that you are a free person living his chosen purpose. Frankl's way out is to develop a new meaning for your life and law practice to pursue.

Getting in Touch With Your Individual Life Purpose

Many of us ended up in law school because we weren't certain about what we wanted to do with ourselves as we approached college graduation. Many of us got out of law school without a strong preference for a particular field of law or type of law firm. We then bounced around for a period of years, often having regrets about career moves that were more impulsive than planned.

Without forming a road map for his career and life, a lawyer is just floundering around and reacting to chance events. Sorting out your priorities is crucial to being happy. If you don't know what good you hope to get out of your legal career, you're prone to depression. A lawyer is likely to feel better about himself if he takes the time to know himself and create a practice that serves his values, interests, talents, strengths and passions.

The process of getting to know oneself is an invaluable piece of psychological and spiritual work that lays the foundation for an existence that is purposeful and meaningful. For lawyers in mid-life an excellent resource is *Transitions* by William Bridges. You can also hire a life coach.

TECHNIQUES FOR GETTING IN TOUCH WITH WHAT'S IMPORTANT

Using Your Unconscious

There are a variety of techniques for accessing your life's purpose that bypass the rational mind and do not rely on conscious control. One is automatic writing. You get a pen and a writing pad, set a timer for 10 or 15 minutes and then just write down everything you'd like to do in your life without reflection. You then sift through what you wrote to find the gems. Another approach is to work with a hypnotherapist.

A third approach is timed creation of art around a theme. You could give yourself 10 or 15 minutes to create a drawing, a painting or a collage about your life's purpose. You can bring your artwork to a Jungian or other psychologist skilled in interpretation of symbolism.

Taking Time Out to Focus Completely on Your Life's Meaning

San Francisco psychotherapist Eric Maisel, Ph.D., has written a book called *The Van Gogh Blues: The Creative Person's Path through Depression*. Like Frankl, he sees depression as a loss of meaning. Unlike Frankl, Maisel emphasizes the use of creativity to restore meaning and overcome depression. Maisel counsels artists and writers. He relates that quite a few of his clients fall into depression soon after they achieve a success, like publishing a best-selling novel on the first try.

How come? Because they learn rather quickly how false was their hope that such a success would make everything in their lives right, and keep them permanently happy.

Once they publish a bestseller, their publisher, agent, family members and friends all develop expectations for a repeat success. The author puts more pressure on himself to make the second book a bigger success, and then the worst happens, The author gets writer's block and falls into self-doubt. The longer he goes without new ideas, the more he doubts himself and the more depressed he becomes.

I relate to Maisel's scenario. I would throw my entire being into preparing for the trial of a big, challenging case. After a successful outcome I would experience a brief feeling of elation. Yet each time, my expectation that other clients with big, interesting cases would flock to my door never panned out. My successes would be met with deafening silence like a tree falling in a deserted forest.

Months would go by when only small, boring cases trickled in. Fairly soon taxes, bills, new case expenses and family expenses would eat up my profit, and I would grow discouraged again. My career was always a seesaw. Given my natural human desire for steady progress, this aspect of law practice was frustrating and disheartening. I would wind up blaming myself and feel bad. In retrospect I was depending way too much on external circumstances, on the world's reaction to what I did. I wasn't focusing on or appreciating the personal meaning of what I was doing

Maisel tells his patients their depression has come from a loss of meaning, which is a crisis. He tells them that the task of fashioning a meaning for their lives rests squarely on their shoulders. If they ask for clarification, he says, "You haven't come to grips with what you intend your life to mean. Until you do, your depression can't lift." The typical client will reply, "How am I supposed to figure out what life means?"

Maisel then instructs: "Not what life means. What you intend *your* life to mean. You must stop everything and decide upon the purpose of your life. Once you've articulated your personal creed, you put it into action. You force life to mean what you intend it to mean." How do you get to the point of articulation? Maisel says, "Everything remains up for grabs in the meaning realm until you decide where meaning resides and what your life will mean. Even after you make a decision, nothing will be settled. You will have to make new, updated meaning as you learn from your experiences and as your circumstances change."

Maisel challenges depressed individuals to fashion a meaning tailor-made for their lives. But there is no one-size-fits-all plan. You have to have the courage, the patience and the will to sit down for however long it takes to envision and articulate a new meaning for your life. How can you do this? You could try a meditation retreat, a vision quest or camping in the woods on your own to walk through the forest and listen to your heart. Whatever it takes, it's a worthy project.

Exploring Your Human Need For Vocation

Brian J. Mahan says that from time to time we are exposed to people, situations or events that inspire us and "recruit us" to a higher purpose that he calls "vocation." Yet in nearly every case, we find ourselves drifting rapidly back to our routines, making excuses for why the time to change has not yet come and quickly forgetting about the experience. At any moment in our lives we are either moving toward ambition (which is all about wealth, possessions, status or power) or toward vocation (which is about purposeful service that provides spiritual nourishment).

Mahan says we are divided beings. We have a spiritual self that is empathic and compassionate, a self that can be inspired by an idealistic lecture and aspire to find meaning in serving others who need our help. This is the self that can feel the pain of others, a state of being he calls "blessed woundedness."

From this place of empathy, the spiritual self can respond with specific actions to help others, rather than turn away with excuses. The spiritual self doesn't say "get a job" when it encounters a homeless person with his hand out. This self feels a sense of inclusion with all humanity. It takes delight in the good fortune of family, friends and even strangers. It is sometimes called the big self or the true self, as distinguished from the little self or the false self aka the ego.

The false self represses and drowns out the voice of the spiritual self. When the two are in tension, the ascendant social scripts of our culture tend to prevail most of the time, unless there is "an epiphany of recruitment" to a larger cause. Even then the spiritual self moves us to pursue a vocation only when the individual stays in touch with the epiphany, keeps it before him and takes small, progressive steps in the real world to incorporate it into his life.

Mahan says epiphanies can range from the airy and subtle to the heavy and obvious. He likens them to the four horses described by the Buddha: the one that senses the rider's wishes without being touched, the one that responds with the slightest touch, the one that requires a harder touch and the one that has to be smacked to move. Mahan says most of us are like the fourth horse, and that's OK, because that's just the way people are—we are so immersed in our daily tasks, conflicts, pleasures and fantasies that we are out of touch with our deeper selves. We literally need to be smacked by life to have an epiphany.

Quoting Thomas Merton, Mahan says the spiritual self seeks to know itself by posing two questions: "If you want to identify me, ask me not where I live, or what I like to eat, or how I comb my hair, but ask me what I think I am living for, in detail, and ask me what I think is keeping me from living fully for the thing I want to live for."

What is the unique vocation that each person truly wants to live for? Mahan quotes Beuchner. It is "The place...where your deep gladness and the world's deep hunger meet." How do you know you have found your vocation? When you feel like a person named Marilyn whom Mahan uses as an exemplar in his book. When Marilyn found her vocation, "her life took on a kind of single-mindedness, a directedness, that she had never experienced before. There was no better place to be, nothing better she could conceive herself doing, nothing else calling to her from the wings, competing for her attention of re-evaluating her performance. Her life was a piece. She was alive—fully, exuberantly and incontestably."

Think about your energy level. If you're fatigued most of the time, and you don't have a medical illness or a psychiatric illness like major depression, then chances are your fatigue is related to lack of meaning or vocation in your life. Yes, we all work a lot of hours, but when you have meaning and vocation, the hours fly by and your energy feels limitless.

Mahan's book contains useful exercises for self-discovery and self-actualization, which I commend to all of you. The hardest thing about being a lawyer in a world ruled by ambition and invidious comparison of winners with losers, is to stay in touch with the youthful idealism and compassion which lie repressed beneath everyday consciousness. As we feel our younger selves and our nobility slipping away, we come up with one rationalization after another to stop feeling grief and angst.

Eventually we have such a hard time looking at ourselves in the mirror that drinking or using drugs will no longer do the trick, and we become suicidal. If you're not living authentically, please buy Mahan's book and start doing the exercises as a way of self-help.

ACTIVELY MAINTAINING BALANCE IN YOUR LIFE

The psalm in Ecclesiastes which says there is a season for everything under heaven, the Buddha's Middle Way and the Native American medicine wheel are three powerful illustrations of the concept of life balance. The saying that "all work and no play makes Jack a dull boy" gets the same point across in folksy language.

Lawyers can get their jobs done very effectively without being somber, serious and grim-faced all the time. They can be completely competent without giving up time for pleasure, fun, smiles and laughter. Without balancing work with leisure and play, our lives feel less and less worth living. For our mental and physical health, it's essential that we restore balance to our lives.

Imbalance Causes Stress and Resentment

Many jobs in our economy are either 9-5 or part-time. You show up. You do what's required of you, and then you go home to eat in front of the TV, coach kids' sports, wash the car or whatever you like. Law is different. It demands everything. It eats up our time, our mental and physical energy and even our souls—if we allow it.

Life balance gets on our radar when we keep getting flack from the important people in our lives for not being with them when they need us. Gradually we recognize we have given up a lot to spend so much time in the office. This realization becomes sharper as our kids sprout up, as our bodies sag from age and lack of exercise, as we look at the stacks of pleasure books we never read and the vacation brochures we never used to take a vacation. We begin to develop resentment against the law as something that has robbed us of opportunities to experience freedom, pleasure, playfulness, creativity, socializing and travel.

You can't be happy if the demands of work cause you to miss out on the activities that give you the most pleasure and joy. Life is not a dress rehearsal. This is it, folks. If we do not find ways to enjoy ourselves during our working years, we've blown it. If you've done nothing except sacrifice your life for others, then you're likely to feel angry and resentful.

The clients who are always needing or wanting something from you can never be grateful enough to replace what you gave up for them, whether it's the magic moments of parent-child bonding, the beauty of canoeing on a river in the fall or having an undisturbed, candlelight dinner at a fine restaurant with your spouse. How do we stop feeling like prisoners of the law office, whose jobs have never allowed us to have fun?

Creating and Sustaining Balance in Your Life

Would you like to work, socialize, play and pray with a feeling of ease and a sense of flow? Would you like to engage in these activities without conflict, tension and guilt? The secret is life balance.

In *Perfect Balance*, life coach Paul Wilson says that all of us have activities we want or need to perform respecting our bodies, our work, our social life and spiritual life. All of us have goals, needs, responsibilities and values that we want or need to attend to in some manner. The problem for most of us is that we have not given conscious thought to balancing these elements of our lives or used conceptual tools to help us find our center of balance. We remain unbalanced by blaming the people we serve for taking all our time. We fail to notice that we are the ones setting our priorities and deciding how we'll spend our precious time.

You cannot afford to wait until you retire to create balance in your life. The clock on your life as lawyer and as a human being is ticking. If you fail to do justice to all of your important needs and take good care of yourself, no one else will. Now is the time to get going.

Don't beat yourself up for not having created life balance in your twenties, thirties or even your forties. Balance tends to come with the reflectivity and maturity that begins in middle age. As Byron Katie says, "Everything in the universe happens on time." If you haven't thought about life balance before, there's a good possibility you simply weren't ready. Perhaps an episode of depression has prompted you to think about it now. If that's what it took, then there was value in your depression.

Defining Life Balance

In *Perfect Balance,* Paul Wilson says leading a well-balanced life means integrating your work life, social life, spiritual life and the life of your body into a satisfying whole in which all major aspects of life are accommodated. For lawyers expressing emotions, valuing them and making them an important part of daily life is a key element in balanced living.

Wilson teaches clients not to see balance as exact mathematical equality in how much time or attention they give to each element. Rather, "the ideal is a balanced, harmonious whole, where all parts are interconnected and relevant." Wilson explains that this means giving each important area of your life its due, rather than living in such a way that each area competes with other areas and creates a sense of painful tension.

When our lives are balanced we feel good and we tend not to think at all about balance. But when our lives are out of balance and we are feeling painful tension (say, between work and social), the issue of restoring balance becomes crucial to our happiness. The obstacle is that we tend to passively blame others for imbalance, rather than taking personal responsibility.

Let's say I'm working 60-70 hours per week at a law office. I come home feeling drained, exploited and cranky. All I want to do is have a drink and get toasted, gobble down some dinner and plunk down on the couch in front of mindless TV. But I have a spouse or a spouse and children who want my attention and who are hoping for a positive interaction with me. If I feel too tired or too cranky to interact positively they will withdraw from me and I will feel bad. If I blame them for my workaholism with justifications like, "I'm working for you—so you can have a nice house and that's why I'm feeling so crappy," then I'm going to resent their response to me.

What if I looked in the mirror and saw that I chose to spend all that time in the office? When I recognize I'm both the puppet and the puppeteer pulling the strings, I'm no longer blaming anyone else for my choices. I become free to choose again in a way that restores balance to my life. To preserve that freedom it's much better to say, "I *choose* to spend more time with my spouse and kids" than "I *should* spend more time with them." "Choice" statements free us, while "should" statements impose obligations which breed resentment.

Using the Balance Diagram
to Figure Out What Needs Balancing

Wilson bids people seeking balance to create a circle with the poles of work and social at west and east and the poles of physical and spiritual at north and south. You are then to pencil in two lines connecting the four poles at the middle. With respect to work and social draw a small circle along the connecting line which represents which one you emphasize most. Depending on circumstances, the circle could be closer to work, closer to social or closer to the middle.

Now draw a line between the physical and spiritual and put a small circle near the one you emphasize most. If your life is in perfect balance, the two little circles will merge at the very middle of the large circle. However, the odds of that are low if you're a lawyer! Use the diagram to figure out which areas of your life you are neglecting the most. Could it be your body and your need for touch or your spiritual life?

Balance and the Body

Lawyers who spend endless hours in containers like cars and law office cubicles under fluorescent lights watching computer screens are out of balance. They are not using their bodies. They are not getting outside to bicycle the hills, hike in the woods, walk on the beach, kick a soccer ball or whack a tennis ball across the net. Physical activity is vital because it turns flab to muscle, improves your self-image and generates feel-good endorphins in your brain and body.

Physical activity helps you forget all about the irritations and anxieties of the law office and restores you. When you perform your exercise outdoors you gain the added benefit of perceiving and appreciating the beauty of nature. Beauty is healing. So is sleep. Lawyers who sacrifice sleep in order to work crazy hours will break down like machines that have overheated from constant operation.

Balance means we respect our body and make it a full partner in our lives rather than treating it as an object. We show respect for our body when we nourish it with good food and exercise; rest when we're tired; bathe and brush our teeth regularly; get regular teeth cleanings and medical checkups to prevent disease (like colonoscopies for lawyers over fifty); use rollers, stretching and massage to unbunch the tight muscles; soak in hot tubs to relax; or sit in saunas to sweat out toxins.

Balance and Touch

Human beings are covered in skin, which is extremely sensitive to and responsive to touch. Our bodies crave physical contact with others from the moment we are born, and we derive emotional warmth, reassurance and pleasure from it.

The scientific research showing humans have a lifelong emotional need for touch is set forth in a book by Ashley Montagu called *Touching: The Human Significance of the Skin*. Touching that makes us feel good includes sex with your spouse or partner, holding hands with a family member, massage from a therapist, self-massage, hugging friends, and petting your dog.

As a parent I love to let my son sit in my lap while we watch a movie at home. I still hug my son and his older sister and kiss them on the head. When my kids were younger I loved to carry them on my shoulders, play-wrestle with them and swing them around by their hands. I still remember the joy of letting my kids and their friends do a "dog pile" on me, when they jumped on one by one until I got up and everybody fell off laughing.

People who work in jobs involving touch, like the barbers who wash and cut your hair, tend to form personal bonds with their customers that can last years, even decades. Lawyers work in an occupation that involves virtually no touching except the occasional, stiff hand-shake. Long periods without touching or being touched are isolating and emotionally dehydrating.

I'm not suggesting that you start hugging judges, clients and opposing counsel. But I am suggesting that you find ways in your life to increase the frequency of appropriate touching. This could mean regularly holding your spouse's hand, gently patting a client on the back as he leaves your office and more physical play with your younger children. Joyful sex with your spouse or partner is great. Even a sensual massage can set your world right.

Balance and Spirituality

Balance requires meaningful involvement with the spiritual aspects of life. Some people get their spiritual needs met through a traditional religion like Judaism, Christianity, Islam; their well known offshoots; or their esoteric and mystical versions. For others it is paganism, shamanism or a nature religion. For still others it is a form of meditation such as Buddhist or TM. Some people find their spirituality in helping others, whether it's working in a soup kitchen or building dwellings with Habitat for Humanity.

Spirituality requires perceiving and being affected by aspects of reality that go beyond material forms. Spirituality is concerned with unifying what seems to be separate, healing our human pain and becoming whole. It is indispensable for a balanced life. If you've neglected spirituality and you're really uncertain about which form of spirituality would most appeal to you, then take time to experiment.

Restoring Balance by Working Smarter, Not Harder

If you're reasonably competent at what you do, you should be able to finish your work at the office and leave enough time for pleasure, socializing and recreation. If you get home at nine p.m. or later each work night, Wilson says there's probably an unconscious agenda that hasn't been brought to light in therapy. Some of us are straining fruitlessly to prove our worth to long dead parents; to hide childhood shame by creating a big professional reputation; or to gain the approval of a spouse, sibling or other person.

The problem is that dead parents can't say, "You've finally made it." The project of gaining someone else's approval is flawed, since none of us can control the thinking of another. If we're going to balance work with other activities, we need to reframe the meaning of work so that work ceases to be an addiction. If this means healing childhood pain from never satisfying critical parents, then it's worth spending the time in psychotherapy, hypnotherapy, drama therapy or any other therapy that heals you.

Obstacles to Balance

Lawyers are compulsive. While many humans try to cram as much activity in a day as their energy will allow, lawyers are notorious for it. We pride ourselves on being multi-taskers. If we can eat lunch at our desks while conversing with others on the speakerphone, signing checks, reviewing emails and scanning our home page for breaking news developments, we feel as if we are justifying our presence on earth as well as our salaries.

In *Crazy Busy*, Edward Hallowell, M.D., tells us that this nonstop frenzy of activity is stressing us out, depleting our energy, making our work mediocre, robbing us of real human contact and leaving no time for relaxation, reflection, creative pursuits or the search for meaning in our lives. Without balance in your life, you are as unstable as a three-legged table. Depression, immune system dysfunction, ill health and other problems are soon to follow.

Why are we so compulsive in the first place? Eckhart Tolle says the main reason is seeing ourselves as a work in progress, and believing falsely that we can only become happy when we reach a certain level of success (one that keeps rising as we accomplish more). To get there we must constantly labor, struggle and accrete things. Yet we're not human becomings, we're human beings.

Tolle says that stopping and enjoying stillness is the portal to deep enjoyment of the preciousness of life. Taking a pause and becoming still is the antithesis of the lawyer's way, but it's one thing we desperately need to become less stressed, more balanced and more in touch with life. A spiritual master like Tolle walks around with a constant sense of stillness within. For the rest of us, using meditation is a great way to perceive inner stillness.

Strategies for Restoring Balance

There is no "one size fits all" approach to restoring balance in your life. You have to find the one that works for you.

Paul Wilson's Calm Way

In order to use the Calm Way, we Type A lawyers need to ratchet down our compulsivity to do everything better than everybody else. The Calm Way won't work if we turn the quest for balance into a "Rocky"-style boot camp complete with headband, grunting, sweating and "Eye of the Tiger" theme music. It's crucial we don't move the pendulum from not pursuing balance at all to pursuing it with tightness and tension.

The first step in finding perfect balance is getting calm. Wilson recommends sitting in an erect posture (as if you were a marionette with the puppeteer pulling your head and neck straight with a string), slowing your breathing and turning your focus within. Now that you're centered, Wilson says it's time to let go of your compulsions, let go of your frenetic worries about the past and future and settle down.

In this relaxed state of mind you can go through the exercises he has in his book for sorting out your life priorities. Wilson has a Life Priorities Calculator in his book that incorporates a long, well thought out list of human values to live by and a chart for balancing your goals, responsibilities, needs and values. He says that if you use these tools in a calm frame of mind, you will not only enjoy the process but gain a better result by accessing your intuition.

Indeed, the only way to access the deepest levels of your being is through intuition, not rational thought. If you find Wilson's approach appealing, I suggest you get a copy of his book and go through the exercises. You can find him on the Internet at www.thecalmway.com.

Using the Rational Mind to Set Priorities

In *Crazy Busy*, Dr. Hallowell recommends using the conscious mind to set priorities. First, sit down in a quiet place and make a list of your priorities in life. This means figuring out what activities are most important for you, the things you most want to do before you die. Next you make a systematic assessment of how you actually spend your time, and the personal value you receive for each unit of time spent. Take note of how little time you spend doing what you love, and how much time and effort you put into doing things you can't stand out of a sense of obligation or for fear of some adverse consequence like being yelled at, being fired from a job or being abandoned by friends.

Then you rewrite your time budget so it's consistent with doing the things that most matter to you. The time budget should eliminate as much as possible the boring, unpleasant and undesirable things that waste your time and effort. By doing this you are actually taking back some control over your life, and building a life that is much more satisfying and likely to create happiness. Don't wait until retirement to clear your mind and finally get to work on figuring out why the universe put you here. By then it's too late.

ACCESSING YOUR RIGHT BRAIN TO BECOME WHOLE

To lead a balanced life with a full range of emotional expressivity, social interactions, creativity, and spirituality, a lawyer must access the remarkable powers of intelligence that lie largely unused in his right brain.

The Functions of the Left and Right Brain

The human brain has a left and a right cerebral hemisphere. The differences in their function were first appreciated in the 1860s by neurologist Paul Broca in France. Dr. Broca discovered that the motor impulses for articulate speech came from a small area located on the left front side of the brain. The discovery came initially from his autopsy of a stroke patient who could not speak except to utter the word "tan" over and over.

During the past 150 years, neuroscience has established certain basic differences in function between the two cerebral hemispheres. The left brain is known to be verbal. It handles words rather than music, pictures and shapes. It excels in sequential, linear reasoning. It's good at breaking down information into small bits and analyzing them logically. Left-brainers are good at remembering names, solving riddles and crossword puzzles and memorizing time charts for when events occurred.

People who live primarily through their left brain fail to develop their empathy, intuition, artistic abilities or creativity. They are the Mr. Spocks who are computer-like, logical, literal and textual. They have difficulty picking up on social cues and in receiving or expressing love and affection. Daniel Pink says left-brainers are epitomized by computer programmers, accountants, lawyers and engineers who excel at number-crunching, analysis and logic.

The right side of the brain is known to be non-verbal, visuo-spatial and emotional. It relies on intuition and hunches. The right brain recognizes faces, interprets the emotional messages of facial expressions and non-verbal gestures, perceives things simultaneously, understands situations holistically, and synthesizes data into a big picture or gestalt. People with a right brain style of thinking are simultaneous, synthetic, holistic, big picture, metaphorical, aesthetic and contextual.

Right-brainers focus on relationships and tend to be warm, empathic and caring, the reverse of left brain people who tend to be cold, self-contained and insensitive to other people's feelings. Right brainers excel at artistry, intuition, invention, pattern detection, empathy, taking the long view, pursuing meaning and seeking the transcendent. They are makers of and lovers of art and music.

Pink says right-brainers are exemplified by teachers of meditation, yoga or spirituality; people who design cars, interior environments, household products or clothes to meet human needs for utility and beauty; visionaries who write or teach about emerging artistic, social, economic or political trends; creative people such as painters, photographers, fiction writers and poets; and caregivers such as nurses, social workers, drug and alcohol counselors and stress reduction counselors.

How the Left and Right Brain are Connected

The two hemispheres of the human brain are interconnected by a vast network of 300 million nerve fibers called the corpus callosum. Its purpose is to facilitate cross-transfers of information between the hemispheres at lightning speed. Birth defects and acquired brain damage from stroke or trauma may limit the function of the corpus callosum.

What Happens When the Left and Right Brain are Disconnected?

Much of what we know about the cognitive effect of physically disconnecting the two brain hemispheres comes from the work of Cal Tech professor Roger Sperry who won the Nobel Prize in physiology in 1981. Beginning in the 1960s Sperry began his work on split-brain patients. These are people who had frequent, severe epileptic seizures that threatened to kill them and ruined their quality of life. These patients were not helped by any combination of medications or even by partial, surgical removal of temporal lobe tissue.

To save their lives and give them back quality of life, neurosurgeons completely severed their corpus callosum. The theory was that initial seizure activity could not blossom into a grand mal seizure (an uncontrolled electric storm across the whole brain) unless it crossed the corpus callosum, so that cutting the corpus callosum should cause seizures to taper out. The surgeries worked. The patients no longer had grand mal seizures, but they did act strangely.

Sperry worked with split-brain patients to show that normal human perception, learning and behavior come from the two halves of the brain sharing information. His experiments showed that surgical separation of the two hemispheres prevented them from sharing information, and led to a person functioning as if he had two separate brains which did not know what the other brain was perceiving or thinking.

For example, the left brain analyzes the literal meaning of words, while the right brain detects the emotional content of words and interprets non-literal, metaphoric language. A person with a split brain who heard "I hate you" spoken in a sweet, soothing and seductive way would not know the speaker was expressing attraction to him. A person with a split brain who was told, "You have a heart as big as Kansas" would be at a loss to understand that expression, because it is absurd when taken literally.

What It's Like to Live Only in Your Right Brain

Lawyers are very verbal and live in their left brain. What would it be like to get stuck in your right brain? This is what actually happened to Jill Bolte Taylor. Inspired by her brother's schizophrenia, Ms. Taylor went into neuroscience research. For many years she studied the brains of normal people and people with severe mental illness on a sub-cellular level in the Department of Psychiatry at Harvard Medical School.

On December 10, 1996, she awoke with an ice pick headache behind her left eye. Within the space of four hours, she lost the ability to understand or speak words, due to a massive stroke on the left side of her brain. With a great deal of effort she dialed the phone number of a colleague and made some incoherent sounds into the receiver. He figured out she had suffered a stroke and sent an ambulance in time to save her life.

Ms. Taylor spent the next eight years recovering her ability to read, write, speak and use her right arm and right leg normally. During her recovery, especially during the early portion, she spent most of her waking hours living in her right brain. Consequently, Ms. Taylor underwent a dramatic personal and spiritual transformation from her experience.

She speaks all over the country telling us that we can expand our consciousness by choosing to live more in our right brain. You can read her book *A Stroke of Insight* or save time by listening to the talk she delivered under the same name on March 12, 2008, sponsored by www.ted.com.

In her book and her talks, Taylor stresses that our two brain hemispheres have different styles of thinking and different personalities. She describes the right side as having circuitry that produces emotional warmth, a sense of connection with all other beings and feelings of peace and calm. She calls it the "We" consciousness that is plugged into the present moment and which lets us know what the present looks like, sounds like, feels like, smells like and tastes like. The right side exists in a timeless realm with no urgency to act.

Taylor says the left side of the brain is the ego, the "I" consciousness, the single and solitary individual who is cut off from everyone else. She says the left hemisphere is focused purely on survival. It races back and forth from past memories to projections of what it fears will happen in the future, in an anxious effort to control the environment and avoid harm.

Are You More Left- or Right-Brained?

If you're not sure if you're left- or right-brain dominant, there are many different ways of finding out. Daniel Pink suggests you try Tecmo's Right Brain Game (www.tecmogames.com), Right Brain Paradise (www.bluelavawireless.com), and doing the drawing exercises in the famous series of books called *Drawing on the Right Side of the Brain* that Betty Edwards launched in 1979. Pink's book has many exercises to strengthen your right-brain function, for those of you who have ignored or suppressed the talents of your right brain.

Ways to Promote the Integration of Your Left and Right Brain

Ninety percent of people are right-handed and left-brain dominant. But this doesn't mean you can't work at integrating your two brain hemispheres so you can be a more complete and creative person. If you like art, try the exercises in the book series *Drawing on the Right Side of the Brain*. You can learn a musical instrument or attend more music concerts to activate your right brain.

Visualization exercises strengthen cooperation of the two hemispheres. You can buy a book or CD on visualization exercises to help you have a question answered, overcome a fear, enhance a skill or rehearse a presentation. Training in non-violent communication will help you strengthen the empathy and social connectedness associated with the right brain. Meditation, which is non-verbal and connects people with the formless and timeless aspects of existence, helps access the right side of the brain, too.

To be a complete person requires being a full-brained person. When we are half-brained, and operating only from our non-empathic, analytic, left brain we feel emotionally and socially disconnected from clients and the other lawyers we must work with to resolve disputes. If you believe Daniel Pink, developing your right brain and increasing your use of it in your career as a lawyer is not just a luxury. It's an imperative for survival as a lawyer because the "Information Age" is passing out of existence and making way for the "Conceptual Age" in which right-brainers will dominate the economy.

Charles Schulz, the warmhearted and wise author of "Peanuts," said: "Life is like a ten-speed bicycle. Most of us have gears we never use." When we start using all the gears in our brains, we will move beyond the limitations of legal formalism. We will experience a gush of sociability, creativity and spirituality. We will know balance and wholeness for the first time.

CHAPTER TWELVE: SUGGESTED READINGS

Daniel H. Pink, *A Whole New Mind* (Riverhead Books, 2006)

Edward M. Hallowell, M.D., *Crazy Busy: Overstretched, Overbooked, and About to Snap!* (Ballantine Books, 2006)

Victor E. Frankl, *Man's Search For Meaning* (Beacon Press, 2006)

Ashley Montagu, *Touching: The Human Significance of the Skin* (Harper & Row, 1986)

CHAPTER THIRTEEN

Learning to eat and exercise to protect your physical and mental health

Good Nutrition is Essential for a Long Lifespan, a Long Healthspan and Optimal Daily Functioning

AN ESSENTIAL PART of making and keeping your life an upward spiral is staying healthy, strong and energized. What you eat and drink and what sort of exercise you do on a regular basis will determine your quality of life. Lawyers need to consume foods that provide slow burning energy to get them through long days of hard work while sustaining high levels of mental concentration. They should also eat foods that are protective against depression and against preventable metabolic illnesses that could shorten their life span or healthspan (the time in your life when you are healthy, vigorous and vital).

By sticking to a good nutrition and exercise plan lawyers can avoid obesity, insulin resistance, diabetes, hypertension, heart disease, stroke and cancer. If they consume appropriate foods and supplements, lawyers can support their brain health, keep their wits sharp and delay or prevent cognitive decline.

Unfortunately far too many lawyers neglect good nutrition and exercise, and they wind up paying for it. One example is the apple-shaped lawyer with the protruding pot belly who is a candidate for Type II diabetes, cardiovascular disease, sleep apnea, depression and early dementia. But staying slim doesn't mean you're healthy if you stay slim by skipping meals, eating non-fat foods without any good Omega 3 fats, smoking or using dangerous weight loss supplements. It's time we took nutrition and exercise seriously. This chapter will lay out the basics of nutritional science and exercise physiology to help you get on track.

Why Lawyers Need Help with Nutrition

The demands of legal work cause us to skip meals entirely, consume Coke and candy in place of a healthy meal or delay a healthy meal to the point where we go into starvation mode and convert all calories to belly fat. The stress of legal work prompts many of us to consume loads of empty calories.

How often have you consumed beer or margaritas with bowls of chips or multiple glasses of wine with baskets of bread and butter before dinner at a restaurant? How often have you opted for the brownie à la mode or the cheesecake with caramel sauce after dinner? Did you take a long walk before going to bed so your body could process that caloric orgy or did you go right to bed?

Good Nutrition—The Basics

Sheer busyness at the office leaves lawyers with insufficient time for the planning, shopping and preparation of healthy meals and snacks that will sustain their health and energy throughout and beyond their careers. Take some time now to learn, or re-learn, the basics of good nutrition, so you can take control over what you eat with your own health as the prime directive.

What are the foundations of good nutrition? In *Enzymes: Go With Your Gut*, Karen DeFelice identifies three: (1) Have adequate nutrition going into your body (high quality nutrient-dense ingredients that will be broken down and digested for energy and bodily maintenance); (2) Have adequate gut enzymes to release, absorb and make use of these nutrients; and (3) Have adequate means to eliminate waste, residue and toxins (which means drinking enough water and keeping your liver, kidneys, stomach, small intestine and colon healthy).

The Harm Done by Poor Nutrition

Skipping meals sets off a primitive brain mechanism for survival that scoops up all unused calories and stores them as belly fat. Eating gargantuan portions will make you gain excess weight no matter what you're eating (except raw vegetables). When it comes to useless flab, the two biggest culprits are excess sugar (which causes hyperglycemia, insulin resistance, diabetes and damage to nerve cells, including brain cells) and bad fats like polyunsaturated fats and trans fats (which turn rancid through oxidation and clog arteries, producing heart attacks and strokes).

For adequate hydration, urination and defecation you need to drink 8 glasses of water a day and consume adequate fiber. Tap water is safe in a glass or in a metal container, but not in plastic bottles. Many plastic bottles contain lexan polycarbonate resin (the stuff used to make CDs, DVDs, mobile phones, computers and iPods) which can release a potent hormone disrupter called BPA (bisphenol-A). Most Americans consume only a small fraction of their daily requirement for fiber. This leads to bloating, constipation and markedly elevated risk of colon cancer. Eating whole grain breakfast cereals, breads, pastas and grains will boost your fiber intake, as will eating whole fruits (like grapefruits, oranges and apples) instead of drinking fruit juices.

HOW TO ESTABLISH AN EATING PLAN AND CONTROL OVEREATING

Why Your Belly Must Go

Bellies grow from poor nutrition, lack of exercise and stress-induced elevation of cortisol. There are two kinds of bellies one can grow while working as a lawyer. The relatively harmless one that we're not too concerned about here is composed of soft, jiggly, subcutaneous fat that gives you a pear shape, because the fat is deposited mainly around your hips, thighs and buttocks.

The dangerous belly is composed of dense, hard fat known as visceral fat because it's deposited under the abdominal muscles, in and around the liver and other organs. This gives a lawyer an apple-shaped body, because his arms, legs, buttocks and thighs are normal, but he has a protruding belly with a ratio of 1 or greater when you divide his belly circumference by his hip circumference.

The World Heart Federation (www.worldheart.org) will send you a free belly fat measuring kit consisting of a plastic measuring device with tape measure and a card explaining how to use it. You are supposed to measure your belly (in a relaxed state while breathing out) midway between the top of your hip bone and the bottom of your rib cage. If you are over 35 inches for women or over 40 inches for men, the WHF suggests you go to your doctor for measuring of your blood pressure, HDL cholesterol, LDL cholesterol, triglycerides and blood sugar.

Belly fat is metabolically active. It releases toxic substances into your bloodstream that can cause diseases. In post-menopausal women it releases estrogen, and this is believed to contribute to breast cancer. Belly fat releases a range of inflammatory compounds that increase LDL cholesterol, triglycerides, blood pressure and blood sugar. Belly fat is associated with increased risk of heart disease, stroke, insulin resistance, Type II diabetes, hypertension and cancer. Belly fat also stores toxic chemicals that people have been exposed to in their work and home environments.

If you've tried dieting and exercise, but your hard apple belly will not go away, it's time to see a certified dietician.

Consulting a Certified Dietician

Dietitians can give you a lot of very important information. This includes your metabolic rate (the total number of calories you need to eat per day to survive); how much of your body is composed of muscle and how much of it is fat; whether you need testing for deficiencies in vitamins or trace minerals like zinc, copper, selenium or magnesium; whether you suffer from digestive dysfunction and why; whether you're so constipated as to require treatment; whether you should be tested for gut pathogens like yeast, harmful bacteria or viruses; and whether you need to step up your exercise program.

Certified dieticians can also advise you on healthy choices for foods and beverages and pinpoint bad eating habits for you to phase out—like eating too quickly, eating too little fiber, drinking too little water, etc. They can help you sort out accurate information from unproven claims on the labels of food packages and supplements.

When consulting with a dietician, choose one who has been registered, licensed, or both, depending on the law of your state. The American Dietetic Association has a website at www.eatright.org that you can use to find one in your community. The ADA was founded in 1917 and has approximately 67,000 members worldwide. It has chapters in all 50 states.

A dietician will get your height and weight, calculate your BMI (body mass index) and ask you to write up a food log that shows when you ate, what you ate and how much, usually for a three-day period. The purpose of BMI is to assess your risk for cardiovascular disease by determining if, for a person your height, you are normal weight, overweight or obese. If you are overweight or obese they will help you lose weight in a natural, healthy way through food choices, portion control and the timing of meals and snacks.

For a BMI calculator go to www.nhlbisupport.com/bmi. BMI can over-predict risk in athletic people with a higher than normal percentage of bulk muscle weight. It can under-predict risk in the elderly who have atrophied muscle mass and higher fat composition than younger folks their height.

Keep a Food Diary to Prevent Overeating

A food diary is a proven means to promote weight loss. On July 8, 2008, researchers at Kaiser Permanente's Center for Health Research in Portland, Oregon, released the results of their study on food diaries. The researchers divided a group of 1,685 middle-aged men and women and tracked their weight over six months. Half kept a daily food diary of everything they ate and drank, and half did not. The half that kept the food diary lost twice as much weight as the control group.

Victor Stevens of Kaiser said the diary works because it makes us aware of and accountable for what we eat. The diary shows us what we're actually putting in our mouths. The food diary not only educates us, but allows us to take control by cutting out non-nutritious foods and reducing portion size. Stevens said it does not have to be a formal document kept on a computer. Hand scribbling is sufficient.

Portion Control Strategies

Something you can do to control portion size is to bring lunches and snacks to work in small plastic baggies and eat off a small plate. When you use a bowl to eat, keep the bowl small, which makes the portion look bigger. A study published in the Journal of the American Medical Association (JAMA) in 2005 showed that people who ate from large bowls tended to eat twice as much because the big bowls made their portion sizes seem small.

Don't Fall for the Trojan Horse Illusion

These days fast food restaurants imply they are giving you the gift of health, when they are really serving up cardiovascular disasters. To meet the demands of resting metabolism (the amount needed to carry out basic functions without strenuous activities) most adults are in the range of 1,800 to 2,200 calories per day. The humongous spinach and cheese omelette at I.H.O.P packs 1,210 calories, which is more than half of your daily caloric needs. Add juice, toast with margarine and coffee with cream and sugar, and you're getting close to the daily max. The tiny amount of spinach in this monstrous concoction doesn't make it good for you.

Fast food restaurants are also serving "healthy salads" in which they give you lettuce and other veggies combined with shredded full fat cheese, croutons and a container of salad dressing loaded with hydrogenated fats and high fructose corn syrup. At family restaurants beware the healthy baked potato drenched in butter and topped with gobs of whole milk sour cream.

How to Deal with Food Cravings and Hunger Surges

Legal work involves intense brain activity that makes us incredibly hungry because it burns lots of calories and stresses us out. Since we're often hungry in the middle of a project that takes all of our attention, we order food without regard to quality and then we shovel it down our throats mindlessly, which grows fat.

If we manage to eat well at the office, we may let our guard down at home and give in to the craving to eat a half gallon of ice cream instead of stopping at a cup or even a pint. Such cravings have nothing to do with hunger. They are driven by restlessness, agitation, anxiety or depressed thoughts.

Here are some ways to deal this problem. After dinner go for a walk. The fresh air and the exercise will help you digest your food and relieve the embedded tension of the day. When you come back home you'll want water on account of sweating from exercise, rather than sugar-laden drinks or foods. If you can't get out to walk, try meditating, which will calm you down.

If nothing works and you still have to have ice cream, put half a cup in a bowl, eat it and you're done. If you eat directly out of the half gallon container, the amount in the giant container keeps shrinking and as it shrinks you tell yourself, "Aw hell, it's just a little more!" until it's all gone. The guilt, shame and extra fat calories aren't worth it.

One approach to dealing with food cravings is called PIG (the Problem of Immediate Gratification). The brainchild of University of Washington psychology professor G. Alan Marlatt, Ph.D., it refers to recognizing the urge to stuff yourself, accepting that you have it and then working with it instead of letting it dominate you.

Marlatt's suggestion is that you see craving as a wave and ride it out, instead of trying to control it or surrender to its control. This is similar to Dr. Ruden's approach to dealing with alcohol cravings. Let them pass like gas. Just wait them out. Stuffing yourself isn't harmless. Recent studies show that chronic overeating keeps distending the top of the stomach until the nerves located there stop signaling the brain that the stomach is full. When this mechanism fails, it becomes easier to overeat because there is no longer a sense of fullness to stop you.

Learn To Eat Mindfully For Improved Health and Enjoyment of Your Food

How can one eat mindfully? Take a deep breath before eating and rate your hunger on a scale of one to ten to gauge it before you prepare or order your meal. Sit down at a table to eat, notice how the food looks and smells and then eat small bites, chewing slowly and savoring what you eat. It takes about 20 minutes for the gut to notify the brain that you've eaten and thus 20 minutes to begin having a sense of fullness. If you shove food down your gullet you're eating way too fast to register fullness and so there is no limit as to how much you can eat that quickly.

Weight control and digestion both require slow chewing of food. The more you chew, the smaller the pieces you will swallow and the longer they will be in contact with saliva. Eating small pieces of food is healthy. Large chunks of food are harder to eliminate and can damage the intestinal lining. They also cause food allergies by gaining attention from microbe-killing cells in the gut that mistake them for pathogenic invaders.

It's helpful to pause midway through the meal, breathe and take stock of where you are. Ask yourself, do I need to finish what's left on my plate? Do I really want dessert and, if so, can I be satisfied with a simple lower fat/sugar dessert instead of the big kahuna? Part of making wise choices is giving yourself a treat every now and then so you don't feel totally deprived and rebel. Go ahead and eat a chocolate soufflé with vanilla ice cream for a special occasion. Just don't make it a habit.

Pre- and Post-Meal Tricks to Reduce Hunger

For people who always feel hungry, there are some things you can do. Research shows that chewing gum (sugarless is more healthy) after a meal can decrease your need for snacks. Taking a tablespoon of cider vinegar or balsamic vinegar with a meal (on a salad) slows the digestion of starch, so you won't get a post-meal sugar crash with rapid return of hunger.

Sometimes when you feel hungry between meals, it's because you are thirsty. The way to figure this out is to drink an 8 oz. glass of water next time you think you're hungry and see what happens. If the hunger sensation goes away, you've answered the question. Since drinking water helps your kidneys flush out the toxins broken down by the liver, it's almost never a bad idea to drink water. Drinking filtered water dilutes the HCL in your stomach and slows the sensations of hunger.

If you know you're going to a restaurant for lunch or dinner, make sure you snack on something healthy (like string cheese with an apple or whole grain crackers) before you leave the office. If you show up starving, you may go through two or more bowls of bread and butter before you even look up. This hunger surge at restaurants can be compounded by drinking wine on an empty stomach. The alcohol will be rapidly absorbed and just as rapidly it will unleash your hunger.

Drinking alcohol on an empty stomach can damage the mucus membrane linings. If you like wine and you know you're going to drink it, coat your stomach with a healthy fat like olive oil. Some restaurants supply a saucer with extra virgin olive oil that you can dip hunks of crusty bread into. Organic EVOO is good for your liver and your lungs. If you go to a restaurant be careful not to drink freezing cold water, because it causes the stomach to contract and empty more quickly, making you more hungry faster. Slightly cool water is fine and the more you drink the more fat you flush away.

How Mood and Environment Affect Appetite and Digestion

Anxiety causes an empty feeling that can be misread as hunger. The worst time to eat is when you are emotionally disturbed, because your digestion will be impaired. If you're feeling anxious, then go for a walk, take a soothing bath, listen to classical music or talk to a friend. If you're bored, then do something interesting like read a book or watch a favorite movie on your TV or computer.

Environment is important when eating. A peaceful setting is conducive to an enjoyable and well-digested meal. It allows you to be present and to be grateful for your food. If you can meet a friend and have a nice conversation, so much the better. If you have to eat alone, then enjoying a good novel can give you a mental holiday. Reading the day's news about war, crime, epidemic disease and the home foreclosure crisis isn't the best thing when you eat lunch.

Eat High-Fiber, Low-Calorie Foods
Like Apples and Jicama

If nothing seems to knock out the hunger that springs up rapidly between meals, eating apples, bananas or oranges is a good strategy. They taste great. They're low in calories. And they pack loads of insoluble fiber to make you feel full and keep you regular. Apples have choline (for memory) and lots of soluble pectin in their skin to reduce LDL cholesterol. Pectin stops the flow of fat into cells and shrinks fat cells.

Scientists at the Université Paul Sabatier in Toulouse, France, fed apples to genetically modified hamsters which had super high bad (LDL) cholesterol and very low good (HDL) cholesterol. After eating a diet rich in apples, these hamsters showed a reversal with big reductions in LDL and big increases in HDL cholesterol. Nutritionists say it's fine to eat two or three apples a day. For more health information and recipes check out www.usapple.org. Bananas pack potassium and oranges are loaded with Vitamin C.

You can also eat jicama or celery. Both are crunchy, high fiber veggies that are mostly water and carry very few calories. Celery stuffed with pure (no trans fat) peanut butter is a great snack. Jicama is not only high in fiber but high in Vitamin C and potassium. It can be enjoyed raw by itself or added to salads. People who like Mexican food tend to love jicama when it is sprinkled with salt and chile powder, then marinated in lime juice in the fridge.

Rev Up Your Metabolism in a Healthy Way

You can increase your metabolic (fat-burning) rate safely and naturally. Drinking green tea and eating spicy foods (like Indian food with cumin or tumeric) helps. Building lean muscle through push-ups, squats and weightlifting helps too. That's because muscle cells have a much higher metabolic rate than fat cells. Muscle cells burn calories even while you sit or sleep, whereas you need to do very intense physical activity for a prolonged period to use fat cells for energy. To accelerate belly shrinkage, take saunas as often as you can (subject to your doctor's approval).

Don't take supplements. This kind of shortcut to rev your metabolism is a dangerous illusion. These kinds of supplements don't work and they contain ingredients that can be toxic, addictive or both. As this book goes to press, lawyers are filing lawsuits all over the country against the maker and sellers of Hydroxycut, a product that was marketed massively to shrink bellies and give you cosmetically perfect six-pack abs. I express no opinion on the merits of the case, but I do urge extreme caution in taking supplements to shrink your belly. Better to take some pilates classes, which are healthy, challenging, effective and will help strengthen your body and improve your posture.

THE GOOD FATS AND HOW THEY BENEFIT YOU

The Benefits of Omega 3 Fatty Acids and How to Get Them

Eating foods rich in Omega 3 essential fatty acids has a remarkable array of health benefits. Studies have shown consuming these foods helps: shed toxic belly fat; reduce the risk of heart disease and stroke; reduce the severity of existing depression; prevent recurrence of depression; improve brain function; protect people against onset of dementia in their older years; and reduce the severity of rheumatoid arthritis and macular degeneration.

Although our bodies manufacture Omega 3 fats, the supply is insufficient for our needs. It is essential that we consume outside sources. Saltwater fish that are loaded with Omega 3s are salmon, albacore tuna, herring, mackerel, sardines and anchovies. You can get Omega 3s from lake trout. Non-fish sources of Omega 3s are avocados, nuts, seeds, olive oil, flax oil and nut oils.

Seeds offer multiple benefits, because all seeds have Vitamin E which is good for your skin and your heart. Walnuts, almonds, sunflower seeds and pumpkin seeds have zinc which helps prevent prostate cancer. Avocados are bursting with monounsaturated oils and can be eaten and enjoyed every day. You can eat them sliced on salads, puréed in guacamole, diced over scrambled eggs or teamed up with turkey or tuna on whole grain bread to make a sandwich. Adding walnuts or pecans to a salad is tasty and boosts Omega 3s. Toss in some dried cranberries for a big antioxidant boost.

Omega 3 Fats and the Mercury Contamination Controversy

The Omega 3 acids in foods like cold water fish, nuts and seeds include EPA (eicosapentenoic acid) and DHA (docosahexenoic acid). These have been determined to be the most helpful in preventing illness, and they are the ones you will find in Omega 3 supplements. Be aware that saltwater fish have methyl mercury in them, but freshwater fish do not.

Some experts say that the selenium in saltwater fish helps to buffer the mercury, and that our need for selenium outweighs the risks from mercury in fish. In small amounts selenium is necessary for life. It protects our blood cells, keeps our heart and pancreas healthy, combines with Vitamin E to produce antibodies and plays a role in many metabolic processes. Brazil nuts are a very good source of selenium. Men are advised to eat two Brazil nuts a day to prevent prostate cancer.

There are experts who say mercury is just too dangerous to consume in large quantities, and the only studies showing that selenium buffers mercury were done in animals. They say it's smarter to reduce consumption of ocean fish in favor of other sources of Omega 3 acids and selenium.

Using Omega 3 Supplements

If you want Omega 3s but hate the taste or texture of fish, try fish oil supplements. You will probably burp up a fishy taste for a few days, but it will then disappear for good. Fish oil supplements must have at least 500-1,000 milligrams of EPA/DHA to be effective. If they are extracted from krill they will have less mercury than from the fish that eat krill.

Using Non-Fish Foods to Protect Your Cardiovascular Health

To keep the arteries to your heart and brain clear of the fatty plaque that causes heart attacks and strokes, you'll have to reduce the

LDL cholesterol which gets oxidized to plaque. If you choose not to eat fish or use fish oil supplements, you could consume plant-based supplements containing ALA (alpha-lineoleic acid). The good news is that our bodies convert ALA to EPA and DHA and plants have no methyl mercury. The bad news is that our bodies convert ALA to EPA and DHA inefficiently, so using plant-based supplements offers less cardiovascular protection.

It's hard to beat eating whole nuts like walnuts, almonds, pecans and pistachios, which are loaded with Omega 3 fatty acids. Breakfast cereals, breads, eggs and other products fortified with Omega 3 are the least beneficial, but better than nothing. To maximize health benefits from cereals and breads at breakfast, go with kamut, flax, spelt or aramanth instead of wheat. Ezekial offers cereals, breads and tortillas with these grains.

Protecting your cardiovascular system from artery-clogging plaque caused by oxidation of LDL cholesterol can also be done with foods that are rich in fiber and natural antioxidants. Good examples are the Vitamin C in oranges, polyphenols in dark chocolate, bioflavinoids in blueberries, the pectin in apple meat and the quercetin in apple skins. The oats in oatmeal have been shown to reduce LDL cholesterol without also reducing HDL (the good) cholesterol, because they contain a soluble fiber called beta glucan. Other foods loaded with soluble fiber are spinach, beans, peas, lentils, barley, cabbage, carrots, split pea soup and garbanzo beans (the stuff used to make hummus).

How Omega 3 Fatty Acids Protect Brain Cells and Improve Brain Function

Brain cells are covered in membranes with millions of receptors consisting of tiny barrel-shaped channels that are selectively porous. These receptors facilitate brain cell functions by letting some ions out of the cell (e.g., potassium) and some ions inside the cell (e.g., sodium, calcium or chloride). Brain cell membranes are composed of fat (either the good or the bad fat depending on what you eat).

When a brain cells fires, it sends an electric signal down the axon at one ten-thousandth of a second to cause the axon terminal to release a neurotransmitter. The axons of brain cells (the long, thin tubes that release neuro-transmitters to adjacent neurons) are coated with myelin, an insulation material composed entirely of fat. Without healthy myelin the electric signal from the brain cell required to race down the axon won't go, will go too slowly or will go erratically, which will disrupt normal neurotransmitter delivery.

The human brain functions much more efficiently if it has fat that is soft and flexible at normal body temperature of 98.6 degrees Fahrenheit. While Omega 3 fats (mono-unsaturated fats) meet this requirement, transfats and saturated fats are solid and relatively rigid at body temperature. Think about peanut butter or margarine with hydrogenated oil. At room temperature they stay solid and are good to spread on bread. Is that what you want your brain cells coated with?

Omega 3 fats are supple at body temperature and thus better able to admit ions into or out of brain cells. They also improve the capacity of the myelin sheath to insulate axons and conduct micro-volts of electricity down the axon, to release neurotransmitters across the synapses. The more efficient these processes, the more effectively our brains function with regard to memory, learning and mood regulation.

Foods rich in Omega 3 fatty acids inhibit inflammation, and are protective against stroke, memory loss and dementia. While Omega 3s reduce inflammation, Omega 6 fatty acids promote it. The ideal ratio in the body should be 2-4 times more Omega 6 than Omega 3, yet many Americans (especially those with inflammatory diseases) have 14-25 times more Omega 6 than Omega 3. Higher concentrations of Omega 3s are protective against depression.

Supplements That Improve
Brain Health and Brain Function

Neurosurgeon Larry McCleary, M.D., is atypical of his profession. Rather than limiting his practice to surgeries on the brain and spinal cord, he has researched and written a book on how to prevent brain problems through proper nutrition. It's called *The Brain Trust Program*. Dr. McCleary claims his program has helped his patients increase mental vigor, clear up "brain fog" (the mental dullness, sluggishness and confusion some people experience) and amp up their memories.

His program for avoiding Alzheimer's and promoting the health of your brain entails nourishing your brain with the right whole foods and supplements; engaging in specific mental exercises as well as cardiovascular physical exercise; and making sure to get adequate sleep. Dr. McCleary says that following his program will stimulate the formation of rich synaptic interconnections between brain cells at any age.

Here's a list of the supplements Dr. McCleary finds essential for everyone, even the healthy middle-aged adults who have not yet shown appreciable mental fog or memory dysfunction: Fish Oil; B-Complex Vitamins; Chelated Magnesium; Taurine; CoQ 10; L-Carnitine; Lipoic Acid and Vitamin D. The fact that he leaves Gingko Biloba off his list shows he's on the ball. A five-medical-center study published in the November 2008 issue of *The Journal of the American Medical Association* shows that taking Gingko Biloba did not reduce the incidence of dementia or slow the rate of progression of Alzheimer's.

Dr. McCleary put magnesium on his list to promote night-time sleep, which must be deep enough to promote brain maintenance and consolidation of memories from the day's learning. The only substance he urges people not to take is extra iron, because iron is a pro-oxidant that stimulates oxidative rust of brain cells. A normal diet has more than sufficient iron for the body's needs.

How Each Brain-Enhancing Supplement Works

Dr. McCleary recommends Omega 3 fatty acids to keep brain cell membranes flexible, strengthen myelin sheaths around axons, lower triglycerides and combat inflammation. He is concerned about mercury accumulation in large cold water fish and says you're better off buying fish oils that have been prepared with a method called molecular distillation to remove mercury, PCBs, dioxins, furans and other ocean pollutants.

Dr. McCleary's highest recommendation is for krill oil, which he describes as the best and safest source of essential brain fats, not just EPA and DHA, but also phospholipids which provide choline for acetylcholine (the neurotransmitter needed for memory formation) and are used for the construction and maintenance of myelin. Krill are at the bottom of the ocean food chain, so they have the least concentrated amount of mercury.

The B vitamins play essential roles in the functioning of the nervous system and reduce the level of homocysteine (a marker of cardiovascular inflammation and heart disease). They help brain cells produce the energy they need to function, balance brain hormone levels and help make neurotransmitters. Because they are water soluble and cannot be stored long-term in fat, they must be replenished every day. While people who eat lots of nuts and dark, leafy greens get all the B vitamins they need, not everyone does this, so supplementation is a good idea.

Dr. McCleary recommends magnesium not only to promote sleep, but to reduce the movement of calcium into brain cells through cell membranes. While small amounts of calcium are necessary for brain cell function, too much calcium can over-excite and even kill brain cells. Magnesium is a natural calcium channel blocker, which has none of the side effects of prescription medication for that purpose. Spinach is high in magnesium.

Taurine is an amino acid containing sulfur that works in tandem with magnesium to block excess calcium from entering brain cells. It also makes blood platelets less sticky, which reduces the risk of the most common type of stroke, an occlusive stroke caused by a blood clot blocking a cerebral artery.

Acetyl L-carnitine (ALC) is most plentiful in meat, but these days fear of cholesterol has reduced meat consumption. The carnitine part of ALC drives fat molecules into the mitochondria of brain cells where they are burned to produce energy. This is very important, because even though the brain is just 2% of the entire mass of our bodies by weight, it consumes 20% of our daily calories, and it needs lots of fuel to burn. The acetyl part of ALC goes to make acetylcholine which plays a crucial role in memory formation.

Alzheimer's drugs like Aricept work by blocking the re-uptake of acetylcholine so more of it is available in the synapses of the hippocampus for memory formation. Sadly, these drugs help very little and their effect diminishes as the disease progressively destroys the hippocampus.

Hard-boiled eggs are a great supply of choline and protein, and can be eaten every day as a meal or snack.

A-Lipoic acid is an antioxidant that is soluble in fat and water. It can fight free radicals in the fat-filled membranes around brain cells and in their water-filled interiors. It can even get inside the mitochondria (the organelles inside the brain cells that burn fuel to produce energy) to quench free radicals there. It's known to fight diabetes and protect against neuro-degeneration.

Coenzyme Q10 is a fat or oil soluble substance found in all brain cells. Its highest concentration is inside the mitochondria. In research on mice it has been shown to fight degenerative brain disorders including Alzheimer's Disease, Parkinson's Disease and ALS. Most people do not eat enough salmon and liver to get their daily requirement of this anti-oxidant.

Statins, Coffee and Degenerative Brain Disease

Dr. McCleary regards the cholesterol-lowering statin drugs (which block production of CQ10) to be a risk factor for Alzheimer's disease. If you have very high cholesterol, you may need a statin drug to protect your heart. Balancing benefits vs. risks of taking or not taking any drug or supplement is something best done in consultation with your own physician.

Dr. McCleary notes that consumption of two or more cups of coffee a day reduces the risk of neuro-degenerative diseases like Alzheimer's and Parkinson's. His view is consistent with many studies I have seen. Coffee has been found to increase insulin sensitivity and reduce the risk of Type II diabetes. All of this is great news for lawyers, but be sure to stay energized by exercising and sleeping, not just by gulping coffee. Buying Fair Trade coffee is the socially responsible thing to do, and it's now available at Starbucks, Peet's, Whole Foods, health food stores, many grocery stores and online vendors.

Vitamin D is known as the sunshine vitamin because exposure to sunlight produces it from the cholesterol in our skin. Adequate amounts of Vitamin D make us feel good, which is why people who live in sunny climates tend to have sunny dispositions and people who live in countries with long, dark winters tend to be depressed, something now called SAD or seasonal affective disorder.

Researchers who gave people suffering from SAD 800 international units of Vitamin D every day for five days observed a lifting of their depression. Vitamin D is a fat-soluble vitamin that can readily enter the brain. Vitamin D protects brain cells from the inflammatory compounds that cause Alzheimer's disease. Since the body can store Vitamin D in fat, it can build up to toxic levels if you take too much. Dr. McCleary recommends 400-800 IU a day, but in no event more than 2,000 IU.

The World's Best Foods For You—The "Super Foods"

The identification of Super Foods that are extra rich in the highest quality nutrients that our bodies and brains need for peak health and peak performance is another major breakthrough. In *Super Foods Rx* and *Super Foods Health Style*, authors Steven Pratt, M.D., and Kathy Matthews set out a list of the 14 most nutrient-dense, health promoting foods, along with recipes to enjoy them.

To come up with the list, they combed through the databases of the American Heart Association, the American Cancer Society, the National Cancer Institute and the U.S. Department of Agriculture for whole foods that were richest in antioxidants, fiber and micronutrients. Super Foods have the property of synergy, which means they combine the broadest, most complete array of nutritional substances that most effectively fight heart disease, stroke and cancer. Super Foods are so good for us we can eat them without guilt.

Super Foods pack the biggest wallop of three different kinds of micronutrients—vitamins, minerals and phytonutrients. What are phytonutrients? They are the nutrients in plants that protect us from inflammatory diseases, gene mutations that can cause cancer and the proliferation of cancer cells in our bodily tissues.

Phytonutrients include polyphenols (powerful antioxidant, anti-inflammatory substances) found mainly in green tea, nuts, berries, grapes, red wine and dark chocolate; carotenoids (which function as antioxidants, anti-cancer and anti-aging substances) found in red, orange and yellow fruits and vegetables; phytoestrogens (which can help prevent prostate and breast cancer) found in soy foods, whole wheat foods, seeds and some vegetables and fruits; lycopene (which prevents skin and other cancers and macular degeneration) found in tomatoes, red watermelon, guavas, rose hips and pink grapefruit; and luteins (which prevent cataracts and macular degeneration) found in spinach and orange bell peppers.

Understanding the Health Benefits of Antioxidants

We hear the term "antioxidant" all the time. It's posted on supplement labels, touted in advertisements for nutritious foods, and discussed with great frequency in magazines devoted to health, fitness, weight loss and nutrition. We are warm-blooded mammals who generate heat to stay alive. We burn oxygen and metabolize nutrients (including carbs, protein and fat) to create energy needed to warm our blood and run our brains.

A byproduct of energy production (from digestion or exercise) is the creation of free radicals, which are oxygen molecules minus one electron. These molecules are highly unstable. Free radicals steal electrons from and damage the molecules that compose enzymes, proteins, DNA and cell membranes.

On top of the free radicals our bodies create, we absorb free radicals from smoking (first-, second- and third-hand), indoor and outdoor air pollution and foods laden with saturated fats or transfats. Our genetics play some role in determining the level of free radicals vs. the level of antioxidants in our tissues and plasma. In order to survive, we must have antioxidants to neutralize the free radicals by donating electrons to them and stabilizing them before they can cause harm by stealing electrons from our tissues.

Most tissues and chemical compounds in our bodies (like peptides, proteins, enzymes and hormones) have just enough electrons and cannot spare any. When free radicals steal their electrons, they go into a deficit state and start degrading. Some nutritionists have likened this process to rust. A common example they give is leaving a slice of apple on a plate and watching it. In a very short time the exposed sides of the apple slice will turn brown. This is oxidative rust. Antioxidant compounds are so rich in electrons that they can donate enough to neutralize free radicals while keeping enough to maintain stability.

Foods are rated with ORAC scores which refer to their Oxygen Radical Absorption Capacity. Foods with the highest ORAC scores have the greatest capacity to absorb free radicals and neutralize their capacity for harm. The USDA has rated what Dr. Pratt calls Super Foods with the very highest ORAC scores. The premise of Dr. Pratt's books is that eating antioxidant-rich Super Foods will give you the longest lifespan and healthspan, while eating inferior foods will reduce longevity, health and quality of life by promoting chronic diseases.

As of 2004, when *Super Foods Rx* was published, the authors estimated that two out of every three adults in this country were overweight or obese and that every year in the United States 300,000 to 800,000 preventable deaths occurred due to poor nutrition that contributed to atherosclerosis, diabetes and certain cancers. Where can you find tasty recipes that make use of the Super Foods? Check out Dana Jacobi's *The Twelve Best Foods Cookbook* published by Rodale in 2005—or you can just go to the Internet and download thousands of recipes for free.

So let's get healthy already! Here are Dr. Pratt's 14 Super Foods, each of which has "sidekicks" that pack nearly as much nutrition and protection from inflammatory diseases of all kinds, including heart disease and cancer:

- Beans
- Blueberries
- Broccoli
- Oats
- Oranges
- Pumpkin
- Wild Salmon
- Soy (organic and non-GMO)
- Spinach

- Tea
- Tomatoes
- Turkey (Skinless Breast of)
- Walnuts
- Yogurt

The Benefits of Nuts

Eating nuts every day (just 2-3 ounces) will significantly reduce your risk of heart attack by as much as 40%. Nuts lower your total cholesterol and raise your HDL cholesterol. Contrary to popular belief, nut consumption does not make you gain weight. That's because the protein and fiber in nuts is more filling than refined foods so you eat less. Nuts increase calorie-burning, and not all of their fat is absorbed. (4-17% passes through the body). When added freely to a calorie-controlled diet, nuts don't cause weight gain, and sometimes make weight loss easier.

Since they're so good for people, how did going crazy get known as going "nuts"? In the *New Whole Foods Encyclopedia*, Rebecca Wood tells us. She says nuts were used in traditional folk medicine to give a burst of wild sexual energy, making the affected person "nutty."

You can eat nuts directly out of the bag or make sandwiches from nut butters by themselves or combined with berry jams or preserves. Peanut butter can dramatically lower the risk of Type II diabetes, because its monounsaturated fats make people more insulin-sensitive, and its high fiber and magnesium content reduce the demand for insulin.

Baking or flash-sautéing fillets of fish or skinless, boneless chicken breasts in EVOO with a crust of nuts or seeds is delicious and healthy. All you need is a dash of salt and black pepper and a squeeze of fresh lemon. Brazil nuts are high in selenium which reduces your risk of prostate cancer. So do pumpkin seeds which contain zinc. Sesame seeds are rich in arginine as are peanuts, walnuts and cashews.

Aginine or L-arginine is a semi-essential amino acid; the body makes it, but not in sufficient quantities, which requires supplementation by food. Arginine improves blood circulation and male fertility, reduces blood pressure, detoxifies the liver by eliminating ammonia from urine, keeps blood sugar stable, promotes the health of skin, joints and muscles and stimulates the immune system to crank out T lymphocytes (T-cells) from the thymus.

Arginine combats the effects of stress which include depression of the immune system with shrinking of the thymus. Although the thymus shrinks naturally with age, there's no harm and only benefit in doing what you can to protect it with sesame seeds and various nuts.

The Benefit of Seeds

Neurosurgeon Larry McCleary, M.D., says the best four seeds for keeping ourselves healthy are flaxseed, sunflower seeds, sesame seeds and pumpkin seeds. These seeds are loaded with potent antioxidant Vitamin E. Ground flaxseeds contain alpha-linoleic acid (an Omega 3 acid), fiber, protein, Vitamin E and carotene. Sunflower seeds have protein, monounsaturated oils, potassium, magnesium, phosphorus and B vitamins (which lower homocysteine). Sesame seeds (the stuff tahini paste is made from) have more protein by the gram than eggs and also contain B vitamins and calcium. Pumpkin seeds have Omega 3 fatty acids, vitamin A, calcium and protein.

Flax oil can be added to your smoothies. Sesame oil is great for cooking Chinese food. Pumpkin oil can be used on salads instead of olive oil. It kills pathogens in the colon. For great snacks loaded with seeds check out the website for Seeds of Change.

The Benefit of Berries

Think berries. All berries contain fiber, which promotes digestive health. Raspberries contain ellagic acid which has anti-cancer properties. In a study of 72 middle-aged people reported in the American Journal of Clinical Nutrition, people who ate one cup of mixed berries a day (including strawberries, raspberries and dark blue bilberries) for two months had higher levels of HDL (the good) cholesterol and lower blood pressure.

Berries lower blood pressure because their polyphenols increase the level of nitric oxide which relaxes blood vessel walls. Polyphenols from berries have also been shown to decrease the rate of bone loss in post-menopausal women. For a citrus-berry shake, like the kind consumed in training by Dana Torres (America's dynamite 42-year-old swimmer who won a silver medal in the 50-meter freestyle in Beijing), put the following into your blender and blend until smooth: 1.25 cups of fresh berries; .75 cup of lowfat plain yogurt; .5 cup orange juice; 2 table-spoons protein powder; 1 tablespoon of wheat germ and one of honey; and .5 teaspoon vanilla extract.

Blueberries are the New Brainberries

It turns out that blueberries with walnuts have a powerful synergistic effect when consumed together. You can eat them plain, with yogurt or with nonfat sour cream. Neuroscientist James A. Joseph works in the field of anti-aging at the Human Nutrition Research Center on Aging at Tufts University in Medford, Massachusetts. He is particularly interested in how to delay and even reverse cognitive decline in older folks. He has discovered that the deeply pigmented flavonoid phytochemicals in blueberries known as anthocyanidins affect the human brain in a beneficial way on a molecular level.

According to Dr. Joseph, anthocyanidins help switch certain genes on and certain genes off to promote the growth of new brain cells and make brain cells maximally responsive to incoming messages from other cells. They help preserve the integrity of the brain and are known to protect the memory cells in the hippocampus from oxidation and inflammation. They also reduce inflammation inside our coronary arteries to protect our hearts and keep our blood pressure normal.

Dr. Joseph's research shows that when blueberries are consumed with walnuts (which are high in Omega 3 fatty acids, especially alpha-linolenic acid), they combine to make the membranes of our brain cells extra flexible and more efficient in neural signaling. In the aging brain of people who do not eat right, the cellular membranes become rigid and this blocks the flow of neurotransmitters between cells. Because of this he dubbed blueberries "brainberries."

Dr. Joseph's recommendation is to eat one cup of blueberries (or other dark berries) a day with some walnuts, almonds or pecans. This can be done with breakfast cereal, yogurt or a salad. Dr. Joseph also recommends getting sufficient folic acid in your food to preserve memory and sufficient zinc to ward off Alzheimer's Disease. Certain breakfast cereals are packed with folic acid.

Pre-menopausal women lawyers who are noticing some decline in memory or other cognitive functions may want to have their iron levels checked. Blood lost through menstruation can cause mild anemia or a pre-anemic state which reduces cognitive sharpness according to a study by John Beard, Ph.D., at the Pennsylvania State University. The frontal lobes (the seat of working memory) and the hippocampus (which performs memory retrieval) are both very sensitive to iron depletion.

The iron can be replaced by eating dark leafy greens, beans, meat or soy. Spinach and edamame are good choices. Women whose blood levels of iron improved significantly in the study had 5- to 7-fold increases in cognitive performance. Never assume you are iron deficient unless you are tested. A woman with no iron deficiency who takes iron supplements can cause problems with her heart, liver or blood sugar.

Preventing Type II Diabetes by Eating Low GI Foods

Type II diabetes is caused by poor nutrition and lack of exercise. Right now 20 million Americans have Type II diabetes, which is being described as an epidemic, with fast-rising numbers. Diabetes is a cause of heart attack, stroke and dementia.

Smart utilization of the glycemic index (GI) guards against obesity, insulin resistance and Type II diabetes. The GI was invented by David Jenkins, M.D., Ph.D., of the University of Toronto. It rates foods based on how quickly your body breaks down the carbs inside them and converts them into glucose (blood sugar) for utilization by your brain and your muscles. Simple carbs, like granulated white sugar and pulpless fruit juice, are converted to glucose very rapidly so they are high GI food. Complex carbs like oatmeal or beans are converted more slowly and gradually to glucose, so they are called low GI foods.

When your glucose level is too high, the pancreas secretes insulin to convert the excess glucose into fat, which is stored in your belly to be used later when you're hungry but there is no food available. Unless you're truly starving your body will not melt belly fat, because when your blood sugar drops very low the pancreas secretes the hormone glucagon which prompts the liver to release glycogen (stored glucose).

People who eat high GI foods run into trouble. Why? Because, the rapid conversion of these foods to glucose dumps way too much glucose into the blood all at once and forces the pancreas to keep squirting out insulin to store the excess as fat. There follows a rapid drop in blood sugar that makes the person quite hungry relatively soon after eating. So he eats more high GI foods, and the poor pancreas is forced into a continual state of over-secretion of insulin.

Eventually the body becomes resistant to insulin and you live in a state of hyperglycemia (too much blood sugar) known as Type II diabetes. Diabetes is a very dangerous disease. It can produce lethal diabetic coma. It can cause kidney damage, blindness from diabetic retinopathy and loss of fingers, hands, toes, feet and legs from poor blood flow. You need to eat low GI foods that are slowly, gradually converted to glucose.

You can't cut all carbs out of your diet. Glucose is the only food your brain consumes, and your muscles need glucose just to help you stand erect. If you're exercising, performing sports or doing hard mental work, you need extra glucose. To regulate your intake of glucose, you can use a book like The *GI Diet* by Rick Gallop. It sets out a simple eating plan that uses the GI to keep you feeling full while eating healthy, low GI foods that will take the weight off and keep it off and protect you from insulin resistance and diabetes.

The GI eating plan involves daily intake of 25% protein, 20% fats and 55% complex carbs. The traditional diet allowed just 15% protein and 30% fat, but this was inadequate for muscle maintenance and provided too much fat (the only purpose of which is to release sugar when blood sugar drops). Gallop consulted with two cardiologists while writing the book. He continues to add new information on his website www.gidiet.com.

Regular consumption of beans will help you reduce your risk of diabetes. Spinach is a low GI food loaded with fiber and magnesium (which decreases insulin resistance). Spinach tastes great sautéed in olive oil with a dash of lemon, crushed garlic and salt. You can eat it plain or mix it into scrambled eggs, whole wheat pasta or brown rice.

How to Maintain a Healthy Small Intestine for Proper Absorption of the Nutrients in Food and Elimination of Gastrointestinal Distress

How many lawyers do you know who are highly stressed, drink too much and have gastrointestinal problems? Stress and alcohol consumption are associated with GI problems including ulcers, gastric reflux, constipation and others. It's hard to practice law when your stomach is churning or your irritable bowel is acting up and you have to rush out of a meeting to the bathroom because of diarrhea.

In *Enzymes: Go With Your Gut*, nutritional expert Karen DeFelice says that people suffering from gastric reflux, food intolerance or constipation may well have a deficiency in their digestive enzymes. These enzymes are not nutrients but help the body absorb and utilize nutrients. They reside primarily in the small intestine.

The tube-like interior of the small intestine has many loops (villi) covered with micro-villi that project outward to absorb water and nutrients. Micro-villi are like the root hairs of plant roots. Healthy villi produce adequate quantities of digestive enzymes known as lactase (for milk digestion), disaccharidases (for digestion of complex carbohydrates) and peptidases (for digestion of proteins). Simple sugars like glucose (blood sugar) and fructose (fruit sugar) are absorbed directly without an enzyme to break them down.

Toward the base of each villus are goblet cells that secrete mucus to protect the villi from toxins and bacteria. If the villi are damaged, the result is a decrease in enzyme production, nutrient absorption and utilization of food and energy production with fatigue. You can damage your villi and reduce secretion of digestive enzymes by drinking too much alcohol. You can also cause your intestine to leak, and set off an immune response with inflammation of the intestinal lining and food intolerance, when you gulp down your food instead of chewing it slowly into very small pieces.

DeFelice advocates that consideration be given to the consumption of digestive enzymes when there are gut-related problems like food intolerance, gastric reflux, constipation, low energy, fatigue and certain neurologic problems that are not responding to conventional treatments.

We need a good supply of digestive enzymes to properly digest food and make its nutrients more available to improve cellular metabolism and produce health and energy; to help the villi produce adequate mucous to clear away gunk, debris and harmful pathogens; and by doing these things to free up the immune system to protect the entire body rather than attack food particles leaking out of the gut.

Something not widely known is that 90% of the serotonin receptors in the human body are in the small intestine. DeFelice says that chemical, microbial or auto-immune damage to the intestine which interferes with serotonin reception can lead to depression, and to insomnia, because the supply of melatonin (which is a breakdown product of serotonin that helps us sleep) is dependent on the supply of serotonin in the gut.

Melatonin sets our biological clock and keeps it in sync with circadian sleep cycles. Melatonin deficiency disrupts sleep. People who don't sleep well develop memory and sensory processing problems. DeFelice's book discusses the different types of digestive enzymes you can buy at health food stores to improve digestive health.

EXERCISE—GOOD FOR YOUR MOOD AND THE LIFELONG HEALTH OF YOUR BODY AND BRAIN

When the contemporary human body was designed about 40,000 years ago, it was made to move, because our ancestors had to leave their caves to forage for meals. Yet some of us stopped exercising with the death of President John Kennedy, the only president who gave significant attention to physical fitness in the public schools.

Not exercising is a huge mistake. Our bodies crave it, it's vital to preserve our health and it makes us feel good. It strengthens the heart and lungs and stimulates the brain to make more brain cells (a process called neurogenesis). When we exercise we stress our muscles and bones to keep them strong. As we age we tend to experience muscle atrophy and osteoporosis unless we exercise regularly and eat foods with sufficient protein, calcium, phosphorous and magnesium.

Keeping our spines straight, our posture upright and our bones strong protects our mobility and our independence. When you see an older lawyer walking around stooped so low toward the ground he can't see what's in front of him, and using a cane to hobble around, this could be your future, unless you exercise regularly.

If you want to avoid heart attacks, strokes and cognitive decline, it's time to get out of your chair and put on your running shoes. Physical exercise promotes way more blood flow to your brain than doing brain gym exercises on your computer.

Exercise Stimulates Production
of Key Hormones and Neurotransmitters

Human growth hormone (HGH) promotes deep sleep, lean muscle mass, fat reduction, beautiful skin, thick bones and strong connective tissue. It's abundant in our youth but declines with age. After the mid-twenties, HGH production falls off precipitously, about 24% per decade. Beginning in middle age men lose five pounds of muscle per decade. If they don't exercise, but maintain weight, the fat composition of their bodies will keep climbing.

You can go to a clinic for injections of HGH, but this is an expensive and potentially dangerous shortcut. HGH researcher William Kraemer, Ph.D., of the University of Connecticut, says that 15 minutes per day of vigorous exercise will cue the middle-aged pituitary to spurt out new supplies of HGH.

Physical Exercise Preserves Mental Acuity
and Reduces the Risk of Dementia

Keeping cognitively sharp requires that you stay active physically. Challenging your brain with crossword puzzles, staying socially engaged and having a positive attitude all contribute to mental acuity later in life, but you've got to exercise your body, too.

Two studies published in the September 2004 issue of JAMA showed that walking benefits your brain. In the first study, researchers at the Harvard School of Public Health found that older women who walked at a leisurely pace for two-three hours per week did better on tests of memory and thinking than inactive older women. Women who walked six hours per week had an extra 20% gain in cognitive function. In the second study at the University of Virginia, researchers found that older men who walked less than one quarter of a mile per day were twice as likely to develop Alzheimer's Disease as those who walked two miles per day.

In 2005 Suvi Rovio and colleagues at the Karolinska Institute in Sweden studied the relationship between physical activity and the risk of dementia in a group of middle-aged people over two decades. They established that exercising twice a week for 20-30 minutes to the point of sweating and heavy breathing reduced the risk of dementia by 52%. Psychologist Stanley Colcombe of the University of Illinois and colleagues published a paper in 2006 showing that six months of regular exercise in healthy, sedentary people aged 60-79 restored losses in brain volume that continued to progress in control group members who didn't exercise.

Staying Motivated to Exercise

What exercise will work for you? The one that requires the least external motivation, which is the one you find most fun and enjoyable. Some people prefer an indoor trainer for running, stair climbing or spinning that lets them read or watch TV. Some people prefer intense indoor workouts at a heath club using free weights and dumbbells, the Bosu, large exercise balls, elliptical machines, rowing machines, artificial rock wall climbing or racquetball.

Exercising alone can be dull and get lonely. Going to a health club enables you to socialize during group exercise and afterward in the sauna, steam bath or hot tub. Health clubs offer group classes in water aerobics, circuit training, fitness boot camps, yoga and pilates, which will give you a great workout and chances to talk and laugh.

Other people prefer outdoor activities that enable them to get fresh air, sunshine and changing scenery as they run or bicycle. I love doing hills on my bike, because it makes me sweat and it's really satisfying to climb up a series of steep hills, and then experience the rest, ease and pure joy of flying downhill.

Diehards will run or bike in a downpour. If the sun is out, training outdoors will give you a double boost of serotonin. Bright light has been used successfully to treat depression from SAD through daily 30-60 minute indoor exposure to a light box, typically in the early morning. Sunlight is many times brighter than a light box, it's free and you can catch it while you are walking or running. To control your risk of skin cancer you can use sun block, wear a hat or both.

What else can you do? Training for a marathon, a half marathon or century ride with others will bring you challenge, friendship and a sense of accomplishment when the event is done. Many of these events are fundraisers for good causes.

Exercise Basics—Strength, Balance, Cardio and Spinal Lengthening

Strength training and cardio are both highly beneficial, and should be done on alternating days. You can do strength training with exercise bands or tubes, dumbbells, manual resistance (such as dips, pull-ups, pushups or calf raises in which you are working to lift your entire body weight), lifting barbells or using weight machines. Strength training can be done standing, sitting or putting some part of your body on an exercise ball. Using an unstable surface, like a ball or BOSU, makes your muscles work harder.

Strength training maintains muscle tone and bone strength, reduces flab and keeps you strong. If you combine strength training with balance training in a circuit-style workout at the gym, you gain still more benefits. At home you can do one-legged squats or brush your teeth on one leg. Maintaining good balance will reduce your risk of falls and improve your ability as an athlete. Strength training should be done twice a week with cardio three times a week for best results. Make sure you get at least one full day of rest and recovery per week.

What is cardio exercise? Exercise involving constant exertion which elevates your heart rate well above resting levels and makes you sweat and breathe hard. Cardio raises your metabolic rate, so you continue to burn calories at a higher than normal rate for hours afterwards. Cardio keeps your heart walls flexible and enables your heart to pump more blood with each contraction, which makes your heart a more efficient pump and lowers your resting heart rate. Cardio also raises HDL cholesterol and keeps blood pressure down. High blood pressure is associated with dementia in older people.

Cardio stimulates the release of endorphins, reduces stress and improves your mood. You can get your cardio indoors on a treadmill or elliptical machine, in an aerobics class, a spin class or fitness bootcamp. For those who like to mix it up, you can try martial arts or cardio-boxing. Running, swimming or time-trialing on a bike are all great forms of outdoor cardio. For cash-rich lawyers, hiring a personal trainer to motivate you can help. For cash-poor lawyers, you can hire an online coach very cheaply. Take a look at Steve Ilg's www.wholisticfitness.com.

With age comes two posture killers—dehydration with thinning of our intervertebral discs and atrophy of the muscles that hold up our spine (the transverse abdominus and spinal erectors). If you want to avoid shrinking and stooping as you age, do Pilates to strengthen those muscles and lengthen your spine. Swimming will help do the same trick. Don't forget to stretch to stay mobile. Yoga is a wonderful way to stretch; it has a meditative element and provides opportunities for group socializing.

Here's the Payoff—14 extra years of healthy living

An 11-year study of 20,000 people from Norfolk, England, found that people who don't smoke, are physically active, drink alcohol in moderation, and eat at least five servings of fruits or vegetables a day live 14 years longer, on average. The subjects in the study were aged 45-79 at the start, with no known cancer or cardiovascular disease, and the results held regardless of social class or body weight.

CHAPTER THIRTEEN: SUGGESTED READING

Stephen Holt, M.D., *Combat Syndrome X, Y and Z* (Wellness Publishing, 2002)

Philip Ades, M.D., *Eating Well for a Healthy Heart* (Eating Well, 2008)

Joseph C. Maroon, M.D., *Fish Oil: The Natural Anti-Inflammatory* (Basic Health Publications, Inc. 2006)

Dr. Johanna Budwig, *Flax Oil As A True Aid Against Arthritis, Heart Infarction, Cancer and Other Diseases* (3rd ed.) (Apple Publishing Company, Ltd., 1994)

Terces Engelhart, *I Am Grateful* (North Atlantic Books, 2007)

Chris Idzikowski, *Learn to Sleep Well: A Practical Guide to Getting a Good Night's Rest*, (Chronicle Books, 2000)

Brian Wansink, Ph.D., *Mindless Eating: Why We Eat More Than We Think* (Bantam Books, 2006)

Gwin Grogan Grimes, *Nuts: Pistachio, Pecan & Pinon* (Rio Nuevo Publishers, 2006)

Peretz Lavie et al., *Sleep Disorders: Diagnosis, Management and Treatment*, A Handbook for Clinicians (Martin Dunitz, Ltd., 2002)

Steven Pratt, M.D., and Kathy Matthews, *Super Foods Rx* (Harper, 2004)

Steven Pratt, M.D.. and Kathy Matthews, *Super Foods Health Style* (William Morrow, 2006)

Sonia Uvezian, *The Book of Yogurt* (Ecco, 1978)

Larry McCleary, M.D., *The Brain Trust Program* (A Perigee Book, 2007)

Bruce Fife, C.N., N.D., *The Coconut Oil Miracle* (Avery, 2004)

Rick Gallop, *The G.I. [Glycemic Index] Diet*, (Workman Publishing, 2002)

Rebecca Wood, *The New Whole Foods Encyclopedia*, (Penguin Books, 1999)

William Dement, M.D., *The Promise of Sleep* (Delacorte Press, 1999)

Gabe Mirkin, M.D., and Barry Fox, Ph.D., *20/30 Fat & Fiber Diet Plan* (Harper Collins, 2000)

Mark Hyman, M.D., Ultra-Metabolism, (Scribner, 2006)

Barbara Kafka, *Vegetable Love* (Artisan, 2005)

Jean Carper, *Your Miracle Brain*, (Harper Collins Publishers, 2000)

CHAPTER FOURTEEN

Using the new science of happiness to become a happier lawyer

What is Happiness?

THERE ARE TWO MAIN types of happiness, hedonic and eudaimonic. Both involve pleasure, but there's a difference. The pleasures of hedonic happiness are brief and superficial, while those of eudaimonic happiness are deep and lasting.

Hedonic happiness is an emotion. It comes and goes like soap bubbles. It stems entirely from external events like waking up to a sunny day after a week of rain, getting a great parking spot, reaching a personal fitness goal or winning a professional achievement award. Hedonic happiness is what we refer to when we talk about "feeling happy." It can't be conjured up or held onto when you need it. It never lasts. Buzz Aldrin felt great on July 20, 1969, when he walked on the moon with Neil Armstrong, but afterward he suffered from alcoholism, depression and two divorces, according to his interview with Marc Lee on July 8, 2009.

Eudaimonic happiness isn't about feeling happy for a moment. It's about stable contentment—being happy for a lifetime. Eudaimonic happiness is a strategy for living and a life path. Someone with eudaimonic happiness cultivates happiness through deliberate adherence to practices that promote sustainable happiness. He is ever mindful of the value of his happiness, and on a moment-to-moment basis he consciously chooses happiness over its alternative (envy, anger, depression). Lionel Ketchian is the founder of the Happiness Club (see www.happinessclub.com). He says eudaimonic happiness is power. Not power over anyone else, but a power within to decide to stay happy no matter what challenge to one's happiness comes along.

Ketchian is no fool. He knows that human beings have problems like leaky roofs, cars that won't start, debts to pay, business setbacks, failed relationships, and so forth. His approach to problems is not to make them the center of your life or allow them to dominate your consciousness. As Candace Pert, Ph.D., says, the fundamental characteristic of the human mind is its capacity to choose where to place its attention. If you're always focusing on your problems, Ketchian says your life and your problems will become one and the same. This is a guaranteed recipe for unhappiness.

Is happiness frivolous? Is it something that serious lawyers handling serious matters have no business pursuing? It depends on your perspective. Happiness expert Aymee Coget, Ph.D., co-founder of the American Happiness Association, asks, "Do you want a peaceful world populated by truly happy people living in harmony with each other?" If your answer is yes, then Ms. Coget says you have a duty to acquire eudaimonic happiness and be a happy person. If you don't and you allow yourself to be as miserable as the people who make our world unhappy, you're just adding to the collective misery instead of boosting the collective happiness.

Wayne Dyer says we all know people who have reason to suffer (like a loved one or friend with cancer) and of tragic situations in which whole groups of people have been made to suffer (like war refugees facing starvation, contaminated drinking water and epidemic disease). Yet no matter how much we suffer on their account, our suffering cannot do anything to heal them, help them or make them happier. Our suffering will only drain our energy and make us less able to help. On the other hand, the happier we are, the more positive energy we can bring to making the world better.

Moreover, life isn't just a vale of tears. Life is filled with countless blessings. If we would take our mind off our problems, we could see, feel and appreciate these blessings. Imagine a brilliantly colorful and intensely fragrant spring flower, a child's spreading gap-toothed smile, walking along a beautiful trail in the pine-scented woods with your beloved pet dog on a crisp fall day, eating a warm gooey dark chocolate soufflé, your lover's deep lingering sensuous kiss or a gorgeous orange and red sunset over the ocean. To be fully present to these wonders, to absorb their magnificence into every cell of your body and to deeply appreciate them is transformative.

The counter-argument is that problems are real, and closing our eyes to our problems won't solve them. You live in a high-density area where the agonizing commute through stop-and-go traffic takes hours. You have a mean boss who makes wounding remarks. You have a bad back that's been hurting a lot lately. The winter rains are so heavy this year, your old roof is leaking. Your kids need private tutoring and dental work, but money is scarce. Your spouse has been cold and testy toward you for months. Ketchian's approach is not to ignore your problems, but to take stock of them. Figure out which unpleasant situations can be changed and which of them can't.

As to fixable problems, do all you reasonably can to fix them instead of passively bemoaning them. As to those painful situations that cannot be changed, stop fighting them, just accept that they are part of your life and put your focus on being happy. If you resist situations you dislike but cannot change, they will occupy your consciousness like noisy, unwanted visitors who never leave.

In his chapter on Acceptance in *Happy 4 Life*, Bob Nozik says that acceptance frees up our energy to lead a happy life. Eckhart Tolle has summed this all up by saying that our biggest problem is that we think we have problems. Wouldn't it be better to appreciate and enjoy the gift of life we have been given? Life doesn't exist in the past or future. Life is now. If you're not living in the present you have no possibility of being happy. Catch yourself next time you say you can't be happy because of what someone did to you in the past or because you haven't yet received something you must have before you can be happy.

The new science of happiness restates ancient wisdom recognizing that we can be joyful in a world where change, aging, sickness and death are inevitable. Once you accept conditions of life that cannot be altered (like being blind), you will not become stuck in disappointment and complaint. You will focus on being happy, and your so-called problems will no longer trouble you.

Whenever a painful event occurs, you can always ask yourself, "Is this event (over which I have no control) worth giving up my happiness for?" and then decide no. Eckhart Tolle says nothing outside of us can make us unhappy. He believes that we generate our own unhappiness by resisting, fighting and opposing "what is" and by fleeing the present moment (which he calls "the now") to seek happiness elsewhere. Indeed, real happiness happens when our absorption in the present moment is so great, we have no thought or desire to be anywhere else.

The Benefits of Happiness

Social science research shows that happy people have higher levels of physical and mental health, longer life spans, more energy, more resilience in the face of setbacks, better relationships, larger social networks and more money. It's not money that creates happiness. It's the happiness that attracts money.

Practicing Eudaimonic Happiness

How do you know if your happiness is eudaimonic? One good working definition is from Lionel Ketchian, who says: "Happiness is an inner state of wellbeing which enables you to profit from your highest thoughts, wisdom, intelligence, common sense, emotions, health, and spiritual values in your life."

Sonja Lyubomirsky, Ph.D., a professor of positive psychology at U.C. Riverside, is a prolific researcher, writer and speaker on happiness. In her book *The How of Happiness: The Scientific Basis for Getting the Life You Want*, she defines happiness as "the experience of joy, contentment or positive wellbeing, combined with a sense that one's life is good, meaningful and worthwhile." This kind of happiness is sustainable even in the face of challenges.

You can be happy in the moment, while not liking the moment. Happiness challenges for lawyers include sudden, acrimonious law firm breakups; getting laid off; getting sued by a former client; facing state bar disciplinary charges; getting divorced because you were too busy to participate in your marriage; and so forth.

In order to stay happy in the face of a strong happiness challenge, it's important to avoid labeling your experiences as fortunate (good for me) or unfortunate (bad for me).

Instead, see life as a whole. Recognize that every episode of disappointment and pain precedes another moment of success and satisfaction, and the converse is true. Events that start off looking like disaster frequently become stepping stones to a better, happier existence in life's rear-view mirror. The universe contains wisdom unfathomable to any individual. If you can trust that wisdom, you will understand the universe always has something better in store for you when you don't get what you want.

Do you believe the universe is out to support you or to get you? People who practice sustainable happiness are able to find meaning in and to grow from experiences that—on the surface—involve nothing but tragedy, loss and suffering.

The most remarkable example I know is Don Piper, author of *Heaven is Real* and *90 Minutes in Heaven*. Mr. Piper was the youth minister at a Baptist church in Texas when an 18-wheel truck ran over his car and crushed his body like an eggshell. Piper says his spirit traveled to heaven, and then returned to his lifeless body which regained life.

Mr. Piper has spent the last three decades speaking all over the country to inspire other people to face life's hardest challenges in a body that is covered with scars, has a crooked arm and legs that hurt all the time. Certainly he consoles dying people, and the families of dying people, by letting them know that incredible joy awaits people in a perfect heaven after they die. Yet he counsels people who are not dying on how to achieve a meaningful life here and now, one marked by a lasting inner contentment that survives all circumstances.

Mr. Piper hears from and meets with people who are at their wits' end, and who may be contemplating suicide due to chronic pain, paraplegia, addiction, divorce, the death of a child, etc. He tells each one that God has a specific plan for them, that he wants them here to fulfill that plan and that doing so will give their life meaning. Mr. Piper's example gives them the hope and inspiration they need to take his advice to heart. He has succeeded in helping thousands of people to accept their losses, find meaning in them, feel relief and become much more positive and functional. These people go back into the world and help others with the sorts of problems that had pushed them into the most severe depression.

There is a marvelous collection of stories in the book series *Thank God I...* from people who found their way to eudaimonic happiness. Each author endured an event that was extremely painful—like being raped, going blind or having their child murdered—yet none of them threw in the towel and gave up his happiness permanently.

Each author gained new empathy, insight and purpose that helped power the rest of their lives in a positive way. Each ended up helping and inspiring many other people lead better lives. Handled the right way, tragedy can lead one from unhappy self-absorption (in which life is all about the thwarting of *my* wants) to a happy life of caring about and connecting with others.

While preparing this chapter, I met with sustainable happiness expert Aymee Coget, Ph.D., in San Francisco. Ms. Coget is a truly happy person, who has developed a three-month Happiness Makeover to teach clients to create their own eudaimonic happiness (www.make-mehappytv.com). Her makeover includes learning and practicing the scientific principles of happiness, improved nutrition, body cleansing on the molecular level and energetic healing (Reiki).

Ms. Coget has read virtually every book available in the contemporary happiness and positive psychology literature. Even though some people snicker when they hear what she does for a living, her clients (who include lawyers and psychiatrists) are incredibly grateful. Ms. Coget wrote a chapter for the second book of the *Thank God I...* book series. Her chapter was titled "Thank God I Was Fat, Ugly, Poor, Divorced and Live in Chronic Pain." You should see her now!

Going through the experiences listed in her chapter title taught Ms. Coget that her happiness was not dependent on being beautiful, rich, married, living in a pain-free body or any chance circumstance. She doesn't *feel* happy. She *is* happy because she practices the science of eudaimonic happiness. She transmits her happiness to other people like electricity. When you're around her, you can feel it.

Positive Psychology and the Science of Happiness

Martin Seligman is a very accomplished mainstream psychologist who was President of the American Psychological Association in 1998. Along with Barbara Frederickson, he did much of the pioneering work that laid the foundation for the new field of positive psychology. The millennial issue of the APA's journal *The American Psychologist* in 2000 was devoted to this emerging field.

Dr. Seligman is the Director of the Positive Psychology Center at the University of Pennsylvania and he maintains a website called www.authentichappiness.com. He is the author of *Authentic Happiness*, the most widely read popular book that introduces the new field to the public. In the Summer 2005 issue of *The American Psychologist*, Dr. Seligman co-wrote an article titled "Positive Psychology Progress" in which he reviewed the developments and contributions of his field.

In the article he says his motivation for creating the new field was the desire "to have a more complete and balanced scientific understanding of the human experience—the peaks, the valleys, and everything in-between." He was interested not just in understanding pathology and how to relieve suffering, but in happiness and how to increase it. This meant going beyond the data acquired to study mental illness, and collecting new data to be used "to create an evidence-based practice of positive psychology" that would make people "lastingly happy."

Positive psychologists are not researching mental diseases, but "positive emotion, positive character and positive institutions." Their goal is to use basic science methodology (including randomized, placebo-controlled tests) to find out "what makes life most worth living" and develop positive interventions to make people happier on a permanent basis. Classical psychology has a disease model focused on abnormalities that produce distress. It relies for diagnosis on the DSM. Seligman and his colleagues have developed the CSV which stands for *Character Strengths and Virtues: A Handbook and Classification* (2004). The general scheme of the CSV relies on six "overarching virtues that almost every culture across the world endorses: wisdom, courage, humanity, justice, temperance, and transcendence."

Seligman has devoted decades to the study of happiness. Although he is a highly intellectual man and a very successful academic, he concludes from his research that "strengths of the heart—zest, gratitude, hope, and love—are more robustly associated with life satisfaction than are the more cerebral strengths such as curiosity and love of learning." This is a huge point for lawyers that they should really allow to percolate into their subconscious.

Why put so much effort into happiness research (including happiness assessment tools and happiness interventions strategies)? Seligman is convinced that happiness is not frivolous. The research shows that "Happy people are healthier, more successful and more socially engaged, and the causal direction runs both ways."

The Factors That Go Into Making People Happy Over Time

Dr. Seligman says there are three different routes to making people happy: (a) positive emotion and pleasure (the pleasant life); (b) engagement (the engaged life); and (c) meaning (the meaningful life). His research shows people differ over which route they prefer, and that the people who are most happy over the long term orient their pursuits toward all three, with the greatest weight carried by engagement and meaning.

This is another very important point. There is nothing wrong with pursuing pleasure. Dr. Candace Pert rightly says that enjoyment of personal pleasure without guilt is our birthright as human beings and that our frontal lobes are wired for it. Morten Kringelbach says that most forms of mental illness (including depression) involve the inability to experience pleasure.

Thus pleasure is an essential ingredient for happiness. However, Dr. Pert and Dr. Seligman would caution us not to limit our pleasure to the self-gratification that comes from personal consumption (the hedonic treadmill). They say that sustainable happiness depends on broadening your pleasure outward through friendship and participation in groups that benefit others.

In her book, Dr. Lyubomirsky says that 50% of our ability to live happily comes from genetic predisposition (much like body shape and eye color). This statistic is based upon studies of the happiness levels of identical and fraternal twins. Based on other research she concluded that 40% comes from conscious, deliberate implementation of principles of happiness and that 10% of our happiness comes from variable life circumstances, such as who you are married to, what job you do, what city you live in or how much money you have. Lionel Ketchian and Aymee Coget take issue with the 10% figure. They contend that variable life circumstances create 100% of hedonic happiness but 0% of eudaimonic happiness, which is all about attitude and life strategies.

Whether life circumstances make up 10% or 0% of your happiness, clearly it's a small fraction. The irony is that most of us put all our energy into pursuing happiness by trying to create and hold on to these variable life circumstances. The experts say that getting divorced and remarried, buying your dream home or getting a big job promotion are examples of things that do not provide lasting happiness.

Why not? It's because people very quickly adapt to external life changes, and what seemed so amazing and wonderful at first soon gets taken for granted. This phenomenon of "hedonic adaptation" explains why lottery winners are extra happy for a period of months, but then revert back to their lifetime baseline of happiness. If they were miserable beforehand, then that's what they will be.

If wanting to be happy or being lucky enough to win the lottery are not sufficient to make you happy, then what is? Dr. Lyubomirsky says there has to be a will and a way, meaning a personal intention to be happy and a reliable method for achieving and sustaining it. She recommends putting your energy on a day-to-day basis into the 40% area, because it can yield long-term happiness, unlike the 10% that comes from losing weight, buying a new car or meeting someone who appeals to you on Match.com. The weight can return. The car can get dented, smashed up or stolen. The special someone can turn out to be a stalker.

Dr. Lyubomirsky says the biggest obstacles to using the 40% of the happiness pie chart to create long-term happiness for ourselves are myths of happiness. These myths lead us to seek happiness in the wrong place or in the wrong way. The myths of happiness are:

1. Happiness can only be found, not made by taking action. If you are not happy today, the odds are you will not be happy tomorrow. If you believe Myth #1, then you probably believe something along the lines of, "I will only be happy if one day I meet Mr. or Ms. Right, he or she is single and he or she falls for me."

2. Happiness lies in changed life circumstances, such as winning the lottery or becoming a partner at your law firm.

3. You either have it or you don't, which means we are either born happy or unhappy and nothing we can do will ever make a dent in our fate. This is fatalism, the religion of good and bad luck. People who believe #3 also believe you cannot be taught how to create happiness or take steps in the real world right now to decrease your misery and increase your happiness. The myths stop people from developing sustainable happiness by making them passive and convincing them their happiness depends on something other than their own attitudes and choices.

Dr. Lyubomirsky's research has shown her that anyone can be happy with the right attitude, regardless of life circumstances. To the skeptic she says: "So, although you may find it very hard to believe, whether you drive to work in a Lexus hybrid or a battered truck, whether you're young or old, or have had wrinkle-removing plastic surgery, whether you live in the frigid Midwest or the balmy West Coast, your chances of being happy and becoming happier are pretty much the same." How can this be?

Research shows that acquiring shiny, impressive and expensive possessions does not produce a lasting increase in happiness. Almost as soon as you get the big raise in salary or the new Lexus, you adapt to having it, you take it for granted and want more.

Far better than extra money in your bank account is having a sense of humor, loving your kids and having a large social support network. These three things are wonderful to have when times are good. When times are rocky, they will get you through much better than money or material goods. You can't get empathy from your new Lexus, hugs from your art collection or compassionate warmth from your big-screen TV when you're feeling down.

The Eight Characteristics of Happy People

If happiness is teachable, then it makes sense to figure out what characteristics the happiest people have in common. Dr. Lyubomirsky has spent a great deal of time researching this and she has come up with a list of eight common factors, which are: spending a great deal of time with family and friends and nurturing those relationships; expressing sincere gratitude for all you have; being the first to offer a helping hand to a co-worker or stranger; practicing optimism when envisioning your future; savoring life's pleasures and really living in the moment; engaging in frequent physical exercise; being deeply committed to lifelong goals and ambitions; and being able to cope with stress, crises and tragedies.

She is convinced it is within your power to change how you think about yourself and the world around you by nurturing a spirit of optimism and building self-esteem as you help others and see the results (relief of their pain and a rise in their joy).

Mark Twain said that cheering others up is one of the best ways to be happy. It distracts us from our own complaints, while helping us see and feel our efficacy in making life better for others who have suffered.

By engaging in intentional activities consistent with these eight modes of living, you can raise your happiness level above your genetic set point and keep it up, which is just the opposite of hoping for a favorable change in life circumstances. The fantasy of endless happiness from a financial windfall is just that, a fantasy. I know a man who soon began alcoholic drinking after selling his business for five million dollars. For years he spent much of his time alone in his house getting smashed, since he had nothing to live for. More recently he began volunteering in the community and his mood finally started to pick up.

Dr. Lyubomirsky says that genes are predispositions, and how they express themselves is due partly to environment, which is largely beyond our control, and partly to intentional behavior, which is under our control. By putting persistent effort into doing things that have the potential to create lasting happiness, you are on the right road. She also counsels that happiness requires learning to forgive rather than holding grudges. Grudges keep the anger alive and make us victims. We need to be careful about this, because some of our clients come to us on account of their grudges. In fighting their battles, we may develop grudges of our own.

Wayne Dyer, a very happy man and a teacher of happiness, has spoken in very moving terms about tracking down the alcoholic father who left him, his brothers and his mother and never called, wrote or sent money before he died. Dyer found the grave. He screamed for hours telling his dead father how much he hated him for leaving, for being so irresponsible and uncaring, for not having the courage to stop drinking and for making his life so difficult because his mother could not afford to keep the family together and had to put the boys in separate foster homes. And then suddenly, all the anger left his body, and he felt the warmth, light and ease of forgiveness. He made a conscious decision never to become resentful and angry when his father's name came up. Remarkably, after he forgave his father, Dyer says that his life, his career and his relationships all improved rapidly and he has stayed on a positive trajectory.

STRATEGIES FOR MAKING LAWYERS HAPPY

(1) Savor the goodness of the present moment.
Buddhists say patience is to life as salt is to meat. You need one in order to enjoy the other. To feel calm, peaceful and alive requires being present for this moment, rather than distancing yourself from reality by mentally racing to the future. The resentment we form in response to always feeling pressured is self-caused. We can slow down, become more present and take in what is funny, interesting, inspiring or beautiful in this moment. John Izzo, author of *Five Secrets to Discover Before You Die*, says if we use each moment as simply a ladder to the next, and all our days are lived solely to get to something that will occur in the future, then we are not enjoying or being grateful for the gift of life. Izzo quotes Seneca as saying, "Treat each day as a lifetime."

(2) Engage in continuous, lifelong learning.
Lawyers who feel trapped in a legal assembly line without an opportunity to learn and grow are bored, restless and unhappy. One of the worst things about law is doing the same kinds of cases the same way for the same sorts of clients over and over again. Human beings need variety, novelty, new learning and constant enrichment of the mind to be happy. Brain scans show parts of our brains that only light up when we are faced with novelty, complexity and challenge.

When we stop learning, we ossify; yet many of us have stopped reading anything but law and we avoid classes outside the law that would enrich our minds and expand our horizons. There are community classes, university extension classes and online classes on every imaginable topic. Why don't we take advantage? We're so invested in winning cases and making money, we don't want to give up a spare minute for self-education because it doesn't contribute to either of these goals. Yet lifelong learning stimulates the growth of new brain cells, and it's a source of energy, excitement and joy in our lives.

(3) Practice craftsmanship

Providing your clients with the best possible service, service that you know contributes to their lives, service that you can be proud of, is a core value that makes sense. This means valuing quality over quantity. Law is a profession and a business. Some of us fall into the trap of thinking that good business is taking on as many cases as humanly possible without careful screening of their value or of the objectives and expectations of the claimant. Small-potato cases can become your biggest headaches. When we take on too much work, we end up disappointing ourselves and our clients. There is only so much time in the day for sustained concentration and quality productivity. When you exceed your allotment, what you generate is subprime, to use a word that appears in the newspapers so much today.

Part of being happy requires finding a ratio between productivity and craftsmanship that enables you to do your highest quality legal work. What sound reason could possibly justify taking on those crappy little cases with questionable merit, trivial damages or both? What's holding you back from doing your best work on cases that deserve your full attention? If you are too busy to do your best work every day, then it's time to eliminate some of your cases.

(4) Value process as much as winning

We are hired by clients to protect their rights. The idea that we are hired to "win" and that only if we "win" have we carried out the terms of our engagement strikes me as false. In many cases figuring out who won and who lost is rather complicated and really depends more on your perspective than any objective standard. Just ask any mediator.

If you have a compulsion to win and losing is a source of shame, it will be very hard to flourish, let alone survive, as a lawyer. Josh Waitzkin is a national chess champion and world champion in the martial arts discipline of Tai Chi Chuan Push Hands who wrote *The Art of Learning*. He says learning how to win matches is important, but must never become the sole focus or edge out playfulness, creativity, self-expression and enjoyment. How many of you are using your playfulness and creativity to express yourselves and enjoy the process while practicing law?

Waitzkin has noticed that competitors who fear losing, because they see it as a source of shame, do not progress in their art. They are paralyzed by their fear and will not risk facing stronger opponents who might beat them or try out new, untested techniques that might fail. Such people were raised by parents who gave them conditional love, and who did not love their kids regardless of the outcome of their matches. He describes a father who scowled at his son, turned away in disgust and gave the boy the cold shoulder after his son was beaten in the championship match of a chess tournament.

Winning can become an unhealthy obsession which is fueled by greed for medals, trophies, fame, fan adulation and endorsement money. In 1995 Dr. Robert Goldman supposedly asked 198 Olympic athletes if they would be willing to die in five years in exchange for taking a drug that guaranteed they would win a gold medal in their event, and received a yes from more than 50% of those polled!

Process is about trying things out, learning and growing. Fear of losing is an obstacle to enjoying process. Josh Waitzkin says there are two main theories of intelligence: the entity theory (which discourages learning) and the learning theory (which encourages it). The entity theory says that each person is born with a finite, ingrained and unalterable level of intelligence, aptitude and talent. If you believe that, then you're stuck believing that no amount of training or hard work will improve your results. You're just plain smart or dumb and just plain good or bad at activities as diverse as math, language, chess, martial arts, brief-writing, cross examination, oral argument and so forth.

People who believe in the entity theory had parents who focused on their results, not the process they went through (Buster, you're great at math, but you stink in English, so don't bother trying to be a writer—become an engineer instead; Sally, you're a whiz at languages, but you can't dance, so you might as well forget about ballet and work at the United Nations). Such parents never praised you for setting a goal and pursuing it with hard work and diligent effort. They didn't care about you showing up, taking part and doing your best; they gave approval only when you won.

The learning theory of intelligence sees mastery as something achieved incrementally by working hard over time to grasp a subject or skill with increasing depth. If you are praised for concentrating, for hard work, for lessons learned and for making baby steps in your progress from novice to master, you will not make global judgments like "I stink at this" and give up in frustration. You see your own potential rather than your limits. You can handle pressure, because you see each contest as a step forward or a temporary setback in a long-term process of incremental mastery, rather than a once-and-for-all test that can shatter your confidence.

The learning theorist is the opposite of a perfectionist. He is process-oriented and committed to going through a never-ending process of learning as he moves toward goals. He understands that learning itself has value and beauty. Waitzkin poses the question: Would you rather live in a shell of static, safe mediocrity or embrace an organic, long-term learning process that lets you push your limits? Waitzkin says that: "In the long run, painful losses prove much more valuable than wins—those who are armed with a healthy attitude and are able to draw wisdom from every experience, good or bad, are the ones who make it down the road."

(5) Pack kindness into your professional interactions and personal relationships.

In the book *The Power of Kindness*, psychotherapist Piero Ferrucci says people need care and attention as much as oxygen. When people are neglected or abused they become depressed. When they receive a simple act of kindness, they spring back to life like a flower that was dying for lack of water does when someone finally waters it.

Ferrucci says we are now living through an "Ice age of the heart," manifested by the hurried and impersonal quality of communications, the valuation of profit and efficiency above human warmth and genuine presence, the transience of friendships and the use of machines to do jobs that people used to do. Yet he urges us to be kind anyway, because: "Kindness itself might seem lightweight, and yet it is a central factor in our lives. It has surprising power to transform us, perhaps more than any other attitude or technique." He illustrates with a quote from Aldous Huxley. "People often ask me what is the most effective technique for transforming their life. It is a little embarrassing that after years and years of research and experimentation, I have to say that the best answer is—just be a little kinder." Do you agree with the bumper sticker "Mean People Suck," while believing it's okay to be a total jerk in litigation? Think about it.

(6) Release the poison of envy

Envy is common in highly competitive people, and lawyers are no exception. We are envious of people who have what we desire to possess but which we do not have ourselves. In *The Kabbalah of Envy*, Rabbi Nilton Bonder says it is easy to empathize with someone who has suffered failure and loss, but hard to be happy for someone who has experienced success and happiness. Most people are jealous and mad when they see others receive what they covet, even when those others are family members or friends.

When are we most vulnerable to experience envy? When we are not clear on who we are or what we want to do with our lives, and we see people who are certain of their path in life and enjoying the path they chose. People who put no effort into divining their unique purpose in life will unconsciously adopt our society's default definition of the good life—being rich and having the most toys. Since less than 1% of our population has most of what our culture sees as truly impressive goodies (like mansions, country estates and private jets) and these people are splashed across the cover of ubiquitous magazines, it's easy to see how envy can strike. The funny thing is that people within that 1% are stratified by wealth and there is loads of envy within the 1%, too.

Envy hurts. Rabbi Bonder says we can allow our envy to destroy us, until we become like vampires—incapable of feeling good about anything we do or have, but feeding on the vitality of others. When Moses, toward the end of his life, was asked to remain outside of the Holy Tabernacle, while his successor Joshua entered alone to meet with God, he said, "A hundred deaths are preferable to the pain of envy." It was on that day that he asked God permission to die. People consumed with envy build huge structures of injustice in their minds that they continually nourish with their emotions and their energy—a colossal waste.

Do you envy your colleagues who have a bigger house, a bigger salary, a bigger office with a nicer view, a fancier car or a better looking spouse? In *The Power of Karma,* Mary T. Browne writes of people who have splendid lives yet feel nothing but bitterness because they are consumed by obsessive envy of a sibling or relative with more money. These people suffer because they are so attached to the idea of having more that they push away what they do have and are unable to enjoy it. Rabbi Bonder says that all of us have a choice as to how we deal with envy, how long it stays with us, and what consequences we allow it to trigger in our lives. If you make your life about loving relationships and meaningful work, it no longer matters who owns what things.

(7) Cultivating gratefulness

The opposite of envy is gratefulness. The mindset of gratefulness is a potent source of happiness. In *Attitudes of Gratitude*, author M.J. Ryan uses quotes, examples and exercises to help people cultivate gratitude. Ryan counsels us to stop seeing only what is wrong, lacking, inadequate or painful. Instead we can look for and appreciate the many good people and good things in our lives and be thankful for the bad things we don't have, such as blindness, chronic pain or cancer. Gratefulness lets us experience beauty, fullness, excitement and wonderment. Grateful people feel younger than their chronological age. They want to keep living to experience more joy.

Choosing gratefulness will spare you a life of complaint, boredom and monotony. In *Thanks!*, Robert A. Emmons, Ph.D., says the famous optimist C.K. Chesterton set a conscious goal of preserving the child within and his sense of awe, so he would not fall prey to the boredom and monotony that saps so many lives of joy and purpose.

People who research gratitude say that finding reasons every day to be grateful improves your mood, boosts your immune system and physical health and improves your relationships. They say that grateful people make better leaders in the workplace, because they openly appreciate their employees. Grateful leaders thank their employees for their positive qualities, contributions, efforts and self-sacrifice. Knowing they're appreciated for who they are and what they do, their employees flourish.

Gratitude researchers say that ungrateful people stir up bad feelings in the workplace because they are quick to find fault, they are harshly critical of others and never say thanks. Staying grateful opens your heart and makes you enjoy being around other people. You cannot be grateful and keep your heart closed. It isn't possible. Instead of counting your blessings once a year on Thanksgiving, try doing it every day.

Some people can do this in their heads, while others find it helps to keep a written gratitude journal.

(8) Hang out with happy people

Nicholas Christakis, Professor of Medical Sociology at Harvard Medical School, published a paper in December 2008 showing that happiness is contagious. On three separate occasions between 1984 and 2003, he had 5,000 participants in the Framingham Heart Study fill out detailed questionnaires about their emotional status. After crunching the numbers, here's what he learned. Every happy friend you have increases your own chance of being happy by 9%. If you have a happy friend who lives nearby, you have a 25% higher chance of being happy. For every unhappy friend, the likelihood of happiness decreases by 7%. Dr. Christakis also found that these effects held true over three degrees of relational separation. Thus, when one person becomes happy, the social network effect reaches friends of friends. Happiness loves company and one way to be happy is to share it with others in a group. The group, in turn, will share it with you.

ADVICE ON HOW TO BE HAPPY FROM HAPPY PEOPLE

Anna Quindlen's Philosophy of Happiness

Anna Quindlen IS A prize-winning journalist. In *A Short Guide to a Happy Life*, she sets out her own philosophy of happiness. Quindlen reminds us that if you win the rat race, you're still a rat. She cautions that the manic pursuit of a promotion, a bigger paycheck or a larger house takes you away from life, and the sad thing is that many people realize this only when they become seriously or terminally ill. She urges people not to be alone. She prizes her relationship with her husband, her three children and her friends. Whenever they need her, she shows up, listens and tries to laugh. She does not put her career before these relationships.

Ms. Quindlen tells us to look around, see how glorious life is, celebrate it and never take it for granted. She encourages us to hug the people we love, to be generous, and to care so deeply about goodness that we spread it around. That means taking money you would have spent on idle pleasures to help a charity, to work in a soup kitchen or tutor a child. To see and appreciate the good in life and to give some of it back to others is a key to a happy life.

She encourages us to love the journey of life and not its destination. Ms. Quindlen reminds us how easy it is to waste our lives and asks us to remember that life is short. She says the awareness of mortality is a gift, because it can spur us to live life to the fullest and share it with love.

The Dalai Lama's Comments on Money and Happiness

The Dalai Lama is respected, admired and beloved across the globe by virtually everyone except the Chinese government. If you can measure wealth in friends, he may be the wealthiest man on earth. He is a man with a warm, kindly face who is always smiling despite living in exile for decades and having seen many atrocities.

In *10 Questions for the Dalai Lama*, documentary film maker Rick Ray asks His Holiness why he thinks people in poor countries are happier than people in rich countries like America. In response, the Dalai Lama says that once poor people have fed their children and themselves, they have taken care of business and are free to enjoy themselves. They have very little in the way of material possessions, but are rich in spirit because they're content with the love they give and get in their families. On the other hand, rich people are always wanting one more thing, so no matter how much they acquire, they feel poor, because there is always some new possession that eludes them.

Randy Pausch's Keys To a Happy Life

Randy Pausch, a computer science professor at Carnegie Mellon University, was asked to give a last lecture in connection with his retirement. Randy was married with three children. A few weeks before the lecture he learned he had terminal cancer, so this would literally be his last lecture. In his last lecture Mr. Pausch offered seven keys to a happy life: always have fun (be a fun-loving Tigger, not a sad sack Eeyore); dream big; ask for what you want; dare to take a risk; look for the best in everybody (if you wait patiently, in time people will surprise and impress you); make time for what matters to you (time is all you have); and let your kids be themselves (be a parent who does not impose his dreams on his kids, but one who gives his kids a joy for life and the tools to make their own wishes come true). Randy is dead now, but you can see and hear him give his last lecture on YouTube.

Summing up the Lessons of Happiness

Spiritual people say that happiness is a product of Karma, the law of universal cause and effect. If you're kind and giving you will be happy, and if you're cruel and selfish you'll be unhappy. Positive psychology maintains that happiness is the result of intention, choice and action, but they base this conclusion on scientific research data, rather than an ancient wisdom tradition. The important point is that lawyers can become happier by making a conscious effort to live by principles of happiness.

If we define our professional lives in terms of money only, we will live with anxiety as our cases move toward resolution, and we will choke on shame when we lose cases or receive financial results below our expectations. If we're ever to be happy, we must make a decision to adopt happiness as our life path. We must take to heart the philosophies of people like Dr. Lyubomirsky, Anna Quindlen, the Dalai Lama and Randy Pausch. The proof is in the pudding. If you begin living the principles of happiness every day, you will become much happier regardless of the ups and downs of your law office net income, and at some point you will you see the connection. From that point on you will consciously generate your own happiness rather than passively wait for happiness to fall from the sky into your lap.

CHAPTER FOURTEEN: SUGGESTED READING

Roger von Oech, *A Whack on the Side of the Head: How You Can be More Creative* (Warner Books, 1990)

James Allen, *As You Think* (New World Library, 1998)

Kent M. Kieth, *Do It Anyway: Finding Personal Meaning and Deep Happiness by Living the Paradoxical Commandments* (New World Library, 2003)

Bob Nozik, M.D., *Happy 4 Life: Here's how to do it* (Trafford, 2004)

Rick Foster & Greg Hicks, *How We Choose To Be Happy* (The Berkeley Publishing Group, 1999)

John Castagnini (Ed.), *Thank God I...* (Inspired Authors, LLC, 2009)

Bridget Grenville-Cleave and Ilona Boniwell, *The Happiness Equation* (Adams Media, 2008)

Josh Waitzkin, *The Art of Learning* (Free Press, 2007)

Sonja Lyubomirsky, The How of Happiness: A Scientific Approach To Getting The Life You Want (The Penguin Press, 2007)

CHAPTER FIFTEEN

Attitudinal changes that foster wellbeing

The Big Picture

DIVIDE UP YOUR LIFE into thirds. Calculate how many hours you devote each day to sleeping, working as a lawyer (including the commute to and from work, work at the office and the work you do at home on nights and weekends) and everything else (self-care, family time, house chores, errands, fitness, socializing, recreation, vacation, pleasure reading, personal growth and worship).

Most probably the biggest third is working. This means you spend more hours being a lawyer than interacting with your spouse and kids or pursuing the interests, hobbies, vacations, sports, creative activities or spiritual activities you love. Given the time spread, your overall quality of life must include how you spend your time at the office. If your goal is to be a loving, authentic and happy person, doesn't it make sense to be that way all the time instead of trying to squeeze that mode of being into your smaller allotment of hours away from work?

Let's face it. No one really succeeds at the Jekyll-Hyde game anyway. You can't be a rude, mean, angry jerk at the office and a kind, patient, considerate person at home. You can't wash the cortisol out of your blood that quickly or that easily. How you relate to other people at work has a huge impact on every aspect of your life outside the office including your sleep, appetite, sexuality, mood, energy level, emotional expressiveness, emotional availability and sociability. You're going to have to make a choice.

One day, at a moment we can't predict, we will die. It could happen thirty years from now or next week. In this moment, right now, we have the gift of life. Why squander it? Why miss out on it? Why pollute it with blame and anger? Yes, there are clients who have been wronged, who are upset and who want our help. Yes, we have to argue with other people to help our clients, and these people may prove difficult, uncaring, even hostile. And yes, when we're in the office we have to work hard to help our clients and prove worthy of our hire.

On the other hand this life has an abundance of energy, freshness, beauty and mystery that can fill us up with endless awe and wonder. Our Source has given us an infinite capacity for learning, growth, pleasure, joy and bliss. Why trade these gifts away, to stew in petty resentments?

I'm not suggesting that you ignore or excuse illegal conduct or that you refrain from protecting or pursuing your clients' rights in a vigorous, professional manner. The legal system exists to do justice when a wrong has been done, and we get hired to make sure justice is done. I am saying you can adopt a new attitude while you practice law. You can see yourself operating within the big picture rather than taking it all personally.

Buddha described the big picture when he said everything changes and dissolves in time. The Bible described the big picture when it said all is vanity. We're all going to die, each and every one of us. With the passage of time, there will be no one left to remember our name, who we were or what we accomplished. Every trace of our existence will disappear. No one in the future will know about or care about what we happen to think is so important right now.

Does it really make sense to twist ourselves into hard knots of anger over our petty squabbles with opposing counsel? Why should we hold onto hate because of what opposing counsel said or did to us during the course of litigation? Isn't it certain he's suffering and that he would love to be happy too, if only he knew how?

Stop the Blame Game

As it exists right now, the adversary system is a blame machine. Each side blames the other for the event(s) that form the basis of the claim. Lawsuits are mechanisms to prove your opponent is blameworthy so you can vindicate your rights and obtain money or property. As lawyers we need to be careful about taking blame home with us at the end of the workday. If we're not conscious of it, we are likely to use blame everywhere and in every situation where things don't go according to our plans.

Blaming causes unhappiness in two ways. First, it leads to the desire for vengeance. There is an old saying that's appropriate here: "When you're out for vengeance, dig two graves." Vengeance literally or figuratively kills the object of vengeance and the person who carries it out.

Second, blaming others makes us passive and irresponsible. A lawyer can blame his loss at trial by his adversary cheating without having to examine his own lack of preparation and execution. A lawyer who submitted mediocre work because he never expected to make partner can blame the partnership committee for not appreciating his brilliant legal mind when they passed him over. He can blame his spouse for incredible selfishness in having an affair, even though he was always at the office and became a virtual stranger at home. A lawyer who ignored his colleagues' repeated pleas to join AA can blame the stress of work for hitting a pedestrian with his car after getting drunk.

We can't be happy if we are out for vengeance or refuse to take responsibility for our own misery by blaming others for causing it. If we really accepted the truth that all things dissolve, we would not get stuck blaming others for our suffering. We would understand it's the nature of existence (not the decisions or actions of any particular people) that frustrate us in our efforts to grab hold of and keep what we envision as the perfect life situation for us. Only when we accept that grasping leads to despair and that (in the words of Mick Jagger) we can't always get what we want, can we be happy. When we blame others for our unhappiness, we hate them and wish to see them harmed.

Each time you blame, hate and wish harm to others, you change the biochemistry of the cells in your body for the worse and your health suffers. In *Feel Good, Feel God*, Dr. Candace Pert mentions a cancer patient who screamed for a whole day at her brother while taking a walk alone to release a lifetime of anger toward him. Two days later her huge tumor had shrunk almost to nothing, and her surgery was cancelled. This release of toxic hate changed her biochemistry.

Take Charge of Your Inner Environment, Your Genes and Your Life

In *Spontaneous Evolution: Our Positive Future*, molecular biochemist Bruce Lipton, Ph.D., says our values, temperament, personality and behavior are not dictated for life by the genes we were born with. Human beings can alter the outer environment of Nature and their inner environment of human nature.

How we see and treat ourselves, each other and our planet are malleable and can be changed for the better. For one thing, every seven years all the cells in our body are replaced and in that sense alone we do not remain the same person. But it goes much deeper. Dr. Lipton says our mental orientation (be it one of compassion and kindness or hate, envy and depression) directly affects cell membrane function, gene expression and protein synthesis in our bodies.

Our genes do not rigidly determine who we are or how we live. Dr. Lipton cites extensive research showing that biochemical signals within our bodies play a much stronger role in shaping and reshaping our bodies and its functions than our genes do. This is because the genes are simply blueprints for protein synthesis that can be used in thousands of different ways depending on what instructions they get. The instructions that tell our DNA which proteins to make actually come from the membranes that cover our cells. These cellular membranes act like "tiny brains" by picking up biochemical signals from inside the body, decoding these signals to determine which proteins are needed to adapt to our fluctuating environment and then telling the DNA within the cellular nucleus which proteins to make.

Darwinism says all modifications in organisms result from chance genetic mutations, and the organisms that survive get selected by Nature, because their random mutations best fit them to changing environments. Modern biology is veering toward the view that organisms have some capacity to modify their own bodily structures and functions so they can adapt to the environment. When scientists stressed lactose-intolerant bacteria by giving them only lactose to eat, the bacteria generated scores of mutations in a very short time (a process called hyper-mutation) until they hit upon one that enabled them to digest lactose. They then snipped out the DNA that coded for lactose intolerance and replaced it with DNA that codes for lactose tolerance.

In lower animals cell membranes respond solely to cues from the external environment, like changes in the food supply. In humans, cell membranes respond to cues from the internal environment created by our psyches. If we subscribe to the materialist view that life is a winner-take-all, dog-eat-dog competition, we are creating an inner environment marked by high stress, anxiety and anger. That's the kind of inner environment that influences cell membranes to direct DNA to make harmful proteins that cause heart attacks, strokes and dementias.

If you believe your DNA makes you a depressive or an alcoholic, then that's the life you will live. We'll never know, but it could be that poor Jim Fixx never believed he could overcome his genetic family history of severe coronary artery disease by running. Dr. Lipton says that if you want to build a joyful life, you can do it. Practicing gratitude and forgiveness and encouraging yourself to experience joyful thoughts and emotions will send biochemical signals to your cells that will select for the DNA that enhances your joy.

Dr. Lipton says human beings have the potential to move from mere survival to thrival, which is a higher functioning and happier state of being than subsisting.

Thrival is marked by human beings cooperating with each other to contribute to and support global harmony. By global harmony Dr. Lipton means humans are living in a conscious, awakened state that is good for animals, plants and other humans and good for the Earth.

Materialism says only matter exists and there is no place for spirituality. When you combine materialism with the lust for money and the use of machines to acquire it, you end up where we are today. We now face a situation where animal species, plant species and humanity lie at the brink of extinction through our heedless natural resource depletion, habitat destruction, pollution of the Earth by manufacturing and dumping of toxic wastes, and warfare. Dr. Lipton warns we are at a choice point for the survival of all living things, us included.

He says the original meaning of the term religion (*religare*) in Greek was to "bind," and religion was seen as something that connected the individual to his community, society and the world. Materialism has set each person against the other. Its message is that evolution is random, we are accidents, only the strongest survive and the strongest are the ones with better genes who amass the most money and power. If we continue to blindly follow these false beliefs, then life on Earth is history.

On the other hand, if we acknowledge the reality of spirit and matter, we can overcome the dualism of religion and science and have time to save the world before it's too late. Dr. Lipton sees the point of evolution as human beings learning to work together to come into balance with the Earth. Acceptance of this view would enable us to stop all the trends that threaten to destroy life, and make life safe and fulfilling for all of us. The message of *Spontaneous Evolution* is that the Earth is sending out signals to people that it's time to live in harmony, lest we keep seeking to control, dominate and abuse the Earth and end up dying out from resource depletion, pollution and war.

You can seek thrival within the legal system. To do this requires that you stop seeing fellow lawyers as competitors in a zero sum game where the only role you can play is that of winner or loser. Dr. Lipton reminds us that the original meaning of the term competition in Greek was not to strive against, but to strive together. In ancient Greece competitors used each other's energy to enhance their own, and brought out the best in each other. This is far different than today's concept of competition, which is to crush or annihilate the other side.

Thrival requires that you set an intention to work with other lawyers to create a legal system that meets people's needs fairly and justly and that you take responsibility for your attitude, your words and your actions so they are aligned with an intention to do good, to avoid harm and to treat others as you would have them treat you.

Choosing Gratitude

Lawyers guided by materialism rather than spirituality feel entitled to money and possessions. They grasp feverishly at them, and become disappointed and angry when they don't get what they feel they are owed. When they do get what they want they quickly grow accustomed to it and tire of it, after which they feel empty and hungry for more. Their happiness is shallow and brief and depends totally on what life gives them.

If you're ready to step off the hedonic treadmill, and attain lasting happiness, the twin portals are gratitude and forgiveness. They will make you feel peaceful and safe so you don't want to hurt anyone. They will enlarge your heart, and enable you to bring more heart to your everyday encounters with other people. The more heart you bring to life, the happier you and the people around you will be. Albert Schweitzer said that gratitude is a motive to do good in the world.

Robert Emmons, Ph.D., says gratitude is not a response to what someone gives you. It is a worldview and a pervasive orientation toward life—one that sees life as a gift, and which has a deep, abiding thankfulness for life. Dr. Emmons says a grateful person views life through the lens of abundance, gifting, providing and satisfying rather than scarcity, burdening, denying and depriving. He urges people to embrace gratitude because it has the power to heal, to energize and to change lives for the better.

Dr. Emmons' research over the past two decades has shown that gratitude promotes human health, happiness and wellbeing. It decreases hostility, lowers blood pressure and makes people less isolated and lonely. It makes people more alert, energized, enthusiastic and attentive. Grateful people sleep better, exercise more and have fewer symptoms of anxiety or depression. They are more helpful to others and more connected socially.

When we are grateful we are less likely to see the world as obligated to make us happy, and we are less likely to seek to control the world to make it serve us. We are less likely to get caught up in power struggles over money, possessions and recognition, struggles that produce anxiety and anger and take us out of the present moment. Grateful people notice and even magnify the good in life, and are able to celebrate the present. They experience more positive emotions and are able to block out negative emotions like regret, resentment, envy and hostility. They are more resilient in the face of stress.

Why don't people embrace gratefulness? Sometimes they suffer from pervasive negativity. Sometimes they have a sense of entitlement or they are entirely unable to humble themselves and acknowledge they depend on anyone for anything. Sometimes they have suffered a loss, and they hold so tightly to their pain they cannot let go. If you don't feel grateful, but you're ready to embrace gratitude, I suggest you buy a copy of Dr. Emmons' book *Thanks!* and read the chapter on practices to cultivate gratitude.

Practicing Forgiveness for Your Own Health and Happiness

The reason to forgive is to heal yourself—to let go, move on and reclaim your happiness. Too many lawyers forego happiness for the small ego satisfaction of anger. They cannot imagine forgiving the person they blame for their suffering, because that would let him win. They also get to feel superior to the other by virtue of their anger and their certainty that he is a scoundrel, a cheater, a villain, etc. Do you have the conviction that people in the law business have done things to irreversibly change the foreordained trajectory of your life, and that you're not going to get where you would have in the absence of these events?

While trapped in hate, it never occurs to you that your dream might not have come true anyway or, if it did, you would have encountered a whole new raft of problems, worse ones than you have now. When you stop hating you can see that, having lost something you wanted, you are now free to gain something that may be better for you in the long run. Wisdom is knowing we cannot see good reasons for bad things happening when they happen, but in the fullness of time even the worst events can be tolerated, accepted and used as openings for a happier, more meaningful existence.

When you stay stuck in hate, the source of your current pain is your hate rather than anything that may have been done to you years before. Forgiveness brings you the peace to move on and build all the health, love and prosperity you can. When you stay angry you lose all your flexibility and adaptability and you cannot envision a different but equally good or better future for yourself. You look back to all the potential you once had and to the wrong done you. Stuck in anger and gloom you can't enjoy the present moment or open up the potential for new growth.

Psychologist Frederic Luskin, co-founder of Stanford University's Forgiveness Project, says forgiveness involves a double shift. You change your focus from your past hurt to the love, beauty and kindness that surrounds you now, and you move from being the victim of your life story to being the hero. Forgiveness is a heroic action that raises one's self-image and self-esteem.

In *Finding Forgiveness: A 7-Step Program for Letting Go of Anger and Bitterness,* author Eileen R. Borris-Dunchunstang, Ed.D., provides many remarkable accounts of harm and forgiveness. Kim Phuc's two siblings were killed the day an American soldier authorized the napalm drop that destroyed her village, burnt off her clothes and sent her running naked from her burning village. Azim Khamisa's only son, whom he loved as much as any father could love a child, was murdered senselessly by a 14-year-old gang initiate while he delivered a pizza. Irene Laure's son was tortured nearly to death, her friends in the French resistance were murdered and buried in a mass grave and she spent WWII in a state of chronic starvation.

Each one of these people forgave the person who harmed them, and benefitted immensely by letting go of hate, by healing and laying the groundwork for a new and better life. If Kim, Azim and Irene could forgive the horrors done to them and their loved ones, then surely lawyers can forgive each other for the phony posturing, the rude personal comments, the acts of oppression and the threats of seeking sanctions or going to trial we use against one another in litigation.

A point that Dr. Dunchunstang makes in her book is that forgiving another does not require you to forget, condone or excuse what he did to hurt you or require you to waive any discipline imposed by the law that he would otherwise receive. Forgiveness does not require you to act like a doormat and say "That's OK" to someone who has harmed you or harmed a loved one.

Rather, forgiveness is an act that empowers and strengthens the person who gives it, by releasing the toxic anger that binds his heart so he can see new possibilities and choose new ways of acting that support his healing from a state of woundedness.

As lawyers, and as people, we are all victims and perpetrators. None of us is wholly good or bad, wholly innocent or guilty. None of us wants to acknowledge we have failed in our responsibilities to others or hurt others. It's much easier to see others as the cause of our pain, and to see ourselves as their victims. But when we refuse to acknowledge our role in causing pain, and put all the blame on others for our woundedness and our suffering, then we live in a state of constant anger, and we never know a moment of peace and ease.

More than any other profession, we are caught up in the blame game. We marginalize our client's role in getting into the mess that sent him to us; we maximize the role of the opposing party as the cause of the mess; we feel sorry for ourselves because we have to clean up the mess; we demonize the opposing party's lawyer as someone trying to profit from whitewashing his client's misdeeds; and we feel angry about the whole damn thing.

Distilled to its essence, the theme of *Finding Forgiveness* is that most of us spend our lives being angry at some person or persons for causing our suffering—for putting us into a place, a situation, a career or a relationship that brings us pain. By seeing ourselves as victims, we remain passive, trapped and without responsibility for transcending our pain. Healing means taking responsibility for our own happiness.

Who most deserves the role of making you happy, and who is most likely to succeed in doing it, if not you? Building happiness is a process. It won't happen in a day. While you're building happiness, give yourself a break when you feel down. Jack Kornfield says compassion must include ourselves to be complete.

You Can Move From Daily Misery
To Lifetime Wellbeing

To make this move is to journey away from letting everything wrong with our current legal system chip you down into an angry victim who seeks solace in alcohol, drugs or suicidal thinking. It's a journey toward reclaiming your physical health through exercise, proper nutrition and stress management; reclaiming your authentic self and life balance through guided exercises; reclaiming your mental freedom and spirituality through meditation; reclaiming life-serving social relationships through nonviolent communication; and becoming the hero of your own life story, one in which you take pride and pleasure in your work as a lawyer and happiness in being alive.

CHAPTER FIFTEEN: SUGGESTED READING

Gerald Jampolsky, M.D., and Diane Cirincione, Ph.D., *A Mini Course for Life* (Mini Course Publishing, 2007)

Eileen R. Borris-Dunchunstang, Ed.D. *Finding Forgiveness: A 7-Step Program for Letting Go of Anger and Bitterness* (McGraw-Hill, 2006)

Bruce Lipton, Ph.D., and Steve Bhaerman, *Spontaneous Evolution* (Hay House, 2009)

The Arbinger Institute, *The Anatomy of Peace: Resolving the Heart of Conflict*, (Berrett-Koehler Publishers, Inc., 2008)